Denys Turner is H.G. Wood Professor of Theology at the University of Birmingham. He has previously held teaching positions at University College, Dublin, and the University of Bristol, and was a founding member of the Centre for Medieval Studies at Bristol. Educated at Mount Saint Mary's College, Derbyshire, University College, Dublin, and St Edmund Hall, Oxford. Professor Turner is married and the father of three. His previous publications include *Marxism and Christianity* (Oxford 1983) and *The Darkness of God* (Cambridge 1995).

CISTERCIAN STUDIES SERIES: NUMBER ONE HUNDRED FIFTY-SIX

EROS AND ALLEGORY

Medieval Exegesis of the Song of Songs

CISTERCIAN STUDIES SERIES: NUMBER ONE HUNDRED FIFTY-SIX

EROS AND ALLEGORY

Medieval Exegesis of the Song of Songs

by

Denys Turner

Cistercian Publications
Kalamazoo, Michigan–Spencer, Massachusetts

The work of Cistercian Publications is made possible in part
by support from Western Michigan University to
The Institute of Cistercian Studies

Library of Congress Cataloging-in-Publication Data

Turner, Denys, 1942-
Eros and allegory : medieval exegesis of the Song of Songs / by Denys Turner.
p. cm. -- (Cistercian studies series ; no. 156)
Includes bibliographical references and index.
ISBN 0-87907-956-8 (alk. paper). -- ISBN 0-87907-756-5 (pbk.: alk. paper)
1. Bible. O.T. Song of Solomon--Criticism, interpretation, etc.--History--Middle Ages, 600-1500. I.Title. II.Series.
BS1485.5.T87 1995 95-21341
223'.906'0902--dc20 CIP

Printed in the United States of America

TABLE OF CONTENTS

ACKNOWLEDGEMENTS

Any author owes some debts which are easily identified in the final text and were it not for the criticism, at once positive and honest, of two anonymous readers for Cistercian Publications, and were it not the combination of sympathy and meticulous care with which Dr Rozanne Elder edited a rather sloppy text, this book would still contain some important omissions, errors of fact and of judgment which I hope I have been able to rectify. Nichola Pinn helped me with questions of the hebrew text of the Song of Songs and Dunstan O'Keeffe OSB of Downside Abbey supplied me with helpful material about Alan of Lille. Rachel Fulton helped me with some important references and with other advice. Paul Thompson read a draft and made useful suggestions as to structure. Ian Wei of the Department of Historical Studies at Bristol University helped me with some matters of translation as also did Susannah Braund of the Department of Classics at Bristol. Dr Lyndon Reynolds, now Director of the Aquinas Institute at Emory University, was Downside Research Fellow and then Newman Fellow in the Department of Theology and Religious Studies at Bristol University during the period of this book's composition. Lyndon patiently discussed nearly every aspect of my work as it progressed over those four years. He will be able to identify the extent of my debt more easily than I; what he will not be able to identify so clearly is the degree of my reliance on his experience, on the breadth of his knowledge of mediaeval thought and of scholarly tenchnique, and on his encouragement.

Other forms of contribution, more basic, humble perhaps, but more necessary to an author, have been made by people who, in different ways, formed the class of the *sine quibus non*. In this class I must first thank Mrs Vicki Jones, who put much of the first draft of the manuscript on disc from an original which matched the hand of Thomas Aquinas in this alone, that it was a true *littera inintelligibilis*. In twenty-five years of academic experience I have not known a more accurate, intelligent and careful typist—or, for that matter, Departmental Secretary—than Vicki. My former colleagues at Bristol University, Kenneth Grayston, John Ziesler, Malcolm Lambert and Meg Davies, would probably not admit how much their support and friendship encouraged me in the writing of this book. Nor will my wife, Marie and my children, Ruth, John and Brendan, who not only helped me with details of the final manuscript but over several years somehow contrived to convey the impression that the absurd demands which authorship makes on a writer's immediate family were a normal part of life together. Truly, they own this book as much as I do.

Finally, a few brief snatches of translation and some fragmentary notes on what they might mean began to take the shape of a book during two periods of study at Saint Deiniol's Library, Hawarden. I am grateful to the hospitality of the Warden and Staff in Britain's friendliest academic library. But those periods of study were supported by scholarships from the Tom Jarman Trust which were awarded to me on the initiative of Mrs Mabel Jarman, a true friend of scholars and a friend of true scholarship. It is to Mabel, and to the memory of her late husband, Tom, that I dedicate this book.

D. T.

ABBREVIATIONS

AHDLMA	*Archives d'histoire doctrinale et littéraire du moyen âge*
CH	pseudo-Denys, *Celestial Hierarchy*, in Luibheid.
CW	*The Collected Works of St John of the Cross*, trans. K. Kavanaugh OCD and Otilio Rodriguez OCD, ICS Publications, Washington, 1979.
AMC	*The Ascent of Mount Carmel*, in CW
DNS	*The Dark Night of the Soul*, in CW
SC	*The Spiritual Canticle*, in CW
LFL	*The Living Flame of Love*, in CW
CCSL	*Corpus Christianorum, Series Latina.*
CCCM	*Corpus Christianorum, Continuatio Medievalis*
DN	pseudo-Denys, *The Divine Names*, in Luibheid.
EH	pseudo-Denys, *The Ecclesiastical Hierarchy*, in Luibheid.
EN	Aristotle, *Nicomachean Ethics.*
Greer	*Origen, Selected Works*, trans. Rowan A. Greer, Paulist Press, New York, 1979.
JB	Jerusalem Bible.
JTS	Journal of Theological Studies.

Luibheid	*Pseudo-Dionysius, The Complete Works*, trans. Colm Luibheid, Paulist Press, New York, 1987.
LXX	Septuagint.
PG	Migne, *Patrologia Graeca*.
PL	Migne, *Patrologia Latina*.
Rev. Ben.	*Revue Benedictine*.
RSV	Revised Standard Version.
SC	Sources Chrétiennes.
Sermons	Bernard of Clairvaux, *On the Song of Songs*, Vols I–IV, trans. Killian Walsh OCSO *et al.*, Cistercian Fathers Series 4, 7, 31 & 40, Cistercian Publications, Kalamazoo, 1977–1980.
ST	Thomas Aquinas, *Summa Theologiae*.
Vg.	Vulgate.

FOREWORD

Current interest in the history of exegesis as a key to the understanding of medieval thought is not a fad. When Beryl Smalley's *The Study of the Bible in the Middle Ages* appeared in 1940, medieval exegesis was the little-known preserve of a few specialists; today it is the happy hunting ground of a host of investigators from every discipline involved in medieval studies. Each year the list of dissertations, books and articles devoted to aspects of the history of exegesis grows impressively. Indeed, one of the urgent needs in the field is more adequate bibliographical tools to keep pace with a rapidly expanding discipline.

Even more needed are good introductions that will both satisfy the canons of rigorous scholarship and give students access to the riches to be found in pursuing the uses of the Bible in medieval culture. This is why it is a pleasure for me to provide this brief Foreword to Denys Turner's *Eros and Allegory*; it is a major contribution to the history of the interpretation of the Song of Songs in the Middle Ages.

Perhaps no book of the Bible was more central to medieval spirituality and mysticism or more problematic to contemporary readers than the Song of Songs. Much modern historical-critical biblical scholarship has relegated the Song to the margins of what is identified as the 'core' of the biblical message. Lingering Victorian attitudes toward the opposition between sex and religion find the Song's frank erotic language embarrassing and even distasteful. Those who are not squeamish in the face of its many descriptions of breasts, embraces and kisses, but accept the book as a poetic evocation of human love, often deplore the mystical interpretation which nourished centuries of devout christian and jewish readers. In 1899, W.R. Inge in his noted *Christian Mysticism* spoke for these readers in his forthright declaration:

> As to the Song of Solomon, its influence upon Christian Mysticism has been simply deplorable. A graceful romance in honour of true love was distorted into a precedent and sanction for giving way to hysterical emotions, in which sexual imagery was freely used to symbolize the relation between the soul and its Lord. Such aberrations are as alien to sane Mysticism as they are to sane exegesis.[1]

Fortunately, the work of numerous scholars of theology, art, and history has demonstrated over the past forty years just how shortsighted Inge's peremptory judgment was.[2] The past decade especially has seen the publication of a number of significant studies dealing with the origins of the song of Songs and with its later uses, studies that have added much to our understanding of the spiritual interpretation of the book.[3] Denys Turner's *Eros and Allegory* makes a significant addition to this literature.

Professor Turner's work performs a dual function. First of all, through its translations of twelve commentaries on the first eight verses of the first chapter of the Song, it provides a model for one kind of introduction to a crucial segment of the history of medieval exegesis. These selections span almost a millennium—from Gregory the Great (c. 590) to John of the Cross and his *Spiritual Canticle* of 1578. Turner's texts are well-chosen and accurately translated, providing both the general reader and the medieval student a good cross-section of the major stages in the history of the exegesis of the Song. These translations will doubtless be particularly helpful in courses concerned with the history of exegesis and its relation to medieval spirituality, but Turner's book is more than anthology of texts. And herein lies its special contribution.

The translations in *Eros and Allegory* have been chosen to illustrate an original and provocative interpretation of the meaning of the medieval reading of the song. In his lengthy introductory essay, Turner goes far beyond the usual boundaries of historical accounts of the medieval multitudes and modes of Song interpretation to explore the internal logic beneath the surface. The penetration of Turner's analysis is equaled by the boldness of his claims to reveal the underlying themes at work across a thousand years of commentarial effort. Such speculative daring marks a new moment in the history of the study of medieval exegesis of the Song. Turner's major hypothesis—that the medieval reading of the Song of Song was fundamentally based upon a fusion of 'erotic metaphysics' dependent on the writings of the Pseudo-Dionysus with ascetical monastic eschatology—provides a new and revealing perspective on medieval understandings of the song. This argument—brilliantly displayed, to my mind—is just one element in a rich and fascinating essay that is bound to provoke discussion, debate, and probably disagreement. One thing is clear. Turner's account cannot fail to be of interest to anyone concerned with the medieval use of the Song of Songs and with the intellectual and cultural significance of the history of exegesis.

I shall not spoil for the reader the opportunity to confront Professor Turner's rich and rewarding argument firsthand by saying more here about other aspects of his case. It is enough for me to express my pleasure in being asked to introduce this significant volume to the interested public and to thank Cistercian Publications for making it available to enrich current scholarship on the medieval uses of the Bible.

Bernard McGinn

The Divinity School
The University of Chicago

NOTES

1. W.R. Inge, *Christian Mysticism* (London: Methuen, 1899) p. 43.

2. Two indispensable German works both appeared in 1958. Friedrich Ohly, *Hohelied-Studien. Grundzüge einer Geschichte der Hoheliedauslegung des Abendlandes bis zum 1200* (Wiesbaden: Steiner, 1958); and Helmut Riedlinger, *Die Makelossigkeit der Kirche in dem lateinischen Hoheliedkommentaren des Mittelalters* (Münster: Aschendorff, 1958).

3. For an overview of some recent works, see B. McGinn, '"With the Kisses of the Mouth": Recent Work on the Song of Song', *Journal of Religion* 72 (1992) 269–275.

PREFACE

I HAVE COMPILED this volume in part to document and in part to explain a curious fact of western christian history. Male celibates, monks and priests, have for centuries described, expressed and celebrated their love of God in the language of sex. They did this in many genres of writing, occasionally in poetry, more often in set treatises on love, but most prolifically and characteristically in a thousand years of commentarial tradition on the Song of Songs. The apparent anomaly of their celibate condition taken together with their enthusiasm for the spiritually erotic is what I document and, in part, seek to explain.

Had I thought that this anomaly could be comprehensively explained in the way most obvious to the twentieth century mind, as the phenomenon of a psychopathology, I should not have found it curious. It might have been worth documenting, but it would not have been worth much effort explaining. But though freudian explanations are, in my view, often illuminating, they are unconvincing as a generalised account of the male celibate enthusiasm for the imagery of *eros* in the Middle Ages. Mediaeval monks do not seem all to have been repressed. Most seem to be happy. They *like* sexual imagery, and if a Freudian would require of repressed subjects that they are ignorant of the forces which they sublimate and that they misrecognise them in their sublimated form, then the mediaeval monk, by and large, lacks an important symptom: he *knows* what he is doing, he *intentionally* denies to himself a genital outlet for his sexuality and *deliberately* transfers his sexual energies upon a spiritual object.

In any case, no responsible Freudian, seeking an explanation of so long-standing a literary tradition as that of the Song commentary, would countenance a foolhardy 'reductivism' which simply ignored the reasons the monks themselves gave for their preferences. And if readers insist upon adding another kind of explanation to that which I offer, I merely ask them to begin from the commentators' own accounts of what they were doing, since these must form the primitive data of such an explanation. My own explanatory objective is limited to the sort of account which the monks themselves could have recognised in their own terms, and these are theological, spiritual, and hermeneutical.

My explanatory purpose is therefore of set purpose limited, and it might be worthwhile admitting what else is missing by way of a comprehensive explanation of mediaeval spiritual eroticism. First of all, I confine myself to male writers, not *because* they are male, but because I confine myself to writers of formal commentary on the Song of Songs, and they are all male. It would, of course, have been quite wrong to have said 'as a matter of fact' they are all male, as if the fact demanded no explanation, or as if none could be of any intrinsic importance. Almost certainly there is an explanation and within the illuminating work on gender and genre in mediaeval theological writings which is being done today it may be possible to account for this fact. To have neglected to state a position in relation to this work, as also in relation to much other interpretative material from which I have profited, is indeed to have left a second thing visibly missing, though the reader may be relieved, as I am, at a text relatively uncluttered by reference to secondary scholarship. Thirdly, in confining myself to the Song commentary, I have restricted the scope of my study of the erotic traditions of spirituality to but one out of a constellation of traditions to an extent which I describe in more detail in Chapter One. Fourthly, I have even neglected to provide much evidence beyond the minimum needed to lend some plausibility to my explanatory and historical hypotheses about the mediaeval Song commentary. Fifthly, I have attempted no general taxonomy of Song commentaries, though there are different styles and kinds both of exegesis and theology, even within the monastic traditions. I have looked for general features shared in common and I have neglected those issues which arise from the differences between one style and another. In all these ways, and in others too, I have restricted the scope of my discussion. In view of this it would be worth explaining more positively the purpose which this volume is intended to serve.

It is, *prima facie*, puzzling that men dedicated to a life of celibacy should find so natural a mode of expression for their spiritual aspirations in the erotic poetry of the Song. At any rate, if it is not so puzzling in itself—after all, these men wanted to talk about love, they needed a human model for it and sexual love is at least one obvious candidate—the intensity of their interest in the Song's eroticism and their unwillingness to bother with the credentials of other candidate models of love, certainly demands explanation. So the question 'Why the Song?' is the point of departure of my enquiry; and since, as I argue, it was *because of* not *in spite of* the Song's eroticism that their interest was aroused, the question 'Why *eros*?' is the natural counterpart to the first.

Furthermore, since these questions are not just asked *of* the Song commentary but are, as it were, addressed *to* it in its own terms, I seek an answer to them for the most part within those commentaries themselves. Here, however, contemporary readers are to some considerable degree thrown back upon their own resources of reconstruction, for the Song commentaries do not always address themselves explicitly to these questions. On the other hand, what they do say provides ample material for that reconstruction, sometimes in what they say in an explicit mood about the proper hermeneutical method of reading the Song, sometimes implicitly in how they gloss particular passages of the Song. I think it is possible to answer the question 'Why *eros*?' in terms which the commentators at least could have made their own, in reference to their sources, their theological presuppositions, and their perceptions of what they needed spiritually. I think it is possible, therefore, to explain why it was that, among all the books of the hebrew Scriptures, the Song leaped out of the page at them as maximising the spiritual resources of the erotic model of love.

I offer the proposition that the reasons why the erotic model of the love of God so appealed to the monastic commentator of the middle ages—and the vast majority of these commentators were monks—had to do with very fundamental preoccupations of the monastic theologian and that these, in turn, were intimately connected with the monks' perception of their *Sitz im Leben*. I shall not anticipate here the account I give later of what those preoccupations and perceptions were; suffice it to say that they are rooted in the monks' theological eschatology, in their sense that their life of partial withdrawal from the world situated them at a point of intersection between this world and the next, between time and eternity, between light and dark, between anticipation and fulfilment. This meant that the concept of love as a 'yearning' or 'longing'—as an *amor-desiderium*, or, in Greek, *eros*—exactly expressed what they wanted by way of a language of love.

But if love as *eros* was what they wanted, the language of love in those terms had been made available to them, as an answer to that need, by earlier, independent theological developments in which, in fact, the monks took little interest: christian speculative neo-platonism. It is fashionable today to play down the direct influence of neo-platonism on monastic theology and I share the conclusion of contemporary scholars that this was normally slight. Nonetheless, though christian neo-platonism in its form of metaphysics made little impact on the mediaeval monastic mind, it had a lot to do with the fact that the monk had the language of the erotic to hand, retrieved from its unacceptably pagan sources, christianised, apt for the purposes of monastic spirituality. In good part it was Origen who did this and in good part the pseudo-Denys; there were others, Gregory of Nyssa being one, whose influence was brought to bear, directly or indirectly, upon the latin West; and much of that influence was mediated through John Scottus Eriugena's translations of christian neo-platonic material, particularly of the pseudo-Denys and of Maximus the Confessor. These transmitted to the Latins greek christian refinements and accomodations with pagan *eros*. Had they not done so, had the speculative theologians of the greek and latin traditions not had urgent and deeply-rooted motives for accomodating the pagan inheritance of neo-platonic *eros*, the monks, who by intellectual temperament would not have done it for themselves, would have lacked a model of love to answer their needs.

It is the main purpose of this essay to claim plausibility for the hypothesis that the monks' conscious and acknowledged preoccupations with a biblical and eschatological theology met and cross-fertilised with sources in neo-platonic metaphysical eroticism in the Song commentary, even if they lacked interest in speculatively metaphysical neo-platonism in its own right. I offer no more than a case for this hypothesis and for no more than its plausibility. One of the reasons for the extensive documentation in the second part of this book is therefore to provide the reader with some of the materials from which the evidence for this hypothesis is drawn. This is done in the interests of fairness to the reader. For the reader might very well be able to doubt whether the evidence is sufficient and to draw a different conclusion from mine.

I have something to offer also by way of an historical hypothesis, this drawn on a broader canvas even than my account of the Song genre itself. The mediaeval Song commentary, as I argue in Chapter One, has a part to play in accounting for the fact that even today the language and imagery of the erotic is embedded in the contemporary experience of the love of God. John of the Cross stands at the point of contact between the Song commentary and our own discourse and I try to explain how and why this is. The fact that John of the Cross inherits and fuses influences both from the Song commentary and from mediaeval neo-platonism may, I concede, have skewed my thinking in favour of the hypothesis that the mediaeval Song commentary fuses both too, if only less consciously. I do not think that it has done so at the expense of a fair argument. In any case, my historical hypothesis is that we have inherited from John of the Cross the faded blooms of a spiritually erotic metaphor. He gets the metaphors from the mediaeval sources. But as he employs them they are no longer rooted in the soils in which they once flourished, either of monastic eschatology or of neo-platonic metaphysics. This, I emphasise, is not a comment on the power and vivacity of John's metaphors. But it is a comment on their relative decline in theological resonance. And if this is right, I think we can see how and why this happened in the development of the Song commentary from Gregory the Great to the late middle ages. John of the Cross' *Spiritual Canticle* is the natural outcome of those processes.

The how and the why lie in the history of mediaeval Old Testament hermeneutics. This is too vast a matter to have been dealt with adequately on the limited scale offered here. The levels of generalisation enforced by brevity elide nuance and I am particularly troubled by the element of counterfactual conditional entailed by my case that things could have turned out quite differently had there been, as there was not, an alternative practice of Song commentary based on the minority hermeneutic of a Thomas Aquinas. This may look to some just too speculative. Still, it is an illusion of some historians to suppose that counterfactual conditionals can be altogether expunged from historical explanations. Any claim that one thing happened because of another entails *some* claim about what would not or might not have happened had the causes been otherwise. In practice, too, sometimes the counterfactual illuminates the fact: what could have happened but did not can help us to see why what did happen did. In this case, the predominant hermeneutic of a Gregory is revealed in its tendencies to a formalised 'metaphorical' employment of the Song's eroticism by the contrast which is provided by the occasional more historically based hermeneutic of a Nicholas of Lyra, and more particularly by what we may suppose to have been the tendency of the theoretical hermeneutics of Thomas Aquinas. I make no general deconstructionist case: but I do find significance in the *absence* of a Thomist Song commentary, just as I think others ought to do in the absence of women Song commentators.

This volume, therefore, offers hypotheses of systematic, historical and hermeneutical kinds. Hypotheses are made to be challenged and are worth challenging if they are worth proposing, though their worth derives not alone from their power to illuminate, but also from their plausibility. I confess to being more confident of mine in their power to illuminate than in the quantity of direct evidence for them. In the meantime there is, I hope, a residual value in this book which may survive criticism even of its substantive theses. There is an increasing number of students, whose interests in these matters continues often to outstrip their knowledge of Latin. I shall at least have made available to them a wider range of the sources than they now possess with which to test such hypotheses, whether mine or anyone else's.

D.T.

1

Why Eros?

THE LANGUAGE of the love of God in the western christian tradition is notably erotic. This is unmistakably, even notoriously, true of the spanish Carmelites of the sixteenth century, John of the Cross and Teresa of Avila, who have so marked Catholic thought, language and experience in the subsequent three centuries. It is less well known in the patristic and mediaeval sources from which John and Teresa draw. But to whatever degree it is acknowledged in these sources, the language of erotic love inherited from them is so deeply embedded in the way Christians talk about their relationship with their God as to have become the near universal, spontaneous and unselfconscious idiom of that relationship. Nor only of how Christians speak of it, it is as much the idiom, the mood and the feel of their experience.

The western Christian has traditionally been a female soul in love with her Bridegroom. She has fallen in love with him, *my beloved is mine and I am his* (Sg 2:16). That love afflicts, soothes, consoles, thrills with the anticipation of consummation (Sg 8:3); the Bridegroom caresses (Sg 8:3), arouses (Sg 7:11), kisses *with the kiss of his mouth* (Sg 1:1); the soul and God are betrothed, they marry, they consummate and the soul becomes pregnant; the story of the soul is a love story, it tells of the vicissitudes of erotic love, of absence and longing for the presence of the beloved (Sg 3:1), of presence and delight (Sg 3:4), of possession and of elusiveness (Sg 5:6); there is wounding, there are tears, partings, forgiveness and reconciliation; the union of lovers is penetration, dissolution and absorption of each into the other in ecstatic self-abandonment. This is not the language of friends in conversation or of companions on a journey, of soldiers at war, or of kingdoms at peace; here are no images of a royal race, a wandering people, or even of a people made one by *agape*. These are the tones distinctively of *eros*, the language of hetero-sexual love.

Nor is this the language of some secondary tradition, for among the great teachers of the christian West there is hardly any rival, unless it be the language of friendship preferred by a minority, though admittedly that minority includes authorities of the stature of Aelred of Rievaulx[1] and Thomas Aquinas.[2] The language of *eros* is the language of Augustine and Gregory, of Bernard and William of Saint Thierry, of Alan of Lille; it is the language of Hadjewich and Mechtild of Magdeburg, of Francis and Bonaventure, but equally of Eckhart and the Rhineland School, of Jean Gerson and of Denys the Carthusian, of Nicholas of Cusa and of Catherine of Genoa. Beyond the Middle Ages proper, this language pervades the thought of Luis de Leon, of John of the Cross and Teresa. At first sight this preponderance in favour of the erotic must seem puzzling in view of a number of immediate and obvious considerations.

Most obviously, we must ask, Why *eros* in view of the rival candidature of agapeic love which, from the earliest christian years, Christians have made their own? Why *eros* in view of the manifestly pagan provenance of the word? Why *eros*, particularly in view of the morally doubtful associations of the word in common usage, attested to by both Origen[3] and the pseudo-Denys,[4] who, on the other hand, are among the christian writers who did most to commend the language of erotic love to the christian tradition? Taking into account the generally poor view which the christian tradition took of human sexuality in the very period in which the language of *eros* is most alive, why adopt, for the expression of the relationship between the human soul and God, the very model of love which the tradition least valued?

There is an argument, canvassed most systematically and forcefully by Anders Nygren,[5] that *eros* is essentially pagan, unchristian; that the attempt to marry neo-platonic *eros* with more genuinely christian agape—an attempt which, for Nygren, could have scarcely been more aptly illustrated than by the source-material contained in Part Two of this book—has produced a hybrid of irreconcilable opposites. On very different grounds, Fergus Kerr has more recently argued that the influence of platonic eroticism on the christian understanding of love 'has had fateful effects in the development of Christian spirituality and asceticism'.[6] Kerr voices a recurrent christian reserve about the erotic model of christian love—though his statement of the case against it is sometimes closer to an expression of personal distaste than an argument—a model which he compares unfavourably with his preferred aristotelian-thomistic model of charity as friendship:

> [in friendship] there is no question [as there is in *eros*] of one partner losing his or her identity in the other. The lover is not infatuated with the beloved. There is no annihilation of the self in submission to, or submersion in, the absolute other . . . We are friends with God. We do not lose ourselves in that self-hating spirituality which has afflicted so many people's lives nor in some ascetical detachment that would save us from the vulnerabilities of love.[7]

I will occasionally return to these and other general evaluations of the erotic model of christian love at points in the discussion where it will be possible to confirm or deny the suspicion that Kerr's account of the role of *eros* in western christian spirituality is a tendentious caricature.[8] Not having in common with either Nygren or Kerr any purpose of advocacy on behalf of or against the traditions of spiritual *eros*, and on the other hand lacking interest in psychoanalytical reductivist explanations of this tradition, I confine myself for the most part to documentation and theological explanation. Why *eros*? is the question, and it seems worthwhile seeking the mediaeval theologians' answers to it. On what theological grounds do those western Christians, whose language is so saturated with the imagery of *eros*, justify this discourse when, even to them, it was so manifestly a choice out of a range of available alternatives? Why, starting from within their own theological positions, did they find this language so commonly appealing to them when they themselves supplied all the reasons for distaste? What theological problems did this language enable them to articulate and resolve?

I ask these questions in relation to a particular genre of western christian writing, that long sequence of commentaries, written over the period from Gregory the Great in the late sixth century to John of the Cross in the late sixteenth, on a group of hebrew poems, the Song of Songs. With the exception of John of the Cross' Spanish re-writing of the Song, these are Latin prose works on a text read in the Latin of Jerome's Vulgate. In spite of their great generality, my questions may be legitimately asked of these commentaries because, throughout that millenium of christian theology, they form a connected tradition of writing, immensely popular with theologians of all schools, with mystics and with preachers and indeed with poets and liturgists, but above all with monks. These commentaries have a quite decisive part to play, though not an exclusive one, in the story of the integration of erotic language into the christian discourse of the latin West. Since, however, very little of this material is available to the contemporary non-specialist reader, I have put together in Part Two of this book a selection of extracts in translation, which is intended to be in some small measure representative of the traditions of commentary from which they are drawn.

THE TEXTS

From the outset it should be made clear both what are the limitations of purpose in publishing these texts and to what degree the selection is representative of the genre. So far as concerns the purpose of this anthology, the texts are to be read by hindsight—if not precisely to be seen from the standpoint of the post-mediaeval writings of John of the Cross and Teresa of Avila, then at least to be seen as a continuing tradition which reached a certain stage of development in their writings. For this reason, though the remaining texts are all mediaeval or earlier, I have placed a translation of John's *Spiritual Canticle* at the beginning of this anthology. At least superficially, the justification for this policy is obvious. John's *Spiritual Canticle* is written in conscious imitation of the Song of Songs. It contains innumerable literary references to its biblical source, both in dramatic structure and in imagery.[9] Moreover, his prose work of the same name is a commentary on his own poem, showing many parallels with the mediaeval traditions of commentary on the poems of the Song. Even in this procedure of commenting on his own version of the Song, John is not without mediaeval precedent. In the early fifteenth century the mystic and Chancellor of the University of Paris, Jean Gerson, did the same,[10] although his rewriting of the Song is a mechanical, wooden thing, scarcely above the literary level of a mnemonic. By contrast, John's *Spiritual Canticle* is regarded as a major work of Spanish literature. Nonetheless it is fair to say that his conception of the relation of prose commentary to poetic text is distinctly mediaeval, not modern: at any rate he shows no evidence of sharing that modern antipathy towards a technique of commentary which threatens to displace the poetic original, as if with its prose 'equivalent'.[11] That John should practice this solecism not even on the work of another but on his own poem displays a literary mentality which to us is puzzling, not to say gross; but it is capable of puzzling us only to the degree to which we yield to the temptation to read John as a 'modern'; whereas in this respect at least, he is best read against the background of mediaeval commentarial traditions.

Indeed, the story of the poem's composition is an object-lesson in the pre-romantic attitude to poetic writing. The *Spiritual Canticle* was written for the most part during John's imprisonment in Toledo. Subsequently he was asked by his friend of the Carmelite reform, Madre Ana de Jesus, to explain the meaning of the poem, to which he had by now added seven further stanzas. In his Prologue to the resulting prose commentary, John admits that the difficulty of his poetic imagery rivals that of the Song itself:

> If these similitudes are not read with the simplicity of the spirit of knowledge and love which they contain, they will seem to be absurdities rather than reasonable utterances, as will those comparisons of the divine Canticle of Solomon and other books of Sacred Scripture where the Holy Spirit, unable to express the fullness of His meaning in ordinary words, utters mysteries in strange figures and likenesses. The saintly doctors, no matter how much they have said or will say, can never furnish an exhaustive explanation of these figures and comparisons, since the abundant meanings of the Holy Spirit cannot be caught in words. Thus the explanation of these expressions usually contains less than what they in themselves embody.[12]

Nonetheless, in the spirit of those same 'saintly doctors', John proposes to give what he can by way of prose explanation of his own poetic imagery and is even prepared to rearrange the order of the stanzas to assist intelligibility of structure. In much of his commentary he not only expounds his poetry in the manner of the mediaeval Song commentator, he employs standard mediaeval glosses in his expositions of passages which he had borrowed directly from the Song.

All in all, we may say that in genre as well as more obviously in content and imagery, in the relation of poetic source to prose commentary upon it, John looks back towards the mediaeval traditions; and that, more generally, there is much to be said for reading the sanjuanist corpus as a whole against its background in the Middle Ages. Equally, I will argue that there is something to be said for reading the mediaeval tradition of commentary on the Song prospectively, as reaching forward to a point beyond the Middle Ages proper in John of the Cross. This may seem to be an improperly teleological assessment. But I do not in fact propose a judgment of John's writings as some apotheosis of that tradition, or of anything else, whether of mediaeval 'mysticism' or of latin 'mysticism' as such. That would be a value judgment which, at least in respect of the tradition of commentary on the Song, I do not happen to share; if I were to offer any at all, I would rather take the view that John's *Spiritual Canticle* represents at least theologically, if not in spiritual and psychological insight, the nadir of the mediaeval tradition. It seems, nonetheless, not improper to suggest an historical conjecture. Contemporary Christians are largely unaware of the mediaeval commentary on the Song. But if, within our own language and imagery we have inherited much from patristic and mediaeval eroticism, it is by and large through John of the Cross that we have done so. John's writings face simultaneously both ways: back to the Middle Ages, forward to our own age. The intention, therefore, in presenting these mediaeval texts is to go some way towards documenting, through first-hand materials in translation, how those continuities of erotic discourse develop from patristic and mediaeval sources to the modern era, through the mediation of John of the Cross.

Secondly, and as regards the limitations of the selection itself, the texts chosen for this anthology nearly all come from commentaries on the Song of Songs, with the exception of three from the twelfth, thirteenth and fourteenth centuries which are chosen to illustrate theoretical principles of hermeneutics which in some important respects challenge the majority practice of interpretation. The place of these three extracts, from Hugh of Saint Victor, Thomas Aquinas, and Nicholas of Lyra, will be explained later. But though the commentarial tradition from which the rest of the texts are drawn has, without question, an important role in the development of western mystical eroticism, it is by no means the only, or even the only important influence. As a result, looked at even from the standpoint of the sources of John of the Cross, the selection hardly does justice to the complexity of the converging flows of influence, still less, in more general terms, to the sourcing of western mystical eroticism as such. I shall be arguing that the mediaeval, particularly the mediaeval monastic, fascination with the erotic as the language of divine love, owes much to the coming together, particularly in Origen, of pagan neo-Platonism with the Hebrew Song of Songs. But let it be said here and now that I by no means offer this hypothesis as a complete explanation of anything: for, first, the erotic mysticism of the neo-Platonists makes its influence felt on the latin West elsewhere, indeed in other places more forcefully, than in and through the Song commentary, and often directly—upon, for example, Meister Eckhart and the *Cloud* Author. Secondly, there are other sources, in themselves independent of either neo-Platonism or the Song, which feed erotic language and imagery into theological discourse, most notably the so-called 'courtly love' tradition, whose effects are so markedly felt in the language of the women mystics, Hadjewich and Mechtild of Magdeburg. They, at any rate do not write in the predominantly monastic and male genre of the Song commentary. They were much more inclined, like John of the Cross, to rewrite the Song in their own poetic forms—but, unlike John, they do not commonly gloss further in prose. Thirdly, there is evidence for the hypotheses both that the Song commentary influenced secular love literature in the later Middle Ages and that the courtly love tradition also fed into the monastic commentary,[13] perhaps especially in the twelfth century and most especially of all through Bernard of Clairvaux, whose influence, in turn, on the mediaeval commentaries of the later Middle Ages is unquestionably decisive.

But however complex this tangle of influence may be, it remains true that mediaeval commentary on the Song is capable of being studied broadly in its own terms and that it repays that study in knowledge of how erotic discourse comes to occupy so central a place in the western Christian way of understanding divine love. Within that tradition of commentary I have selected the extracts which form Part Two of this volume.

Thirdly, then, within that genre of the Song commentary, though my selection is by no means arbitrary, the extracts fall far short of an adequate representation. They range from Gregory the Great in the late sixth century to Denys the Carthusian in the mid-fifteenth. Under-represented is the period between Gregory and the twelfth century and there will be those who will particularly regret the absence of Bede;[14] the inclusion of a brief extract from Alcuin, whose commentary is a mere compendium of Gregory and Bede, may allow a glimpse of something of the desire for continuity which so dominates in that period. Others, who know the field in more detail, will note the absence of Honorius Autun[15] and Rupert of Deutz.[16] Moreover, though I have included three commentarial extracts from the twelfth century—from Bernard of Clairvaux, Alan of Lille and from Thomas of Perseigne—and one theoretical piece from Hugh of Saint Victor, no such brief extracts can do more than offer a taste of the richness and variety which that century has to offer in this genre. Again, there is much to regret in the omission of Anselm of Laon[17] and of Richard of Saint Victor.[18]

Moreover, the degree of representativeness of my anthology is further reduced by the fact that only one of my commentarial extracts extends beyond Chapter 1, verse 8. The reason for this lies in the historical *terminus a quo* of the anthology in Gregory the Great. There is evidence that Gregory wrote a commentary on the major part of the Song and throughout the Middle Ages commentators believed that they possessed the complete text. In fact what they possessed was but a torso of genuine gregorian writing taking his commentary up to and including verse 8 of Chapter 1, the rest being made up by a commentary of Robert of Tombelaine written in the eleventh century.[19] What is contained in this volume is the translation of all that is available to us of Gregory's own commentary. To facilitate the study of the continuities and changes of commentarial fashion in the tradition which flows from Gregory, the selections from subsequent commentators, with the exception of those from Nicholas of Lyra, are likewise confined at the most to the first eight verses of the Song, and sometimes to less. No doubt much is thereby lost in variety and something is gained in repetitiveness—not to say tedium—which could have been avoided by excerpting more consciously with an eye to contemporary preference and taste. But we do gain therefrom a basis for comparisons, and the reader is, I hope, introduced at least to the sheer foreigness of the mediaeval style by an anthology compiled on no principle of flattery to contemporary preoccupations.

It follows from this that neither the intrinsic merit nor the degree of influence of the authors anthologised is in any particular ratio to the length of the extracts. The enormously influential *Sermons on the Song of Songs* of Bernard of Clairvaux are available in complete translation[20] and for this reason I have instead translated an excerpt from the very much briefer precis of the first thirty nine of his

Sermons, the *Brevis Commentatio*, compiled, it is thought, by his friend and fellow Cistercian, William of Saint Thierry. While comparatively dull stuff, it contains with sufficient precision the outlines of the doctrines and priorities of the *Sermons*. But if we do not lose much in substance, we lose dramatically in style and rhetorical force. Denys the Carthusian, on the other hand, who, it seems, could only write at length, provides passages of rhetorical exuberance and vitality scarcely rivalled in the mediaeval period except by Bernard of Clairvaux himself.[21] Such passages are far between and are, as it were, volcanic eruptions set in an arid desert of prolixity. Compared with the terse concentration of the bernardine *Brevis Commentatio* or of Alan of Lille's *Elucidatio*, it is much inferior. To have excerpted more of Denys' purple from his plain merely for the sake of a shorter and more superficially appealing read would, however, have been untruthful.

In other respects, the selection is governed by some general principles. The tradition of commentary on the Song is predominantly monastic and so therefore are my selections. Nonetheless, there is a more academic, school-based tradition which flourished from the twelfth century to the end of the Middle Ages and this is represented by the later thirteenth-century Augustinian master of Paris, Giles of Rome, and by the fourteenth-century Franciscan, Nicholas of Lyra. Much sets the scholastic apart from the monastic style, though both the degree and nature of these differences ought not to be set quite as firmly in concrete as some have done, for example Jean Leclercq.[22] According to Leclercq, the scholastic emphasis is on the collective and ecclesiological interpretation, on faith, on the knowledge of the mysteries, and on the presence of God in the world through the Incarnation. The scholastic commentary addresses the intellect, is almost always concise and complete, and explains the entire letter of the text. The monastic commentary, on the other hand, emphasises God's relations with the soul, Christ's presence within it, and the spiritual union realised through charity. It is in effect a treatise on the love of God, aimed to touch the heart rather than instruct the mind, and is written in a fervent style and normally left unfinished. As a generalisation, perhaps this will do, but even the minimal selection contained in Part Two of this book hardly bears this classification out. Even if we disregard Thomas Gallus' 'mixed' interpretation as being untypical in its explicit acknowledgement of scholastic neo-platonist and monastic biblical sources, few of the more typical authors fit neatly into Leclercq's categorisations: Giles', for example, is undoubtedly a 'scholastic' commentary, but it emphasises the priority of charity over knowledge of the mysteries; Gregory's is undoubtedly 'monastic' as is Alan's, though both set individual interpretations against an ecclesiological, 'collective' background.

Leclercq's over-tidy categories can, however, be verified at the end of the Middle Ages by comparing the conservative, extreme allegoricism of Denys the Carthusian with the consciously polemical 'literalism' of Lyra or with the 'philosophical' exegesis of Giles. But from yet another point of view—that of exegetical theory—we need to be cautious about an over-ready categorisation into monastic and scholastic styles. For though there are quite considerable divergencies of exegetical theory in the Middle Ages, these do not always correspond neatly with *any* such distinctions as can legitimately be made between monastic and scholastic styles, least of all with Leclercq's. In any case, both the continuities and differences on theoretical matters may be studied through the long methodological introductions of Gregory and Denys and through the more systematic 'alternative' treatments of hermeneutical method contained in the extracts from Hugh of Saint Victor, Thomas Aquinas and Nicholas of Lyra. It ought also, thereby, to be possible to find some clues not only to how in practice the mediaeval commentators read the Song but also to why they thought they were justified in reading it in the way they did.

A second purpose which this anthology may go some way towards serving is to illustrate the theory and practice of mediaeval exegesis of the Old Testament. I shall be discussing later how the hermeneutical doctrines of the mediaeval commentator mesh with the interest in the erotic.[23] In the meantime we should note that in one way the commentary on the Song is truly representative of that hermeneutic, for the Song is perhaps, after Genesis and Psalms, the most frequently expounded book of the Old Testament in the Middle Ages.[24] In another way it is unrepresentative, for the Song is a very special case, in which the mediaeval predeliction for allegorical and typological readings is reinforced by the very particular difficulty the mediaeval commentator had in accepting any literal interpretation of a blatantly erotic and apparently secular poem. As early as Origen it is possible to see how that difficulty in accepting a 'literal' interpretation creates a pressure to theorise the necessity of an allegorical interpretation[25] and at the very end of our period we find Denys arguing quite simply that the Song cannot 'literally' refer to the actual love between Solomon and the Shulamite girl, or else it would be nothing but a secular love poem (n. 4). Even Nicholas of Lyra, an enthusiastic advocate of a new 'literalism' in the fourteenth century, agrees that whatever the Song *is* literally about it is not literally about sexual love (n. 19). From Origen to the end of the Middle Ages, then, the Song's overtly sexual eroticism provided a powerful *argument* for the general principle of the allegorical interpretation of the Old Testament as such and not just an instance of its application. For this reason, through the study of the mediaeval commentary on the Song it is possible to get at one of the motivating forces of mediaeval biblical hermeneutics. On the other hand, mediaeval commentators by and large recognised the exceptional character of the Song and one could easily be led into an unbalanced assessment of mediaeval 'allegoricism' through an excessive concentration on this particular genre of mediaeval Old Testament commentary.

WHY THE SONG?

All this being said, we are left with the question, Why? Why did mediaeval commentators so favour this text? Any answer to this question will have to be given at a number of levels and perhaps no answer at any level will do for the whole history of the genre. At one level the answer needs to be studied in terms of what individual commentators, or at the most groups of commentators in particular periods, thought they could get out of the text, and here some broad trends are detectable. Gregory valued the Song at least partly because it forced the issue of allegorical interpretation, but as much and more because by means of the allegorical interpretation of a narrative of erotic love, betrothal and marriage and their vicissitudes, he could extract a model through which to develop and deepen simultaneously an ecclesiology, an account of the progress of the christian soul in its contemplative quest for union with God and of the interactions between these two dimensions.[26] In Gregory, the ecclesiology predominates and above all the Song provides him with a model of the enduring love of God for his people and of theirs for their God; for Gregory, the Song is a divine love-story whose reference stretches across all time and history, from the creation, through the Covenant with Israel, the incarnation of Christ, the emergence and expansion of the Christian Church, to, finally, its ultimate fulfilment in the Kingdom. It is onto this vast ecclesiological narrative of history that Gregory plots his story of the particular journey of the individual soul. The personal story interacts with, but is decidedly dependent on, the ecclesiological.[27]

By the twelfth century the emphasis had changed and was relatively stronger on the 'moral' or personal reading: the love of Solomon and the Shulamite models the individual's relationship with Christ, and as a result the language of the commentary itself—particularly in Bernard—becomes more personal, more directly expressive, less detached and explicative, as if the model has become incorporated into the monk's own personal relationship with God. Then there are other, more particular, purposes—the most striking being Alan's—which is to find in the Song an allegorical, scriptural basis for the emergent mariological preoccupations of his century. There are qualifications which must be added to this picture, which reduce these differences to a matter of emphasis. In one of the finest passages in Gregory's commentary, he develops the familiar gregorian theme of *conpunctio*, the touching of the individual soul with sorrow and repentence, likened to the 'kiss of his mouth' which the Bride longs for in the first verse of the Song (n. 18). Contrariwise, within his mariological interpretation, Alan never allows the reader to forget that praise of Mary, the mother of God, is rooted in her role within the Church (n. 31). By and large we can say that, though emphases change and increasing weight is attached to moral interpretations in the twelfth century, the concerns continue to be with the interdependence of ecclesiological and moral interpretations. Only in the very late mediaeval commentary of Denys the Carthusian do the ecclesiological, the individual, and mariological readings become separated out from one another along clear lines of demarcation. It is hard not to think of Denys' three-fold commentary as indicating a decline from a twelfth-century ideal of an integrated reading.[28]

In short, a first answer to the question why the mediaeval commentators took so enthusiastically to the Song must be given in terms of the ecclesiological, ascetical, and devotional gains the writers thought they could win from the allegorical reading of it. But this first step towards an answer leaves the most pressing question unresolved. Many other Old Testament texts provided opportunities for allegorical interpretations, yielding much the same theological output, whether ecclesiological or moral. Very little is contained in what we possess of Gregory's Song commentary which is not contained more amply in his massive

Moralia in Job. My notes to his text to some degree illustrate this theological dependence. Later, in the Middle Ages, the impression is reinforced that the theological and spiritual results won by the commentators' exegesis are not so much wrested *de novo* from that text as given in advance and read into it. In Alan, perhaps, the text of the Song provokes new connections of imagery and thought, but we would hardly say this of Alcuin, Giles or Denys the Carthusian, in whom everything said in connection with the Song appears already theologically formed independently of it. As in so many other ways, the outstanding exception is Bernard, for whom the Song is a central biblical source. His *Sermons* integrate important, novel theological insight with a genuine, exuberant pleasure in the Song's own repertoire of discourse and imagery. But sadly, the integration of theology and imagery is nowhere near as successful in much mediaeval exegesis of the Song.

Here we may as well anticipate a later question: if the Song provided the mediaeval commentator with abundant material for very varied theological reflections, why is it that not one mediaeval Song commentary makes anything at all of the theological topic the text throws in the commentator's face: the theology of sexuality and of marriage? Search the catalogue of mediaeval Song commentaries for even a hint of this theological interest. Result, zero. It is not as if there was no discussion of these matters. Authors who write Song commentaries also write formal treatises on marriage.[29] But never in their Song commentaries. Why?

The question becomes all the more puzzling when we consider that, even if the Song was not itself always the originating source of the theological content the mediaeval commentator found in it, neither is it true to say that it was only a secondary source of a disposable, if particularly congenial and appropriate, imagery. Rarely does the commentator treat the language of the Song merely as a decorative metaphor with which, as if out of a contingent aesthetic preference, pre-formed theological propositions are merely embellished. This must especially be said of Bernard. There is something specific to the Song which the mediaeval christian mind needed and could get only, or at least most authoritatively, from the Song. Bearing in mind the immense popularity of the Song, bearing in mind the enthusiasm and pleasure with which mediaeval commentators poured their best efforts into its elucidation; taking into account, on the other side, the reasons for eschewing this text altogether with which their own somewhat negative attitudes towards human sexuality supplied them, and taking into account finally their unproblematically positive appreciation of other forms of human love, especially of friendship—bearing all these factors in mind, we seem to conclude that the Song had to offer the mediaeval commentator something which only the Song could supply; and that that something was precisely what was most specific to and characteristic of it: its exuberant celebration of *eros*. We are, if this is so, forced to conclude that it was not in spite of the Song's eroticism, but because of it, that Gregory, Bernard, Alan, and Denys, and a hundred other mediaeval commentators, warmed to this text. To the authors of this unbroken thousand years of commentarial tradition, the natural, spontaneous, but also reflectively apt, human model for divine love is love in its erotic expression.

WHY EROS?

Our question 'Why the Song?' therefore becomes 'Why *eros*?' Why think of the love of God as an erotic mutuality? Why is the drama of this love, in history, Church, and individual, best reflected in the discourse of falling in love, betrothal, marriage, and consummation? Why is this unashamed delight of the lovers in each other's bodies—face, hair, breasts, eyes, limbs—the root image of the mutual pleasure of God and the soul in each other's presence? Why is the Incarnation a 'kiss of his mouth'? Why did Bernard,[30] and before him Gregory,[31] and Origen,[32] hold that, of all the great canticles of the hebrew and christian scriptures—songs of victory, of exhortation, of aggression, of rejoicing and of gratitude—this song of uninhibited eroticism in which there is not a single mention of Israel's God, was nonetheless the highest of all songs, *the* Song of Songs?

The historical answer to these questions lies, I suggest, in a complex tissue of relationships between two broad streams of influence present throughout the Middle Ages: first, the greek tradition of *eros* which flows ultimately from Plato's *Symposium* through the erotic mysticism of pagan neo-platonism into Origen and the pseudo-Denys, thence to be transmitted to the western theological tradition through the latin translations of Scottus Eriugena in the eighth century; and second, a package of theological preoccupations which are specifically monastic, above all those of a theology of history and an eschatological biblical hermeneutic. At times these two streams flow together, uniquely perhaps in Thomas Gallus; more commonly they flow separately and as they flow they develop, sometimes to converge in transmuted forms, at others not to meet. Even from the evidence which has been carefully studied we know this history to be far too complex to be told in a single volume. And by no means all the evidence is in which would be needed to secure this hypothesis on firmer foundations.

Nonetheless a sufficient basis exists in the evidence compiled in Part Two for affirming the conjoint causality of these two streams of influence as having generated and sustained the mediaeval fascination with the erotic. Naturally, in its most general form, not each and every mediaeval commentary, or even most of them, show explicit evidence of this parentage; but the classical mediaeval commentary on the Song of Songs is intelligible if one reads it against the background of the neo-platonic and monastic preoccupations which converge upon it. No doubt there could be other explanations. No doubt to establish more conclusively that these two streams of influence not only might, but do, explain the Song genre, would require a source-critical investigation on scales both of breadth and detail which I do not here undertake. My claims are more limited than those of proof: neo-platonic eroticism *was* a powerful influence upon many aspects of mediaeval theology, even if only relatively indirectly upon the monastic tradition; the monk *did* read his Bible from within an eschatological hermeneutic which, as we will see, can very well explain his receptiveness to a neo-platonic model of love as *eros*; and if the monk was unlikely to have been much influenced by speculative neo-platonising theology, he could nonetheless receive the model more happily from a biblical source—and he found it in the Song of Songs. If not for proof, my case is that there is evidence at least for very strong plausibility.

NOTES

1. Aelred of Rievaulx even recasts the foundationally erotic imagery of 'the kiss of his mouth' (Sg 1:1) in terms of spiritual friendship and adapts Bernard's threefold distinction of kisses into 'corporeal', 'spiritual', and 'intellectual' to his purposes, see *Spiritual Friendship* 2.22–27, Cistercian Fathers Series, 5 (Kalamazoo: Cistercian Publications, 1977) pp. 75–77.

2. Thomas Aquinas twice discusses the question of charity as friendship, in his *Scriptum super Libros Sententiarum*, III, dist. 27, q. 2, a. 1; and in the *Summa Theologiae*, 2–2ae, q. 23, a. 1.

3. Prologue to the *Commentary on the Song of Songs*, in *Origen*, trans. Rowan A. Greer (New York: Paulist Press, 1979) pp. 219–220—referred to hereafter as 'Greer'.

4. *Divine Names*, 708B–709D in *Pseudo-Dionysius, The Complete Works*, trans. Colm Luibheid (New York: Paulist Press, 1987)—referred to hereafter as 'Luibheid'.

5. Anders Nygren, *Agape and Eros*, A Study of the Christian Idea of Love, Part I, trans. A.G. Herbert (London: SPCK, 1932) pp. 23–27.

6. Fergus Kerr OP, 'Charity as Friendship', in *Language Meaning and God*, Essays in Honour of Herbert McCabe OP, ed. Brian Davies OP (London: Chapman, 1987) p. 7.

7. Kerr, p. 22.

8. See pp. 63–64 below.

9. I have annotated the text of the *Spiritual Canticle* to show at least the most literal points of dependence.

10. Jean Gerson, *Super Canticum canticorum*, in *Jean Gerson, Oeuvres Complètes*, Introd. textes et notes, Mgr P. Glorieux, Vol. VIII (Paris, 1971) pp. 565–639.

11. I have more to say on this subject below, pp. 191–196.

12. *The Spiritual Canticle*, in *The Collected Works of St John of the Cross*, trans. K. Kavanaugh OCD and Otilio Rodriguez OCD (Washington: ICS Publications, 1979) pp. 408–409.

13. E. Anne Matter in *The Voice of My Beloved: The Song of Songs in Western Mediaeval Christianity* (Pennsylvania: University of Pennsylvania Press, 1990) pp. $–$, presents evidence of a varied influence of the Song genre on religious and secular, vernacular and latin literature from the twelfth century on.

14. Bede, *In Canticum canticorum libri VI*, in *Bedae Venerabilis Opera*, Pars II, Opera Exegetica, 2B, ed. D. Hurst OSB, CCSL, 119 (Turnholt, 1983) pp. 165–375.

15. *Expositio in Cantica canticorum*, PL 172:347–496.

16. *Commentaria in Canticum canticorum*, ed. H. Haacke, CCCM, 26 (1974).

17. *Enarratio in Canticum canticorum*, PL 162:1187–1228, though this is a shortened version of a text existing only in MS, neither being any longer attributed to Anselm of Laon himself.

18. *In Cantica canticorum expositio*, PL 196:405–524.

19. P. Verbraken, 'La Tradition manuscrite du Commentaire de St Gregoire sur le Cantique des Cantiques', *Rev. Ben.* 73 (1963) 277–288.

20. *Sermons on the Song of Songs*, trans. Killian Walsh OCSO and Irene Edmonds, Cistercian Fathers Series, 4, 7, 31, 40 (Kalamazoo, 1977 *et seq.*).

21. See below, pp. 434–438.

22. See *The Love of Learning and the Desire for God*, trans. Catherine Misrahi, (London: SPCK—New York: Fordham University Press, 1978) p. 107.

23. See below, pp. 71–80.

24. Matter says, without any qualification, that 'the Song of Songs was the most frequently interpreted book of mediaeval Christianity' (p. 6). Even though this cannot be right, she is able to list over one hundred Song commentaries before 1200.

25. Origen, *Prologue to the Commentary on the Song of Songs*, in Greer, pp. 217–244.

26. Of course there are many other particular theological topics which are nearly universally treated even in the small number of extracts in my anthology: the incarnation, the Trinity, the problems between the early Church and Israel, schism and heresy being only the most common.

27. In Gregory's commentary above all it is possible to see what is lost from view by an over-rigid application of Leclercq's distinction between scholastic and monastic styles of commentary: what is subtle about Gregory's commentary is the *interplay between* individual and collective interpretations; he, at least does not set them at odds with one another and it seems equally implausible to think of Bernard's *Sermons* as if he did.

28. See below, pp. 168–173.

29. See J. Leclercq, *Monks on Marriage, A Twelfth-Century View* (New York: Seabury Press, 1982).

30. *Sermon*, 1.7.

31. Nn. 6–7.

32. Greer, pp. 236–239.

2

EROS AND ECSTASY

CREATION AS ECSTASY

IN ACCOUNTING for the neo-platonic sources of the eroticism of the mediaeval Christian West, one authority is, if not uniquely, at least decisively influential. Probably early in the sixth century of our era a shadowy figure, representing himself as 'Denys the Areopagite', the Athenian convert of Saint Paul, and universally known as such until the late fifteenth century, wrote of the mutual love of God and the soul, and also of the cosmic relation of all created being and God, as an *eros* and an ecstasy. For this Denys (or, as we must now call him, 'pseudo-Denys') the appropriateness of the language of *eros* to God is rooted in a primordial truth. Creation itself is an explosion of erotic energy, the ecstasy of a God who, in his act of creating, stands outside himself, perhaps literally 'beside himself' with love. Denys' word for that love is *eros*:

> . . . in truth it must be said that the very cause of the universe in the beautiful, good abundance of his benign yearning (*eros*) for all is carried outside of himself in the loving care he has for everything. He is, as it were, beguiled by goodness, by love (*agape*) and

> by yearning (*eros*) and is enticed away from his transcendent dwelling place and comes to abide within all things, and he does so by virtue of his supernatural and ecstatic capacity to remain, nevertheless, within himself . . . (*DN*, 712A–712B)

Concerned lest in a theological context this explicit use of the word *eros* might scandalise, Denys nevertheless firmly insists upon the appropriateness of the word as one being, in his time, scarcely distinguishable in meaning from the more traditional christian term, *agape*: 'in my opinion the sacred writers regard "yearning" (*eros*) and "love" (*agape*) as having one and the same meaning' (*DN*, 709B).[1] Witnessing to the depth of biblical precedent lying behind this usage, he comments,

> Now if [in this usage] I would appear to be misusing holy scripture, let the critics of the word 'yearning' (*eros*) listen to this: *Yearn for her and she shall keep you; exalt her and she will extol you; honor her and she will embrace you* (Prov 4, 6 & 8, LXX). And there are many other scriptural passages in which the yearning (*eros*) of God is praised . . . (The scriptural writers) added 'real' to the use of 'yearning' (*eros*) regarding divine things because of the unseemly nature such a word has for men . . . to those listening properly to the divine things the name 'love' (*agape*) is used by the sacred writers in divine revelation with the exact same meaning as the term 'yearning' (*eros*) . . . (*DN*, 709A-C)

If the created order, and if we ourselves, are the ecstatic outflow of God, then our return to God is our reciprocating ecstasy, our standing outside ourselves in God:

> This divine yearning (*eros*) brings ecstasy so that the lover belongs not to self but to the beloved. This is shown in the providence lavished by the superior on the subordinate . . . and it is shown by the subordinates in their divine return toward what is higher.

> This is why the great Paul, swept along by his yearning (*eros*) for God and seized of its ecstatic power, had this inspired word to say: 'It is no longer I who live, but Christ who lives in me'. (Gal 2:20) Paul was truly a lover and, as he says, he was beside himself for God, possessing not his own life but the life of the One for whom he yearned, as exceptionally beloved. (*DN*, 712A)

What is more, thirdly, that *eros* which is the dynamic of the soul's return to God is one and the same with the erotic outflow from God which is our creation. The soul returns to God as *to* the source *from* which it flowed; and it returns *by means of* the same *eros* to which it returns. It is round that the cycle of creation goes and it is *eros* which makes that circle go round:

> Why is it . . . that the theologians sometimes refer to God as Yearning (*eros*) and Love (*agape*) and sometimes as the yearned-for and the Beloved? On the one hand he causes, produces and generates what is being referred to, and, on the other hand, he is the thing itself. He is stirred by it and he stirs it . . . He is yearning (*eros*) on the move, simple, self-moved, self-acting, pre-existent in the Good, flowing out from the Good onto all that is and returning once again to the Good. In this divine yearning (*eros*) shows especially its unbeginning and unending nature travelling in an endless circle through the Good, from the Good, in the Good and to the Good, unerringly turning, ever on the same center, ever in the same direction, always proceeding, always remaining, always being restored to itself. (*DN*, 712C–713A)

THE PROBLEM OF CREATION

For the pseudo-Denys, then, the dynamic of creation is *eros* and the dynamic of the return of creation to its source is *eros*. There is just one *eros*, a single, homogeneous stream in contrasting movements of flow and ebb. And there is no doubt that the pseudo-Denys' choice of this term as a key to his theological system is as a governing, constructive image. In any sense in which metaphors are ever 'mere', this is no mere metaphor. On the one hand, the pseudo-Denys' metaphysics needs the language of *eros* and, on the other hand, the language of *eros* is stabilised and controlled by the metaphysics.

On the side of need, there are two overwhelmingly difficult problems for the christian platonist metaphysician and both concern the doctrine of creation itself. For the Christian, orthodoxy requires the representation of the act of creation as the free act of the divine will *ad extra*. On the other hand, for the Platonist the difficulty with this conception of creation arises both on the score of its character as a free act and as concerns the possibility in principle of God's acting 'outside' himself. The concept of creation as an erotic ecstasy goes some way towards meeting both difficulties.

For the platonising Christian, God is above all else unity, a oneness beyond all differentiation. Creation, on the other hand, is multiplicity. If anything at all *other than* God exists, then God's absolute oneness appears threatened. For if there is anything other than God it would seem to follow that there is something in God which is his otherness than creation, some character of being differentiated. But if there is anything from which God has to be differentiated, then it further seems to follow that God is a being whose nature is, in part, that by virtue of which he is different from anything else. It seems to follow, in short, that God is but one kind of being among a multiplicity of kinds of being, a being among others. This cannot be so: as the pseudo-Denys comments: '. . . God is not some kind of being' (*DN*, 817D); 'He does not possess *this* kind of existence and not *that*' (*DN*, 824B). In that case, it would seem, there cannot be anything other than God, nothing can exist *ad extra*, if the absolute unity and undifferentiation of God is to be preserved.

If there is a difficulty about how anything can exist other than God, there is even greater difficulty, deriving equally from the oneness of God, concerning how God could *cause* anything to exist other than himself. How can that which is absolutely 'one' cause multiplicity without itself falling from oneness? The mere existence of anything other than God would appear to set God within a complex of *external* differentiations. But worse, for God to *cause* anything other than himself would *prima facie* be to suppose differentiation *within* the very being of the godhead itself. And there cannot be differentiation within that which is the cause of all, for internal differentiation and multiplicity is a characteristic precisely of creatures. Consequently, God cannot cause multiplicity to exist without himself becoming multiple. But for God to become multiple is for God to cease to be God. Therefore, God cannot cause anything other than himself to exist.

This, in excessively condensed form, is the neo-platonist's problem with the doctrine of creation. But even if these problems could be overcome, further difficulties would lie in wait with the orthodox christian doctrine that God's act of creation *ex nihilo* is a *free* act. Just as neo-platonist theology rests upon the absolute oneness of the godhead, so it depends upon the characterisation of that godhead as 'necessary being'. Nor is that connection of properties incidental. The reason why the godhead is 'necessary being' lies in the absolute oneness of God.

For we may not conceive of God's creative activity *ad extra* as his choice of one action out of a range of potential alternative actions, whether the alternatives envisaged are to have created some other universe than the one he has created or to have not created anything at all. 'Could have, but did not' cannot be said of God as if implying any potentiality, any unrealised capacity in God. Correspondingly, to think of God's creating the universe he has created as something he might *not* have done—to predicate of God 'Did, but might not have done'—is likewise to think of the act of creation as the realisation of the capacity to create. Hence, we can allow neither the predication 'God could have created other universes, but did not' nor the predication 'God created this universe, but might not have' in any sense which would entail potentiality, whether unrealised or realised.

For in principle, potentiality cannot be predicated of God. Potentiality is predicable only of creatures, and this is because potentiality implies multiplicity and multiplicity implies limitation. Potentiality implies multiplicity because within any being which has the potentiality to be or to do something we must distinguish between that potentiality and its realisation. I am not absolutely 'one' if it is possible to distinguish in me between what I can be and what I am. And potentiality implies limitation because it implies dependence. That which can be, but is not, depends upon something else for its realisation.

Now if, in describing God's activity of creation, we can neither say 'God might have created other things, but did not' nor 'God created the universe, but might not have' in any sense in which it is entailed that God is a potential being, then we have no sense available to us in which we can describe God as 'free'. For if we have to rule out all language of alternatives to what is, what is can be described only as 'necessary'. God *has* created the universe, therefore *necessarily* he created the universe.

There is no doubt that the pseudo-Denys recognised these difficulties in reconciling his avowed platonism with the christian doctrine of creation; equally, there is no doubt that he thought of these difficulties as occupying the centre of the agenda of the christian follower of platonism. This to say, however, that for him these difficulties were central within the problem of whether we can say anything about God at all. Platonism—whether we have in mind the thought of Plato himself or the revised platonism of

Plotinus and Proclus, on whom the pseudo-Denys drew so extensively—is a world of thought in which the dialectics of unity and differentiation and of freedom and necessity predominate over all other matters. It is hardly an exaggeration to say that platonism *is* the thinking through of these dialectics. But when this dialectical preoccupation of pagan platonism intersects with the judaeo-christian doctrine of the free creative activity of God, the tensions are so acute as to threaten the very project of their reconciliation.

CATAPHATIC AND APOPHATIC THEOLOGY

The pseudo-Denys' solution at the level of dialectical theology is found in a sophisticated and complex doctrine of language about God. This is not the place for more than a sketch of that doctrine, for here we are concerned less with the dialectical theology itself than with the way in which it at once calls for and then underpins the imagery of *eros*. The pseudo-Denys' account of language about God presupposes the fundamental rhythm of flow and ebb, of creation *ad extra* and return *ad intra*, to which correspond, respectively, the affirmative and negative moments of theological language, the cataphatic and the apophatic.

Because, the pseudo-Denys says, all creation flows from God, and because in that outpouring of the divine being into creation every creature retains within it a trace of its divine source, every creature in some way reflects, or is in some way an image or 'similitude' of, the divine nature from which it flows. That being so, every description of a creature is a potential source of language about God (*DN*, 597A). No doubt, as we will see, *all* language fails in its representation of the divine, and some images fail more than others do, but before anything we say of God fails it leads us some part of the way back up the ladder of language to that exact point at which it fails. All language about God has to be stretched before it snaps. But everything we can truly say about something God has created can be stretched out towards the representation of God. And this is because in its creation each thing is the stretching out of God towards it.[2]

For the pseudo-Denys, language about God is truly unrestricted in range. Anything can be said about God which describes something God has created.[3] Far from the pseudo-Denys' conception of appropriate talk about God is that attenuated vocabulary of specialised terms of art which the expression 'religious language' suggests today. We may even say that for the pseudo-Denys there is nothing particularly 'religious' about religious language at all. 'Religious language', had he had any meaning for the expression, would have meant for him simply ordinary language stretched to the limit of its significance. There, where it is overstretched to the point of breaking, talk about creatures comes to be talk about God. It is, therefore, intrinsic to the logic of theological language as he conceives of it that we not only may, but must, exploit to the fullest the possibilities of human experience and imagination in the attempt to utter God. The 'wise men' of the scriptures praise 'the Cause of everything that is' in using 'names drawn from all the things caused' (*DN*, 596B). 'Every attribute may be predicated of him . . .' (*DN*, 824B). And he is not reluctant to illustrate at length the variety and complexity of the imagery which the biblical authors have passed down to us (*DN*, 596A-B; 597A-B), not fearing in this to descend, for necessary purposes, to vulgarity:

> I have spoken of his anger, grief and rage, of how he is said to be drunk and hungover, of his oaths and curses, of his sleeping and waking and indeed of all those images we have of him . . . (*MT*, 1033B)

The renewal of interest in the pseudo-Denys' theology in our own time rises predominantly from his exposition of the *via negativa*, the recognition that when all talk about God has been exhausted, the rest is silence. There are no doubt very good reasons for this—but we misconstrue the point of the *via negativa* if we tear it out of its context of relationship with the *via affirmativa* and represent it as an independent or even as an alternative theological strategy[4]—or, more paradoxically still, as an independent avenue of knowledge of God. The metaphor of the 'exhaustion' of religious language is perfectly apt. The 'silence' of the negative way is the silence achieved only at the point at which talk is exhausted. The *via negativa* is not the requirement that we talk as little about God as we can, but that we talk as much as we can about God. Theologians are, as it were, embarrassed into silence by their very prolixity, as if they know they must stop because they have talked too much. It therefore represents the pseudo-Denys' position perfectly well to say that theologians must *talk* their way into the silence of the *via negativa* by means of the very superabundance of affirmation. As the pseudo-Denys puts it: 'these and similar terms concern a denial in the sense of a superabundance' (*DN*, 640B).

Without the affirmative way there is no negative way. This is not only for the obvious, purely formal, reason that there can be no negation where there is nothing to negate, but for a more materially interesting and dialectically more complex reason. We will not, the pseudo-Denys suggests, learn to recognise that *any* of our imagery fails of God until we have discovered the failure of that imagery through the exploitation of its self-correcting variety. We do and must speak of God as a 'person'. We may very well suppose that we know what we mean when we call God a 'person' until we discover why we have to say that God is 'pure spirit'—which no person of our experience is. Then again, we may, after much familiarity with the description of God as 'spirit', begin to think of God as 'disembodied', until, that is, we see why we must also 'seek his face' (Ps 26:8) or experience his voice shaking the wilderness (Ps 28:8). And, to acknowledge a more contemporary preoccupation, it is notoriously easy to assume the special aptness of talking about God as male. We learn to see what is deficient about doing so only when, by construing God also as female, it becomes clear that gender language *as such* fails. That is, we know that gender language fails precisely when we have exhausted *both* its possibilities.

The *via negativa* and the *via affirmativa* are not, for the pseudo-Denys, independent theological strategies; it is not that, first, as it were, we are permitted the naive and unself-critical indulgence of affirmation, subsequently to submit that affirmation to a separate critique of negation (*MT*, 1000B). The *via negativa* is not the way simply of saying nothing about God, but the encounter with the failure of what we *must* say about God to represent God adequately. If talk about God is deficient, this is a discovery made within the extending of it into superfluity, into that excess in which it simply collapses under its own weight (*DN*, 640B). It is at that point that theological language is revealed to be, in a phrase of Nicholas Lash's, a 'broken language'.[5]

THE DIALECTICS OF *EROS*

Out of his dialectical sensitivity to these tensions within religious discourse—the interplay between prolixity and silence, between its necessity and equal deficiency—the pseudo-Denys insists upon the real, practical dangers which lie in high-sounding, 'sublime' language about God. It is not wrong to speak of God as 'spirit', 'light', 'majesty', but it is potentially more misleading than to speak of God as 'a rock' or as 'a lion' (*CH*, 141A-B). God is manifestly not a rock or a lion whereas it might be all too easily supposed that we have a conception of 'spirit' adequate to the description of God. The point is not without its relevance today when it is absurdly difficult to persuade the contemporary Christian of *any* reason for suspicion about the description of God as a 'person'. In any case, when the pseudo-Denys raises the question of how appropriate it is to speak of the divine *eros*, with its many dubious associations, he has no very serious difficulty in that connection. After all, if we may legitimately think of God's moods as like those of a soldier with a hangover, then there need not be too many scruples, on the score of vulgarity, in speaking of the erotic frenzy of God.

Erotic discourse is not for the pseudo-Denys merely permissible, it is necessary to his theological purposes. His christian metaphysics, as I have said, requires it, for pulled as that metaphysics is in one direction by the platonic pole of unity and necessity, and in another by the christian pole of the free creative activity of God, some discourse is needed which at one and the same time will exhibit and reconcile the apparently contradictory forces. Here, it might seem that we have passed from the consideration of how erotic discourse might be justified in theological contexts to the role that that language plays in meeting the requirements of a particular theological synthesis, that between Platonism and Christianity. For the contemporary Christian to shelve the problem in the redundant file of merely historical problems would be a misjudgment. The tensions between the unity of God and his internal differentiations are to be found in the very sources of Christianity itself, for they are found in the tensions between the rigorous monotheism of its jewish inheritance and the trinitarian implications of the divinity of Jesus. Furthermore, that very monotheism of the jewish scriptures is itself in internal tension with the equally jewish emphasis on the freedom of the divine creative and providential activity within history. The contemporary fashion—in some little short of an unthinking compulsion—of playing off what are undiscriminatingly described as 'greek' elements in christian theology against the hebraic, can disguise the fact that much within platonising Christianity is but the recognition, in other terms, of deep tensions in the hebraic sources themselves; tensions which are not dissolved by gestures of distaste directed at the 'greek' formulation of them. The problem of a discourse in which to articulate these tensions is not *caused* by Denys' neo-platonism; his neo-platonism is significant because it dictates the particular form in which the problem and so its solution appears to him; but the problem is one which it is inconceivable any Christian theology should be without.

Besides, and on a more general canvas still, the polarities of freedom and necessity, of oneness and differentiation which so dominate the christian neo-platonist agenda are polarities which are internal to the very nature of *eros* itself. To say this is to shift the ground of the discussion away from any occupied exclusively by the exigences of christian neo-platonism and away even from any peculiar to Christianity and Judaism. It is to see human *eros* and its discourse no longer as in an external way meeting the needs of any particular mode of human thought and experience, but as being able to do so because in any case it contains within its own nature the dynamic polarities in question. Erotic discourse is the language *in which* those polarities find their natural mode of expression, because it is, in fact, the language *of* those polarities.

A few platitudes of erotic love will illustrate this well enough. To love erotically is to yearn for an identity of lover with the beloved which surpasses that which can be attained within any other kind of relationship between them; it is simultaneously to achieve a fuller differentiation within that union than either can possess without it. Within erotic love I am both more *me* and more *than* me. The search for erotic mutuality is the search for a union which does not conflict with differentiation and for a differentiation which is not set at odds with union; and so it is at least implicitly the yearning for a condition in which the very contrast between union and differentiation is itself transcended, a condition in which the affirmation of the one is not bought at the price of the denial of the other.

In a parallel way the language of *eros* is the language in which the transcendence of the dichotomy between necessity and freedom is achieved. *Eros* imposes obligations more binding—and so in a sense more 'necessary'—than any which the force of moral laws could impose; and yet, within *eros*, the language of 'imposition' and 'obligation' is itself wholly inappropriate, insofar as 'imposition' and 'obligation' can only be construed in contrast with the freedom of lover and beloved. For within the 'necessities' of erotic mutuality, lover and beloved exchange with one another the gift of their own freedom, so each lives within the one freedom of both. Within that freedom they make and respond to absolute demands on one another. Erotic love is necessity lived in the mode of freedom and freedom lived within the mode of necessity. Within *eros*, necessity and freedom live within each other and transform each other just as lover and beloved do. Into what? We can only say, into *eros*. For *eros is* their transformation. Love makes only love.

Regardless of genre or historical period, the best erotic writing, whether sacred or secular, characteristically resists the dissolution of the dialectical tensions of identity and difference and of freedom and necessity into the polarisations of a mutual exclusiveness. It is true that erotic language is spontaneously hyperbolic and that the natural hyperboles of *eros* are all on the side of the identity of the lovers with each other and of their mutual absorption into something which they both are and could not be separately. And yet, the mode of erotic love which Kerr plays off against 'charity as friendship' is a caricature; erotic union does not entail the extinction of the lover's identities.[6] Far from it. On the erotic model, that which the lovers both are makes each to be more truly himself or herself than separately either could be. *Eros* is intrinsically paradoxical; and what is distinctive about the language of *eros* is entirely lost if it is misread as the one-sided language of union, at the expense of the language of differentiation.

In *Wuthering Heights*, Catherine Earnshaw tells Nelly she loves Heathcliff, 'not because he's handsome, Nelly, but because he is more myself than I am'.[7] Just so for Augustine, for whom God is 'more intimate to me than I am to myself'.[8] 'Whatever our souls are made of', says Catherine, 'his and mine are the same'.[9] So too Donne, for whom

> When love, with one another so
> Interinanimates two souls
> That abler soule which thence doth flow
> Defects of lonelinesse controules.
> Wee then, who are this new soul, know,
> Of what we are compos'd, and made,
> For, th'Atomies of which we grow
> Are soules, whom no change can invade . . .[10]

'But surely', Catherine goes on, 'you and everybody have a notion that there is or should be an existence of yours beyond you . . . Nelly, I *am* Heathcliff . . .'[11] Just so Catherine of Genoa, for whom 'My being is then God',[12] for they are one. And every act of the one is an act of the other: 'he is always, always, in my mind—not as a pleasure, any more than I am always a pleasure to myself, but as my own being—so don't talk of our separation again—it is impracticable'.[13] So too, John of the Cross, for whom the union of the soul with God brings about a transformation of agency such that God and the soul become, as it were, a single agent:

> As a result all the operations of the memory and other faculties in this state are divine . . . it is He who divinely moves and commands them according to his spirit and will. As a result the operations are not different from those of God; but those the soul performs are of God and are divine operations.[14]

Unless we understand such language—whether of Emily Brontë or Augustine, whether of John Donne or John of the Cross—as deliberately paradoxical, as striving, through paradox, to combine in equal measure the apparently opposed, then it collapses into sheer unintelligibility—or, more commonly, it is read as exhibiting an excessive, perhaps even an obsessively morbid, emphasis on the union of the lover and beloved, at the expense of human identity and the freedom of the soul's own agency. But when John of the Cross says that 'my' actions become 'divine', he is decidedly *not* saying that they cease to be mine; when he says that my exercises of memory become 'divine operations', he does not deny that they are at one and the same time true exercises of my human powers of memory. When Catherine of Genoa says, without qualification, that the divine fire so transforms the soul that it 'becomes God' she manifestly has no intention of denying that I remain me. There is no doubt at all about what John or Catherine *want* to say; their thought lives only in the oxygen of such paradoxes. To dissolve the paradoxes, to try to read their thought in the terms of a non-dialectical and purely linear logic, which would entail the possibility of pushing to the limit the language of union with God only at the price of evacuating wholly the language of personal identity, or vice-versa, is to dissolve their thought. The structure of their theology relies on a single foundation, namely, that we begin to glimpse what union with God can mean, and equally what true human identity can be, only when the languages of both are pushed to the limit and are there *held together*. And there, where we meet with the limits of language, we also discover why it is that we could not possibly understand *how* they are held together. There, at the limits of language, we must fall into the silence of the *via negativa*.

But if we can be sure about what John and others want to say, the question remains whether they may be allowed to say it, whether there is a discourse in which such paradoxes may breathe freely, without being crushed between the millstones of formal contradictoriness. Plainly, it is no use appealing to 'paradox' if what is in question is ordinary nonsense. Nor, for any of our writers, is there any difficulty in answering this question, for they know that they are talking the language of love, and assume with equal confidence that the language of love is the language of *erotic* love. They share with John Donne and Emily Brontë the instinctive realisation that the language of *eros* thrives on these paradoxes, that it is the language which naturally inhabits the boundaries of language itself: *eros* comes into its own just where the 'way of negation' begins.

What is more—to return to our subject—the paradoxes of *eros* are none other than those of the neo-platonic theological agenda, the paradoxes of unity and differentiation, of oneness and distinction, of freedom and necessity. Dionysian neo-platonism is the logic and the metaphysics of that language. In short, dionysian theology is but the dialectics of the divine *eros*.

These dialectics of oneness and differentiation are therefore the dialectics of transcendence. The epistemic progress of the mind towards God, laid out in a series of ascending stages in Chapters Four and Five of the pseudo-Denys' *Mystical Theology*, moves from complexity of image to simplicity, from 'dissimilar' (or material) similarities to 'similar' (or mental and spiritual) similarities, from concrete to abstract, from prolixity of words to terseness and ultimately to silence. As the mind ascends through the hierarchy of language, it moves, therefore, from that which is most obviously distinct from God to that which is progressively less obviously so, from the more 'unlike' to the more 'like'. God is more obviously not rock than he is not spirit, more obviously not a shape than he is not a mind (*MT*, 1033B), more obviously not a mind than he is not being, more obviously not being than he is not divinity, and so on, until everything that God can be compared with, however 'like', is negated. But the progression by which we eliminate what God can be compared with must also be the progressive elimination of everything with which God may be contrasted. For, as later, Aquinas,[15] following Aristotle,[16] liked to put it, *eadem est scientia oppositorum*—the knowledge of opposed pairs is just one knowledge, or, more colloquially, to know what something is like is to know what it contrasts with. As comparisons fall away, therefore, so, logically, must contrasts. As we move from complexity to simplicity, from the multiplicity of creatures to the oneness of their cause, from differentiation to lack of differentiation, we must encounter and then also transcend the last differentiation of all: *the difference itself between unity and difference.* We cannot, the pseudo-Denys is saying, describe the oneness of God in terms of how that oneness contrasts with the multiplicity of creatures; for to know how God's oneness is to be differentiated from anything other than it would require our knowing what kind of thing the One is. And we cannot know what kind of thing God is because, as we have seen, *God is not any kind of being.*

We cannot therefore know God's distinction from and transcendence of creatures through our knowledge of how oneness differs from multiplicity, because, if God transcends *all* differences, then God transcends also that difference between oneness and differentiation. To put it more plainly, it is not, for the pseudo-Denys, that before the absolute oneness of God differentiation falls away; it is rather that, before the absolute transcendence of God, *both* oneness *and* differentiation fall away. What falls away, therefore, is the language itself of oneness and differentiation: or, which is to say the same, *language as such.* As the pseudo-Denys himself puts it: 'The Cause of all . . . is not similarity or dissimilarity . . . we make assertions and denials of what is next to it, but never of it, for it is both beyond every assertion and . . . beyond every denial' (*MT*, 1048A-B). Before the transcendence of God even our negations fail.

The divine transcendence is therefore the transcendence even of difference between God and creatures. There is no knowable distance between what God is and what creatures are, and so there is no language in which to state that difference, for there are simply no terms. All our terms of contrast state differentiations between creatures. There are none in which to state the difference between God and creatures. God is not, therefore, opposed to creatures, cannot displace them, which is why, for the pseudo-Denys, the language of the oneness of the soul with God in erotic ecstasy is not, and cannot be, the language of the displacement of the created identity of that mind; nor is Catherine of Genoa's 'the soul becomes God' any more the denial of the soul's identity than is Catherine Earnshaw's 'I *am* Heathcliff' the denial of her own selfhood. On the contrary, it is for either Catherine the assertion of her identity. These are the paradoxes of *eros*. They are none other than the dionysian paradoxes of God-talk.

THE METAPHYSICS OF *EROS*

But if the pseudo-Denys' dialectics of language about God is the logic of *eros*, his metaphysics describe the underpinning reality. We return here to the second of the christian neo-platonist's dilemmas about divine creation: the dilemma of freedom and necessity. In the pseudo-Denys' grappling with this dilemma two great images predominate, that of the sun and that of erotic ecstasy, and they are used together to reveal the complex interpenetrations of freedom and necessity within the divine action of creation, an action which, for the pseudo-Denys, is, at root, an expression of the divine goodness.

It was Boethius, not the pseudo-Denys, to whom mediaeval writers commonly ascribed the formula *bonum est diffusivum sui*—'the good of its nature extends itself'. Eight hundred years later Meister Eckhart constructed the image of creation as a divine *ebullitio*, a 'boiling over', an overflowing of the divine being into creatures, generated, as it were, by the internal heat of the divine *bullitio*, its 'seething' or 'boiling'.[17] Both the boethian formula and the eckhartian image are perfectly expressive of the pseudo-Denys' understanding of creation, an understanding which seeks room both for the absolute solitariness of God and for God's creative expression *ad extra* (*DN*, 649B). For the one, he says, the 'sacred writers . . . call the divine subsistence itself "goodness"' (*DN*, 693B), that is to say, they use the word 'good' to describe the divine nature in itself and independently of any relations in which creatures stand to that nature. For the other, just as 'good' is the term expressive of the divine being in itself, so it is expressive of the divine activity *ad extra*, issuing in creation. For, 'This essential Good, by the very fact of its existence, extends goodness into all things' (*DN*, 693B). 'Good', therefore, is the term which holds together the solitary transcendence of the divine being (its 'subsistence') with the outpouring of that being into the pluriformity and multiplicity of created beings (its 'relatedness').

Immediately, however, the pseudo-Denys turns to the platonic image of the sun; there the energy and tendency of the image is all on the side of the *necessity* of the creative activity of God:

> Think of how it is with our sun. It exercises no rational process, *no act of choice*, and yet by the very fact of its existence it gives light to whatever is able to partake of its light in its own way. So it is with the Good. (*DN*, 693B)

We have already seen why a neo-platonist will resist any obviously anthropomorphic account of creation as a free act. The picture of a neo-liebnizian God discursively reviewing the possibilities (as a rational agent would have to), whether to create or not to create and, if to create, which of the infinite number of possible worlds to create, is clearly offensive to the neo-platonic mind. For God cannot possibly be conceived of as having to make up his mind about what would be good, or even best, to do, since the goodness of anything is the *product* of divine activity, not the cause, or even the motive of it. As the pseudo-Denys says, the divine light in its outflow, 'exercises no rational process, no act of choice'. Nor, as we have seen, may we represent creation as the fulfilment of a capacity in God, for then God's not creating all the possible alternative worlds would entail unfulfilled capacity in God.

For the same reasons, then, relative to any analogy drawing on human free choice, the act of creation is best construed as 'necessary'. On the other hand, the language of necessity falls equally short of the mark, as the deficiency of both the boethian formula and of the pseudo-Denys' image equally suggest. For that which acts 'necessarily' acts subject to constraint, whether imposed by causes externally or internally by its own nature. Clearly, the divine will cannot be subject to external constraint, but neither can its actions be determined by its own nature, though that is what the dionysian image of the sun does suggest. In this respect the pseudo-Denys' image does not do full justice to the thought, for he is perfectly clear that the divine being does not have a nature, is not in that sense 'a kind of thing' in which a creature is (*DN* 593C), such that anything can be determined about its actions by reference to the kind of thing it is. Neither God, nor 'the Good' can be said to have a nature which determines what it can or does cause, in the way in which chemicals have properties which determine their reactions; nor even in the way in which humans have a nature which restricts or enables possibilities of free choice. 'The Good', and so God, is absolutely free; so, then, is the divine creative activity, because it is the outflow of goodness itself. This is why Thomas Aquinas says of God the creator that he does not calculate, even with a view to achieving some good, about what or whether to create; for 'it is not how the first cause . . . acts . . . that he should do so for the sake of any gain; he has in mind only to communicate his own perfection, that is to say, his own goodness . . .[18] And so he alone is absolutely free-handed, because he acts not for his own benefit, but only out of his own goodness.'[19]

In the less sober, more excited language of the pseudo-Denys, creation is the divine ecstasy. It is in the nature of *eros*, as of goodness itself, to pour out into the other, and it can do so without any loss to itself, for

> He is, as it were, beguiled by goodness, by love and by yearning (*eros*) and is enticed away from his transcendent dwelling place and comes to abide in all things, and he does so by virtue of his supernatural and ecstatic capacity to remain, nevertheless, within himself. (*DN*, 712B)

And yet, *eros* is not a 'nature' determining action; it is not a response to stimulus or a response to another's goodness; the divine *eros* is a love which creates that other which it loves, for it creates *out of* goodness, not *because of* any supererogatory goodness it can thereby secure. It is out of that 'necessity' which is love that God creates; but creation is for that same reason an absolutely free act and we should be entirely lost for the words in which to construe this paradox if we had not the language of *eros* in which to utter it.

More than that. We possess the human language of *eros* in which to speak of the divine precisely because our own being is the creation of that *eros*. Because we are the divine ecstasy, because we and all creation are God-standing-outside-himself in love, we ourselves participate in the divine *eros* and possess the language in which to name the source of our being. We are most fully that which we are in our source. And the passionate yearning for the source from which we originate is at one and the same time a passion for God, a passion from God, and a passion for ourselves. There, where God is to be found, am I. 'I *am* Heathcliff'. 'My being is then God'.

Thus it is that the identity of my being with the divine being is construed in the theology of Denys and, subsequently, in so much western christian literature, especially that which has come to be called 'mystical'. There is no doubt that the influence of the pseudo-Denys' neo-platonism is crucial for the survival within that tradition of the discourse of the erotic. But decisive as the influence of the pseudo-Denys undoubtedly is, we cannot account for the overwhelming domination of the model of *eros* alone in terms of that influence and this for a number of reasons.

NOTES

1. Cp. Origen, Greer, p. 227.

2. See Gallus, ¶ 1. But note that in his reception of the pseudo-Denys' theology, Gallus can differ from him quite radically. Two differences are worth mentioning. First, whereas the distinction between the cataphatic and the apophatic in the pseudo-Denys is made *within* our intellectual knowledge of God, in Gallus it is made *between* intellectual knowledge and affectivity. Intellectual knowledge, for Gallus, can give us grounds for saying affirmative things about God on the basis of inferences from creation; affectivity, through the negation of those intellectual affirmations, is what leads to real union with God. This is because, secondly, intellectual knowledge (the cataphatic) is the knowledge naturally available to pagans, whereas the apophatic is the knowledge acquired by grace alone. Neither of these two distinctions, between the intellectual and the affective, between nature and grace, are made in this way by the pseudo-Denys.

3. It is important to be careful what one says here. The pseudo-Denys does not hold that anything true of a creature is true of God. Doubtless some creature is a cunning and deceitful hypocrite. This is not true of God. God has not created the hypocrite's hypocrisy as such; nor is it true that the hypocrite creates his hypocrisy without dependence upon the divine creative power. Hypocrisy is an evil and as such is not anything created because there is nothing which hypocrisy *is*, it is a failure, a lack. See the discussion of evil in *DN* 4. 713D–736B.

4. This, in fact, represents one of the chief points of difference between the pseudo-Denys and Proclus. For Proclus only negative language may be used of the One, affirmative of the lower beings who emanate from the One. The negative and affirmative ways are, for Proclus, different routes to different goals. Compare the pseudo-Denys, who says: 'We make assertions and denials of what is next to [the One], but never of it, for it is both beyond every assertion . . . and . . . beyond every denial' (*MT*, 1048B).

5. Nicholas Lash, *A Matter of Hope, A Theologian's Reflections on the Thought of Karl Marx* (London: Darton, Longman and Todd, 1981) p. 144.

6. See Chapter 1, n. 6.

7. *Wuthering Heights*, c. 9.

8. Augustine, *Confessions*, III. 6: *tu autem eras interior intimo meo.*

9. *Wuthering Heights*, c. 9.

10. The Extasie, in *John Donne, A Selection of His Poetry*, ed. John Hayward (Harmondsworth: Penguin Books) pp. 56–57.

11. *Wuthering Heights*, c. 9.

12. Catherine of Genoa, *Purgation and Purgatory*, trans. Serge Hughes in *Classics of Western Spirituality, Catherine of Genoa* (New York: Paulist Press, 1979) p. 80.

13. *Wuthering Heights*, c. 9.

14. John of the Cross, *The Ascent of Mount Carmel*, III. 2. 8. p. 216.

15. Thomas Aquinas, *Quaestio Disputata* de Veritate, q. 2, a. 15, corp.

16. *Prior Analytics*, I, 1, 24a 30.

17. Cf Eckhart's *Commentary on Exodus*, in *Meister Eckhart, Teacher and Preacher*, ed. B. McGinn, *Classics of Western Spirituality* (New York: Paulist Press, 1986) p. 46.

18. *Summa Theologiae*, I, q. 44, a. 4, corp: *Sed primo agenti . . . . non conuenit agere propter acquisitionem alicuius finis; sed intendit solum communicare suam perfectionem, quae est eius bonitas.*

19. *Et ipse solus est maxime liberalis: quia non agit propter suam utilitatem, sed solum propter suam bonitatem.* (ad. 1).

3

Pseudo-Denys and the Latin Song Commentators

SPEAKING IN the most general terms, we may first remind ourselves that the need for a discourse which will do justice to the conflicting tensions within the christian doctrine of creation arises quite independently of the particular expression of those tensions within dionysian neo-platonism. The human experience of *eros* is itself the human experience of those same antinomies and it is perfectly natural, not to be accounted for exclusively in terms of the *de facto* hegemony of neo-platonism in the Middle Ages, that resort should be had to the model of *eros* in the human quest for an adequate theological language.

The second reason is more particularly connected with the themes of this book. All the commentaries on the *Song of Songs* in Part Two, with the exception of those from Giles of Rome and Nicholas of Lyra, are by authors who were monks or else, as in the case of Alan of Lille, had an explicitly monastic connection. In this, the selections reflect the preponderance of monastic authorship in the genre. But the pseudo-Denys' speculative theology impacted notably less directly on the monastic traditions of theology than on the theology of the schools, less still than it impacted on the great mediaeval mystical writers. The bearers of the neo-platonic inheritance from the pseudo-Denys are the great systematic theologians, Albert, Thomas, Bonaventure, and Nicholas of Cusa; or they are the so-called 'mystics', particularly the northern european mystics of the fourteenth century, Eckhart, Ruusbroec, Tauler, Suso, and the *Cloud* Author; not Gregory, Rupert of Deutz, Bernard of Clairvaux or William of Saint Thierry. Doubtless there are exceptions to this, cases where the convergence of neo-platonic metaphysical eroticism with the monastic biblicism is explicit and acknowledged, as in the twelfth century school of Saint Victor—particularly by Richard—which exercised so important an influence upon the whole theological agenda, on biblical, scholastic, and mystical theology and did so from within a conscious debt to the pseudo-Denys.

Moreover, there is the case of Thomas Gallus, a Victorine of the thirteenth century, a rare case of an enthusiastic Song commentator who explicitly sought to bring together these twin influences within a Song commentary. And yet, though Gallus' commentaries stand out in this respect, the argument for saying that the monastic and the neo-platonic converge in the eroticism of the mediaeval Song commentary cannot rest upon the existence of just one exemplar. Besides, the case of Gallus is not only exceptional, it is also equivocal in this regard. Undoubtedly his commentaries are 'dionysian', perhaps, even, 'unmonastic', in setting the 'practice' of the Song against the background of a clearly articulated speculative metaphysics of *eros* (n. 3). But the detail of his Song exegesis relies much more fully on the parallel he discerns between the stages of the soul's encounter with God and the orders of the Angelic Hierarchy than upon the erotic metaphysics as such. The appeal to the pseudo-Denys is more decisive, certainly, on epistemological matters, in his reliance upon the distinction between the cataphatic and apophatic ways of theology, and this is crucial in determining the detail of his exegesis of the Song, for it dictates the distinction between, respectively, the lower (cataphatic) and higher (apophatic) levels of spiritual attainment. Nonetheless, even here there are respects in which Gallus' reception of the pseudo-Denys might be said to be relatively 'monastic'—if Leclercq is right to place the emphasis of 'monastic theology' on this point—in his more 'affective' than 'intellectualist' account of the *via negativa*, and in his emphasis on the priority of charity over faith. Consequently, if Gallus is an exception to the mainstream of monastic commentary in the degree of his reliance on a neo-platonic metaphysic and epistemology—and this is undeniable—this distinctiveness ought not to be exaggerated. In the last resort the true point of Gallus' dependence on neo-platonic *eros* is there, where Bernard's or Denys the Carthusian's is to be found: in their enthusiastic espousal of a general world-view in which erotic love, or love modeled on the erotic, is the prime mover, the moved, and the end of all motion, whether in the orders of nature, of the human, or of grace. In short, where Gallus' dependence on the pseudo-Denys most differs from the monastic mainstream it is least relevant to my case for the convergence of monasticism with neo-platonism in the Song commentary; where it is most relevant, it is least distinctively different.

Still more ought that other enthusiastically dionysian Song commentator, Denys the Carthusian, be treated with caution. Again, certainly, his intellectual priorities ill fit excessively neat categories. He is, however, distinctive mainly by virtue of his eclecticism. Denys is a reclusive monk who can write like a schoolman, a dialectical theologian who can also compose conservatively monastic biblical commentary, and a monastic commentator who belongs within the history of Rhineland mysticism. In this respect he stands alone, or perhaps together with Jean Gerson, though with few others. Yet even in Denys the three traditions—scholastic theology, monastic biblicism, and mysticism—rarely combine in any single work, and his *Commentary on the Song*, excerpted here, reveals little of the analytical temperament so evident in either his commentaries on Denys the Areopagite or in his *De contemplatione.*[1] Indeed, the case of Denys the Carthusian illustrates with especial clarity the late mediaeval division between scholastic theology and monastic biblicism in regard to the influence of the pseudo-Denys. For both his formal theological treatises and his mystical writings betray the marked influence of the *divus Dionysius*, as he is fond of calling him, and the Carthusian wrote commentaries on his namesake's entire corpus. But his biblical commentaries show little or no trace of his influence, at any rate directly.

The case for explaining monastic eroticism as the product of specifically monastic theological preoccupations combined with neo-platonic influences cannot rest, therefore, upon the meagre support of a few instances where this two-fold debt is admitted. That case begins from the fact that, whether or not under the influence of the pseudo-Denys, the monastic traditions of theology share with his a marked preference for the erotic imagery of love. Among the reasons for the lack of enthusiasm for the pseudo-Denys in the monastic world Leclercq notes the 'abstractness' of his ideas and 'their little basis in sacred scriptures',[2] the first love of all monastic authors. And yet, for all the obvious differences of style and theological method, there remain profound thematic continuities, especially in the matter of the ecstasy of love. What the pseudo-Denys found in Plato and Proclus, the monk found in the Song of Songs. But there is no need to say any more than this: we do not need to say that what the generality of monks found in the Song of Songs they *consciously identified* as that which the pseudo-Denys had found in Plotinus and Proclus. If the monk knew his pseudo-Denys he appealed to that knowledge but rarely. More specifically, we do not need to rely upon the sort of argument, now largely discredited as merely conjectural, which Gilson once attempted to provide in support of greek theological influences on twelfth-century cistercian theology.

All the same one must say, as with so much else of Gilson's work, that his case is more valuable and interesting, even when wrong, than is many another, even when right. It was Gilson's concern, rightly, to defend Bernard of Clairvaux's credentials as a truly constructive, systematic theologian and his hypothesis was that Bernard's theology draws upon three great 'knots' or 'blocs' of theological source:[3] the great discourse on *agape* in the First Letter of John; the theme of ecstasy or *excessus* of love which he found in Scottus Eriugena's translation of the *Ambigua ad Johannem* of Maximus the Confessor;[4] and finally the *Rule* of Saint Benedict. From the first, John's *Letter*, Bernard took the language of *caritas*: God is charity, and our love is that same charity of God, received by us as the gift of the Holy Spirit, for *caritas ex Deo est*. Charity, moreover, *is* knowledge of God: *for no one has seen God* (1 Jn 4:12) and in the darkness of the unknowing mind, the affectivity of love is the only knowledge of God possible to us. Following Gregory the Great here, as in so much else, for Bernard *amor ipse notitia est*,[5] 'love is itself a kind of knowing'. Because God alone is charity, the central fact of love is that God has loved us first; but for precisely the reason that all depends, not on our uncertain love of God but on the certainty of God's having first loved us, the birth of love in the soul expels fear and insecurity, and is the birth of confidence, trust, *fiducia*.

What John's *Letter* gave Bernard, therefore, was the centrality in the life of the Christian of gratuitous *caritas*. What, on Gilson's account, Bernard may have derived from greek theological sources, was a theme connected in those sources not so much with the *agape* (*caritas* or *dilectio*) of John, as with *eros* (or *amor* as the Latins translated it), and that was the theme of ecstasy. Where, then, did Bernard derive this theme? There is, Gilson had to concede, no evidence of more than likelihood for the direct influence of the pseudo-Denys:

> We may ask, then, whether he ever read Dionysius, or rather we might have asked it if the thing, likely

> enough in itself, were not made the more so by the fact that he had certainly read, and in Scotus Eriugena's translation, a text of Maximus the Confessor and turned it to good account.[6]

It was, Gilson argues, either from the pseudo-Denys or, if not, from Maximus' treatise on obscure passages in the pseudo-Denys, that Bernard borrowed the term for ecstasy and together with the term, *excessus,* a whole cluster of allied themes familiar from dionysian sources. God is unchangeable, unmoving, but all things move towards God, driven by love, and, finding their place in God, each thing 'is made wholly to be in the whole beloved' (*fiat totum in toto amato*).[7] This *excessus,* a natural movement in the natural world, an *excessus* of knowledge and love in intelligent beings, dissolves (*liquescit*) the lover in the Beloved, making the one to be like the other, its true exemplar; but this, the 'melting' of lover and beloved into one another, does not negate the lover's identity, but rather reaffirms it. Moreover, though never complete in this life, this *excessus* of the lover in God is a true deification: *in* God we *become* God.

Gilson's thesis, then, is that in Bernard's theology a synthesis is achieved between the *caritas* of the New Testament and the *amor et excessus* of neo-platonism:

> in the act of borrowing [from Maximus], St Bernard so welded it with the Johannine bloc that the two became altogether one. God is charity; He gives us charity, and thus dwells in us and makes us to dwell in Him. How? By way of the restoration of that image, which each of us substantially is, to the likeness of its Exemplar; by stripping us of our own will thus to unite us to His, by liquefying us, so to speak, so that we may already pass into Him by ecstasy, while awaiting the day when we shall pass wholly into him by glory; by no means there to be dissolved and lost, but confirmed forever in perfection.[8]

There is no doubt that those elements whose presence in Bernard's theology Gilson attributed to greek sources are to be found there. It is, furthermore, highly illuminating, to a degree not yet fully explored, to be required by Gilson's case to see Bernard's understanding of love as a synthesis of johannine *caritas* with neo-platonic *amor*.[9] In fact, the presence of elements of neo-platonic *amor* in Bernard's understanding of christian love ought not to be seen as the issue, for that presence is undeniable. All that needs to be contended is Gilson's assertion that they are there by conscious transmission from Bernard's supposed reading of greek sources. There is, after all, no evidence that Bernard did read Maximus' *Ambigua*. But then there is no need to suppose that he had read Maximus to explain the presence of the terminology of *excessus* and *liquescere* in his language of love.[10] Michael Casey lists more obvious sources for *excessus* in the Vulgate Ps 67:28 and in 2 Cor 5:13, in John Cassian, and in Gregory the Great.[11] And as far as concerns the much less familiar metaphor of 'liquefaction', it is strange that Gilson failed to note the use of the word in the Vulgate text of the Song itself: *anima mea liquefacta est* (Sg 5:6). This is a much more likely source of Bernard's vocabulary.[12]

In a way all this is beside the point. It is certainly true that Gilson's speculative source-criticism does not stand the test of more recent scholarship, but it does not very much matter from our point of view from whose hands precisely Bernard received the neo-platonic doctrines of *amor* and *excessus*. For in the more general terms of Gilson's skeleton, it is beyond question one of the more striking things about Bernard's theology of the love of God that he has most successfully synthesised the two great streams of tradition about that love, the tradition of *caritas* and *dilectio* with the tradition of *amor* and *excessus*. If, as the pseudo-Denys had said, the words *agape* and *eros* had come to mean much the same, it is nonetheless clear that what *he* means is that *agape* had come to mean much the same as *eros*.[13] By contrast, when, in the thirteenth century, Thomas Aquinas came to write his Commentary on the pseudo-Denys' *The Divine Names*, for him the meanings were reversed: the pseudo-Denys' *amor* was made to mean Thomas' *dilectio*.[14] But for Bernard, as also for Thomas of Perseigne (n. 5) following Bernard, we have the impression that such questions, whether purely semantic or more substantive, did not much matter: *amor* is for him a term of multiple possibilities, including within its scope the whole register of neo-platonic notes together with all those which meditation on the biblical and patristic sources could provide him with. He does not argue about it, for it is not for him a theoretical or practical question; as a consequence, from the standpoint of any theory on which they are opposed to one another—such as Nygren's—his terminology would appear to oscillate arbitrarily between the characteristics of the one and the characteristics of the other. But from within his own standpoint there is simply no issue. *Amor* is perfectly expressed in christian *caritas*, *dilectio* is convertible with both, and *caritas* has its own ecstasy for which the ecstasy of *eros* is a perfect model.

It is certainly unhistorical to overplay the divergences between the speculative theology of the schools, in which the debt to neo-platonism is admitted, and the 'biblicism' of the monastic theologies, in which it is not. Nonetheless, it is equally true that what Bernard can be said to have inherited from the *eros* of neo-platonism, he radically transformed to his own purposes and within a quite different theological structure. What, in the neo-platonist, is the driving force of a metaphysic, the dynamic of an overarching ontology in which the human subject finds a place, but not at any exclusive centre; what in the pseudo-Denys is an *eros* and an ecstasy of *mind*, of intellect, reaching beyond itself into the dazzling darkness of God, has become in Bernard detached from the logic and ontology of neo-platonism. Bernard, we may say, inherits the *language* of *eros* from the neo-platonic tradition, but for him that language is no longer the necessary mode of expression of an objective ontology, as it is, one hundred years later, in Gallus. It is the experientially apt discourse of a soul in love with God, a language which expresses that love with an immediacy and spontaneity available to him in no other more appropriate image. Bernard, moreover, does not *explain* the love of God as modelled on *eros*, as does Gallus. Bernard is in love with God erotically. It may not be rooted in the neo-platonic metaphysics of Denys; but it is not, for all that, an unrooted language. It is sustained and vivified by the lived experience of the love of God which it perfectly expresses. As Bernard says, 'Only the touch of the Spirit can inspire a song like this, and only personal experience can unfold its meaning.'[15]

All this is certainly true, often said, and possibly misleading. To say that Bernard's eroticism of language is the language of his experience is not to say that it does not serve any formal, acknowledged theological purpose. The mistake of supposing that Bernard can only write 'expressively' or 'affectively' and that he has nothing to offer by way of a 'systematic' theology was long ago exposed, once and for all, by Gilson to be the shallowness which it undoubtedly is. Leclercq moreover, has shown Bernard's theology to be profoundly and truly a 'monastic' theology[16] and only a deepseated and unwarrantably *a priori* prejudice that would identify theology in the Middle Ages with the theology of the schools sustains the judgment that Bernard lacks a theology. There are deeply theological and not merely personal and psychological roots to Bernard's preference for erotic discourse and they lie in what he shares with the common traditions of monastic theology; this shared inheritance of monastic theology we will examine in the next chapter.

In the meantime we can say that what neither Bernard nor the majority of the monks inherit from neo-platonism is its speculative metaphysics of *eros*, nor particularly the dialectics of its negative theology. What they all inherit, especially through the powerful influence first of Gregory and later, together with Gregory's, that of Bernard himself, is the language and imagery of *eros* which they are able to integrate into their own truly theological perspective. Yet it is a biblical rather than a speculative theology, an ecclesiological and historical rather than a dialectical theology. What is more, those particular theological interests were dictated to them by their particular situation as monks, with all that that implies in terms of asceticism and personal spirituality. It is, I suggest, for this reason that the Song of Songs meant so much to the monk of the twelfth century and later: it fused, within a single text, his theological preoccupations, his personal spiritual requirements, and the language which best gave expression to both; but the language, if not the theology, came to him replete with neo-platonic assumption.

NOTES

1. *De contemplatione*, in *Doctoris Ecstatici D. Dionysii Cartusiani, Opera Omnia* 2, IX, *Opera Minora*. (Tournai, 1912).

2. J. Leclercq, 'Influence and non-Influence of Dionysius in the Middle Ages', in *Pseudo-Dionysius*, Luibheid, p. 31.

3. E. Gilson, *The Mystical Theology of Saint Bernard*, (London, 1940-. Kalamazoo: Cistercian Publications, 1990).

4. Maximus, *Ambigua* in John Scottus Eriugena's Latin translation, PL 122.

5. Gregory, *Homila 27 in Evangelium*, PL 76:1207.

6. Gilson, p. 25.

7. Maximus, *Ambigua*, PL 122:1202A.

8. Gilson, pp. 27–28. For the sake of completeness, though it is not strictly relevant to our concerns, I note that Gilson argues that Bernard's synthesis harmonises with these two 'blocs' the third 'bloc' of the Benedictine Rule, *see* Gilson, p. 31.

9. Michael Casey, *Athirst for God, Spiritual Desire in Bernard of Clairvaux's Sermons on the Song of Songs* (Kalamazoo: Cistercian Publications, 1988) pp. 189–290.

10. On this matter, see B. McGinn, 'Pseudo-Dionysius and the Early Cistercians' in *One Yet Two: Monastic Tradition East and West*, ed. Basil Pennington (Kalamazoo: Cistercian Publications, 1976) pp. 200–241.

11 Casey, p. 290.

12. Or, possibly, as in Gallus, Gregory the Great; see Gallus, n. 19.

13. *DN* 709B. Though the pseudo-Denys had already taken a decisive step away from the pagan neo-platonic account of *eros* as need and towards an account of it which draws it closer to christian *agape*. For the pseudo-Denys *eros* is a love which creates all things in a cosmic community and in an order of differentiations. It is by no means the individualistic love of the plotinian mystic.

14. *In divinis nominibus*, c. IV, lect. ix, 424. Bonaventure, discussing the same question, concludes, on the authority of the pseudo-Denys, that the terms both describe an *affectio*, but from different points of view. *Amor* refers to an *affectio* which is unitive of lover and beloved. *Dilectio* adds the element of choice, as in the Song 5:10: *dilectus meus electus est milibus*. *Caritas* further adds the high valuation of the beloved. See *In Sententias* I dist. 10, dub. 1.

15. *Sermons*, 1.11.

16. *The Love of Learning*, c. 9.

4

Eros and Allegory

WHATEVER MAY have been the influence of neo-platonic ideas on the monk it was theological and personal interests specific to the monastic vocation itself which led the monk to take so great an interest in the Song of Songs. If the christian neoplatonist had a metaphysical agenda which drew him to the same text, the agenda which drew the monk to the Song was primarily historical, ecclesiological, but above all, biblical. These theological interests are, however, closely integrated with one another, as we may see if we consider, first, how the monastic commentator envisaged the setting, the *mis-en-scène*, of the Song.

THE SONG'S *MIS-EN-SCÈNE*

In the course of his discussion of why the Song cannot 'literally' refer to the sexual love of Solomon and the Shulamite, Nicholas of Lyra offers a revealing, if parenthetical, remark. No more than any other writer in the tradition of Song commentary can Nicholas yield to the thought that human love might serve as the literal sense of the text, for there is, he says, always something suspect about sexual love, even if 'confined within the bounds of marriage'

(n. 19). Now the Song represents a problem for the mediaeval commentator not only if he harbours suspicions about the moral worth of sexual love in general, but for the more particular reason that the text is careless in providing clear indications that the lovers are even married. In other words, it is not entirely clear from the Song that their love affair had even that minimum justification which marriage could provide. We may speculate, if not in any way to provide direct evidence, that Origen intended a, perhaps unconscious, solution to this difficulty when he declared the Song to be an 'Epithalamium, that is a wedding song, written by Solomon in the form of a play, which he recited in the character of a bride who was being married'.[1] This neatly solves the problem of the lovers' desires for sexual union, the intensity of their physicality, and their erotic fantasisings about each others' bodies. Because this is their wedding day, the consummation of their love may be legitimately longed for, though it cannot yet have taken place. For a wedding day is midway between the promise of betrothal and its fulfilment in sexual union. It was a 'solution' adopted universally by commentators from Origen to John of the Cross and it determines the commentarial nomenclature of the chief *dramatis personae, sponsus et sponsa*, 'bridegroom' and 'bride'.[2]

Rather more to the point, and certainly less speculatively, this *mis-en-scène* of a wedding day is exactly appropriate to the *specific* eroticism of the Song, which is of that most erotically intense condition of all, sexual arousal at the not quite immediate prospect of fulfilment. 'May he kiss me with the kiss of his mouth' are the Bride's opening words and, Giles of Rome drily comments, the grammatical mood is optative (n. 6). But not only grammatically, for the emotional mood is above all that of *amor* and *desiderium*, of arousal and desire, not that of *fruitio* and *delectatio*, completion and delight.[3]

In fact, the Song is a poem charged with a sense of sexual fulfilment *anticipated*. Probably the best translation of the commentators' *amor*[4] is, as with the Greek *eros*, 'yearning' or 'longing', words which exactly express the tensions of *eros* itself, the tensions of interplay between 'presence' and 'absence', between 'now', but 'not yet', between the 'possession' of the beloved and his 'elusiveness', of 'oneness with' and 'otherness than'. These, as we have noted, are the structuring polarities of erotic love itself and the reading of the Song as an epithalamium exactly captures these dialectics, the shifts of feeling and mood, at a high point of their intensity, in the wedding day's 'now' but 'not yet'.

EROS AND SALVATION HISTORY

If the symbol of the wedding day aptly represents the Song's specific eroticism, we begin to see how that eroticism could also be seen to meet, with equal aptness, the theological and ascetical preoccupations of the commentator. In speaking of these preoccupations we are, of course, speaking quite generally, for the particular agendas of individual commentators may, as we have seen, vary quite widely. We are therefore speaking of those shared theological interests which make the Song's eroticism attractive to a great number of monks over a very long period.

The theology of history which in general terms, appears to be shared by our commentators, is itself structured on the interplay of overlapping moments of 'now' and 'not yet'. There is, indeed, but one Church, stretching across all time, from Adam to the Second Coming in the Kingdom, but that one Church exists in successive phases of anticipation and fulfilment—we might even say, of arousal and consummation. One after the other, our commentators represent the Bride's longing for the Bridegroom's kiss as the longing of the patriarchs and prophets for the coming of Christ—as Bernard says, their longing can outstrip in intensity the Christian's complacency in his possession of Christ.[5] And Gregory insists that 'the whole human race, from the origins of the world to its end, we now represent as one single Bride who in the Law received a pledge of the spiritual gift; but now she seeks the presence of the Bridegroom himself and says, *May he kiss me with the kisses of his mouth'* (n. 12). Nicholas of Lyra likewise affirms that there is but one love of the Old and the New dispensations: they differ only in degree of explicitness (n. 22). Following Gregory—indeed, directly quoting the passage above—Denys the Carthusian adds that what in the Covenant was promise of Christ was, for the pre-covenantal human race, itself a fulfilment of its natural desire for redemption; and then, in turn, the fulfilment of the covenantal promise in Christ releases in the Church a new longing for her Bridegroom, the risen Christ, and ultimately for fulfilment in the Kingdom of heaven (nn. 18–19). Every fulfilment, therefore, is a previous longing now satisfied and yet is also a further promise generating a new, as yet unsatisfied, longing. History is a fabric of overlapping strands of longing and satisfaction, of promises and fulfilments, stretching across all time. Every epoch of history is, as it were, a wedding day. At the theological centre of this great sweep of historical ecclesiology is the Ascension of Jesus. Here the tensions of presence and absence become acute: the gospel of John (16:7) represents Jesus as having to go away in order to leave space, within history, for the Spirit: 'Unless I go, the Advocate will not come to you'. *Draw me after you* is the pivotal verse from this point of view; thus does the Song prophetically proclaim the longing of the christian soul to follow Jesus in his Ascension (Alcuin, n. 4). Alan of Lille presents only a more sharply focussed, not an unrepresentative, image of these tensions in his picture of the Virgin Mary—who more than any other person shared a physical intimacy with her Son in his historical life—mourning his physical withdrawal at the ascension and longing to be 'drawn up' with him into his presence finally in the Kingdom (n. 14). And Denys presents a touching vignette of Mary nostalgically revisiting the places of her

Son's birth, passion, and death, yearning to be restored to him by her assumption into heaven (n. 62).

Presence, absence; now and not yet; possession, elusiveness; identity, separation; longing, fulfilment. These couplets which are the structuring tensions of *eros* itself, its emotional dialectics, lend themselves aptly to the mediaeval theologian of history because they exactly correspond with his sense of the Church's place in history, situated between the promise which fulfils and the fulfilment which brings new promise. But as they provide the formal pattern of salvation history, these dialectics are reflected in the personal, spiritual response of the soul to Christ. If with less exuberant emotion than in Bernard, the feel of Gregory's asceticism is saturated, as Leclercq puts it, by 'the dialectics of presence and absence, possession and non-possession, certainty and uncertainty, light and darkness, faith and eternal life'.[6] The christian soul longs for contemplative union with God in 'interior peace fulfilled' (n. 19); but here and now, *in via*, that contemplative fulfilment is present in the form of *conpunctio*, a desiring, suffering, repentant sense of separation caused by our historical, sinful condition. So the presence yearned for is for that which cannot yet be achieved fully. Conversely, the soul's longing for her Bridegroom, 'as if for one absent' is, even in this life, capable 'suddenly', if only briefly, of being transformed into a sharp sense of presence, as it was for Cleopas and his companion on their way to Emmaus: the absence of the beloved can sometimes take the form of immediate presence (n. 13).

This interpenetration of 'presence' and 'absence', the sense of the christian way as that of a longing for that which cannot yet be, together with a sense that the presence is somehow already given in the longing itself, is very characteristic of the gregorian spirituality. It profoundly affected the monk's perception of his situation as that of someone caught at the point of intersection between the 'now' of fulfilment and the 'not yet' of anticipation, and this perception retains its hold over monastic asceticism to the end. In a passage of quite remarkably hyperbolic rhetoric, Denys the Carthusian speaks of the desire for the sweetness of God, 'an unfathomable, limitless, measureless stream', as the desire to be 'carried away, transformed and absorbed into him and, all enraptured, be plunged into the most joyful, vast ocean of his happiness'. And yet, the 'poor silly little soul' is 'thrust into this heavy weight of matter, tied to the millstone of the body' and can scarcely have the presumption to desire that 'kiss of his mouth' of him 'before whom the highest of the supreme spirits tremble'; but, confined as it is in this 'land of unlikeness', it makes bold to do so, by its love, which 'fretting at separation, compels' it. The soul is intoxicated by desire, a desire intensified by the very separation which it seeks to overcome; it suffers from the separation, from its enforced exile in the *regio dissimilitudinis*, but the suffering is a longing and the longing is a suffering (nn. 41–42).

More prosaically, indeed rather more typically, Alan of Lille describes the monk's sense of being poised eschatologically between this world and the next in a comment on the verse of the Song, the *King has brought me into his cellars*:

> The word 'cells' or 'cellars' is just the right word, for it signifies what belongs to the 'celestial'. For, bearing in mind the overtones of the word, the wines which fill and inebriate and release the mind from the cares of the world are stored in cellars; in the same way celestial happiness inebriates the mind and thereby detaches it from company with and altogether removes from it the love of earthly things . . .
>
> And just as a person who lives in a cell, as does a solitary hermit, is withdrawn from the clamour of the times, so is a person in heaven withdrawn from the clamour of the world. (n. 16)

Individual soul, monk, Church, history, all are poised within tensions of time and presence which are exactly those of *eros* itself. It is only in the light of this overarching theology of history on the one hand, and the monk's personal sense of being balanced on an eschatological knife-edge on the other, that we can begin to understand the appeal of that most characteristic of mediaeval teachings, the allegorical-typical interpretation of the Bible. To this we must turn next.

THE FOUR 'SENSES' OF SCRIPTURE

It is, speaking in the most general terms, quite impossible to understand any mediaeval doctrine of biblical hermeneutics except as rooted in a corresponding theology of history and eschatology. Any differences between mediaeval biblicists in the one will show up in differences in the other. Insofar as there is a difference, the common interpretative schema of the mediaeval biblicist allows for a fourfold layering of scriptural 'senses': the literal (or historical or narrative), the allegorical, the tropological (or moral), and the anagogical. The terminology occasionally varies: the tropological is occasionally called the 'individual' sense and the anagogical is sometimes called the 'mystical' sense, which can be confusing since all commentators are agreed that the three non-literal senses are different forms of the 'spiritual' or 'mystical' sense of Scripture. Any biblical text may contain one, more than one, or all of these senses, but the particular balance of the relationships among these senses can be distributed in quite different ways by different commentarial traditions. In every case, however, the account given of how the senses relate to one another is governed by the relations of temporality and history in which the events and epochs of salvation history are described as standing with one another. In other words, mediaeval biblical hermeneutics is dependent upon its theology of history.

In the briefest and least contended form, however, the allegorical reading of the Old Testament is the theological interpretation of the literal record of the facts, things, persons and events of Israel's history as being *anticipations* or 'types' of Christ and the Christian Church; the events of jewish history recorded in the Bible have to be understood in the nature of *promises* whose significance can be fully grasped only in the light of their fulfilments in Christ. The anagogical or mystical reading of the Christian Scriptures, in turn, is the reading of the events of the Incarnation or of christian history in the light of their ultimate fulfilment in the kingdom of heaven, of which Christ is the promise. Hence some events of the Old Dispensation may be interpreted twice, first allegorically on the basis of the literal sense and then anagogically on the basis of the allegorical sense. Finally, the tropological interpretation of the Scriptures is the reading of the implications of those texts in their significance for the life and behaviour of the individual Christian, but only in and through their allegorical and anagogical significance.[7]

'All these four senses', Nicholas of Lyra tells us,

> may be explained by way of illustration by the name 'Jerusalem'; in its literal sense it refers to a certain city which was once the capital of the kingdom of Judea, founded in the first instance by Melchisedech and later expanded and fortified by Solomon. But in its moral sense it refers to the faithful soul; it is in this sense that Isaiah says: *Rise up, Jerusalem, take your seat* (52:2). But in its allegorical sense it refers to the Church militant, as when it says in Revelation 21 (v. 2): *I saw the holy city, the new Jerusalem coming down from heaven, like a bride dressed for her husband*. In its anagogical sense it refers to the church triumphant, as Galatians 4 (v. 26) says: *She who is above is Jerusalem the freed-*

woman: and she is our mother. We have given as an example a single word; in the same way a single passage could be given and as in the one case so in others. (n. 2)

On a relatively superficial acquaintance with the detailed interpretative practice, it is all too easy to think of the four senses of Scripture as having been accepted without important qualification and without debate throughout the Middle Ages. After all, the example given by Nicholas would have been acceptably formulated to any mediaeval scholar from at least the twelfth century and would hardly have been a novelty to Gregory, for Nicholas borrowed it from Cassian.[8] This impression is, however, misleading. Beneath the surface of a common terminology of interpretative method there are important differences not merely of application, but also of theory and doctrine.

The tensions which lie beneath the surface easily break through if one attempts to move beyond the most minimal and nearly vacuous formulae. For example, the writing of the first two paragraphs of this section was almost impossible without compromising the position of at least one of the commentators in our anthology, limited as that selection is. Any account which allowed for Gregory and Denys the Carthusian would have probably done well enough for Alcuin, Alan of Lille, or Thomas of Perseigne; but had it advanced beyond the generality of those two paragraphs it would certainly then have misrepresented Hugh of Saint Victor, Thomas Aquinas, and Nicholas of Lyra. In fact, it is hard to advance beyond the proposition that there are four senses of Scripture and the names for each without hitting rocks of controversy. The impression of uniformity is reinforced by the fact that most mediaeval authors preferred to represent their positions as traditional than to highlight their differences with each other. Sometimes, however, the contended issues do not have to be forced to the surface, for they are openly stated: Hugh of Saint Victor (nn. 4–6) and Nicholas of Lyra (n. 7) enthusiastically polemicise against the over-hearty allegorisings of the tradition and Denys the Carthusian is not in the least reluctant to respond in kind (n. 4). Sometimes disagreements are unstated but manifest, as in Thomas Aquinas. Plainly, for all that the magisterial calm of his exposition may suggest that he was but abstracting a common position—as he liked to claim, Augustine's—Thomas could not have hoped or intended to disguise the fact that he is in open theoretical conflict with majority practice, including Augustine's. That he was unconscious of his differences with the tradition is all the more unlikely in a *Quaestio* which amounted to the inaugural lecture of his first Parisian mastership and so was in some way a manifesto of his own distinctive contribution to the subject.

METAPHOR: 'LITERAL' OR 'ALLEGORICAL'?

The central problem, when they were conscious of it, appeared to the mediaeval interpreters to be the standing to be given to the literal sense of Scripture relative to the other, 'spiritual', senses. As we will see, there are enthusiasts for allegory to the virtual neglect of the literal sense, such as Denys the Carthusian. There are enthusiasts for the literal sense who show undisguised distaste for excessive allegorising, such as Nicholas of Lyra. And there are others, such as Hugh of Saint Victor and Thomas Aquinas, who are happy enough with allegory, but only when it is firmly rooted in a good, sound text and in a clearly established literal sense. When they were conscious of a debate, this was the debate mediaeval commentators were conscious of.

We, however, might view the debate somewhat differently. For us the problem is only secondarily that of the weight the literal sense should be given; it is, in the first instance, of what is meant by the word 'literal' and to some degree what is meant by the word 'sense'. On the other hand this is a debate which by no means all mediaeval commentators had a taste for and most were unaware of any issue. As for our chances of understanding what this problem of theoretical hermeneutics amounts to, these are further reduced by the fact that we are in no better position to count on an agreed definition of the literal than were mediaeval theologians—even if our uncertainties relate to different issues. We need some terminology and some distinctions of our own if we are to find our way through an exceedingly confused tangle of argument.

The word 'literal'—and so also, what is to be understood by the 'literal sense' of a text—appears to have been used by most mediaeval commentators in two quite distinct ways, the meaning of the term varying between them as a function of one of two kinds of *non*-literal locution with which the word is paired in contrast. The first contrast in which the literal stands is nearer to our modern usage and is that between literal speech and figurative speech—let us say, in short, between the literal and the metaphorical. The second contrast is wholly patristic and mediaeval and is the contrast, thought to be present uniquely in scriptural writings, between the literal sense of Scripture and its spiritual senses. In our terms (or at least in terms intelligible to us), the first distinction, between the literal and the metaphorical, is a *semantic* distinction between two different kinds of linguistic meaning which the text in question might bear. Mediaeval commentators can, however, seem confused about this. On the one side they could readily concede that straightforward and unambiguous narrative reports of historical events had the literal meaning of referring to those events. And in the most straightforward sense of the term, the 'literal' meaning of the text can sometimes be thought of, minimalistically, as what the text factually reports. Nor is the literal meaning, in this first sense, confined to statements of fact. Plain moral exhortation is, as Thomas Aquinas says (a. 2, ad 3), often literally intended by the text and is capable of immediate application to our lives just as factual reports, literally meant, are capable of direct factual corroboration.

But on the other side is the source of confusion: what is to be said about the very frequent scriptural use of metaphor, even in narrative reports or moral exhortations? Here our authors appear to be divided into two camps of theory, the lines of division cutting across those between the two senses of the word 'literal'. One camp, to which belong the vast majority of our authors, with varying degrees of theoretical explicitness, but with virtual unanimity in practice, assigns metaphorical expressions to the side not only of the *semantically* non-literal, but also, and in the *second* sense of the non-literal, to the allegorical.

This practice of treating scriptural metaphors not as part of the literal meaning of the text but as a form of spiritual sense, begins in the earliest sources known to the Latin tradition for the very distinction between literal and spiritual senses, in Origen. Having established, on general grounds, the distinction between the literal and the spiritual sense of Scripture, Origen asks how we are to know when a passage of Scripture is to be read as bearing a spiritual, as distinct from a literal, sense. He answers that we are led to suspect that a spiritual interpretation is required of a passage from its intractable obscurity, from its factual impossibility or falsehood or from its being plainly self-contradictory:

> . . . the divine wisdom has arranged for there to be certain stumbling blocks or interruptions of the narrative meaning, by inserting in its midst certain impossibilities and contradictions, so that the very interruption of the narrative might oppose the reader, as it were, with certain obstacles thrown in the way. By them wisdom denies a way and an access to the common understanding; and when we are shut out and hurled back, it calls us back to the beginning of another way, so that by gaining a higher and loftier

> road through entering a narrow footpath it may open for us the immense breadth of divine knowledge.[9]

Fair enough. But when Origen provides us with illustrations of such textual anomalies, most of his examples in fact illustrate only an incongruity caused by the failure to understand what are rather obvious *metaphors* in their metaphorical significance.

> . . . who will be found simple enough to believe that like some farmer 'God planted trees in the garden of Eden, in the east' and that He planted 'the tree of life' in it, that is a visible tree that could be touched, so that someone could eat of this tree with corporeal teeth and gain life, and further, could eat of another tree and receive knowledge 'of good and evil' (Gen 3:8)? Moreover, we find that God is said to stroll in the garden in the afternoon and Adam to hide under a tree (cf Gen 3:8). Surely I think no one doubts that these statements are made by Scripture in the form of a type by which they point toward certain mysteries. Also Cain's going away 'from the face of God' (Gen 4:16) obviously stirs the wise reader to ask what 'the face of God' is and how any one could 'go away' from it. But there is no need for us to enlarge the discussion too much beyond what we have in hand, since it is quite easy for everyone who wishes to collect from the holy Scriptures things that are written as though they were really done, but cannot be believed to have happened appropriately and reasonably according to the narrative meaning.[10]

In terms of our distinctions, Origen has combined into one the two kinds of contrast between the literal and the non-literal meaning. There is, after all, scarcely a hermeneutical problem, but only a literary one, with someone who cannot understand 'the tree of life', 'the face of God' or references to God taking an afternoon stroll, as metaphors.

But Origen seems insensitive to the distinction between the kind of textual anomaly which demands the hermeneutical solution of allegory and a literary anomaly which derives simply from a perverse blindness to metaphor. Because of this failure to distinguish between genuine hermeneutical crux and mere literary crassness, Origen appears to conclude from the fact that certain texts are non-literal in the first sense, i.e. are metaphorical, that they are therefore non-literal in the second sense, i.e., they must be read as having a spiritual meaning only—as 'a type by which they point to certain mysteries'. Metaphor is not part of the literal meaning (in the first sense); therefore it is to be interpreted spiritually (as non-literal in the second sense). As we will see, the majority of our authors follow Origen in this tendency to identify the two definitions of literalness and so in the practical identification of the metaphorical with the spiritual sense. For the purposes of shorthand I shall call this hermeneutical tendency 'metaphoricism'. Of our authors, all but Hugh of Saint Victor, Thomas Aquinas, and Nicholas of Lyra are prone to it.

Contrast with this metaphoricism the attitude occasionally but clearly articulated in Augustine. As a trained rhetorician he knew more than most about the literary use of tropes in both ordinary and in formal secular speech and he was acutely sensitive to their use in scriptural contexts. Where metaphor is anomaly for Origen, demanding a spiritual interpretation, Augustine is able sometimes to be more cautious. He notes, in *On Christian Doctrine,* that the chief cause of unnecessary difficulty with the text of Scripture lies in the failure to see its frequent employment of metaphor for what it is, figurative speech. Sensitivity to the various species of trope is a necessary *preliminary* skill for good scriptural interpretation, being required for the establishing of a sound basic text on which, only subsequently, to build accurate typologies:

> . . . an awareness [of tropes] is necessary to a solution of the ambiguities of the Scriptures, for when the sense is absurd when it is taken verbally, it is to be inquired whether or not what is said is expressed in this or that trope which we do not know; and in this way many hidden things are discovered.[11]

So much is clear enough to be easily mistaken for a formal statement of exegetical principle and not just a rule of thumb for 'hard cases'. As a matter of fact, however, Augustine was not always so clear even in theory that what we call 'metaphor' was part of the literal meaning of Scripture and in his practice frequently neglected his own advice. This can be aptly illustrated by his own parenthetical gloss in *On Christian Doctrine* on the Song 4:2: *Thy teeth are as flocks of sheep that are shorn, which come up for the washing, all with twins, and there is none barren among them.* Noting that the obscurity of some scriptural texts is such as to deceive readers into erroneous interpretations, he admits that others are so obscure that it is hard to get anything at all out of them, let alone an erroneous interpretation. In a passage which was to have significant influence upon later mediaeval theory of interpretation,[12] and certainly a greater influence than had the matching passage from Origen, Augustine explains:

> I do not doubt that this situation [of scriptural obscurantism] was provided by God to conquer pride by work and to combat disdain in our minds, to which those things which are easily discovered seem frequently to become worthless.[13]

The Song passage, Augustine goes on, could have said what in plain terms it means, namely that:

> there are holy and perfect men with whose lives and customs as an exemplar the Church of Christ is able to destroy all sorts of superstitions in those who come to

> it and incorporate them into itself, men of good faith, true servants of God, who, putting aside the burden of the world, come to the holy laver of baptism and, ascending thence, conceive through the Holy Spirit and produce the fruit of a twofold love of God and their neighbour.[14]

So why is all this said in the poetic imagery of the Song, obscurely and indirectly? 'Does one learn anything else besides that which he learns when he hears the same thought expressed in plain words without this similitude?'[15] The answer lies in the greater facility, in the greater aesthetic pleasure with which

> I contemplate the saints . . . when I envisage them as the teeth of the Church cutting off men from their errors and transferring them to her body after their hardness has been softened as if by being bitten and chewed. I recognise them most pleasantly as shorn sheep having put aside the burdens of the world like so much fleece, and as ascending from the washing, which is baptism, all to create twins, which are the two precepts of love, and I see no one of them sterile of this holy fruit.[16]

Why the literal sense should be more pleasantly received when dressed in this metaphorical apparel, Augustine declines to say. What he will say, though, and again in terms which match Origen's, is why we should be put to the trouble of having to strip away the metaphorical dressing to lay bare the spiritual significance:

> . . . no one doubts that things are perceived more readily through similitudes and that what is sought with difficulty is discovered with more pleasure. Thus the Holy Spirit has magnificently and wholesomely modulated the Holy Scriptures so that the more open places present themselves to hunger and the more obscure places may deter a disdainful attitude.[17]

In view of this passage, and of many another which would illustrate an equal readiness to read metaphors as allegories, it would be a mistake to place Augustine's exegetical theory unambiguously into, still less at the head of, either an explicitly 'metaphoricist' or of an explicitly 'anti-metaphoricist' camp. Augustine the exegete neglected the Song: his importance to us, if great, is indirect, and subsequent commentators learned as much, if not more, from his practice as from his theory. Taking his exegesis as a whole—practice and theory—we cannot say that one position may be described, definitively, as 'Augustine's hermeneutic', for he is in turn clear on one side, clear on the other, and ambiguous. It is not surprising, therefore, that his influence on mediaeval hermeneutics is itself ambiguous. His authority is appealed to on all sides in this as in many another mediaeval debate.

ALLEGORY AND TYPOLOGY

We must, in any case, ask how far there *is* a genuine mediaeval debate, consciously engaged in, on the question of the hermeneutical standing of metaphor, and how far what was but a complex of disagreements and differences of emphasis are too easily read by us as a debate only from the point of view of our constructions upon it. The evidence which I have provided in my anthology appears to show that there was, genuinely, a debate but that for the most part it was consciously conducted from the side of a minority of hermeneutical theoreticians who took an 'anti-metaphoricist' position. The majority, in practice, are 'metaphoricists', unproblematically and undefensively. The minority—Hugh of Saint Victor, Thomas Aquinas and Nicholas of Lyra—explicitly warn against the tendency to allegorise without sufficient grounding in a firmly established literal sense and observe that this excessive 'allegoricism' seems to follow from the failure to hold fast to the distinction between literary trope and allegory proper.

Because they were all clear (though in Nicholas' case, as we shall see, less than perfectly consistent) that metaphors were part of the literal sense of Scripture, they were also able to be clear that the three 'spiritual' senses of Scripture are not to be understood as simply kinds of metaphor. Repeatedly they distinguish between the rhetorical employment of *similitudines imaginariae*[18] as figures of speech and the allegorical-typological reading of an event reported by Scripture as a *figura* of Christ or of some other sacred mystery.

At the root of this distinction is a peculiarly strong conviction, shared by Hugh, Thomas, and Nicholas, of the intimate foundation of typology in the historical truth of the biblical text. Typology is distinct from metaphor because whereas metaphor is the product of any significant likeness between one thing and another, however unrelated they may be in causation or in historical sequence, historical sequence and providential causation are the essential foundation of typological significance. Consider how the majority of our exegetes treat the 'kiss' of the Song's opening verse. Thomas of Perseigne's treatment is typical:

> There are three characteristics of the kiss which should come to mind, namely that the lips of those who kiss are joined; that they draw one breath together and that their bodies are drawn close. In the first is the joining of natures; in the second is the uniting of two spirits; in the third is the sharing of things suffered. The natures joined are those of the man and the Word; the spirits which breathe together are the divine and the human; the things suffered are shared by Christ and the Christian. (n. 3)

As it stands, this is but the exploitation of a somewhat forced similitude, an abstract correspondence, between the meeting of lips in a kiss and the meeting of the divine and human natures in Christ; and the problem with this hermeneutical strategy is that it reduces the historical specificness of the kiss of the Song to the level of the abstract likenesses between any kiss whatever and the Incarnation, and so to the level of metaphor. If the kiss of the Song is to function as true type in Thomas Aquinas' sense, the Bride's plea for it has to be read as an historical event which is *prophetic* of, not simply a metaphor for, the Incarnation; there would be a type only if the kiss which the Shulamite is literally said to desire of Solomon could be said to anticipate and by anticipation somehow *enter into the reality of* the meeting of natures in Christ. Thus, the Song's kiss would be capable of bearing the typological weight of signifying the Incarnation only if it could be shown to be an historical event in some way providentially connected with the second.

The issue concerning history may be put into sharp focus in relation to the problematic historical veracity of the Song itself. For Thomas Aquinas no typology is genuine which is not rooted in a true historical sense. And we may suppose that this principle held true for the Song itself, though this matter deserves further discussion later.[19] For Denys the Carthusian, on the other hand, no typological significance would be possible on the supposition that the Song reports a true love-tryst between Solomon and the Shulamite; were it a true factual account of such an affair it would be too morally unworthy a tale to bear the weight of a Christological significance (n. 4). Putting the issue in its sharpest and most uncompromising form, the situation appears to be this: for Thomas Aquinas, the Song can have a typological significance only if it is historically true. For Denys the Carthusian it can have typological significance only if it is historically false.

Now it may be objected that to force the issue between metaphor and typology this sharply is to beg a central question of mediaeval hermeneutics unwarrantably in favour of Thomas Aquinas: and, for sure, few apart from Thomas Aquinas would have as rigorously and consistently insisted as he did upon a true historical sense as the foundation of allegory—Hugh of Saint Victor and Nicholas of Lyra perhaps among them. It would indeed be a pity so to sharpen the conceptual focus of this debate as to make it possible to see it only from one side of the matter, especially given that, as I have said, it was seen as a debate mainly from that one side. This would be all the more unfortunate in view of the fact that Thomas' position is decidedly that of the minority. Finally, Denys too is in a minority in the openness of his rejection of the historical veracity of the Song. When all is said and done, the sharpness of the distinction ought not to be exaggerated and needs to be more closely defined.

All the same, though it will be necessary later to correct this one-sided and over-focussed reading of the 'debate',[20] we may say that it was what they *perceived* to be a common and widespread neglect of the historical truth of Scripture which led Hugh, Thomas, and Nicholas to protest the excessive allegorisings of the majority. All three are clear on one point on which, as they see it, their opponents are at least confused: allegory is not part of the meaning of the *text* of Scripture, but only of the events which the text records. (Hugh, n. 4; Thomas Aquinas, a. 1, corp.; Nicholas, n. 1). All three held that the literal events of the Old Dispensation are types of the New because the Holy Spirit, who is the author of the Scriptures, is also the author of the events which they record. And as the Holy Spirit has determined the literal meanings of Scripture, so the Holy Spirit has determined the meaning of the events which the text, in its literal sense, records. Thus it is that the Holy Spirit, the author of all history, disposes, within the single, continuous sweep of his providence, that some events have the significance of anticipating other events because the first are part of the one historical-providential continuum which results in the second. So the events of the Old Dispensation not only precede the events of the New; nor are they types of them only by means of abstract likeness to them; they are types, as distinct from metaphors for them, *because* they are drawn into the one providential causality whereby both are brought about in history. In a certain sense, therefore, the earlier events *are* the later events, because they enter into the same reality, because in general terms they are anticipations of them: it is thus and only thus that the earlier are capable of being *similitudines* of the later.

It was in consequence of this concern for historical veracity that, again, all three agreed on the proposition that there is one and only one kind of meaning of the *text* of Scripture and that is its literal sense. 'Metaphoricism' in practice treats all metaphors as spiritual meanings, and since metaphors are part of the meaning of the text, there is a tendency to treat the spiritual senses of Scripture as part of the meaning of the text. For Thomas this cannot be so. The spiritual senses are not, as metaphors are, further layers of *textual* meaning, but are the meanings of the events or objects to which the text literally (whether in metaphor or not) refers. Hugh of Saint Victor engages in a dramatic dialectical argument with his opponents on this issue (nn. 4–5). If, as all agree, references to lions in the Old Testament are taken (and in Hugh's view, rightly taken) to be an allegory for Christ, this is not because the *word* 'lion' *means* 'Christ', but because what real lions are and do has a similitude with what Christ was and did. For Hugh, the word 'lion' means, even in scriptural contexts, what it means in any other context, the shaggy-maned beast 'which sleeps with its eyes open'. It does not, even in Scripture, *mean* 'Christ'. Some such actual beast, referred to in a divinely inspired context, can be said to stand allegorically for Christ, but it is only by virtue of that actual likeness between real lions and Christ that the reference can be read in its allegorical significance.

In the *Didascalicon* Hugh puts the nub of the argument succinctly:

> Scripture says: *Be watchful. Your adversary the devil prowls around like a roaring lion* (1 Pet 5:8). If we were

> to say that, in this passage, lion signifies the devil, we must understand that it is the lion, not the word 'lion' (which is referred to). For were these two words, 'devil' and 'lion' to mean the same, it would be worthless to compare one and the same thing with itself. It follows therefore that this word 'lion' means the animal itself, while it is the animal which designates the devil; and all the other examples are to be taken in this same way, as when we say that a worm, a stone, a snake or other such, signifies Christ.[21]

On this point Nicholas follows Hugh and Thomas closely enough. In what looks like a virtual paraphrase of Thomas' discussion in the *Summa Theologiae*, he argues that what is special about Scripture is

> that in it any one text contains many senses. The reason is that the principal author of the book is God himself and it is in his power not only to use words to signify something, which men are able to do as well and in fact do; but also he uses the things signified by the words to refer to other things. Thus, any book uses words to signify something, but it is peculiar to this book that the things signified by the words signify something else. By means of the first signification, that is, by words, we get the 'literal' or 'historical' sense; and by means of the other signification, that is, by the things themselves, we get the 'mystical' or 'spiritual' sense. (n. 1)

It is clear, then, that for Hugh, Thomas, and Nicholas, the 'spiritual' senses of Scripture are not *textual* meanings, but the meanings of the historical events and objects which the textual meaning literally records.

Where Thomas at least is clearer than Nicholas, however, is in his insistence that metaphor is part of the literal meaning. In his *Quodlibetal* discussion (a. 3, corp.) Thomas considers the objection to the doctrine of the four senses that there is nothing in the least distinctive about figurative language, for if, in Scripture, things are said which are figurative of Christ, 'so also are they said figuratively of many other men; as [in Dan 8:5] the king of the Greeks is signified by the he-goat of the she-goats'. Hence, if the spiritual senses are but metaphors, there is nothing hermeneutically to mark off scriptural writing from any other, secular, genre, particularly poetry. To which Thomas replies

> a he-goat, or other such, by means of which persons other than Christ are referred to in the Scriptures, were not themselves actual things, but metaphors, contrived solely for the purpose of signifying those persons; and so the meaning by which those persons or kingdoms are referred to in those metaphors is historical only. But in addition those things which are referred to in actual truth so as to signify Christ are related as shadow to truth; and so that signification by means of which Christ and his members are referred to gives rise to another sense than the historical, namely the allegorical. But if it happens in any text that Christ is referred to by means of a metaphor, that meaning adds nothing to the literal sense; in this way Christ is referred to as a stone cut from the mountain, but not by human hands. (Dan 2:24)

Later in the same *Quodlibet* he adds more laconically that '. . . to signify something by words or merely by the construction of images . . . yields nothing but the literal sense . . .' (a. 3, corp.). And as for poetry: 'poetic images refer to something other than themselves only so as to signify them; and so a signification of that sort goes no way beyond the manner in which the literal sense signifies' (a. 3, ad 2).

If on this issue we might have expected Nicholas to follow Thomas, as on others we surely may, we must admit that his discipleship is less unwavering. He seems unsure of himself. In his Prologue to the *Postillae Morales seu*

Mysticae he says that whereas some passages of Scripture have only a literal sense, other passages have no literal meaning at all and he refers, by way of illustration, to two passages of Scripture which are unambiguously metaphorical:

> For example, at Judges 9:8: *The trees went forth to anoint a king to rule over them*, etc. And at Matthew 5:30: *and if your hand causes you to sin, cut it off and throw it away*. The literal sense is that which is signified by the words, as has been said: and there is no such sense in these passages, nor in others like them. For it would follow that the literal sense of Scripture was false, for trees never did any such thing, nor could they. Likewise, our Saviour did not suggest that anyone should literally cut off his hand. Rather, in these passages there is a mystical sense which is to be understood of the things signified . . . For by 'the trees' are to be understood the citizens of Shechem, who made Abimelech their king to rule over them, as is explained in the text itself, and by the hand which is to be 'cut off' is understood any such acquaintance as provides the occasion for a man's downfall—he ought to cut himself off from the company of such. (n. 15)

This, as it stands, is pure 'metaphoricism'. Nonetheless, even in this Prologue Nicholas goes on to concede that for some (he must be thinking of Thomas and perhaps Augustine) such metaphors are included in the literal sense and that in practice he intends to follow this loose usage. He is on more consistent theoretical ground in his *Postilla* to the Song itself, where he once again follows Thomas closely. Indeed, he appears to reverse the position of the *Postillae Morales*: the literal sense, he now says, 'is not that which is signified by the words, but that which is immediately meant by the things signified' and goes on to say that 'this is illustrated by the example of Abimelech and the Sichimites' (n. 18), the very example he used in the

Postillae Morales to illustrate his retreat from the Thomist position. Now, Nicholas says, because the literal meaning of words is what they refer to, and because the story of the 'trees' metaphorically refers to the citizens of Shechem and to Abimelech their king, it follows that the metaphorical meaning of the passage is the literal meaning. We will see later that in his interpretation of the Song this analysis becomes quite crucial.

Two propositions thus far characterise the hermeneutics exemplified by Hugh, Thomas, and Nicholas. The first is that only the literal meaning of Scripture can be regarded as, in the strict sense, the meaning of its words. The spiritual senses are further meanings not of the text of Scripture, but of the events and objects which those texts literally record. Secondly, metaphors, which are part of the literal meaning of the text, are not to be confused with the spiritual senses of Scripture. In the light of these propositions it seems possible to make a distinction available to, indeed perhaps required by their style of hermeneutic, between allegory and typology. This, of course, is a modern distinction, not a mediaeval one, though the basis on which the distinction is made is none other than that on which Thomas and others very consciously did make the distinction between typology and metaphor.

Allegory strictly speaking, we may say, is a literary device, a narrative metaphor, interpreted by reading off events in the narrative as metaphors for other events whose relation with one another is similar to the relation of the events in the allegorical narrative. Some of Jesus' so-called 'parables' are in this way allegories, for example, the parable of the sower; for in that parable, the story of the varying fortunes of the seed sown exactly matches the story of the variable character of those receiving Jesus' preaching. Typology, on the other hand, is not a literary, but a theological doctrine—or rather is based upon one, namely upon the theology of history according to which earlier events not merely *match* later events in formal outline, but are prophetic anticipations of them; they are in a certain way causative of the events which they anticipate. As I explain in a note to Thomas Aquinas' discussion of the subject (p. 353, nt. 8), there is a certain suggestion that in this way events of the Old Testament are treated as quasi-sacraments, for they, like sacraments, are 'signs of something sacred' which 'effect what they signify' (*effici-unt quod figurant*).[22] Hugh of Saint Victor openly says as much: 'these literally recorded facts, which in this manner represent spiritual realities, are called sacraments' (n. 3).[23]

ALLEGORY AND THE LITERAL SENSE

After having examined these differences of opinion about the meaning of literalness we are in a position to explain the corresponding differences of opinion about the relation between the literal and the spiritual senses, for on this latter issue we find a division of tendencies which parallels that between the 'metaphoricist' and the 'anti-metaphoricist'. Hugh, Thomas, and Nicholas, who shared a strong conviction of the basis of typology in historical truth, were led thereby to attach great importance to the basis of the spiritual senses of Scripture in its literal meanings. Hugh asks in exasperated mood: 'If the letter is taken away, what is Scripture?' (n. 5) And Nicholas complains that the literal sense has become '*multum obumbrata* . . . almost suffocated, being tangled in so many mystical senses . . . by the method of expounding generally handed down in the tradition.' (n. 5) On their theory, and in Nicholas' practice illustrated below, spiritual meanings may be read off only from clearly established literal meanings, which, as Thomas emphasises, have to be historically true to bear any weight of 'spiritual' significance. Given their truth, however, it is possible to read off spiritual meanings from the literal, for it is the shape, as it were, of the events literally recorded in the Old Testament which is the key to the events they typify in the New.

Nonetheless, even a cursory reading of the texts of mediaeval biblical commentaries suggests that by no means all commentators in practice shared Hugh's, Thomas' or Nicholas' view of the primacy of the literal sense and often we are left with the unmistakable impression that the reverse is what is really happening, namely that a spiritual meaning already known is being read into the text, sometimes, as in Denys the Carthusian (n. 4), as *being* its literal meaning.

The theoretical literalism of Hugh, Thomas, and Nicholas had to work against the mainstream exegetical practice, the theory of which, insofar as it was theorised at all, owes much to an aspect of Origen's influence, at any rate as mediated by Gregory the Great. It would be wrong to load responsibility onto Origen, however—as we will see. But there is, for Origen, a very clear point in saying that the spiritual sense of Scripture is 'already there' in the literal sense. For the literal sense of a biblical text is the meaning intended by its author and the author of Scripture and of all its senses is the Holy Spirit. As Origen sees it, the Holy Spirit intends primarily the spiritual meaning of the Old Testament, and wraps this fundamental meaning in a literal account of historical events which at once disguises the spiritual meaning and functions as our key to its disclosure. For Origen, the spiritual meaning determines the structure of the literal, even, as we have seen, to the point of generating a distorted, incongruous or absurd narrative text.

> . . . since the chief aim of the Holy Spirit was to keep the logical order of the spiritual meaning either in what is bound to happen or in what has already taken place, if anywhere He found that what happened according to the narrative could be fitted to the spiritual meaning, He composed something woven out of both kinds in a single verbal account, always hiding the secret meaning more deeply. But where the narrative

> of events could not be coherent with the spiritual logic, He sometimes interspersed either events less likely or absolutely impossible to have happened and sometimes events that could have happened but in fact did not . . .[24]

In the order of composition, therefore, the spiritual meaning comes first and it generates, indeed 'writes', the literal meaning. To that extent, then, the spiritual sense is 'already there', waiting to be disclosed. From the point of view of the human reader, however, the literal meaning is all we have to go on and it is only through the literal meaning that we can read back into the spiritual sense. Indeed, it is only by means of the distortions and anomalies of the literal meaning that we can have any inkling that there is a spiritual sense at all, so heavy is the disguise of the literal meanings.

Just as Augustine is appealed to on all sides of mediaeval exegesis, so also Origen can by no means be held entirely responsible for the more extreme tendencies of mediaeval allegoricism. Nor, in any case, are Origen's views particularly well represented by those influences which can be attributed to him. Hugh of Saint Victor probably had Augustine's *On Christian Doctrine,* not Origen, in mind, when he laid great stress on the responsibility of the exegete to determine an accurate text and to base allegory on a firm foundation in the literal sense. But he could, had he known, have found support for his strictures on this score equally well in Origen's practice.

Moreover, in justice to Origen, it is important to note carefully what he actually says. In the first place he holds that most of the Bible is written in a perfectly plain, morally and spiritually worthy, literal sense. It is available to the ordinary, unaspiring Christian. It is only some texts, a minority, which are so anomalous as to demand a spiritual meaning requiring the neglect of the literal sense, for in such places a literal sense is either missing altogether, being nonsense, or is offensive, or factually incorrect. True enough, such anomalous texts do not demonstrate only that *they* are to be understood spiritually, but that the whole of Scripture has a spiritual meaning. The anomalous texts are, as it were, cracks in the surface of the literal meaning, through which may be glimpsed something of the depths of spiritual meaning which underlie and sustain the whole text of the Scriptures. But it does not follow from this account that the superiority of the spiritual sense allows any wholesale depreciation of the literal sense in all places. Far from it. Both the theory and much of the practice of Origen's exegesis shows a sensitivity to what he saw as a subtle and complex interplay of elements of the spiritual and elements of the literal senses. It is impossible to get an alibi for any generalised neglect of the literal sense out of a fair reading of Origen's exegesis. Moreover, as we have seen, Origen's argument from anomaly is repeated in so many words by Augustine. We do not need to lay responsibility for the use of this argument exclusively on Origen's shoulders, any more than it would be right to read Origen's overall attitude to exegesis in terms of it.

Nonetheless, Origen's reception within the Latin traditions does not always do justice to his complexity, particularly in the case of the Song. Here, within the historical development of mediaeval exegesis, Gregory the Great's influence is immense. As may be seen from the introductory remarks to his Commentary on the Song (nn. 2–5), the implicit reference to Origen's own Preface to his Commentary is pervasive. Moreover, the influence of Origen on Gregory tends to be strongest on the side of an emphasis on the spiritual reading and in Gregory's reading of the Song this does in practice lead to the neglect of literal and historical significance. We might say that, for Gregory, the Song's eroticism makes it, in Origen's sense, 'anomalous' in principle and as a whole, to the degree that the pressure of its anomaly leads to an exclusively 'spiritual' reading. For Gregory, Origen lies behind this.

From whatever source, the willingness to apply the argument from anomaly to the Song can, in the hands of some later mediaeval exegetes, become a veritable enthusiasm. Some appear positively to have welcomed textual obscurities as licence to free-style allegorisings. Some of our commentators are puzzled by how the Bridegroom of the Song can be said to have 'breasts more delightful than wine' (Sg 1:1) since, as Giles reminds us, 'it is the Bride who has breasts, not the Bridegroom'. Giles is alert enough to suspect a corrupt text (n. 8) only to reject the idea on the authority of the *Glossa Ordinaria*, that 'the Bride ascribes breasts to the Bridegroom so as to make it clear that she is speaking figuratively' (n. 11). He then adds his own Christological meaning.

Nicholas, of course, knew that the Vulgate text mistranslated the Hebrew word which is, admittedly, ambiguous between 'breasts' and 'loves' and, in a rather more responsible spirit of scholarship, welcomed the reduction in pressure to allegorise that the textual emendation permitted. But Denys the Carthusian will have none of this (n. 29). Since, he says, the Hebrew word is ambiguous (as even Nicholas concedes) it is preferable to take the traditional and Vulgate reading, with its attendant opportunities for Christological gloss, no matter what the text-critical evidence may say to the contrary. This is late, hyperbolic 'Origenism' taken to a point not at all warranted by Origen's own practice.

For the majority tradition, then, the spiritual sense of Scripture is both 'there' in the text, underlying and determining the literal meaning, and 'not there', for it is disguised by the literal meaning it generates. By a single process and in a single text, the Holy Spirit at once writes the spiritual sense and the language in which it is disguised. It is certainly true, therefore, that for this tradition, the literal meaning is the hermeneutical key to the spiritual sense, but the underlying account of the relations between literal and spiritual senses is quite different from that of our three theoretical 'anti-metaphoricists'. For these latter, as we have seen, the basis of typology lies in the true historical events which the literal meaning of the text records; it is the events themselves which speak prophetically. As we have seen, this is why Hugh and Thomas maintain that the spiritual senses of Scripture are not, strictly speaking, meanings of the *text* which records the events, but the meaning of the *events* which the text 'literally' records. For mainstream Song commentators, however, the historical veracity of the literal text is not crucial and where the historical truth of the text cannot be relied upon, the *only* meaning of the text is the spiritual. Another general difference between these two camps results from this one: whereas for the minority, the events of the Old Testament must have a significance in their own terms to be capable of bearing the weight of their typological sense, this is not so for the majority. There is, again, partial support for this majority view in Origen who was prepared to go so far as to say that there is no ultimate distinction btween the Old Testament and the New at all. Understood in its spiritual sense—that is, in the light of its fulfilment in the New Testament—the Old Testament *is* the New Testament in disguised form:

> I do not call the law the Old Testament if I understand it spiritually. The law is only made the Old Testament to those who understand it carnally . . . But to us who understand it and expound it spiritually and with its gospel meaning it is always new; both are New Testament to us, not in terms of temporal sequence but of newness of understanding.[25]

THE PROBLEM OF THE SONG'S LITERAL SENSE: THREE SOLUTIONS

Even for the most resolute mediaeval allegoriser, for whom, at the extreme point, the literal sense is so reduced in historical reference as to seem but a pretext for the disclosure of the spiritual, the literal sense remains in practice the hermeneutical point of entry. The problem with the

Song, however, is that, to put it in Origen's terms, the text as it stands, by virtue of its explicit eroticism, is so generally 'incongruous' as to tempt the mediaeval commentator into the denial of any value of its own to the literal sense. Not every commentator in our anthology yields to this temptation and none so wholeheartedly as Denys the Carthusian, for whom the literal meaning *is* the spiritual meaning (n. 4). All, however, are defensive, including even Gregory (n. 3), who is otherwise happy enough to defend the appropriateness of erotic discourse. Nicholas of Lyra, however, while no less than any doubting that the literal sense of the Song can lie in its reference to a love affair between Solomon and the Shulamite woman, provides a neat, and so far as I can tell, almost unique solution, by treating the entire first six chapters of the Song as an extended series of metaphors (*parabola*) not for Christological mysteries, but for the history of Israel. This is ingenious. Since, for Nicholas, metaphorical meaning is part of the literal sense, he is able to assign a clear literal meaning to the Song which as metaphor refers literally to actual historical events of jewish history and at the same time is able to avoid having to acknowledge Solomon's actual love affair as itself directly the basis of typology.[26] It is Israel's history which is the type of Christ, the erotic love-play a metaphor of that history. We know what problem this solution solves: he is theoretically committed to historical truth as the basis of allegory. Therefore, were Solomon's love affair itself to be read as the literal referend of the Song text, and so the basis of typology, then that love affair would have to be taken as prophetic of, because through divine providence causally related with, the Christological events which it typified. And this would seem to throw an unacceptable weight of spiritual significance upon what he notes is a dubiously licit sexual liaison. In essence, Nicholas' solution is to take advantage of one half of the argument from anomaly: the Song is too morally repugnant to be accepted as historically referring to Solomon's love affair; and so on the literal side its plain sense is metaphorical; it is only indirectly typological; for by metaphor it denotes literally other historical events which can in turn be read typologically.

Nicholas' solution appears not to be quite unique. A recently published edition of an anonymous *Expositio hystorica* of the Song[27] offers a similar solution, though, to put it a little paradoxically, to a very different problem. This *Expositio* is written *secundum Salomonem,* that is to say, following the hermeneutical strategies of Rabbi Solomon ben Isaac, or 'Rashi', the jewish commentator of the late eleventh century. In fact, the *Expositio hystorica* is an adaptation and paraphrase, as well as a latin translation, of Rashi's commentary, composed by a christian scholar of the late thirteenth century. The author's intention was manifestly to follow Rashi's interpretation of the Song as closely as a Christian possibly could, and this desire had a number of consequences for the construction of the revised latin version, both positive and negative.

On the positive side, the most obvious consequence was that the latin revision was going to have to be, in the most widely accepted christian sense of the terms, 'historical' or 'literal'. For given his desire to follow Rashi as closely as possible, a Christian allegorical reading was out of the question. To this extent, the latin author's *sensus hystoricus* is intended to be effectively equivalent to that *sensus hebraicus* which is at least not inconsistent with Christianity. This, in turn, had the further, though this time negative, consequence that, as the editors point out,[28] the christian author could not follow Rashi in taking the historical reference of the Song up to his, Rashi's, contemporary times. Indeed he had to confine the historical scope of his commentary to the pre-christian era, from Exodus to the roman occupation; otherwise, the christian author would have had to confront Rashi over the significance of the Song in reference to the conflict between the Synagogue and the Christian Church—as Rashi did from the jewish side and in their turn christian commentators did from their side (see Gregory, nn. 32–37, Giles, nn. 40–41). Consequently, the anonymous Christian differed also from Nicholas of Lyra on the period of the Song's historical reference, for Nicholas, for all his commitment to the *sensus litteralis*, was to read chapters 7 and 8 of the Song as an allegory of christian history from the early Church to the time of Constantine.

On the other hand, the christian author does seek to follow as closely as he can the general hermeneutical strategy of Rashi in regard to Song interpretation, and this is where his significance for our discussion is at its greatest. For following Rashi along a path of theoretical hermeneutics which Nicholas was later to tread, he composes an interpretation which is both, in the strict sense, 'literal' and at the same time not, in this literal sense, to be understood as the narrative of the mutual love of the Shulamite woman and Solomon. The author manifestly regards his position as consistent. The Song is both *literally 'about'* and a *metaphor for*, the history of Israel. He says:

> Solomon . . . composed this work as a metaphor of a woman who has been made a widow by her husband's desertion while he was still alive and she desires and longs to be restored to him and to be united to him by love, remembering as she does the love of her youth. The Bridegroom himself suffers for her in her misery, remembering the kindnesses of her youth and her beauty and her honest behaviour, which had united her with him by powerful bonds of love; and he does so on this account, that he has not willingly afflicted her, nor has he rejected her unconditionally, for she is still his wife and she her husband.[29]

Kamin and Saltman argue convincingly that his reading of the Song as pure *metaphora* is consistent with the author's claim that his is an *expositio hystorica* only on an assumption which, they say, was first clearly argued for in the thirteenth century, namely that metaphor is part of the literal sense.[30] The logic of this is unassailable: our author would have had to think this to be consistent. Moreover, it seems at least plausible to say that he did think it. And if it is certainly true that there are precedents, in Augustine and in Hugh of Saint Victor among others, for this view of the metaphorical as literal, there is little doubt that no one had been able to set out the grounds for this view as systematically and convincingly as Thomas Aquinas did in that century. Though there is no evidence that the author of the *Expositio hystorica* had read Thomas, no commentary on the Song could be more 'Thomist' *in principle* than this *Expositio hystorica*; or rather, since we have no idea what kind of commentary Thomas did write or might have written, we can at least say that among christian commentators in the middle ages, only a Thomist could have consistently *defended* the writing of such a commentary.

Moreover, it seems that on the score of theory at least, the position of this christian follower of Rashi seems indistinguishable from Nicholas of Lyra's. For even if they differ on the Song's historical range, they agree on three propositions of Song hermeneutics: first, that the Song is not literally about the love of Solomon and the Shulamite; secondly, that it is a work composed entirely of metaphor; and thirdly that the literal sense of its metaphors lies in their reference to the history of Israel's relationship with Jahweh.

This theoretical hermeneutics is, however, distinctly that of a minority, even after the thirteenth century. The majority of commentators take neither the route of Denys the Carthusian, who denies any literal sense other than the typological and explicitly rejects Nicholas' solution, nor the indirect literalism of Nicholas and the *Expositio hystorica*, but a third way. They ignore the question of the Song's historicity almost entirely and, in practice, use the Song as a rich quarry of metaphor for Christological themes. Thomas of Perseigne draws a typology from a pedantic taxonomy of kisses (the 'kiss of the flesh', 'of the devil', 'of man' and 'of the beloved') and, as we have seen, from the physical characteristics of a kiss (the 'joining of lips', the 'drawing of one breath', the 'closeness of bodies') (nn. 3–4). Alan is more elaborate and theologically dense: the Bridegroom's mouth is a likeness of the Son, the second person of the Trinity, for there is an analogy between the relation of the mouth to the body and the relation of the Son to the Father:

> For many reasons the Son is called the mouth of the Father: For as one person speaks to another with his mouth, so the Father has spoken to the world by means of his Son. For the mouth is the same in nature as the rest of the body; so too is the Son of the same nature as the Father. And a kiss is offered to the mouth; so too does the Father offer the vessel of grace to the faithful soul.
>
> 7. The Virgin asks for three kisses. One kiss is the Incarnation. For as in one kiss two lips are pressed together, so in the Incarnation the divine nature is made one with the human. A second kiss is the Holy Spirit's, by whom the Son kisses the Father, by whom the Father loves the Son, it is he who unites Father and Son, for his is the love of them both, their embrace and their kiss. The third kiss is the kiss of Christ's teaching . . . So, she longs for the Incarnation to be wonderfully worked in her; and she longs for the Holy Spirit to come upon her and the power of the Most High to overshadow her (Lk 1:35); and for the teaching of Christ to be given. These are the kisses by which the Father kisses the Son, or the Bridegroom the Bride, or the Lord his handmaiden, the son the mother, the pupil the teacher . . . . (nn. 6–7)

This exposition represents the very finest mediaeval allegorical interpretation, at once complex in theological and hermeneutical texture and economical in words. The levels of reference are many. The Bride's longing for the Bridegroom's kiss becomes an image for the Virgin's longing for the conception of the Word within her. Gregory had found in the desire for the kiss a reference to the people of Israel's expectation of the Messiah (n. 12). In Alan, this generalised expectation has become personalised in Mary's 'expecting' of Jesus, the symbol of her pregnancy being an implied further level of meaning made explicit later in his Commentary (n. 20). And then there is the kiss itself: for Alan, as for Gregory, the joining of the two lips is a metaphor for the joining of natures in the Incarnation of the Son. But this Incarnation in turn bears the weight of Trinitarian meaning—a meaning, one suspects, which Alan had found in cistercian sources, such as in the following passage from William of St Thierry's *Golden Epistle*, a passage which itself may be derived from Bernard:

> . . . the Holy Spirit . . . the God who is charity . . . He who is the love of Father and Son, their Unity, Sweetness, Good, Kiss, Embrace . . . becomes for man in regard to God . . . what he is for the Son in regard to the Father, or the Father in regard to the Son through unity of substance. The soul in its happiness finds itself standing midway in the Embrace and Kiss of Father and Son.[31]

For Alan it is as if the kiss which is the joining of natures in Christ—the kiss by which the Father kisses the world—is the direct reflection within human history of that kiss by which the Father and Son mutually embrace, the 'economic' reflecting the 'immanent' Trinity. It is as if the allegorical kiss of the Incarnation and the anagogical kiss of the Trinity are one and the same kiss. Thus he hermeneutically fuses these two senses. And it is this one kiss which the Virgin longs for when she replies to the Archangel: *Be it done unto me according to your Word* (Lk 1:38). At the theological level, therefore, Annunciation, Incarnation, and Trinity are fused into a single theological totality within the word 'kiss'; at the hermeneutical level are fused different senses of the text; and on the score of literary sources, the Song and Luke, Gregory, William and Bernard, each of them possessing its own theological and hermeneutical densities not lost on the mediaeval reader, are fused within a terseness of expression which stands on the borders between the exegetically naive and the theologically sublime. In short, in this passage Alan unpacks a dense, compressed theological symbolism.

But is this truly typology? The answer depends on the standpoint from which we ask the question. For all its theological weight and complexity, Alan's is no more a typological exegesis in Thomas Aquinas' sense than is Gregory's plain analogy between the Bridegroom's breasts and the holy men of the Church (n. 29) or the Aristotelian psychologising of Giles of Rome (nn. 13–16). To all intents and purposes, much of the 'typological' interpretation illustrated in this volume is the systematic exploitation for theological purposes of traditional and deeply embedded metaphors. Not one of our commentators is prepared to say that the divine author of Scripture, the Holy Spirit, providentially brought about an *historical* love affair between Solomon and a Shulamite because that actual carnal relationship typifies those mysteries of the christian faith which it prophetically signifies. In this way the Song is in a very different case, exegetically, from, for example, the Exodus narrative, which can typify the redemption because it has a place in the historical events which bring the people of Israel forward to the fulfilment of the messianic promises.[32] The love affair of the Song differs more particularly from that of Ruth and Boaz (Ruth 4:13–22), which can be a type of the Incarnation because its place in the ancestry of Jesus through David has a role in the events which bring about what it signifies. In the Song all is different; no significant historical nexus is established; the question of historicity is either ignored, or, as in Denys, denied. This is why the particularity of the lovers' love does not precisely stand for the love of Christ and the Church; in practice it is the general, formal characteristics of erotic love as such which have the power to signify how Christ and the Church, the soul and God, are joined in love.

But if this is so, then at least the *Thomist* basis for the distinction between typology properly speaking and formal analogy or metaphor appears to have been altogether removed, at least in the case of the Song. And one has to admit that there is, in fact, a certain consistency from his point of view in Denys the Carthusian's open assertion that the Song's literal meaning *is* its spiritual meaning, that it is therefore the *language* of the Song, not any supposed historical events to which it refers, which is the source of the typological sense. Denys' hermeneutical explicitness merely reflects more consciously and consistently what had become a common practice of neglect of the literal sense of the commentators before him. To this neglect we have a witness, some one hundred years earlier, in Nicholas of Lyra (n. 7), as in Hugh of Saint Victor two hundred years before that (n. 4). Both, as we have seen, express a marked distaste for the proliferation of 'mystical' interpretations which, as Nicholas says, serve only to 'suffocate' the literal sense. In view of these witnesses it is, therefore, safe to say that, with the exceptions of the *Expositio hystorica* and Nicholas' *Postilla Litteralis*, there is no 'Thomist' historical-allegorical interpretation of the Song in the Middle Ages. For this reason it may seem perverse to read that mainstream tradition exclusively, or even mainly, from the standpoint of a very small minority of non-practising 'antimetaphoricist' theoreticians.

It would seem to be going too far to draw, from the uncertainty of most mediaeval commentators about the historicity of the Song's narrative, the conclusion that in their commentaries they altogether abandoned typology in favour of ahistorical metaphor, simply on the basis of a selectively Thomist account of allegory. In the first place, though after Augustine's *De doctrina christiana* Thomas' is undoubtedly the most sophisticated and articulate biblical hermeneutic of the Latin West, it would be quite wrong to assume that his account is representative of a commonly held view of the relationship between the spiritual and the literal senses. As we have seen, the majority view differs sharply from Thomas' on precisely this point and was developed much earlier than Thomas'. In any case, Augustine and Gregory were much more influential than Thomas at *any* point in the Middle Ages. In practice, secondly, since most monastic commentary is more 'metaphoricist' in spirit than thomist, at least in its relative unmindfulness of the the historical truth of the literal sense, it would be simply arbitrary to deny the character of the typological to what they were doing. In their own terms, an exegesis such as Alan's would perfectly meet the accepted criteria for typology. In particular, thirdly, even Denys the Carthusian's position can be perfectly well justified on an extension of Origen's principle of anomaly to the whole text of the Song. The Song from beginning to end lacks a morally acceptable narrative sense. Consequently, it far from follows that such passages *lack* a typological sense. On the contrary, it follows that they *must* have one.

Fourthly, even if so extreme an allegoricist as Denys denies that the actual text of the Song has its own narrative truth, he is as firm as any mediaeval commentator in his insistence that in a more general way the Song must be understood against the background of the history of the people of Israel in its relation to its Christological fulfilment. Denys' exegesis is thus firmly set within that theology of history which I described at the beginning of this chapter. The people of Israel repeatedly show, in the events of their history and in their scriptures, how they desired the coming of Christ (n. 8). From Abraham to John the Baptist, the history of the Israelites is the history of their longing for their redemption, and for Denys it is the history of their *eros* for Christ. The Song is the literary apotheosis of that *eros*, the fullest achievement of Solomon's prophetic powers, the consummation of all Old Testament typology. In that sense, even in Denys, the Song is true typology.

We may deny this only on an *a priori* preference for more theoretically adequate and theologically satisfying thomist hermeneutic.

Nonetheless the distinction between a broadly 'metaphoricist' style of allegory and a broadly 'historical' style can be justified and it is valuable to use the theoretical precisions of a Thomas in the process of clarifying the inner logic of the former—particularly since the hermeneutic of Thomas is itself a native product of the same traditions and sources as is the majority 'metaphoricist' practice. I have already suggested that it is possible to trace important continuities between mediaeval exegesis of the Song and the erotic language and imagery of John of the Cross. In the final chapter of this essay I will argue that this is possible because it is possible also to identify a tendency within mediaeval exegesis away from the exploitation of erotic language as historical typology and towards a more general, literary and only loosely historical employment of that discourse as imagery. If there is such a tendency, one would expect to find it *prima facie* within 'metaphoricist' styles of exegetical practice, hardly within exegesis conducted on thomist principles. The 'metaphoricist' inclination to neglect literal truth reduces almost to a convention the distinction between the use of the Bible as prophetic typology and its use as a source of metaphor. As a consequence it is unsurprising that we observe the distinction between metaphor and typology—which for Hugh, Thomas, and Nicholas is sharply focussed—being blurred or even denied within the more common practice of the monastic commentator on the Song.

NOTES

1. Origen; Greer, p. 217.

2. We should note that the Vulgate latin of the Song offers little support for this nomenclature. The female lover is very rarely addressed as *sponsa*, the male never as *sponsus*. The 'Bride' is variously addressed, most usually as *amica mea*, occasionally as *soror et sponsa*, only twice as *sponsa* alone; the 'Bridegroom' is addressed always as *dilectus meus* or *quem diligit anima mea*.

3. Cp. *Brief Commentary*, n. 13.

4. Again, we should note that *amor* is the commentarial word. The Vulgate uses *diligere* and its cognates throughout, a fact which the commentators let pass unremarked.

5. SC 2.1.

6. *The Love of Learning*, p. 32.

7. This last qualification can be quite important. As Thomas Aquinas points out (*Quodlibet* 7, q. 6 a. 2 ad 3), Scripture can contain literal moral instruction which, as such, is part of the literal sense. The tropological sense is that which is generated through a typological interpretation which instructs us how to act in and through a prophetic type of Christ or the Church.

8. *Collationes*, 14.8.

9. *On First Principles*, IV. 2. 9, Greer, pp. 187–188.

10. Greer, p. 189.

11. *On Christian Doctrine*, III. xxix. 41, trans. D. W. Robertson Jr, (New York: Macmillan, 1958) p. 104.

12. It is quoted, for example, by Thomas Aquinas, p. 345 below. Thomas' determination to identify his own position as 'augustinian' ought here, as elsewhere, to be taken with considerable caution.

13. *On Christian Doctrine*, II. vi. 7; p. 37.

14. *Ibid.*

15. *Ibid.*

16. Pp. 37–38.

17. *Ibid.*

18. See a.2, ad 1. It is arguable that in the *Summa Theologiae* Thomas uses the word *parabolum* to mean metaphor (1a q.1 a.10 ad 3) as does Nicholas, nn. 18 and 22 below.

19. See pp. 138–139 below.

20. See pp. 121–123 below.

21. *Didascalicon*, VI. iii; PL 176:791A.

22. *Summa Theologiae* 3a q. 62 q.1 ad 1.

23. Though he qualifies this statement in *De sacramentis*, I. ix. ii; PL 176:317D: 'In the same way as in a human being there are two things, body and soul, so likewise there are two in Scripture, the letter and its sense, just as in every sacrament what is externally and visibly transacted and seen is one thing and what is invisibly and inwardly believed and laid down is another . . . . But because not every sign of something sacred may helpfully be described as a sacrament in the same

way (for the letter of the sacred senses and the shapes and pictures of sacred realities are signs but cannot reasonably be called 'sacraments'), it seems best to regard the description just given as an interpretation or manner of speaking rather than a strict definition'.

24. Greer, p. 188.

25. *Homily 19 on Numbers*, ix. 4, quoted in *Cambridge History of the Bible*, I (Cambridge, 1970) p. 483.

26. Matter correctly says that 'there is no "non-allegorical" Latin tradition of Song commentary', but her bald assertion that 'even Nicholas of Lyra, champion of the historical sense of the Bible, argued that the Song of Songs has no literal sense' (*The Voice of My Beloved*, p. 4) is scarcely borne out by Nicholas' *Postilla Litteralis*: even when, as with cc. 6–8 of the Song, Nicholas gives an allegorical reading, he prefaces it with an unadorned literal interpretation. It seems likely that Matter has failed to grasp that, for Nicholas, an understanding of the Song as *parabolum* is not the same as, nor does it entail, an allegorical reading.

27. *Secundum Salomonem: A Thirteenth Century Latin Commentary on the Song of Solomon*, eds S. Kamin and A. Saltman (Ramat Gan: Bar Ilan University Press, 1989).

28. P. 8.

29. *Expositio hystorica*, 1. 9–16

30. P. 12.

31. William of Saint Thierry, *The Golden Epistle*, II. xv; trans. Theodore Berkeley OCSO, in Cistercian Fathers Series, 12 (Kalamazoo: Cistercian Publications, 1980) pp. 95–96. In turn, William got this idea from Bernard of Clairvaux, SC 8.1–2, pp. 45–46, and it is developed in more theological detail in the *Brief Commentary*, n. 12.

32. Denys the Carthusian, as we might expect, is quite explicit in rejecting Nicholas of Lyra's attempt to read the Song in the light of Exodus; see Denys, n. 36 and Nicholas, n. 25.

5

The Logic of Typology

IF MEDIAEVAL commentators generally agree, though differing in what they mean by it, that the allegorical-typical sense of the Song is derived in some way from its literal sense, a question arises concerning *how* the spiritual sense is thus determined. The question is asked not prescriptively, but descriptively; we want to know what the majority of Song commentators did in practice, not by what theoretical methods the mediaeval commentator thought he could legitimately determine the spiritual sense by the literal. Excessive concentration on the theoretical, prescriptive question would leave us with little to discuss and would, in any case, once again skew the discussion in favour of the few mediaeval theorists who discuss the matter *ex professo*; it would, therefore, bias the discussion in favour of a minority, whose views on theory differ sharply from the majority practice. On the evidence, the answer to the question about majority practice is far from simple.

PHYSIOLOGICAL ANALOGIES

We need to look at different exegetical strategies differently. We have noted that in all our authors—and in this they are as representative of the genre as in any other respect—there is a predeliction for physiological analogies for spiritual realities, a preference which undoubtedly reflects the pervasiveness of physiological language in the Song itself but is also, in this as in so many other ways, a preference which betrays the influence of Origen:

> On the basis of the evidence we have cited it is clearly demonstrated that these names for members (used in Scripture) can by no means be applied to the visible body, but must be referred to the parts and powers of the invisible soul. The reason is that both carry similar designations, but the examples given obviously and without ambiguity bear meanings that apply not to the outer man but to the inner man.[1]

In such terms Gregory explains how, as breasts are attached to the rib-cage, dispensing 'without' the milk which they draw from 'within', so the preachers of the Gospel draw from their interior lives the spiritual sustenance which they give to others in their preaching (n. 29). In a much more complex and sustained analogy, Giles of Rome elaborates from an aristotelian psychology the correspondences between the senses of sight and hearing and 'philosophical' contemplation on the one hand, and between touch, taste, and smell and the different stages of mystical contemplation on the other (nn. 13–16). The neo-Platonist Thomas Gallus had developed the same analogy somewhat more economically earlier in the thirteenth century (n. 14).

In this sort of case the logic of the physiological typology is quite straightforward: it is that of the formal 'analogy of proportion': a:b::c:d. And one of the logical characteristics of such analogies is that the correspondences they are based upon are purely formal and relational. It goes without saying that it is not because *breasts* are like preachers that the typology is justified, but because *the relation between* breasts and the source of their milk corresponds with, or is 'like', *the relation between* preachers and their interior lives.

It seems to be a consequence of this logical feature of

formality, and not always or especially from any merely arbitrary disposition of the commentator, that such analogies are indeterminate as to content and are thus susceptible to indefinite proliferation—given, at any rate, sufficient ingenuity, rarely lacking, on the part of the commentator. In any case, the character of being formal means that such analogies can be constructed without regard to content and so there are no constraints internal to the logic of this hermeneutical strategem. Consequently, from 'breasts' alone we can get Gregory's analogy with the preaching of the Gospel; or we can get Alan's complex correspondences between the breasts of maidens, married women and widows and, respectively, virginity of soul, fallen flesh and 'the harsh discipline of self-control' (n. 11); or again, in the same commentary, between the Virgin's two breasts and her example of chastity and virginity (n. 10). Denys the Carthusian's enthusiasm for such analogies is uncontrollable: the breasts of the Bridegroom typify the wisdom and knowledge of Christ, the two commandments of love, the Old Testament and the New, the commandments of Christ and his evangelical counsels, his mercy and truth, or prevenient and subsequent grace (n. 24). The pure formalism of the typology accounts for its apparent arbitrariness, taken in Denys to such extremes of implausibility as to seem virtually random. He might as well have concluded his list with a lazy *et cetera*. In any case, he evidently took less heed than he might have of Augustine's strictures on the pointless elaboration of such typologies; they should be constrained, Augustine thought, by what Scriptural practice itself warrants—that, and only that, was a justified allegorical reading which could be found elsewhere in Scripture in a literal sense.[2]

As regards their logical structure, such analogies function as 'models' do—except that there are models of very different kinds. In just one respect, that of their formal character, these typologies seem to be 'models' in the way maps are models of what they map. A map stands to what it maps in a relation of purely formal symmetry. A map is a set of relations of distance between two-dimensional symbols which are exactly proportional to the relations of distance between the geographical features which the symbols stand for. Consequently, given the scale of the map, we can work out the actual distance between two points on the ground from the distance between the two symbols which stand for them on the map. Hence the relation between the map and the ground mapped is purely formal; it is a matter of arithmetical proportion only. Unlike a scaled-down relief-model of the same territory, a map does not itself 'look like' the ground it maps, partly because it represents two-dimensionally that which is three-dimensional. Nor even does it 'look like' the ground in the way an aerial photograph does, for a map is not, properly speaking, a picture. It is rather the representation of the ground it maps in terms of equivalent formal proportions: as **a** is to **b** on the map, so **c** is to **d** on the ground.

In that respect, then, the physiological analogies which so frequently occur in Song commentaries have the logical character of a map. They are, we could say, 'topographical' analogies, for in the same way the function and shape of the human limbs and organs disclose the mental and spiritual geography. In another respect, however, these analogies differ in logical character from maps. A map provides a set of determinate proportions between symbols which stand for *individual* features of the ground mapped and so it corresponds uniquely and individually with the one and only ground it maps: a map of the County of Avon is a map *only* of the County of Avon. By contrast, as we have seen, the mediaeval practice of physiological analogy is indeterminate in respect of what it maps and the same bodily limbs may represent a great variety of alternative spiritual realities, even in the same author and context.

The extraordinary degree of elaboration, but also the very great precision with which such analogies can be exploited, is well illustrated in the following passage from Bernard's *Sermons on the Song of Songs*:

> While the Bride is conversing about the Bridegroom, he, . . . , suddenly appears, yields to her desire by giving her a kiss . . . . The filling up of her breasts is proof of this. For so great is the potency of that holy kiss, that no sooner has the bride received it than she conceives and her breasts grow rounded with the fruitfulness of conception, bearing witness, as it were, with this milky abundance. Men with an urge to frequent prayer will have experience of what I say. Often enough when we approach the altar our hearts are dry and lukewarm. But if we persevere, there comes an unexpected infusion of grace, our breast expands, as it were and our interior is filled with an overflowing love; and if someone were to press upon it then, this milk of sweet fecundity would gush forth in streaming richness. Let us hear the bridegroom: 'You have received, my love, what you asked for, and here is a sign to show you, your breasts are better than wine; henceforth you will know that you have received the kiss because you will be conscious of having conceived. That explains the expansion of your breasts, filled with a milky richness far surpassing the wine of worldly knowledge that can intoxicate indeed but with curiosity, not charity; it fills but does not nourish; puffs up but does not build up; pampers but does not strengthen.[3]

EROS AS ANALOGY

Turning from such abstract, formalistic physiological typologies, we may distinguish from them the more general exploitation of the typological potential of human *eros* as such. In what way, if any, is human *eros* describable as a 'model' of the divine love? I have argued thus far that the mediaeval hermeneutic of the Song makes extensive use of quite general formal parallels beween the human experience of erotic love and the course of salvation history from the creation to the final kingdom. That history reads to the commentator 'like' a love story because the love of God for humans and of humans for God has the same 'shape' as a love story. We may ask, however, whether there are any grounds other than the formal coincidence of 'shape' on which the divine providential love may be so described; in particular, we ask whether, in addition to being a formal 'image' in the character of a map, human *eros* is being said to have any constructive, *participative* role within salvation history. For the mediaeval commentators, does making carnal love in any way *make* the salvation history which it maps?

The answer to that question must be no. But in order to make clear precisely why, in their exegesis of the Song, the monastic commentators viewed its typology as primarily formal and 'non-participative', let us make a further distinction of models, a distinction between the kind of model which a map is and the kind of model which is represented by a toy doll.

A map, we have said, has a purely formal relationship with what it maps. The sense in which it is 'like' what it maps is that the internal relations of the map must be exactly proportional to those of the territory it maps. Materially, however, a map is entirely discontinuous with what it is a map of, for, clearly, a sheet of paper printed with ink shares nothing materially with Avon's rolling hills and plains. Indeed a map not only does not have to look like what it maps, it does not even have to be a visual model at all: a map can be programmed into a computer, as a set of mathematical coordinates. Not so a toy doll. A toy doll must 'look like' a baby. No child is going to play happily with an arithmetical formula, no matter how exactly that formula expresses the mathematical relations of the dimensions of a baby. On the other hand, there is no *one* baby that a doll must look like, for a doll is not a replica of any one child. Furthermore, and more to the point, a map is in an entirely passive and reflective relation with the ground mapped; it provides information about something which exists independently of it. On the other hand, a doll's relation as model with a baby depends not merely on its abstract likeness with a real baby, but also, and crucially, upon its role within the imitative *behaviour* of the child who plays with it. A child playing with a doll is imitating an adult's relationship with an infant in a way which is not only *formally* similar to adult behaviour (the child 'washes', 'changes' and 'feeds' the doll) but also so as, by imitation, to *participate* in the adult behaviour. The two behaviours, adult and childish, are continuous with one another; the child at play prefigures a future behaviour by engaging in that behaviour—as we might put it, 'really', but in the mode of participation. Consequently the child is actually learning the adult behaviour of playing with an infant; he plays at playing with an infant by means of playing with a doll; but thereby he in some way really engages in the activity of playing with an infant.

Now when the mediaeval commentators construe the human *eros* of the Song as a type of the divine *eros* of salvation history, or of the soul and Christ, it is very far from their minds that the human love of Solomon and the Shulamite stands to the divine *eros* as a participative model does to what it models. As they see it, the relationship of type to typified is rather more like that of map to ground mapped, a matter of formal symmetries. It is in this connection that the distinction between 'metaphoricist' and 'historicist' styles of typology seems to take on some kind of theological significance. For though on both accounts the interpreter 'reads off' the typological sense from the literal, they differ, as we have seen, in the grounds on which the typological sense is held to be justified. For Hugh, Thomas, and Nicholas, no typological sense may be derived from any but a true historical sense, and this is because it is the events of the Old Testament literally signified to which the

Holy Spirit gives the power further to signify the mysteries of Christ. For these 'historicists', moreover, those events have the power to signify typologically because, through their role in the historical processes of redemption, they are providentially causes of what they signify—they *are*, by participation, what they are types of, as a child playing with a doll truly enters into the adult behaviour by participation. But the events of the Old Law could have this power only if they were true historical events; and if they were true historical events *they must have had a significance of their own*, in terms of jewish history and culture itself.

We do not possess any commentary on the Song by Thomas Aquinas, though he may have composed two,[4] and we have been able only to speculate about how any he may have written would have differed in method from the formal allegoricism of the monastic style. On the principle of Old Testament exegesis, however, Thomas' position is unambiguous. The Old Testament has its own truth, no doubt continuous with, because prophetic of, the New Testament, but capable of standing for the New only by virtue of the sense which it had in its own time and terms. In the *Summa Theologiae*, therefore, he raises the question whether the ceremonial precepts of the Old Law have any 'literal cause', or only a figurative, and his reply—that they have causes of both kinds—is based upon quite general propositions about Old Testament exegesis as such:

> . . . just as the ceremonial precepts prefigured Christ, so also did the historical narratives of the Old Testament, since *all these things happened to them in a figure* (1 Cor 10:11). Yet these had, besides a mystical or figurative sense, also a literal one. Therefore the ceremonial precepts also had their literal causes over and above their figurative ones.[5]

The connection between the literal meaning of the Old Testament precepts and their significance for the people of Israel is brought out more fully in the body of the article:

> Now the end of the ceremonial precepts was twofold; they were ordained for the worship of God at that time, and for prefiguring Christ . . . . In the same way, then, the reasons for the ceremonial precepts of the Old Law may be taken in two ways. First, in relation to the divine worship to be observed at the time. In this aspect they are literal, whether they concern the avoidance of idolatry, or the commemoration of particular divine benefits, or to point to the divine excellence, or else indicate the frame of mind required of the worshippers of God. Secondly, their reasons may be assigned according to their purpose in prefiguring Christ. In this aspect their reasons are figurative and mystical, whether they concern Christ and the Church—the allegorical sense, or the way of life of the Christian people—the moral sense, or the state of future glory to which we are brought through Christ—the anagogical sense.[6]

In the absence of any commentary from Thomas' hand, the value in speculating about what kind of commentary he might have written is limited to that to be gained from the exploration of the logic of his position on Old Testament typology in general. From within that position it might be possible to derive an answer to the question of which of them he might have adapted for the interpretation of the Song.

In this exploration we are offered some constraints on merely idle speculation by the hermeneutical predicament of Nicholas of Lyra. Nicholas shared Thomas' hermeneutical principles. For both, typology must rest on a true literal sense. For both, the true literal sense is the significance it had for the people of Israel in their role as the chosen people, a role which was determined by the providential guidance of the Holy Spirit. For both, the Holy Spirit determined not just the vicissitudes of that history themselves, but also their further significance within the whole economy of salvation history. Consistently with these hermeneutical assumptions, Nicholas sees himself as faced with two possible accounts of the Song's literal sense: either to accept the Song's own claims to be literally 'about' the love of Solomon and the Shulamite at face value, or to read the love narrative as metaphor for what it is literally about, namely events of Israel's history.

Nicholas' reasons for rejecting the first of these choices are curiously similar to Denys the Carthusian's. Nicholas says:

> Some have said that the Bridegroom is literally to be taken as Solomon himself but that the Bride is the daughter of Pharoah, his beloved wife. But this seems not to be true, because granted that this love between Bridegroom and Bride could have been lawful, at any rate if confined within the bounds of marriage . . . it was of a carnal sort and such love often has something not very fitting and unlawful about it; and so a description of a love of this kind seems inappropriate in canonical books of Sacred Scripture, especially as they were written at the dictation of the Holy Spirit. In any case, Solomon's knowledge of his love for his wife and of hers for him and of the pleasure such love yields was a matter of personal experience; he did not learn about this love from that revelation of the Holy Spirit which is the reason why Hebrew and Latin scholars alike list this book among the canonical works. (n. 19)

And, as if consciously reflecting Nicholas, whose *Postillae* he knew, Denys comments:

> . . . it may be gathered that they are mistaken who think this work should be read in its literal and historical sense as referring to Solomon and his Bride, the daughter of Pharoah, and allegorically to Christ and the Church. If this were so then the subject matter of this book would be of no worth, sensual and prurient

> and not spiritual, mystical, most excellent and heavenly; nor would it be a prophetic text, but rather a sort of love song. In any case . . . Solomon took the daughter of Pharoah to be his wife when she was still in her childhood, before she was fourteen years old . . . and this book can hardly have been written at that age, but later. Therefore, had he composed these songs literally about himself and the daughter of Pharoah, this book would have been a narrative of past events and could not have been a description of a spiritual marriage: and the holy and learned teachers, in whom the Holy Spirit dwells and speaks and through whom the Church chooses to be instructed, witness against this. (n. 4)

Remarkable as this convergence between Nicholas and Denys may seem, we ought not to attach much *hermeneutical* significance to it. They are opposed on all important points of hermeneutical theory, after all. The consensus between Nicholas and Denys seems to be rather in the moral and theological valuation of sexual love itself—as they both say, sex is too morally dubious a thing to bear the weight of a christological meaning—and in any case, as Nicholas puts it, you scarcely need the Holy Spirit to account for the wealth of Solomon's sexual experience.

The divergence between Nicholas and Denys lies in fact, on the familiar hermeneutical issue of the status of metaphor. Both read the eroticism of the Song as metaphor: and if they differ on the question of what the metaphor is metaphor of, this is because, as we have seen, in practice Denys identifies the Song's metaphorical significance with its allegorical significance, whereas Nicholas takes metaphor as part of its narrative, historical meaning. Consequently, for Denys the Song's eroticism is *both* metaphor *and* allegory for Christ, metaphor and *therefore,* allegory. For Nicholas, the eroticism is metaphor for jewish history and so is literally 'about' it. That jewish history may, in turn, be read in its christological significance or it may not be. And Nicholas' solution in the *Postilla Litteralis* is to read chapters 1–6 in a purely metaphorical-literal way, chapters 7–8 in both ways; in the *Postillae Morales seu Mysticae* he offers no Song commentary at all, but includes it among other Old Testament writings which, he says, do not need a spiritual interpretation.[7]

What, then, were Thomas' options? Consistently with his hermeneutic, they appear to be those which Nicholas faced, because both give due weight to the Old Testament significance of the Song and both seek a foundation for the spiritual senses in a true literal sense. Nicholas' rejection of the love story itself as the historically factual referend of the literal sense, being based upon a moral judgment of the suitability of sexual love as a source of allegory in its own right, still leaves that option open hermeneutically. Consistently with their shared hermeneutic, both Thomas and Nicholas could have taken it.

To have exploited this option would be to have taken a step beyond the recognition of its hermeneutical consistency into a more positive theological evaluation of human sexuality than Nicholas was prepared to take. Whether Thomas' theological position on human sexuality would have allowed him to take it is another matter, but we can determine at least what his hermeneutics would have required of him theologically were he to have argued for the historical veracity of the love affair as the literal sense of the text, and so the basis of its typological meaning. He would at least have had to have said that the love of Solomon and the Shulamite is not merely a formal stereotype of the love of Christ and the Church but that it is in some way an historical event of real significance for and within the historical course of salvation: that, as playing with a doll participates in and is a continuous reality with the adult behaviour of child-rearing, so that sexual love is a real participation in the love story of Christ and the Church through the prophetic love between Israel and Yahweh. Logically—

that is, consistently with his hermeneutic—Thomas could have said this, as indeed could have Nicholas. And Thomas' theology of Old Testament history entails the same conclusion, for he regards the Old Law as a whole as a proto-sacrament of the New: it effected, albeit but partially, what it signified.

The logic of Thomas' position has been worth examining, if only as a counterfactual conditional, because it brings into sharp focus the very different logic of the 'metaphoricist' hermeneutic of the Song. The 'metaphoricist', for whom the literal sense is barely more than a pretext for a typology, is under no such *hermeneutical* pressure to give intrinsic weight to the eroticism of the Song and, on the contrary, is under a *theological* pressure to deny it that weight, to deny that human sexuality can play a real, more than merely symbolic, part in the economy of grace and salvation. The pressure of a theological depreciation of human sexuality therefore bears upon an hermeneutically open door, opening up into an unproblematically 'pure' typology of the Song in which the role of human *eros* is reduced to the purely formal symmetries with which it maps onto the divine realities which it typifies. Erotic type and spiritual typified are exactly parallel lines. *As* parallel lines, therefore, they may never meet.

'IMAGE' AND 'LIKENESS'

At this point in the argument it is appropriate to return to the difficult question of the influence of neo-platonic thought, in particular that of the pseudo-Denys, on the majority practice of mediaeval Song hermeneutics. I have made no case for this influence in terms of direct transmission, but I would claim a rather high level of what one might call 'ideological osmosis'. Certain key neo-platonic ideas progressively soaked the theological mind of western Christendom, even that of the monk who otherwise had little time for the source-texts in which they are explicitly articulated. Here I wish to attend to one such idea, offering as an hypothesis the proposition that the 'formalism' of the Song commentator's concept of erotic allegory is at least in part the product of quite general neo-platonic epistemological pressures. Operating as a controlling discipline, if hardly consciously recognised, there was, I propose, an assumption of the inverse ratio between the degree to which a type may be said to *participate in* the reality which it typifies and the degree to which the type is a purely formal symmetrical, essentially *mimetic* model of that reality.

The source of that assumption lies, I suggest, within the platonic inheritance of the Middle Ages and is found clearly in the pseudo-Denys. For the pseudo-Denys, theology, as we have seen, articulates two contrary but interrelated movements or 'ecstasies': an ontological *egressus* whereby the divine *eros* boils over into creation in successive phases of differentiation from itself, and a cognitive *regressus*, whereby rational creatures are drawn back, through the presence within them of erotic yearning, into the divine *eros* from which they proceed. Consequently, in different degrees, all *eros* is divine, manifested in different epiphanies. Pretending to quote his mentor Hierotheus, Denys writes:

> I have set out in due order the many yearnings springing from the One . . . but now, once more, let me take all of these yearnings and concentrate them into the single yearning which is the father of all yearnings . . . Come, let us gather all these once more into a unity and let us say that there is a simple self-moving power directing all things to mingle as one, that it starts out from the Good, reaches down to the lowliest creation, returns then in due order through all the stages back to the Good, and thus turns from itself and through itself and upon itself and toward itself in an everlasting circle. (*DN* 713D)

The dialectical relationship between the ontological unity of all *eros* on the one hand and its dispersed differentiations on the other, is complex, since it has to be adequate to a multitude of apparently self-cancelling propositions. In itself, as the creative, differentiating and ordering principle of all things, there is just one *eros*; as existing in its many differentiations, it is, of course, many. On the other hand, in itself, in its oneness of undifferentiation, it is also, as we have seen, inherently dispersive, expressive of itself in created multiplicity; and in its manyness it is the principle and movement of all things back into the unity of their source. Moreover, it is the first without loss of unity and the second without loss of differentiation. This, at the ontological level, is the scale of participation, for it is in the degree of their closeness to the One which is their source that they participate in it, and in equal measures *are* and are *one*.

At the epistemological level there is a parallel complexity. To know a created thing is at once to know it in its source and in its point of return, in its *egressus* and in its *regressus*, and to know a thing both in its coming forth from *eros* and in its return to *eros* is, therefore, at once to know it in its likeness and in its unlikeness to its origin and goal. Here, for the pseudo-Denys, there is a sliding scale of likeness and unlikeness, a scale which he divides roughly into two, between the 'similar similitudes' and the 'dissimilar similitudes'. Created things are all to some degree 'like' their source: but they are more or less like it. This, at the epistemological level, is the scale of likeness or *mimesis*, a ladder described step by step in Chapters Four and Five of the *Mystical Theology*.

In the pseudo-Denys' thought, these two scales—the ontological and the epistemological ways—appear to be related to one another in a number of complex, overlapping relations which we must try to unpick from one another. Let us distinguish two. In the first, the two scales are in direct proportion to one another. On the ontological scale, created realities are more or less close to their source. On the epistemological scale, created things are more or less like their source. So it is with *eros*: the differentiations of *eros* within creation participate ontologically, in degrees of more or less, in the reality of *Eros* as such. In the same way, those created differentiations are epistemologically more or less like the *Eros* of which they are all in some way images. For the pseudo-Denys, the one notion of likeness contains within it both these elements—ontological participation and epistemological *mimesis*—in direct proportion to one another. The more a created reality participates in its divine source the more like that source it is, the better it is as image. Every likeness is a participation, every participation is a likeness, the more the one, the more the other.

That on the one hand. On the other hand lies the pseudo-Denys' distinction between 'similar' and 'dissimilar similitudes'. If all created things to some degree participate in their divine origin, and if their degree of likeness to it is directly proportional to the degree of participation; if, therefore, there is no likeness of the Godhead which does not to some degree participate in it; nonetheless, within the epistemological, mimetic, side of the dionysian notion of likeness the distinction between similar and dissimilar similitudes yields a quite different set of relations between the mimetic and participatory elements. Let us return to maps and dolls. Maps are non-participatory models. Their value as models lies in the formal exactness with which they replicate real relations of distance, not in their material continuity with the real world of the ground mapped. Hence we may say that maps are entirely mimetic models. Dolls, on the other hand, are participatory models: though they replicate babies, they do so indeterminately with respect to any particular baby and they acquire their power as models from their role in behaviour participative in and continuous with parenting behaviour. That behaviour is, therefore, both mimetic and participatory. Now the pseudo-Denys seems to see the distinction, in respect of mimetic power, between the dissimilar similitudes and similar similitudes as like that between maps and dolls. Dissimilar similitudes, being ontologically distant from their source and so low in their degree of participation in it, are mimetically formal, abstract, analogical; similar similitudes, being higher in their degree of participation in their source, are, if also mimetically like it, primarily like it through participation.[8] Indeed, there seems to be an inverse proportionality, within likeness in general, between mimetic and participative degrees of it. In the degree to which a created reality stands at a distance ontologically from its source, to that same degree is its power as a likeness formal or analogical. This inverse proportionality seems to hold particularly of *eros*: because human sexual *eros* is in its substance low on the scale of yearnings for the divine, its power to reflect the divine lies less in its participation in the substance of the divine and more, therefore, in its formal likeness to it. Human sexuality, which, as the pseudo-Denys says, is a 'partial, physical and divided yearning . . . is not true yearning but *an empty image* or, rather, a lapse from real yearning' (*DN* 709 B-C). It is a vastly 'dissimilar similitude', distanced ontologically from the reality it reflects and to that degree reflecting the divine *eros* in its empty shape alone.

The character of this dionysian dialectic suggests a further sense in which human *eros* may be said to be a 'model' of the divine. We have noted that a map is in only a passive, materially discontinuous relationship with the ground it maps; doll-playing, however, is participative of the activity it imitates. Now on the pseudo-Denys' account, there is indeed a certain *causal* continuity between the divine *eros* and human sexual *eros*. For this reason the map model fails to do full justice to the relationship between them. Nonetheless, the causality of that relationship between divine and human *eros* operates in only one direction, from the divine to the human sexual, and so it is only from the point of view of the divine causality that there can be said to be any causal continuity between them. Human *eros* participates in the divine *eros* only as caused by it, only minimally, in turn, sharing in that divine causal power itself. Because human *eros* is caused by the divine *eros*, however, it can dimly, but, as we have seen, only formally, reflect it.

In this respect we might compare the pseudo-Denys' conception of the relationship between divine and human *eros* to that between the heat of a room and the thermometer which records it. A thermometer registers the temperature of its environment in terms of lengths of a column of mercury. It *translates* that which exists in one medium (heat) into a qualitatively different medium (length), but does so with quantitative exactness. Hence, whereas the ground which a map maps can in no sense be said to be the cause of the map which represents it, the heat of the environment, by expanding and contracting the mercury, directly causes the changes in the length of the column which record it. The heat, we might say, causes the phenomenon by which it is measured and reflected. In this way too, for the pseudo-Denys, the divine *eros* causes the human *eros* by which it is measured and reflected.

But, of course, that causal relationship is a one-way relationship only. We read the degree of heat from changes in the thermometer's scale because of the formal symmetries between them; so too, we may 'read' the divine *eros* from its reflection in the human. But as there is only a quantitative correspondence between a degree of heat and a length of mercury, but no qualitative sharing between them (heat and length are heterogeneous 'qualities'), so, for the pseudo-Denys, human and divine *eros* are quantitatively or formally alike, but do not qualitatively share in the same reality.

In the pseudo-Denys, then, qualitative and quantitative likeness—degree of participation and degree of formal exactness of copy—are inversely proportional. The lower the degree of participation in quality, the greater the merely quantitative formality and emptiness as *mimesis*. Denys' 'dissimilar similitudes' are 'dissimilar' because of the distance at which they stand from their Creator; and 'similar', therefore, only in their formal relations.

The 'metaphoricist' style of typology shows signs of yielding to the pressure of this inverse proportionality, for it combines in the same way the features of formal matching and participative emptiness, of quantitative correspondence and qualitative discontinuity. And if there is, in general terms, a connection of doctrines here, then it may be plausible to extend the hypothesis and connect this distinction with another, which drew almost universal support from mediaeval theologians in some version or other—the distinction between 'image' and 'likeness'. To most mediaeval theologians, this distinction, however unaugustinian it sometimes became, was Augustine's; but even in Augustine it seems to have the same ultimate roots as in the pseudo-Denys, in neo-platonism. And, if Thomas Aquinas is right, there is a connection between the prevailing theories of 'likeness' and typological hermeneutics: for, he says, a type is based upon a certain kind of *similitudo* (a. 1, ad 4).

Most mediaeval theologians, arguing from the Vulgate text of Genesis 1:26, drew what they thought was a theologically significant distinction between the 'image' and the 'likeness' of God. God said: *faciamus hominem ad imaginem et similitudinem*, 'let us make man in [our own] image and likeness'. The history of this distinction and of its sources in Augustine are far too complex to trace in detail here,[9] but we may conveniently start with Hugh of Saint Victor, who did much to popularise a particular version of it. For Hugh, an *imago* is a purely formal, non-participatory likeness; a *similitudo* a participative likeness which shares in the reality of that of which it is the likeness.[10]

Thomas Aquinas did not accept this terminology, as we will see, though a majority of mediaeval theologians preferred to follow Hugh. Bonaventure, in his *Commentary on the Sentences*, aptly and representatively illustrates how this distinction was set out by Hugh and, Bonaventure comments, customarily since:

> 'Image' denotes an agreement (*conformitatem*) in quantity, while 'likeness' a sharing (*convenientiam*) in quality. For 'image' denotes a kind of 'shape' (*configurationem*), that is, a quantitative feature of quality or a qualitative feature of quantity; but a likeness attributes the same quality to different things.
>
> From this fundamental difference it is customary to derive three ways of distinguishing between 'image' and 'likeness' in the text: *Let us make man in [our] image and likeness*. The first is given by Hugh when he says: 'Likeness refers to nature and image refers to shape', for 'likeness' denotes the sharing of a natural quality, 'image' a sharing in the determination by shape (*in distinctione figurali*), in the manner of a triangle, in which there are three apices and three lines; just in the same way there are three powers [of the soul] any one of which has a relation with any other; and so too with the three Persons [of the Trinity]; thus a power [of the soul] or a person [of the Trinity] has the character of an apex, whereas a relation of a procession (*emanatio*) has the character of a line.[11]

From this passage it is clear that, for Bonaventure, an image is what I have called a formal analogy. As apices stand to the lines which join them in a triangle, so are the powers of the soul related to one another, and their mutual relations map on to the Persons of the Trinity in their processions. 'Images' are isomorphs, agreeing with what they image in shape (*figura, quantitas*), but not in kind (*qualitas*). Whereas likenesses are a sharing in kind or quality, as the second way of distinguishing between them shows:

> The second way of distinguishing them is that an image occurs in the order of nature and likeness in

> the order of grace; and this [distinction] also has its source in the fundamental distinction between them. For because an image denotes an agreement in shape (*configurationem*) and is exemplified in the case of the natural powers of the soul, namely, memory, intellect and will; so it is that an image is something in the natural order. But because a likeness is an actual sharing, and is the common possession of a quality; and because the quality by which the soul is made like to God is grace; for this reason a likeness is said to be something in the order of grace.[12]

In brief, the way in which a natural object or power can be like God is purely and simply as an image of God: for the powers of the soul have the same pattern of relations with each other as do the Persons of the Trinity, but they do not *thereby* participate in the actual life of the Trinity. On the other hand, grace gives to the human soul a likeness to God, because by grace the soul participates in what God is, in the life of God himself. Now there is nothing in what Bonaventure says here, or indeed elsewhere, which suggests that 'image' and 'likeness' are mutually exclusive; that that which is an *imago* of God cannot by grace become a *similitudo* of God. Far from it. Those powers of the soul—memory, intellect and will—which by nature image God are precisely the powers by which, through grace, the human soul does participate in the divine life. Yet they do not participate through natural *imago* but only through the *similitudo* of grace. The distinction between *imago* and *similitudo* therefore remains important for Bonaventure because he insists that just because a natural object has the natural power to reflect something of God, it does not follow thereby that it shares in any way in the nature of God. An image, just insofar as it is in the same formal relations as God, does not enter into the order of grace, does not just by virtue of its *conformitas* to God thereby have any *convenientia* with him.

This distinction is not found in the pseudo-Denys in so many words and, in terminology at least, Thomas Aquinas is closer to the pseudo-Denys than to Bonaventure. But though he uses the distinction between 'image' and 'likeness' in a different way from Bonaventure (he seems less happy to make it out in terms of a disjunction between nature and grace), Thomas, like the pseudo-Denys, seems equally concerned to distinguish, as Bonaventure does, between the participative and mimetic aspects of the *similitudo*:

> There are two kinds of agreement (*convenientia*) or likeness (*similitudo*): one is by participation in the same quality: in this way two hot things are in agreement (*conveniunt*) . . . the other is by means of a certain proportion: in this way in Scripture metaphors of bodily characteristics are transposed onto spiritual realities, as when God is said to be the sun, who is the origin and source of the spiritual life, as the sun is of bodily life.[13]

But that likeness is more telling, has more power as a representation of one thing by another (*expressissima*), which is

> through a sharing of form (*per conformitatem*), as sight is like to colour, than that which is by analogy, as sight is to intellect, which may be compared as having similar relations to their objects. So the mind has a more telling likeness (*expressior similitudo*) to the Trinity in its knowing God than it has in knowing itself.[14]

The distinction between participative and formal similarity which is found in Bonaventure is made here with the same clarity, but in Thomas it is made within the one concept of *similitudo*. For Thomas, image is related to likeness as species to genus; every image is a likeness, but not every likeness is an image. Only those likenesses function as images which express something and some likenesses fail to express anything at all, as when two things just happen to share the same quality: one white sheep is like another, but neither is an image of the other. But when the sharing of a quality by one thing can *stand for* some other kinds of thing which possess it, then their common participation in that quality serves as the basis for the one's serving as the *imago* of the other.

Thomas' view that every image is a likeness, therefore, entails that every image to some degree participates in what it images. And yet, though in this he differs terminologically from them, like Hugh and Bonaventure, he holds there is a distinction to be made between those images which participate more and those which participate less in what they image. The difference in the way Thomas and Bonaventure describe this distinction appears to be this: Thomas would say: the more participative a representation is, the greater its degree of likeness, and so the greater its power as image. Bonaventure, by contrast would say: the more participative the representation the more it is likeness *rather than* image. For both theologians, however, the same sliding scale operates: as a thing is less participative in what it represents, the more its representation is purely formal, *per analogiam* rather than *per convenientiam*.

Moreover, commenting on the pseudo-Denys' *Divine Names*, Thomas makes clear what for him at least underlies this conception of a sliding scale between participation and mimesis. It is the neo-platonic metaphysic of creative causality:

> that which in a participative and secondary way possesses a property is an image of that which primarily and causally possesses it and the purpose of an image is to reveal that of which it is the image.[15]

'IMAGE' AND FORMAL TYPE

It is but a speculation, though an hypothesis worth proposing, that this neo-platonic, philosophical distinction between a 'formal' image and a 'participative' likeness has a significant connection, if only an indirect and epistemological one, with the hermeneutic of the Song. In the main tradition of Song commentary, whether monastic or scholastic, *eros* is, in terms of this distinction, 'image', not 'likeness'.

That for the neo-platonic tradition of *eros*, all *eros* is in *some* way divine is certainly true. All *eros* in some way, therefore, both participates in and images its principal causal source. For everything possesses in the core of its very nature a tendency to return ultimately *to* that divine *eros from* which it proceeds and that tendency by which it yearns for the divine *eros* is itself in some way a participation in the *eros* to which it returns. This is clearest in Thomas Gallus, who consciously models his commentary on the pseudo-Denys' erotic metaphysics:

> The ninth [hierarchy of the soul] includes the highest aspirations for God, the excesses and infusions which go beyond understanding, the burning brilliance and the brilliant burnings; understanding cannot be drawn into the sublime ecstasies and excesses of all these [lights], but only that supreme love which unites. . . . This order embraces God and is wrapped in the embraces of the Bridegroom, it knows no sight, it takes *Mary's part which will not be taken away* (Lk 10:42). In this order the bed is laid for the Bridegroom and Bride. It is from this order that the torrent of divine life flows down in stages upon the lower orders. (n. 10)

But his view shared by Bernard of Clairvaux who is least of all a conscious platoniser: for Bernard all love is from God and to God; all human love, including the *caritas* which binds humans together with one another is a participation in some way in the love which binds Father to Son through the Spirit in the Trinity: and because of that, the human experience of love, even (as we will see) that of marriage, can in some measure be an image of the one source from which its proceeds. All, however, depends upon our choosing God as the object of love, for human beings, having the power of choice, can divert that *eros* away from God altogether and can, as it were, reduce the power of human love as likeness virtually to zero. As Origen says, just as in human sexual relations (the *eros* of the 'outer man') it can come about that a man

> should love not his bride or wife but a harlot or adulteress, so also there can come upon the inner man, that is the soul, a love not for his legitimate bridegroom, who we have said is the Word of God, but for some adulterer and seducer.[16]

In the same way, the pseudo-Denys notes how easily the erotic language of Scripture may be adulterated by a carnal reading of it (*DN*, 709B-C) and it is the common fear of all our commentators that readers of the Song will be thus seduced. The choice for the soul, as Denys the Carthusian puts it, is between being a Bride of Christ or an adulteress with the devil (n. 42). However, when we turn to the hermeneutics of the Song, one thing we cannot say is that our commentators regard human sexual *eros* as in itself an evil, as a perversion of the divine *eros* from its proper object. If low on the scale of *eros*, sex is not off it. Though many appear to harbour negative attitudes towards human sexuality, mediaeval Song commentaries provide no evidence of a generalised moral disapproval of sex. What, on the other hand they do wholeheartedly, without exception, disapprove of is an interpretation of the Song as being *about* a human sexual relationship. That, they say, is *hermeneutical* adultery. Human sexuality may be an image, indeed a very powerful image of the divine *eros*; but in the Song it gets its power as an image precisely and only insofar as it is not seen as sharing in, itself incarnating, that which it images. What is at stake, therefore, is not the diminishing of sex as such, nor, for that matter, the praise of sex as such; it is rather that, in order that it may function as the hermeneutical key to the Song sex must be diminished as the Song's meaning and praised as that meaning's image. In order to represent the divine *eros* it must be in the bare form and proportion of it that it does so, not by its real participation in that *eros*. The *eros* of the Song must be image, not likeness.

The hypothesis that there is a conceptual connection between 'image' and 'typology' gains plausibility from a further and more direct connection which it is possible to make, this time on the score of content, between the way in which the nuptial imagery is treated in the Song commentary, at least from the twelfth century and after, and the more systematic treatises in the period on the theology of marriage itself.

Marriage, it was universally agreed by that century, was a sacrament. The shared view of the sacraments was that they were all, as Thomas Aquinas was later to put it, 'sacred signs which effect what they signify' (*efficiunt quod figurant*)[17]—the mystery which they disclose they also 'contain' effectively. And for all but one of the sacraments there was in principle no particular difficulty with showing that the two dimensions of 'signifying' and 'containing' coincided. To put it in terms of the Hugh/Bonaventure distinction, just as Baptism is, through the sign of washing with water, a natural *imago* of the cleansing and regeneration of the soul, so it is by grace a true *similitudo,* effecting what it signifies. By grace the natural sign participates in the efficacy of Christ's redemptive work: it *does* what it *says* and the saying is the doing. So, *mutatis mutandis,* for all the other sacraments, with the exception of the sacrament of marriage, in which the coincidence of sacramental signification and sacramental efficacy runs up against a difficulty in principle.

This difficulty did not relate to what or how marriage signified. On that score the starting point was the words of Paul in Ephesians 5:32, that marriage is a 'great mystery' which signifies Christ and the Church. Nor—so long as what is in question is the power of marriage to signify only—is there any difficulty with the fact that what makes a marriage is consummation, the union of husband and wife 'in one flesh' through sexual intercourse. For the carnal union of marriage is a powerful *imago* of the union of natures in the Incarnation of Christ which, in turn, is the theological basis of the doctrine of the union of Christ with the Church, his body.

At the level of the power of marriage to signify, therefore, we are at once brought back to the very same complex of theological symbols which are to be found in our Song commentaries: sexual love, the union of flesh, the kiss and embrace of lovers, typify, through the union in love of the Bridegroom and Bride, that between Christ and the Church and between Christ and the individual soul. Hugh of Saint Victor, who idealised the unconsummated marriage of Mary and Joseph, held that there is no greater likeness of the union between Christ and the Church than the *spiritual* union of husband and wife.[18] For Gregory the best likeness of the union between Christ and the Church was the *carnal* union of husband and wife (n. 8). But for Bernard of Clairvaux, there is no greater likeness of the union between Christ and the *soul* than the *carnal union* of husband and wife (n. 7). Thus far it is evident that the theology of marriage and the interpretation of the Song have important external similarities with one another: in both, the same fundamental typological structure is to be found, for as marriage is a type of the union of Christ with the Church and is the sacrament of them both, so too is the union of Solomon and the Shulamite in the Song.

But we saw that the mediaeval commentator had a problem concerning the role of the literal sense underlying the typology of the Song: how far could the carnal love of the Song be allowed not merely a mimetic, formal analogical role as signifier of the divine love, but also a participative role in the reality signified. Exactly parallel with this difficulty was another mediaeval theologians had with the theology of marriage as sacrament. Though there was the indisputable authority of Paul that the carnal union of marriage *signifies* Christ and the Church, it seemed to them perfectly obvious that the carnal union of marriage could not *effect* a union between Christ and the Church, for that latter union must precede and be presupposed to the possibility of marriage as a sacrament. Unless, that is to say, the union of Christ and the Church is already effected, there are no sacraments, nor has carnal union any power to signify, sacramentally, that 'great mystery'. Therefore, carnal union cannot be said to effect that which is presupposed to its signifying power. It follows that, as Thomas Aquinas put it, the union of Christ and the Church is, as Paul says, 'the thing signified' (*res significata*) by carnal union, but not so as to effect it (*sed non contenta*).[19] In the terminology of Hugh and Bonaventure, the carnal union of marriage is, as it were, an *imago* but not a *similitudo*; it maps the mystery of Christ and the Church, but it has no role in making what it maps.

Three interconnected pairs of terms of contrast therefore seem to meet within a common hermeneutic of the Song's erotic language, and each pair is found in internal relations of inverse proportionality. Insofar as carnal union is an 'image' of Christ and the Church it is not a 'likeness'; insofar as carnal union 'signifies' Christ and the Church it does not 'effect' their union; insofar as, in general, the erotic love of Solomon and the Shulamite is an allegory of Christ and the Church it lacks a real, participative efficacy in that which it allegorises. Remarkable as these parallels are, they have been presented merely as parallels. I must emphasise that they are not connections of thought explicitly made within our commentarial material—a fact which is in itself every bit as remarkable as the existence of the parallels themselves.

I have already remarked how strange a thing it is that, given all the theological opportunities which the commentators did exploit in the Song—some of them, *prima facie* somewhat unlikely—the one most obvious opportunity, that of drawing upon it for the construction of a theology of marriage, is never taken up. The reason for this ought by now to be clear. The monk was not interested in sexual love as such, nor, of course, in marriage for himself. These things he had denied himself in their carnal form. Nonetheless, the monk saw ample opportunity to exploit the eroticism of the Song from the standpoint of his monastic life, for, as 'image' of his own personal vocation and asceticism, it mapped perfectly on to it and on to the theology of history and eschatology within which he situated his vocation. As marriage could be an image of Christ and the Church, so too it could be an image of his way of life; and yet it was *his* way of life, not marriage, which he saw as the true participation in the mystery which marriage images. Therefore, in order to image his personal love story with Christ, erotic love had to be detached from its carnal reality. As carnal reality it could have no place in his life; in order to be a true image of the mutual love of Christ and the Church, erotic love had to be denied its carnal substance, for not even in marriage, still less in his life, was it that carnality which participated in the reality of the mystery. In short, if *eros* is the 'image' of Christ and the Church, or of the soul and Christ, his own celibate life was the true 'likeness' of it. *Eros* is image only insofar as it is *not* likeness. It is the monk who truly effects by celibacy what *eros* signifies by carnality. Carnal marriage is the sign, but mystical marriage is the reality signified.

This duality of signification and efficacy underlies what I have identified as the 'formalism' of the monastic hermeneutic of the Song, the depreciation of its literal meaning. That same duality is found, in different form, in the metaphysic and epistemology of dionysian neo-platonism. The two dualisms match one another, though in our texts they rarely coincide explicitly—unsurprisingly in a genre so generally unreceptive to the speculatively metaphysical. Nonetheless, they breath the same theological air and a common logic: *eros* as ontological dissimilitude is formal similitude; the more the love story of the Song is evacuated of its historical and narrative truth, the more available it becomes as an allegory of the monastic life. The reality of *eros* is found in the inversion of its own significance, that is, in celibacy.

NOTES

1. *Prologue to the Commentary on the Song of Songs*; Greer, p. 222.
2. *De doctrina christiana*, II. vi. 8; p.38.
3. SC 9.7; p. 58.
4. Legend has it that he dictated a brief commentary on the Song on his deathbed; a late thirteenth-century bookseller's catalogue refers to another, though it cannot be known whether this was genuine and now lost. See James A. Weisheipl OP, *Friar Thomas d'Aquino, His Life, Thought and Work* (Washington, 1983) What is certain is that neither of the two Commentaries included in the 1745 Venice edition of the *Opera* is by Thomas; the first is by Haimo of Auxerre, the second by Giles of Rome and is partially translated below.
5. *ST*, 1a2ae q. 102 a. 2 *sed contra*.
6. *ST*, 1a2ae q. 102 a.2 *corp*.
7. 'Here end the *Postille Morales seu Mistice* on all the books of sacred Scripture, with the exception of some which seemed not to need an exposition of this kind'.
8. We could, of course, make a case for saying that maps too are likenesses only through their roles within the activities of finding one's way around the countryside mapped, and so that they participate in that real life behaviour. This, however, would be somewhat forced. And the extent to which the comparison with dolls does hold merely shows what the pseudo-Denys would not have denied, namely that every likeness, however 'dissimilar', is in some degree participatory in what it images.
9. See David N. Bell, *The Image and Likeness, The Augustinian Spirituality of William of Saint Thierry* (Kalamazoo: Cistercian Publications, 1984) which contains excellent discussions of Augustine's development of the distinction.
10. *De sacramentis*, I. vi. cap. ii, PL 176:264C-D.
11. *In Sententiarum* II dist. xvi a. ii, q. iii resp.
12. *Ibid.*
13. *Summa Theologiae, Suppl. 3a*, q. 69 a. 1 ad. 2.
14. *Quaestio Disputata de Veritate*, q. 10 a. 7 corp.
15. *In De divinis nominibus*, c. iv. lect. xviii, 522.
16. Greer, p. 223.
17. *ST* 3a, q. 62 a. 1 ad. 1
18. Hugh of Saint Victor, *De virginitate Beatae Mariae*; PL 176:860.
19. *ST*, *Suppl.* 3a, q. 42, a. 1, ad 4.

6

From Allegory to Imagery

THE DISTINCTLY UNEROTIC, even pedantic, feel of much mediaeval commentary on the Song will, in view of the formalism of its hermeneutic, hardly be a matter for surprise. On the whole the blood is thin. Set hermeneutically at such a distance from the *eros* allegorised, most mediaeval readings of the Song seek out formal, analogical parallels in which the shape, but hardly the substance, of *eros* is projected upon the mystical marriage of Christ with the Church or with the individual, celibate, soul. So manifest is the commentators' fear of a blurring of the lines between human and divine *eros* that one has been tempted to ask if they did not emphasise the formal character of their allegories precisely in order to deny to the human erotic any degree of substantive, participatory continuity with the divine *eros* which it allegorises. There is enough truth in this possibility to raise the temptation, and an irresistible one in the case of Denys the Carthusian; but it will not do justice to a group of central cases, represented above all by the greatest commentator of them all, Bernard of Clairvaux. Bernard and Denys merit a more detailed comparison.

THE LANGUAGE OF *EROS*: BERNARD AND DENYS COMPARED

There is a clear acknowledgement, above all in Gregory and Denys the Carthusian, that what they are doing is dangerous. But the dangers they envisage are not always those alone of a reductivist hermeneutic; sometimes they are personal and spiritual as well. The erotic language of the Song is itself a personal temptation to the reader. And the formalism of the hermeneutic may be seen as at least partly motivated by the desire to contain this personal danger. 'What is to be done', Denys asks, 'with those many religious and canons and others in Holy Orders within the Church who, in the Divine Office, are accustomed to hear or read these words, though they are not yet thus cleansed, who have hardly attained to a true and spiritual understanding and can scarcely read and hear these words at those times and in Church without indecent thoughts?' (n. 17).

Denys' anxiety on this score is scarcely greater than Origen's, who feared from a similar hermeneutical reduction a similar personal danger:

> . . . if anyone who is only a man according to the flesh takes it up, for him there is no little risk and danger from this book of Scripture. Not knowing how to listen to the words of love with pure and chaste ears he turns everything he hears from its inner to it outer and bodily meaning and feeds in himself the desires of the flesh; so, on reading divine Scripture, is aroused to the lust of the flesh.[1]

Jean Gerson was too ashamed to report the things he had heard by way of literal readings of the Song and Denys quotes him as complaining that 'they would offend pious ears' (Denys, n. 16). And Gregory had insisted that we must be 'subtle enough to grasp' the spiritual import of the Song, 'lest, when we hear the words of this external love we become fixed in the things of sense and the instrument which is given to lift us up should rather weigh us down' (n. 4).

Origen, Gregory, and Denys, it therefore seems right to say, fear a literalist hermeneutic *because* they fear that the text itself could be a powerful threat to the individual reader of it, in his personal life; it was a potential temptation to the 'lewdness' which it describes. In short, they fear the language of the Song, because of its capacity for sexual arousal. Hermeneutical disaster is threatened by a reading of the Song in terms of the sexual intimacies it describes; but the intimate eroticism of the actual describing threatened personal spiritual disaster. Together with the more general theological and literary reasons for reading the Song allegorically, a primary ascetical motive was to denature the text itself, to neutralise its power to arouse forbidden passion.

For this reason, too, Gregory emphasises the relationship between hermeneutical levels of the text and the hierarchy of spiritual growth: understanding must go hand in hand with holiness. Thus, Abraham, Isaac, and Jacob; Proverbs, Ecclesiastes, and the Song; the 'moral', the 'natural' and the 'contemplative'; obedience, rejection of the world, and the contemplation of God—all these are rungs of the same ladder by which the individual soul is able to 'reach up to the contemplation of God' (n. 9). The person who cannot read the Song with the requisite degree of spiritual maturity, who comes to 'the sacred marriage feast' not 'clothed in the wedding gown . . . of charity . . . will be cast out from the wedding feast into the darkness outside' (n. 4). In similar vein, Denys counsels that the immature of spirit should be taught to think of the words of the Song at least in general terms as being 'meant in their spiritual and very pure sense; and they should lift up their hearts to the recollection of God, to thoughts of Our Lord Jesus Christ and his Church, and of the glorious Virgin and their most pure love of one another . . . and soon enough they will be rid of every unbecoming thought' (n. 17).

We may suspect, however, that from a practical point of view, Denys had his priorities the wrong way round. It seems unlikely that a monk tempted by the lewdness of the Song at the Office would be relieved of his burden by a theoretical hermeneutic. The monk's normal exposure to the Song was going to come through the liturgy in the first instance, not through personal reading or study. That liturgical context imposed its own primary hermeneutic on the Song. For there, in the Office or Mass text, readings from the Song were set alongside others, not only from the Old Testament but also from the New, and they functioned as a powerful reinforcement of the 'spiritual' reading of the Old Testament texts. It is easy to forget how much spontaneous exegesis is the product of such liturgical juxtapositions; those who are familiar with the texts of the Vespers for the Feast of the Assumption, perhaps through Monteverdi's setting of them, will be able to place Alan of Lille's or Denys' mariological readings of the Song against their liturgical background.[2] Even today, in a Sunday eucharistic liturgy, the placing of readings from the Old and New Testaments in immediate succession within the Liturgy of the Word has the effect of provoking the reading of one in terms of the other in a manner which would have been familiar, through daily practice, to the mediaeval monk.

Against the background of such daily practice of the liturgical interpretation of Scripture the monk would have read the Song—at any rate he would have been exposed to a selection of readings sufficient to reinforce the method of interpretation which he could carry over spontaneously into his own reading, whether in his *lectio divina* or in the more formal written commentary. Leclercq remarks on how the Song was always understood 'in an atmosphere of worship and contemplation. People were preconditioned: they knew it had a spiritual sense, and the biblical and patristic language in which the text of the words was received came between the original meaning and the interpretation spontaneously given to them in the liturgy'.[3] This liturgical hermeneutic meant not only that the Song was made capable of yielding a theology of his monastic life, but also that that theology was integrated into the life it theologised as a common, shared routine and as a personal spirituality. To the monk, the Song came already interpreted by his monastic practice; it was already a spiritual text before he ever embarked on the formal exposition of it.

On the one hand, therefore, the Song had its dangers for weaker souls who could be all too easily seduced by the evocative eroticism of its language. On the other hand, the liturgical medium of its transmission, together with the spontaneous hermeneutic implied by that medium, created a weighty loading of spiritual meaning which at once engaged the reader personally and distanced him from the eroticism of the discourse itself. Within the 'hermeneutic of inversion' he could fill the shape of the Song's carnality with the stuff of his own celibacy. Once he was thus distanced from the carnal meaning of the Song, its eroticism could become not only a safe, but even an apt, vehicle for the personal expression of his love of God.

A crucial question for the mediaeval interpreter of the Song was therefore: what would be an appropriate *emotional* distancing from its secular erotic language. Speaking merely theoretically, if that distance were too great, the commentary would lapse into the uninspired pedantry of spiritual meanings in which the attractive power of the Song's eroticism was so reduced as to diminish its power as a metaphor of the spiritual. If the distance were too small, the danger was run that the spiritual meaning would become a vehicle for a more or less well disguised carnality. This dilemma of feeling was resolved more or less adequately by the mediaeval commentators—more than adequately by Bernard, less than adequately by Denys the Carthusian.

By turns, Denys appears to be impaled on both horns of this dilemma. His commentary displays both the extreme of an ingenious pedantry and that of an ecstatic, first person, hyper-emotional rhetoric—the latter no doubt contributing to his mediaeval reputation as the *Doctor Ecstaticus*, but also raising questions for the modern reader about how completely Denys had been able to integrate the earthy eroticism of the Song into his theological and spiritual purposes. Only a few years earlier, in a text which Denys had certainly read, Jean Gerson had stated his choice of a 'doctrinal and scholastic' study of the Song in preference to 'endless declamations and moral exhortations which serve no purpose . . . of inducing a truly effective love'.[4] In some of Denys' passages one can see what Gerson feared from 'endless declamation':

> Why do you call me back from the sight of my Bridegroom? Why do you hold me back from his embrace? Why do you turn me away from our converse? Why, in this affair which transcends all reason, do you demand an explanation? Do you not know that the eagerness of love is not to be restrained by commonplace decencies? . . . He who pours out his love into me, he also sets that love aflame and encourages it, and it is he who provokes and inflames me to beg for the kiss of his mouth . . . Love, fretting at separation compels me . . . I will speak, therefore, to the Bridegroom and little by little I will recover my breath; and now, aroused to an explosion of desire I will say for the first time, *May he kiss me with the kiss of his mouth*; and a second time *May he kiss me with the kiss of his mouth*; and a third time I repeat, *May he kiss me with the kiss of his mouth.* (n. 43)

Later in the same passage, Denys quotes Bernard's *Sermons* verbatim (n. 45), but very different is the emotional atmosphere of Bernard's *Sermons*. Leclercq rightly says that Bernard is not only in love erotically with God, he is as much in love with the erotic language of the Song itself, with the sheer beauty of its imagery, its linguistic colours and textures.[5] Bernard says as much himself:

> It is impossible to find words of greater sweetness in which to give expression to the feelings which the Word and the soul exchange with one another than those of Bridegroom and Bride; between them everything is shared, nothing belongs to the one alone, there is no division: there is, for both, but one inheritance, one table, one house, one bed, more even than that, but one flesh. Therefore, in view of this, a man will leave his father and his mother and join with his wife, and the two will become one flesh.[6]

Even the less vibrant paraphrase of the *Brief Commentary* carries some feel of Bernard's love of the language of Bridegroom and Bride:

> Of all the kinds of fleshly love that there are, there is none so appealing, none found more commonly desirable, than the union of Bride and Bridegroom; so it is of the spiritual, of the created spirit and the uncreated. In the one case the two become one flesh; in the other the two become one spirit. And so by means of the comparison drawn between the things of the body and the spiritual, of the human and the divine, here are described the Bridegroom and Bride, Christ and the Church or the holy soul. (n. 7)

It is as much the intrinsic beauty of the Song's language as any formal hermeneutical doctrine of the four senses which leads Bernard to the spiritual application of it to God. For Bernard, that beauty of language has an intrinsic power to lead to God directly. Two striking characteristics of Bernard's *Sermons* reinforce this suggestion. In the first place there is a notable absence of the sort of formal hermeneutical theorising which plays so important a part in the introductions to Origen or Gregory or most of the later mediaeval commentaries. Admittedly, Bernard is writing sermons in which he at least pretends to be addressing his cistercian community in person, and formal theorisings would have seemed out of place in a predominantly pastoral genre. Yet Bernard scarcely seems to need the theory, for the practice of the spiritual interpretation is quite spontaneous and direct. Secondly, very rarely does Bernard give expression to that fear of human *eros* which is so frequently encountered elsewhere in the commentarial literature. Perhaps these two facts are connected. Perhaps it was *because* he so little feared the literal eroticism of the Song that he hardly felt the need for a formal theory to explain it away. Perhaps, alternatively, it was because of his feel for the intrinsic transcendent power of the language of the Song that he had nothing to fear from its eroticism. In any case, as Leclercq notes, Bernard seems to fear nothing of the Song's imagery, he is not even reluctant to dig out from beneath the surface of the bowdlerising Latin the sexual explicitness of the hebrew text, thus to exploit to the maximum its erotic possibilities.[7] Throughout the *Sermons* there is a sense that human realism about sex and its symbolic capacity are fused somewhat in the manner in which the music of a text is fused to the text it sets, the beauty of the one contributing to, not diminishing, the beauty of the other. Indeed, the image is Bernard's own, for he described the language of the Song as 'the very music of the heart'.[8] So, for Bernard, human *eros* and spiritual significance are fused into a single literary totality in which the longing for beauty is in perfect harmony with the beauty of the longing itself. Leclercq, again, comments:

> From the first phrase of this spontaneous process he was realistic without being vulgar. And, he never waited until he got to lofty considerations to turn everything into poetry and music by the quality of his imagery and the rhythm of his sentences. It is beauty which transforms everything, even before the spiritual meaning gives human love its full value, whereby the sensual is not denied, but is used and integrated into an experience at once very rich and then surpassed.[9]

In speaking of this fusion of levels we are not referring only to what, in any strict sense, the mediaeval hermeneuticist would have described as the 'literal' and 'spiritual' meanings. There is nothing mechanical about Bernard's employment of this hermeneutical distinction and in one way Bernard takes the erotic surface of the Song more seriously in its own right *as erotic* than even the most committed theoretical literalist—much more so than Nicholas of Lyra, for whom the eroticism of the text is dissipated into a narrative history of Israel. For though Bernard is certainly as quick as any to seize upon the spiritual significance of the text, wresting from it mercilessly the most detailed allegory, no one does as much justice as Bernard to the literary qualities of the Song; no mediaeval commentary leaves us with quite the same sense of the Song's having been allowed to speak in its own terms and tonalities. In short, in Bernard, the language of the Song is respected for what it is.

Compared with this intimate fusion of language, thought, and feeling in Bernard's *Sermons*, Denys the Carthusian's rhetorical outbursts seem hyperbolical, even somewhat neurotic. Denys' stylistic *excessus* comes disturbingly close to tastelessness; it is a generalised, abstract frenzy. His defiance of moderation, for all that it is derived from Bernard, becomes, in context, a trifle unbalanced (n. 45). His discharge of erotic emotionalism upon God is closer to a divine licentiousness than to Bernard's confident, guilt-free and, for all that, sexually more explicit, eroticism. In Denys, one has the impression that fear of sex drives a compulsion to negate its human reality by means of displacement and that the fear is carried over into the displaced form of it. There is a quality of anxiety in Denys' ecstasy which is not found in Bernard. For this reason one is easily persuaded to think of Denys' strenuous rhetoric as symptomatic of a freudian inversion, yet remains reluctant to entertain such speculations about Bernard. My concerns in this essay are, however, distinctly not with psychological, but with literary and, more strictly, theological and linguistic matters. And in this latter connection the quality of excessiveness in Denys is in a different, if related, sense symptomatic, namely, of an abstractness of language, of an emotional distancing, whereby all the urgencies and intensities of feeling characteristic of human sexuality are, as it were, spiritually mimicked; and, in their form as mimicry, they displace the human reality they imitate. It is as if Denys cannot get the distance right, emotionally, between the human and divine *eros*, as if he is condemned, from the literary point of view, to occupy a position set either at too great a distance from or too close to human *eros*. And the language of his commentary displays this ambiguity not only in its wild swings of mood and feel, but also in the contrivance we sense equally in his poetry and his pedantry. Either way, Denys protests too much to be entirely credible.

THE DISINTEGRATION OF THE HERMENEUTIC

By comparison with Bernard, Denys' use of the imagery of the Song as a vehicle of personal spiritual expression betrays a form of emotional and linguistic disintegration. And this breakdown in comparison with Bernard is matched by a parallel hermeneutical disintegration in comparison with Gregory. In Denys there is a marked hardening of the lines in the practical employment of the doctrine of the four senses. Unlike Bernard's, Denys' *is* a mechanical hermeneutic. By hindsight it is possible to read Gregory's commentary in the light of the sharp theoretical distinctions of a Hugh or a Thomas and to identify, with relative clarity, passages which fall within each level of 'sense'. But beyond following Origen and Augustine broadly in their distinction between the 'spirit' and the 'letter' of the text and in the account of the spiritual sense as allegory, Gregory himself is unconcerned with further, and later, precisions between allegorical, anagogical, and moral senses: as Smalley notes, Gregory's hermeneutical ideal is 'to meander like a river' between them.[10] And in practice Gregory's commentary moves easily between these levels of interpretation, seeking always—as I have noted—an integration among them. Even when, in the twelfth century, these distinctions of senses do become more sharply focussed, it is rare to make too much of them and common practice to fuse many levels of interpretation into one gloss (see Alan, n. 10). But while Denys undoubtedly attaches equal importance to each of his threefold interpretations—the 'general', or ecclesiological; the 'individual' or moral; and the 'special' or mariological—the sense of the interplay between them so characteristic of earlier models is now gone. Each is given an entirely separate exposition; often, indeed, though not always, parallel with the others, but lacking Gregory's emphasis on the dependence of the moral on the ecclesiological, or Alan's on the dependence of the mariological on the ecclesiological.

Hermeneutically, therefore, the three levels of spiritual interpretation are, in Denys the Carthusian, relatively independent of one another. And this, in turn, has consequences for the content of the 'individual' interpretation of the Song, for in its hermeneutical detachment from the typological interpretation it is also detached theologically from the ecclesiological content of that interpretation. In short, Denys' individual interpretation is, at least negatively, an *individualist* interpretation, lacking the ecclesiological, and with them, the historical depths and resonances so explicit in Gregory's moral readings. I say 'negatively', because, of course, there is no tendency in Denys to argue for an 'individualist' interpretation; rather, it is 'individualist' by default, by virtue of the implication that it is possible to give an account of how the Song may be read for the individual without any intrinsic reference to the ecclesiological significance which, on the other hand, he undoubtedly does attribute to the text in a separate hermeneutical act.

Denys' detachment of the personal, spiritual possibilities of the Song from their anchor in the bedrock of ecclesiological allegory is equalled by the absence of any alternative anchoring in the metaphysics of neo-platonism. Granted that the explicit conjunction of dionysian erotic metaphysics with the Song is rare in the mediaeval commentarial traditions, it is still a possibility, as the meticulously dionysian interpretation of Thomas Gallus shows. Gallus saw the pseudo-Denys' *Celestial Hierarchy* as the speculative theology, and the Song of Songs as the practice, of the christian life. Just as in Gregory, the practical spirituality of the Song is rooted in the ecclesiological theology of history from which it may be derived, so for Gallus, the spiritual ladder of the soul's ascent through love to *excessus* in God is rooted in and reflects the hierarchy of angelic beings, from the lowest angels to the most exalted Cherubim. The erotic language of the Song, therefore, is stabilised and organised in every detail by its controlling metaphysic: the soul's hierarchy reflects the hierarchy of creation; the *regressus* of the Christian soul reflects the *regressus* of all creation. If Gallus', therefore, is primarily an 'individual' interpretation there is absolutely no temptation to think of it as an 'individualist' interpretation.

I have argued that the influence of the pseudo-Denys' erotic metaphysics is pervasive in certain crucial aspects of the biblical hermeneutic of the Middle Ages, and that it is very rarely direct. In all commentators other than Denys the Carthusian, failure to acknowledge this influence is therefore unremarkable. But in Denys the Carthusian it may be thought curious and, arguably, significant. Denys the Carthusian is an ardent dionysian. In this he is only just excelled by Gallus. He knew and referred approvingly to Gallus' commentaries as he did also to that other, near contemporary, dionysian Song commentator, Jean Gerson. He was well aware, therefore, of the hermeneutical possibilities in a pseudo-dionysian interpretation of the Song and had no personal or theological grounds for disapproval.

And yet he entirely ignores the possibilities of such an interpretation. I think we may usefully, if cautiously, take note of the Carthusian's neglect of the pseudo-Denys in a way which would be unjustified in other monastic commentaries, and, together with that other symptom of disintegration in Denys, relative to the gregorian or bernardine syntheses of the moral with the ecclesiological senses, note it as composing a *double* failure of integration.

As a result, the emotional abstractness of the discourse of Denys' individual interpretation runs together with an hermeneutical and theological deracination. In his individual interpretation, the earthy, human eroticism of the Song is detached not only from its human content, but also from any underpinning significance either in ecclesiology or metaphysics. Consequently, what it draws from the Song itself is primarily an imagery of love, an ecstatic discourse of personal relationship with God, carrying over with it, no doubt, centuries of theological resonance, but heard, as it were, from a distance. Denys' commentary shares with the Song its emotional intensities, but, as I have put it, in the form of a stylised mimicry. Whereas in Bernard there is emotional continuity between the language of the Song and the language of his *Sermons*, in Denys there is emotional inversion. Denys' mystical *eros*, for all its value to him as a personalised imagery, is an emotional, theological and hermeneutical shell.

Emotional fragmentation by the standards of Bernard, hermeneutical disintegration by the standards of Gregory, metaphysical vacuity by the standards of Gallus—these characterise the relative degeneration of Denys' commentary from three ideal-types of mediaeval commentary. I have suggested earlier that a vulnerability to this outcome is implied, at any rate logically, in the very character of the formalism of the majority hermeneutic of the monastic tradition. And, in respect of the evacuation of eroticism, one version of the literalist-historical hermeneutic can have a similar consequence illustrated by Nicholas of Lyra's reduction of the Song's eroticism to the status of *historical* metaphor. In its own way, and on the same standards of comparison, Nicholas' hermeneutic is equally corrosive of the Song's eroticism, if not of its significance for the theology of history. Whereas Nicholas' commentary denies to the spiritual writer the utility of the Song as a 'spiritual' text, Denys' is at its most vigorous when exploiting that text for its possibilities as personalised metaphor, in the process reducing the theological reference of allegory to the personal reference of an imagery.

Because of the convergence in Denys the Carthusian of a number of different tendencies, this shift from allegory to imagery is noticeable, especially in his individual interpretation. First, he takes 'formalism' to the limits: the Song has no narrative truth, but only an hermeneutically inverted, formal relationship with what it allegorises. Second, because of its detachment from any explicit foundation in an ecclesiological sense, or, alternatively, in an objectivised metaphysical system, the individual interpretation of the Song becomes primarily a first-person language of self-expression. Thirdly, Denys' use of the erotic language of the Song is not only hermeneutically, but also emotionally, inverted, for it not only *reads* erotic carnality in the terms of its denial in celibacy, it also *negates* carnal emotions by their reproduction as spiritual. Taken together, these tendencies converge to press the discourse into an increasingly empty expressiveness. There are times when Denys' reading of the Song can seem little more than the exploitation of a metaphor for the love of God, which by the fifteenth century had become little more than a conventional index for standard theological topics.

I make no historical claims for a track of progressive decline from the standards of the twelfth century or of Gregory to Denys, and I have made no attempt to plot any linear historical course of events. Not that an historical proposition of this kind is altogether unappealing. But whatever plausibility for this historical hypothesis may be incidentally provided by a comparison between Gregory or Bernard and Denys on the Song is far too incomplete to count as hard evidence for it. Throughout this essay I have been concerned with the internal logic of the mediaeval traditions of interpretation of the Song's eroticism, not with building the case for some uni-directional line of historical tendency towards an outcome in Denys the Carthusian. Nonetheless, although the distinction on which this account of 'inner logic' has rested—that between a 'formalist-metaphoricist' and a 'literalist-historical' hermeneutics—is, and is meant to be, a stereotype, the distinction has, I suggest, an historical foundation in the texts it is meant to explain. What is more, that which those sterotypes entail *should* happen *does* happen. There are tendencies, within the development of 'formalist-metaphoricist' styles of hermeneutic, towards the reduction of historical, ecclesiological allegory to personalised imagery; we might have predicted such a reduction from the internal tensions of the hermeneutic. And these tendencies are exhibited with some clarity in Denys the Carthusian. There are tendencies within the 'literalist-historical' styles of hermeneutic to the reduction of the Song's significance to depersonalised historical metaphor; they are found in Nicholas of Lyra, and from within the logic of his hermeneutic we can see why they should be. Admittedly, the judgement that Gregory achieves a more balanced and theologically integrated synthesis between the personal and the ecclesiological than do either Nicholas or Denys, that Alan's mariological interpretation is more happily rooted in a theology of the Church than is Denys', that Bernard's personalisation of the Song's eroticism is emotionally more mature than Denys', that Gallus reconciles the biblical hermeneutic more adequately with the preoccupations of the dionysian speculative theology than does Denys are all matters of judgement and, to some degree, of personal taste. They are not offered as an historical thesis by themselves. But I do offer them as defensible propositions which raise an historical question about the late development of the mediaeval hermeneutic of the Song.

NOTES

1. Greer, p. 218.

2. For example, the very ancient reading of the verse *Surge, amica mea et veni*, 'Arise, my love, and come' (Sg 2:10) in the Vespers for the Assumption is only one of the most obvious and striking of such liturgical interpretations.

3. Jean Leclerq, *Nouveau Visage de Bernard de Clairvaux*, (Paris: Editions du Cerf, 1976) p. 129. [ET. by Marie-Bernard Saïd, OSB, *A Second Look at Saint Bernard* (Kalamazoo: Cistercian Publications, 1990) p. 104].

4. Glorieux, 'Gerson', p. 576.

5. Jean Leclercq, OSB, *Monks on Marriage. A Twelfth-century View* (New York: Seabury, 1982) 76.

6. SC 7.2, p. 39; cf also 1.5 and 1.8, where Bernard speaks of the Song's 'figurative language pregnant with delight'.

7. See Leclercq, *Monks on Marriage. A Twelfth-century View* (New York: Seabury, 1982) SC 1.11; Ch. 7.

8. SC 1.11; p. 7.

9. *Nouveau Visage*, p. 133. [ET p. 108, altered].

10. B. Smalley, *The Study of the Bible in the Middle Ages* (Oxford: Blackwell, 1984) p. 33.

7

John of the Cross and the Latin Tradition

I BEGAN this essay, as I begin my anthology, with John of the Cross. Deeply embedded in his language of the soul and God we find an erotic imagery which is no longer employed defensively, as it had been in Origen and the pseudo-Denys, nor even self-consciously. In John it is a spontaneous and natural idiom. No alternative imagery of love comes near to challenging the hegemony of John's eroticism, nor, it appears, is John aware of the need for any other imagery to supplement it, or perhaps to correct an imbalance which *eros* might be thought to have created in the soul's discourse of the love of God. For John *eros* is sufficient for the purpose. It says all that he wants to say *about* the love of God; and, as for Bernard, it expresses all that he wants to say *to* God as a soul in love with him.

In the preceding chapters, I have offered an 'explanation' of one track in the mediaeval historical record of that hegemony of *eros*—an explanation in two senses of the word. The first was a systematic account of why the language of *eros* served the purpose of expressing what some ancient and mediaeval christian writers wanted to say about the love of God. The second was an account of some specific historical processes, extending from Origen to the end of the Middle Ages, which can be identified within the tradition of commentary on the Song of Songs. It is time to harness these two forms of explanation, and their associated hypotheses, to the purpose of illuminating the erotic language of John of the Cross himself.

JOHN AND DIONYSIAN NEO-PLATONISM

The first part of my argument was directed to the explanation of why *in principle* the language of *eros* gained prestige within christian theology in spite of its dubious associations equally with sexual lewdness and with pagan philosophy. I have suggested that the appeal of erotic language lay, from this point of view, in its capacity to resolve a group of problems central to the project of a christian neo-platonism—the problems of creation, freedom, and necessity. Perhaps the word 'resolve' does ill-justice to the complexities of the role of erotic discourse in the construction of a christian neo-platonic metaphysic. It was not as if the metaphysical tensions of unity and differentiation were, on the one hand, conceptually irreconcilable and, on the other, somehow magically 'resolved' in the imagery of *eros*, as if erotic language allowed the neo-platonist to say something *by image* which his theology denied him the right to say *conceptually*. Rather, the neo-platonic metaphysic at once demands and resists the reconciliation of those tensions and so points towards a silence beyond language where alone those tensions may be dissolved; and erotic love serves the ends of this dialectic, for it is itself the tendency and yearning of the mind for that transcendent point beyond language in which the 'undifference' of unity and difference is effected. In short, it is the very capacity of erotic discourse to embody, rather than resolve, these tensions which commends it so precisely as the language of neo-platonism. Neo-platonic apophaticism wants to make language point beyond itself. And the language of *eros* does this. The tendencies of the metaphysic and the tendencies of *eros* are one and the same.

Consequently, in the high neo-platonism of the pseudo-Denys, the erotic is, as I put it, at once required by and sustained in the overarching ontology: his theology as such is an erotic creationism and an erotic recapitulationism. The erotic is not, therefore, a secondary 'imagery', a decorative shell, detachable from the metaphysical mass which it surrounds. But as there is a history of the interactions of *eros* and allegory which I have traced, along just one narrow path, so there is a history, which I have not sought to trace, of the interactions of *eros* and neo-platonic metaphysics, from the pseudo-Denys to John of the Cross. That will be best done on another occasion when, through a corresponding account of the so-called 'mystical' traditions of the Latin West, it will be possible to show how the intimate relation between the language of *eros* and the neo-platonic metaphysics is progressively severed. Here I can at best summarise some aspects of the historical outcome of those processes in John of the Cross.

John's reception of the pseudo-Denys seems to have been mediated partly by the mystical writers of the Middle Ages. Within that stream of influence, and with reference particularly to the Northern European schools, the impact of the pseudo-Denys on the language of mysticism remains undiminished to the end. This impact includes, but extends far beyond, the language of the erotic, for it is traceable in several other partially interconnected clusters of image, above all those of 'darkness' and 'light' and of 'interiority' and 'exteriority'. These, together with the imagery of *eros*, form varying patterns of relationship with one another within the history of the negative mysticisms of the Middle Ages, but they are the constant pool of imaginative resource throughout those traditions, until and within and beyond John of the Cross. And what I have said about the erotic cluster may be said of the other two: that though in the pseudo-Denys they are closely integrated into the dominant metaphysic of neo-platonism, the ties which bind them to it are loosened to varying degrees within the mediaeval period.

These three clusters of imagery, of *eros*, of interiority and of divine darkness, are there in John of the Cross, indeed they entirely dominate his thought and writing. Yet as this imagery survives in John it is unsustained by the classical neo-platonic metaphysics. Nor is it because John has replaced the neo-platonic ontology with any very obvious rival doctrine of creation that this is so evident, though, insofar as he shows any sign of needing one, it would probably be true to say that he thought of himself as a Thomist. Rather, a metaphysics of creation is simply absent from his writing. John, the mystical theologian, is not interested in systematics.

Stronger evidence of neo-platonic influence can be found in the traces of classical dionysian epistemology which can be identified within the deployment of his imagery. No doubt John simply imbibed much of the dialectical 'feel' of dionysian theology from his sources in mediaeval mysticism. Yet he does seem to have known at least the pseudo-Denys' *Mystical Theology*. Among the sparse references in John's writings to earlier authorities there are four to this work, all to the same passage in Chapter One and all to the same effect: the light of God is a 'dazzling ray of darkness'.[1] And in the *Ascent of Mount Carmel* there are several references to the metaphor of the 'cloud of unknowing', almost certainly, again, borrowed directly from the pseudo-Denys and not from the fourteenth-century english work of that name.[2] Otherwise, the most definitely establishable form of his dependence on the pseudo-Denys is more general and pervasive: his employment of the image of the 'dark nights of the soul'—in particular that of the 'dark night' of faith—is classically dionysian.

With the borrowed imagery John incorporates its dionysian dialectics. As the soul climbs Mount Carmel towards the source of divine life, the whole emotional and cognitive capacity, sensory and intellectual, is thrown into ever deeper darkness and pain by the excess of light, perhaps in the way a flash of lightening first oversaturates the world with light, draining it of colour, only instantly to plunge the eyes into deeper obscurity. John's 'cloud of unknowing' shows itself here to be profoundly dionysian, specifically in its intellectualism: John reverses the later mediaeval tendency to read the darkness of unknowing in anti-intellectualist ways and in favour of the knowing of love. For John, it is the intellect which, as it is led forward by its own dialectical tendency of unknowing, is drawn through the darkness of faith into the very life and knowing of God.[3] This is the authentically dionysian cognitive dialectic, authentic in a way that the epistemology of the more consciously dionysian Gallus, or the fourteenth-century english *Cloud* Author is not. For Gallus, 'wisdom is the *love* of God' (n. 14). For the *Cloud* Author, dependent here as elsewhere on Gallus, the 'cloud' is the simple *negation* of intellect, not its dialectical transformation into God, so that, for him, it is in the vacuum of the mind that the 'nakyd entente' of the will supplies the true 'knowing unknowing'.[4]

There is too in John a strong feel for the dialectics of *eros*. It is particularly there in his theology of divinisation, of the final union-in-identity-and-difference between the soul and God. John's is a language of erotic union of a vigour and force which can be exceeded only by an Eckhart working on the boundaries of orthodoxy. In that union 'the soul becomes divine',[5] 'appears to be God',[6] for the Spirit 'deifies the substance of the soul, absorbing it beyond all being into his own being'.[7] And yet, as we have seen, this hyperbolic language of union is never exploited by John to the extent of denying the individual identity of the soul: for 'the union wrought between the two natures and the communication of the divine to the human is such that, *even though neither changes its being*, both appear to be God'.[8]

Both union and distinction are, for John, most fully expressed in the imagery of marriage:

> This spiritual marriage . . . is a total transformation in the beloved in which each surrenders the entire possession of self to the other with a certain consummation of the union of love. The soul therefore becomes divine, becomes God through participation . . . Consequently He is for her an enchanting, desirable garden; . . . here it is as though she were placed in the arms of her Bridegroom. As a result she usually experiences an intimate spiritual embrace, by means of which she lives the life of God. The words of Saint Paul are verified in this soul: *I live, now not I, but Christ lives in me* (Gal 2:20).[9]

Above all, however, the residues of a neo-platonic epistemology are to be found in those places where, occasionally, John does engage in formal speculative theology, where he tries to give some conceptual rigour to his doctrine of divinisation. In *The Ascent of Mount Carmel*, in an attempt to describe in theoretical terms the nature of the union between God and the soul which he will later describe experientially, John distinguishes between what he calls 'essential union' and the 'union of likeness'. 'God', he says,

> sustains every soul and dwells in it substantially, even though it may be of the greatest sinner in the world. This union between God and creatures always exists. By it he conserves their being so that if the union would end they would be immediately annihilated and cease to exist.[10]

This union, which is simply the creative act by which God sustains any being, each in its own way, in the kind of existence which is proper to it, is not to be confused with that achieved between God and the soul by transforming grace:

> . . . in discussing union with God, we are not discussing the substantial union which is always existing, but the union and transformation of the soul in God.

> This union is not always existing, but we find it only where there is a likeness of love. We will call it 'the union of likeness', and the former 'the essential or substantial union'. The union of likeness is supernatural, the other natural . . .[11]

Now the 'union of likeness' is a union by *participation*:

> When God grants this supernatural favour to the soul, so great a union is caused that all the things of both God and the soul become one in participant transformation, and the soul appears to be God more than a soul. Indeed it is God by participation.[12]

By contrast, John says, 'essential union' with God gives no likeness by participation whatever. His denials are emphatic and severely absolute. 'It is noteworthy that among all creatures both superior and inferior none bears a likeness to God's being or unites proximately with him'.[13] 'Everything the intellect can understand, the will experience and the imagination picture is most unlike and disproportioned to God'.[14]

It is clear that these denials of any 'likenesses' between creatures and God have to be understood against the background of his distinction between 'essential' and 'participative' union with God. What is enforced by this distinction is a sharp *epistemological* disjunction between the spheres of creation and redemption; and so between nature and grace. If we forget that what is in question is an epistemological distinction, we will find such passages as these unnecessarily difficult to reconcile with his other, equally definite, if also somewhat more parenthetical, statements that of course grace *perfects* and does not destroy nature. Epistemologically, however, the disjunction is sharp. From the created nature of natural objects, from the images which we can generate from them, from the conceptual ideas which we can work up from the natural images, we can indeed derive an indirect and mediated knowledge of God: but no such knowledge as we can thus derive may in any way, as John puts it, 'serve as a *proximate* means leading to God';[15] none such can serve any purpose of bringing about that *union by participation* which only grace can achieve. Indeed, it is only by the denial of those images and conceptions in the way of negation that the supernatural, and so participative, gift of faith can bring the intellect into transforming union with God:

> It is as if Isaiah had said that the intellect will not be able through its ideas to understand anything like God, nor the will experience a delight and sweetness resembling Him, nor the memory place in the imagination remembrances and images representing him.
>
> Manifestly, then, none of these ideas can serve the intellect as a proximate means leading to God. In order to draw nearer the divine ray the intellect must advance by unknowing rather than by the desire to know, and by blinding itself and remaining in darkness rather than by opening its eyes.[16]

What we have here, then, is a reformulated but still recognisable version of the classical mediaeval distinction between the 'image' and 'likeness' of God—'"image" belongs to nature, "likeness" to grace', as Hugh of Saint Victor put it. Moreover, we have not just the distinction itself but also some residue of the disjunctive logic of it: *insofar* as we affirm image, we deny likeness; *in order to* make room for grace and the union of likeness, we must negate image.

I say that we have 'some residue' of the disjunctive logic of this mediaeval distinction. But something important within the full-blown dionysian dialectics is missing from John's. As we saw, for the pseudo-Denys there is an hierarchy of images and conceptions of the divine, and the movement of the mind and of language is from the lowest, most 'dissimilar similitudes' to the highest and most 'similar similitudes'. All, *in the end*, must be negated in the darkness of the divine light, but not all equally and at once. For the pseudo-Denys, although, absolutely speaking, all fail in infinite degree, not all fail at once and to the same degree as far as *our* knowledge is concerned. Hence, for the pseudo-Denys, there are degrees of likeness and unlikeness and the dialectic is a spiralling movement up the scale.[17] But in John this epistemological hierarchy is gone: 'among all creatures both superior and inferior none bears a likeness to God's being'.[18] And though there is a scale of of superior and inferior, it is epistemologically irrelevant, for 'Truly, as theologians say, all creatures carry with them a certain relationship to God and a trace of him (greater or less according to the perfection of their being) *yet God has no relation or essential likeness to them*'.[19]

In this simplified dialectics of John, therefore, we have a definite, if also somewhat refracted, reflection of the core epistemological theses of classical christian neo-platonism. It will not surprise us to find, therefore, that to a similarly indirect degree, the epistemology spills over, in the way we have observed it to do in the Middle Ages, into what (admittedly little) John has to say about scriptural hermeneutics. John's hermeneutics are distinctly anti-literalist.

It appears that at the time of his initial theological studies as an ordinand at the University of Salamanca, the Faculty of Theology was riven by a familar dispute over the literal sense of Scripture. The 'scholastics' were traditionalists, holding fast to the older style of allegorical interpretation. The 'scripturists', Kieran Kavanaugh explains, 'sought the literal sense of Scripture through a development of scientific methods and the study of languages'.[20] John's teacher, Gaspar Grajal, seems to have been a leading 'scripturist'. If so, John could hardly have sympathised with his master, for in the many hundreds of scriptural references contained in his writings, John shows himself to be a resolute allegoriser.

Nor only in practice. Though we have no words of John on scriptural interpretation as such, we have in *The Ascent of Mount Carmel* a long and detailed discussion of the right way to interpret claims to 'prophetic locutions'. From that discussion it is possible to determine John's view of, in particular, the hermeneutics of Old Testament prophecy. The theory is as 'Origenist' as his practice. His words speak for themselves:

> One should not interpret . . . prophesy literally, for God's spiritual meaning is difficult to understand and different from our literal interpretation[21] . . . souls are misled by imparting to God's locutions and revelations a literal interpretation, an interpretation according to the outer rind. As has been explained, God's chief objective in conferring . . . revelations is to express and impart the elusive, spiritual meaning contained in the words. This spiritual meaning is richer and more plentiful than the literal meaning and transcends those limits.
>
> Anyone bound to the letter, locution, form or apprehensible figure cannot avoid serious error and will later become confused for having been led by the literal sense, and not having allowed for the spiritual meaning which is divested of the literal sense. *Littera, enim, occidit, spiritus autem vivificat* (2 Cor 3:6). The soul should renounce, then, the literal sense and live in the darkness of faith, for faith is the spirit which is incomprehensible to the senses.[22]

As we will see, when we turn to John's reading of the Song, this theoretical Origenism has important consequences for his own literary practice.

We are therefore left in John with all the linguistic resources of the preceding centuries of christian neo-platonism. These resources of language and imagery still carry with them the evidences of the dialectical epistemology to which they were once so closely bound in high dionysian theology. And we may truly say that there are respects of imagery, epistemology, and of hermeneutics in which John is a purer, more faithful disciple of the pseudo-Denys than many of the mediaeval authorities who stand between John and his source. Nonetheless, almost entirely absent—and, where present, irrelevant—is the metaphysical world of dionysian neo-platonism. John's mysticism lacks roots in this metaphysics, or in any other designed to serve the same purpose of, as it were, 'fixing' the imagery within a stabilising world-view. And we will see in the next section that, as a consequence, *eros* in John has become reduced to little more than 'imagery', expressive trope, figure of speech. It was always more than this for the pseudo-Denys. In saying this I am very far from suggesting that John's use of erotic imagery is redundant, for if it is no longer integrated into an explicitly dionysian creationist ontology, that is not to say that it is secondary and marginal to the thought and experiences which it expresses. John, like Bernard, does not just *think of* love as *eros*. He loves God erotically. It is not, therefore, a matter of John's metaphors having nothing to be integrated with. It is, rather, a matter of what they are integrated with; and, beyond that, it is a matter of the literary and theological consequences of the fact that, whereas in the pseudo-Denys the erotic is fixed objectively into the structure of the divine world-order, and whereas in the hermeneutics of the Middle Ages, the erotic was fixed as typology into a universalising theology of history and eschatology, John's eroticism is personalised, highly subjectivised metaphor; it is his, but merely his, personal style.

JOHN AND THE SONG TRADITION

If the dependence of John's theology and spirituality on the pseudo-Denys can be relatively easily demonstrated, the dependence of his *Spiritual Canticle* on the Song of Songs scarcely needs to be. In my notes to the translation of John's poem I have documented the obvious allusions to the Song and these are only those detectable on the very strictest criterion of verbal filiation. On looser criteria there are many others to be detected.

Nor is there any need to labour the equally obvious dependence of The *Canticle's* imagery on the Song. Wine, water, springs, flowers, garlands, valleys, mountains, winds, gardens, birds, lions, stags, foxes, woods, meadows, oils, vineyards, fruits, caverns—these are John's pastoral images of nature. All are the Song's. Bride and bridegroom; hiding, fleeing, wounding, seeking, healing, sickness, surrendering, self-giving, abandonment, loss, finding, captivating, embracing, loneliness, tasting—these are the moods and states of erotic love; again, distinctively, if not exclusively, the Song's. Heart, eyes, hair, breasts, blackness of skin, neck, arms—these are the physical charms of the body. We need not add to these lists; they are too easily compiled.

Less mechanically retrievable and certainly in some ways more significant are similarities in dramatic and narrative organisation. Both the Song and the *Canticle* are dialogues. In both the 'Bride's' role predominates. In both there is a clear sense of dramatic movement. Both tell of the vicissitudes of love organised around the central dramatic tensions of *eros*, of longing and fulfilment, of hurt and absence, of delight and presence, of losing and seeking, of finding and giving. But in neither is there any clear narrative sequence detectable; instead there is a kaleidescope of episodes which are spliced into one another, sometimes overlapping, sometimes superimposed, sometimes simply juxtaposed with an apparent narrative arbitrariness which, however, seems powerfully to reinforce the condensations of the imagery. In these ways at least the *Spiritual Canticle* reveals its relationship with the Song, its model.

But the *Canticle* is dependent not only on the Song; occasionally even the poem itself, more frequently the prose commentary, shows evidence of filiation with the preceding traditions of mediaeval commentary on the biblical text. Consider stanza 33:

> Do not despise me;
> For if you found me dark
> You may well gaze upon me now;
> For then when you looked on me
> What grace and loveliness you left in me.[23]

The reference of the first two lines to the Song 1:4 and 5 is clear: *I am black, but beautiful . . . Do not gaze upon me because I am swarthy . . . .* But the remaining verses of the stanza embody what is for us now a familiar mediaeval gloss. Compare Gregory:

> I am black but beautiful. 'Black' in merits, 'beautiful' in grace; 'black' on account of her past life, 'beautiful' on account of her subsequent record . . . (n. 37). Black for my own part, made beautiful by what I have been given; black on account of my past, beautiful because of what I shall become in the future. (n. 39)

And compare John's own gloss on this stanza:

> . . . the bride dares tell her Beloved not to consider her any longer of little account and not to despise her. If she previously merited this treatment because of the ugliness of her fault and the inferiority of her nature, now, after he has looked at her the first time, by which He arrayed her in His grace and clothed her in His beauty, He can easily look at her the second time and many more times, making this grace and beauty grow.[24]

'The bride in the *Canticle*', he goes on,

> explains the same thing, saying, *I am black but beautiful, daughters of Jersusalem; wherefore the King has loved me and brought me into his inner chamber* (Sg 1:4). This is like saying: Souls, you who do not know of nor recognise these favours, do not marvel that the heavenly King has granted such admirable ones, as even to bring me into his inner love. For though of myself I

> am dark, he so frequently fixed His eyes on me, after having looked at me the first time, that he was not satisfied until He had espoused me to Himself and brought me into the inner chamber of his love.[25]

It would be possible to illustrate further these multiple lines of dependence, of the *Canticle* on the Song, of the prose commentary on the Song, and of both the *Canticle* and the prose commentary on the patristic and mediaeval Song commentaries.[26] There is no need to do so, for there are enough materials provided to trace out more of them even in the restricted sample of texts in my anthology. Further research is likely only to confirm more completely what is in any case evident from the most cursory readings of the sources.

Given John's manifest intention to write a mystical poem closely modeled in style, form and meaning on the received tradition of Song interpretation, what are we to make of his relationship with that tradition? Clearly it would be an unforgivable scholarly reductivism to read the *Canticle* itself simply in terms of what it inherits from the mediaeval commentary on the Song. The *Canticle* breathes a life of its own. Its imagery is fresh, vital, personal. It is not *merely* borrowed, conventional and, as it were, 'hallowed'. If in nearly every word, image and resonance, if in every feature of dramatic structure, the *Canticle* bears the marks of that tradition, there is no denying the credentials of the *Canticle* as an independent and original work of poetry and theology. To fail to acknowledge this would be crass, calling to mind Brahms' remark to a critic who claimed to detect thematic similarities between his First Symphony and Beethoven's Ninth: '*Any* old fool can see that!'

All the same, it remains true that although John's language in the *Canticle* is not merely borrowed, it is borrowed. While it is not merely conventional, one thousand years of unbroken commentarial tradition has allowed him to receive that language unproblematically. And if John does not receive that sacralized language in a naively passive way, but attentively reworks it again, because the ancient tradition which spiritualised it was still very much alive in his own day, John has no need to rehearse the arguments of Origen and the pseudo-Denys to show that it has a spiritual meaning. In the Hebrew Song of Songs God is nowhere to be found until the text is interpreted theologically by jewish and christian interpreters. Divine meaning so saturates the language of the *Spiritual Canticle* that God does not need to be mentioned, so irreversibly spiritualised has that language become in the tradition on which John's poem draws.

But if we are to view the *Spiritual Canticle*—poem and commentary—against the background of that tradition, we will have to see in both a particular development of it which is, in fact, continuous with developments we noted in Denys the Carthusian's exegesis. In the same way that John's neo-platonic eroticism has come unstuck from its moorings in the corresponding ontology, so also has his *Canticle* become detached from the characteristic mediaeval ecclesiology and eschatology. It retains, as we saw, the formalism of the monastic tradition. But we were able to detect in Denys the Carthusian signs of a fragmentation of the schema of interrelated allegory, tropology, and anagogy into relatively isolated interpretative strategies; and the consequence of this, in Denys' tropological interpretation, was a theological tendency towards individualism and a linguistic tendency towards a personalised rhetoricism. For the same reason, the *Spiritual Canticle* tends the same way, but to an enhanced degree. Seen in the light of the mediaeval classification of interpretations, the *Canticle* must be described as a pure, theologically and eschatologically vacuous, tropology. Here, all is the individual soul and God, in personal and solitary dialogue with one another. Gone, even as a distinct alternative reading, is any ecclesiological interpretation of the received imagery; gone is that sense that all time and history is an outpouring of the Holy Spirit in ecstatic love of the human race, of Israel and of the Church; gone, therefore, is the careful dovetailing of moral interpretation with the great sweep of ecclesiological eschatology. Moreover, insofar as the *Canticle* does offer an eschatology—and therefore, in the mediaeval meaning of the term, a 'mystical' sense—it too is collapsed into a purely individualised tropology, into, we could say, a personalised 'mysticism' in the modern sense.

No doubt this is to the advantage of the poetic quality of the *Canticle*. Certainly, in point of personal expressiveness, the poem is closer to the Song itself in its original, preinterpreted form than is the over-theologised, detached, bloodless remnant which survives in the late mediaeval allegorical commentary; consider, in particular, what Giles makes of it, or Denys in his 'general' interpretation. The songs of the *Canticle*, like the songs of its biblical prototype are, at least, genuine love songs. And this, we might say, is a literary gain, though we might add, at the cost of an impoverished theological vision. Because John's personalisation of the Song's imagery liberates it from over-familiar typologies, it could be reworked into a subjectively resonant personal rhetoric. What it loses as typology it gains as imagery. But because John liberates *eros* from typology he sacrifices with it that density of theological texture and breadth of ecclesiological reference which the best mediaeval commentator—Gregory or Alan or Bernard—was able to bring even to his tropological interpretation.

That, however, is not the whole story. For whereas John attenuates the theological vision of mediaeval typology, he retains the logical structure of the formalist hermeneutics. His imagery of the *Canticle* works by means of the same device of symmetrical formal analogy as does the mediaeval commentator's typology: as A is to B, so C is to D. In his prose commentary John relentlessly pursues the 'meanings' of his poem, at times word for word, to the point where one is led to suspect that the poem is functioning, in relation to those 'meanings', more as a cypher or code than as a constructive creator of them. Decoding the poem: that is the hermeneutical strategy of the commentary. Its meaning seems to lie at once on and below the surface of the imagery, at once revealed and disguised by it. Or, to change the metaphor, interpretation appears to require a double movement: stripping away the imagery to disclose the meaning hidden by it; then reassembling, so that, once disclosed, the meaning can then be recognised within the imagery. In practice that is how the commentary came to be written: in response to a request from the carmelite nuns at Beas, who wanted to know what the poem 'meant'.

THE NEMESIS OF HERMENEUTICAL FORMALISM

These remarks bring us back to the difficult question raised at the beginning of this essay: the relationship between the poem and the prose commentary of the *Spiritual Canticle.* There I suggested that the commentary may legitimately be seen to stand to the poem in much the same relationship as the mediaeval commentary does to the Song. This can provide a helpful way to look at the matter.

In one important respect this comparison fails. The mediaeval commentator was the author not of the text he construed, but only of his own commentary on it. The commentator knew that the principal author of the Song was the Holy Spirit. He knew, particularly if he was of a 'formalist' inclination, that the text he was presented with was only a surface; that though the Holy Spirit had shaped that surface, he had done so only to disguise or hide beneath it the deeper, spiritual meanings which, in turn, are the determinants of the contours of the surface. The commentator therefore saw himself as faced with a quasi-geological problem of reading the mind of the creator who had buried unknown meanings in unknown places below the surface. Moreover, when he faced the problem of how to identify the lower geological strata, he was possessed of but one instrument of measurement and one set of clues as to where to apply it.

The clues were the cracks and fissures on the surface, the anomalous ruptures in the literal meaning. The measuring instrument was the power of allegory. Applied to the surface anomaly, that instrument was capable of reading off networks of correspondence between surface and depth with which the commentator could ultimately map the whole of the surface on to its sustaining substructure. Thereafter, if the commentator chose, he could mine those depths too and appropriate the gold of the spiritual meanings to himself in a moral interpretation.

This strategy, so described, is the epitome of the neoplatonic hermeneutical method, especially in its traditional monastic form. Though John of the Cross owes much to this tradition, his commentary cannot stand in the commentator's relationship with his poem for the simple reason that John was the author of both. In every other respect, however, the comparison holds. John, as the author of his commentary, is the interpreter of the Song's spiritual meanings. But he is also the author of the poem which, as interpreter, he expounds. It is therefore *John* who disguises as poet what *John* the interpreter reveals. In short, John is to the conjunction of poem and prose what the Holy Spirit is, on Origen's account, in relation to the double meaning of the Song, the author at once of surface and depth and of the relation between them.

This is not the fanciful suggestion it might seem to be. John himself explains that the analogy holds for the description of the relationship between commentary and poem. Though he pretends to stand back from his authorial relationship with the poem so as to speak of himself in the role of commentator, *as if* of another, nothing can disguise from us, still less from John, that he is also the author of that which he proposes to interpret:

> If [the] similitudes [of the *Canticle*] are not read with the simplicity of the spirit of knowledge and love which they contain, they will seem to be absurdities rather than reasonable utterances, as will those comparisons of the divine Canticle of Solomon and other books of Sacred Scripture where the Holy Spirit, unable to express the fullness of His meaning in ordinary words, utters mysteries in strange figures and likenesses. The saintly doctors, no matter how much they have said or will say, can never furnish an exhaustive explanation of these figures and comparisons, since the abundant meanings of the Holy Spirit cannot be caught in words. Thus the explanation of these expressions usually contains less than what they in themselves embody.[27]

As a model for interpretation, this sounds distinctly Origenist. Let us therefore read again what Origen says:

> [The Holy Spirit's] aim is to envelop and hide secret mysteries in ordinary words under the pretext of a narrative of some kind and an account of visible things . . . Moreover, we should know that since the chief aim of the Holy Spirit was to keep the logical order of the spiritual meaning either in what is bound to happen or in what has already taken place, if anywhere he found that what had happened according to the narrative could be fitted to the spiritual meaning, He composed something woven out of both kinds in a single verbal account, always hiding the secret meaning more deeply. But where the narrative of events could not be coherent with the spiritual logic, He sometimes interspersed either events less likely or absolutely impossible to have happened and sometimes events that could have happened but in fact did not.[28]

That, precisely, is the relationship in which John stands to his *Canticle*, poem and prose.

Yet because he stands to both poem and prose as the Holy Spirit stands to the Song, John knows the meaning of his poem *in advance*. He so writes the poetic surface as at once to disguise and to reveal the depth, for he creates both the surface contours and the depths which sustain them. His poem contains 'absurdities' and 'strange figures and likenesses' (the fractured narrative, the kaleidescopic imagery) because he himself wrote them into it, already knowing what spiritual meanings explain them. In that same sense in which, for Origen, the hidden spiritual meaning generates or 'writes' the surface, literal meaning of the scriptural text, so too, in John's literary output; hence the natural relationship—at any rate as *we* would see it—between poem and prose is reversed. In an important, authorial, sense, the prose was already there as *meaning* before the poem came to exist as *image*. And so it must be for the reader too.

This is not how contemporary sanjuanist scholars prefer to see the matter. Overwhelmingly, the weight of recent critical opinion, hispanophone and anglophone, supports the case for the priority of the poetry over the prose. Willis Barnstone, for example, confidently affirms that 'while the commentaries depend on the poems, the poems do not depend on the commentaries, and are often distorted by them; it is not necessary to know the commentaries in order to understand the poems'.[29] He dismisses as 'literary heresy' and as 'intentional fallacy' the procedure of reading the poetry in terms of the significances which John finds for them in the prose commentaries.[30] More generally, the received opinion favours the priority of the literary, emotional and spiritual qualities of the poetry as they can be understood in their own right, and so it is fashionable to emphasise the poetry's own intensities of passion, the sensuality of the imagery in its own terms, the authenticity of the poet's love of nature for its own sake and, in respect of literary sources and models, the dependence not so much on the prose commentaries as on secular precedents, in particular on the popular love-songs and dance forms of his native Spain.[31]

My interpretation of the relationship between the poetry and the prose of John of the Cross implies the opposite of all this. I think it plain that the commentaries could very easily be made to stand on their own as independent treatises—indeed, for good or ill, they are frequently read this way as making perfectly good, complete, sense. As far as the poetry is concerned, the existence of the commentaries from John's own hand has the result that the poetry *cannot now* stand on its own. Perhaps we could say that if the commentaries had not been written, the poems *could have* stood on their own, but, the commentaries having been written, it cannot be a mistake to take poetry and prose in conjunction. Moreover, the point is not merely a logical one: in the case at least of the *Spiritual Canticle*, the poem is, as we have seen, designed to be so fractured in narrative sequence and in overall significance as to demand a gloss—not merely because of the reader's ignorance of the significance, but because the text is specifically designed to point beyond itself to the sorts of meaning ascribed to it by the commentaries.

None of this denies that the poetry and the prose are different genres, nor does it suppress the importance of their differing literary qualities. Neither could *displace* the other without some loss of what each uniquely provides. John himself says as much. If he acknowledges, in the spirit of the biblical exegete, the need to answer the request of the nuns of Beas for an explanation, he is every bit as emphatic in denying that the prose explanations can exhaust every legitimate significance of the poems: they do not, he insists, supply the only possible meanings of the poems. Nor is any of this to deny that John wrote the poems without any thought for the prose commentaries upon them. Least of all is it to deny that they are fine poetry, and it is consistent to concede that in some ways the poems are the more fundamental and primary literary output within John's *oeuvre*. On the other hand, it is worth countering a modern prejudice, that to insist on their being understood in what is, admittedly, an antique, distinctly pre-romantic relationship with the prose commentaries is to deprive them of their poetic authenticity.

CONCLUSION

Precisely because it is necessary to read John of the Cross in his own terms, it is necessary *not* to read the poetry in isolation from his prose. At the hermeneutical level we are faced with the fact that the poetry and the prose come down to us from John's hand together with an explicitly stated set of principles for the interpretation of the relationship between them. That hermeneutic is late mediaeval, not modern, post-romantic. John shows no sign of valuing any literary product for its own sake and simply *as literary*. Nor does he show any sign of valuing poetry as a uniquely irreplaceable genre. His conviction that the poetry contains a surplus of significances beyond the reach of any commentary, including even his own, owes far more, as I have argued, to an Origenist scriptural hermeneutic than to any late-modern doctrine of the uniqueness and self-sufficiency of the work of art. There is something anachronistic and unhistorical in the contemporary insistence that John's poetry would be devalued by being set in the relation he envisaged for it with the prose commentaries.

The setting of John's poetry against its mediaeval precedents is just as important in assessing the eroticism of his imagery. Here, the twin pressures of neo-platonic, specifically dionysian, erotic ontology and of mediaeval scriptural hermeneutic exert their power more forcefully on John's *Spiritual Canticle* than on any other of our authors. Yet, by the time both pressures have found their way to John, they are scarcely recognisable in their original forms. John's *eros*, from the standpoint of the pseudo-Denys, is metaphysically attenuated. His hermeneutics, from the standpoint of Gregory, has become a completely de-historicised, individualistic formalism. Both processes of degeneration from their originals were already far advanced in the Middle Ages, as we have seen. But in John they converge and each powerfully reinforces the tendency of the other, as it were, leaving erotic discourse free-floating in an ontological and theological vacuum, resonating neither with the overtones of a doctrine of creation, nor with those of a theology of history; and, I should say, not even with any compensating gains of a truly carnal sensuality.

I have said that one gain from John's liberation of erotic language from the constraints of a typological theology is that his *Spiritual Canticle* at least reads more like the love poetry of the Song itself. This is true. Yet if I may, in conclusion, be permitted an entirely personal reaction, as distinct from a rationally argued critical opinion, how different is the Song's red-blooded, carnal delight of woman and man for each other, how different is the Song's concrete immediacy and sexual explicitness from the distanced, abstract eroticism of the *Canticle*. The monk *has* to interpret the Song spiritually, so full is it of erotic danger and risk. The *Spiritual Canticle* runs no such danger, nor ever did for a sixteenth century reader: it is as safe as psalms, for its spiritual meanings—or rather the fact that it has them—are perfectly transparent to any readers John himself could have envisaged, equipped as he knew them to be with a knowledge of the traditions of Song interpretation on which the *Canticle* so manifestly depends.

The language of the *Canticle* betrays all too clearly the formalist pressures exerted upon it to spiritualise. Its eroticism is two-dimensional, a sheet of glass superimposed on its spiritual significances. Like a plate of glass it can shimmer and glitter, reflecting light which strikes the eye, but only at one very precise, carefully contrived, angle of refraction. From any other angle that language is pure transparency and, lacks any density of its own; we are compelled to look straight through it to what lies below. So too, with the erotic imagery of the *Canticle.* Again and again, as in stanza 31, we are given a brief moment of true erotic promise:

> That one solitary hair
> You looked upon it fluttering on my neck
> You gazed at it on my neck
> And it enchanted you . . .

But immediately, the intrusive, calculated, 'Origenist' absurdity of the next line, culled from the Song, pulls us back from the brink of carnality to the safety of the spiritual meaning:

> And in one of my eyes I wounded you.

The stilted, discordant image of a 'single eye' may serve its 'Origenist' purpose of reminding us that this stanza cannot be meant to evoke the carnally erotic stimulus of the girl's fluttering tresses, but is intended to evoke the spiritual sense of the stanza. But it cannot be denied that, for those who seek an autonomous erotic significance, it is a disappointment. From the literary point of view it is a contrived disaster organised for an exegetical purpose: to ensure, by the allusion to the familiar sacred text whose spiritual meaning the reader already knows, that the metaphorical surface can be made to disappear into its spiritual interpretation. For this reason it is possible, if only with some irony, to welcome the comment of the spanish literary critic, Menendez y Pelago: 'So sublime is this poetry that it scarcely seems to belong to this world at all; it is hardly capable of being assessed by literary criteria'.[32]

Just so, comments Peter Hatton. 'The effect created by the *Canticle* is indeed "other-worldly" and deliberately so. The poet strives, it seems, to avoid the concrete image but rather to create a smooth surface which is transparent to the deeper meaning below its surface. The verse points beyond itself, urging the reader not to rest in it but to transcend it.'[33]

I have attempted in this brief narrative of some events in the development of the latin tradition of Song commentary to resituate the study of John of the Cross in the context of his mediaeval precedents and in this way also to illuminate some tendencies within the development of the mediaeval exegesis of the Song. Contemporary reception of John of the Cross would reserve only a marginal place for the Song Commentary. Moreover, we stand, if not in time, at any rate culturally perhaps at an even greater distance from John than he did from his sources in neo-platonist metaphysics and monastic hermeneutics. And yet, as much because of John as of any other christian writer, we still speak his language when we wish to articulate the discourse of divine love. In John's time that language was already theologically and metaphysically deracinated. John himself was able, by sheer literary skill, temporarily to breathe life into the residual metaphors which had been washed up on the banks of a dried-out theological stream. I suspect that today not only the theology but also the metaphors are dead. At least they are exhausted. It would not be without its ironies if the fate of spiritual eroticism turned out to be that said to afflict erotic experience itself: to be exhausted by its consummation. *Omnis homo post coitum tristis.*

NOTES

1. *MT*, 1, 1 997B, quoted by John of the Cross in *AMC*, II.8.5, p. 128; *DNS*, II.5.3, p. 336; *SC*, st. 14 and 15. 16, p. 489; *LFL*, st. 3. 49, p. 629.
2. *AMC*, II,3.4. p. 111; II.9.1, p. 129; II.16.9, p. 152; *DNS*, II.5.3, p. 336; II, 8.1, p. 343; II.16.11, p. 366.
3. See, e.g. *AMC*, II.6–8.
4. *Cloud*, c. 6.
5. *SC*, st. 22.3, p. 497.
6. *LFL*, st. 1.14, p. 584.
7. *LFL*, st. 1.34, p. 594.
8. *SC*, st. 22.4, p. 497.
9. *SC*, st. 22.3, p. 497 and 5, p. 498.
10. *AMC*, II.5.3, pp. 115–116.
11. *AMC*, II.5.3, p. 116.
12. *AMC*, II.5.7, p. 117.
13. *AMC*, II.8.3, p. 126.
14. *AMC*, II.8.5, p. 127.
15. *AMC*, II.8.6, p. 128.
16. *Ibid*.
17. *MT*, cc. 4–5.
18. *AMC* II.8.3, p. 126.
19. *Ibid*.
20. *CW*, Introduction, p. 18.
21. *AMC*, II.19.7, p. 165.
22. *AMC*, II.19.5, pp. 164–165.
23. Stanza 33 according to the order of the stanzas on which John wrote his commentary. The original order of the stanzas was rearranged for the purposes of his interpretation of them—see the two versions, pp. 410–415 and 712–717 in *CW*.
24. *SC*, st. 33.3, p. 538.
25. *SC*, st. 33.7, pp. 539–540.
26. For example, cp. Song, 1,3, stanza 26 of the poem, stanza 26.2, p. 511 of the Commentary and Alan of Lille, n. 16. Or *SC* 26.14 and Denys the Carthusian n. 41. Or Song 1, 6, *SC* st. 1 and Gregory n. 41.
27. *SC*, Prologue, 1, pp. 408–409.
28. Greer, pp. 187–188.
29. Willis Barnstone, *The Poems of St John of the Cross* (Bloomington: Indiana University Press, 1968) p. 30.
30. Barnstone, p. 30.
31. See Robert Graves' Introduction to *The Poems of St John of the Cross*, revised English versions by John Frederick Nims (New York: Grove Press, 1968).
32. Quoted in Roy Campbell, *The Poems of St John of the Cross*, preface M.D'Arcy SJ (London: Harvill, 1952) p. 1.
33. In an undergraduate essay presented to the Department of Theology and Religious Studies at Bristol University, 1986.

TEXTS ON THE SONG OF SONGS

The Song of Songs, Chapter 1, verses 1–8

THE VULGATE TEXT

1 Osculetur me osculo[1] oris sui
quia meliora sunt ubera[2] tua uino

2 fragrantia unguentis optimis[3]
oleum[4] effusum nomen tuum
ideo adulescentulae dilexerunt te

3 trahe me post te curremus[5] (in odorem unguentorum tuorum)[6]
introduxit me rex in cellaria sua[7]
exultabimus et laetabimur in te
memores uberum[8] tuorum super uinum
recti[9] diligunt te

4 Nigra sum sed[10] formosa filiae Hierusalem
sicut tabernacula Cedar
sicut pelles[11] Solomonis

5 Nolite me considerare quia fusca sim
quia decolorauit me sol
filii matris meae pugnauerunt contra me
posuerunt me custodem in uineis
uineam meam non custodiui

6 Indica mihi quem diligit anima mea
ubi pascas ubi cubes[12] in meridie
ne uagari incipiam post greges sodalium tuorum

7 si ignoras te[13] o pulchra inter mulieres
egredere et abi post uestigia gregum
et pasce hedos tuos iuxta tabernacula pastorum

8 equitatui meo in curribus Pharaonis assimilaui te
amica mea[14]

The Song of Songs of Solomon
in Hebrew called *Sir Hasirim*

Chapter 1:1–8

Translated from the Vulgate text

1 May he kiss me with the kiss of his mouth,
For your breasts are more delightful than wine,

2 More fragrant than the finest ointments.
Your name is oil poured out,
Therefore the young maidens have loved you.

3 Draw me after you, we will run
(in the fragrance of your ointments).
The King has brought me into his chambers;
We will rejoice and be glad in you.
Thoughts of your breasts surpass wine.
The righteous love you.

4 I am black, but beautiful, daughters of Jerusalem
Like the tents of Kedar, like Solomon's hides.

5 Do not gaze upon me because I am swarthy
It is the sun which has burned me.
My mother's sons have fought against me;
They made me guardian of the vineyards,
My own vineyard I have not kept.

6 Show me, you whom my soul loves, where you will pasture
Where you will lie down at noon
Lest I should begin to wander astray after the flocks of your companions.

7 If you do not know yourself, O most beautiful of women
Go out, depart in the tracks of the flocks
And feed your goats by the shepherds' tents.

8 I have compared you, my love, to my team of horses,
Harnessed to Pharoah's chariots.

NOTES

1. Gregory usually gives the plural, *osculis*, as does the Hebrew, *neshikot*, 'kisses', though he uses the Vulgate singular at nn. 15 and 18 of his Commentary. In this he follows Origen in Rufinus' Latin translation. The rest of the commentators in this volume usually, though by no means always, follow the Vulgate.

2. Here Jerome evidently follows LXX which gives *mastoi sou* ('your breasts'), rather than the Hebrew *dodeka* ('love'). As Nicholas of Lyra points out (n. 26), the Hebrew vowelless form of *dodeka* could be read as *dadeka* ('breasts'), though in fact the usual Hebrew word for 'breasts' in the Song is *shadai*, as in Sg 1:13.

3. In Gregory this line is replaced by *odor unguentorum tuorum super omnia aromata*, in this, again, following Rufinus' translation of Origen's Commentary.

4. Gregory has *unguentum*.

5. Most of our commentators punctuate *post te* with *trahe me*, the exception being Gregory, who reads *post te curremus* (n. 25).

6. All of our commentators include the bracketed phrase except Nicholas of Lyra, who points out that it is an interpolation, not to be found either in the Hebrew or in the Septuagint (see Nicholas, n. 31).

7. Gregory, *cubiculum suum*.

8. Nicholas of Lyra amends to *amorum suorum*.

9. A mistranslation of Jerome's; the Hebrew translates adverbially as 'rightly'.

10. Gregory, *et* at nn. 36 and 39, otherwise *sed*.

11. Gregory, *pellis*.

12. Gregory, at n. 41, reads *pascis* ('you feed') and *cubas* ('you lie down'), reverting to the future tense of the Vulgate at n. 42.

13. All our commentators follow the Vulgate in giving the reflexive. Again, a mistranslation of the Hebrew word of emphasis: 'If you *really* do not know . . .'.

14. Most commentators read verses 1–7 as a complete poem, treating verse 8 as the beginning of a new one.

John of the Cross

Born Juan de Yepes in 1542 in Fontiveros in Castile, John of the Cross was the son of an impoverished weaver of part Jewish ancestry. His father died a few years after his birth, and his childhood and adolescence were a time of considerable poverty. The family moved to Medina del Campo, where an uncle made provision for his education, and in 1563 he joined the Carmelite Order, taking the name of Juan de Santo Matías.

In 1564 he was sent to the University of Salamanca to pursue philosophical and theological studies and in 1567 occurred the event which was to transform his life: his meeting with Teresa de Jésus, who had recently begun the reform of the Carmelite Order. At the time John was on the point of joining the Carthusians, but Teresa, who was looking for priests to serve her reformed communities of nuns, persuaded him to join the Teresian reform. There he took the name by which he is since known, Juan de la Cruz.

Teresa's reform provoked bitter opposition from the superiors of the unreformed communities and in 1577 John's association with Teresa led to his arrest and imprisonment in the priory at Toledo. Teresa, in a comment of characteristic tartness, wrote in a letter of appeal to Philip II that she would rather John were in the hands of the Moors: they would have had more pity. While in Toledo, locked in what was little more than a cupboard, John composed a number of poems, including the *Cantico Espiritual*, translated below.

In 1578 John made a dramatic escape from his imprisonment. Thereafter, his life combined episodes of administration, spiritual direction, contemplative solitude and the writing of the prose commentaries on some of his poems which form the substance of his prose *oeuvre*. Even to his deathbed he was dogged by the persistent hostility of the unreformed Carmelites. He died in Ubeda in Andalusia on 14 December, 1591.

I have translated John's *El Cantico Espiritual* from the version he revised for the purposes of the prose commentary and from the text edited by Kieran Kavanaugh and Otilio Rodriguez for their translation of the *Complete Works*, Institute of Carmelite Studies Publications, Washington, 1979.

John of the Cross

THE SPIRITUAL CANTICLE

Bride

1. Where have you gone to hide
My loved one, leaving me to grieve?
You fled like a stag[1]
Leaving me wounded,
I went after you calling, but you had gone.[2]

2. Shepherds, you that roam
Over ranges, to the sheepfolds on high,
Were you, by chance, to see
Him whom my soul loves most,
Tell him that I sicken and suffer and die.[3]

3. In search of my loves
I will cross brooks and crags[4]
Not staying to gather flowers,
Not fearing wild beasts,
I will pass through forces and frontiers.

A question to the creatures

4. O woods and dense thickets,
Planted by my lover's hand,
O meadow green and
Brilliant with the blossoms of flowers,
Tell me if he has passed you by.[5]

Reply of the creatures

5. Scattering a thousand gifts,
He pressed on through these groves
And with but a glance
Of his face alone
He left them clothed in beauty.

Bride

6. O who is able to heal me?
Now give yourself to the last!
Desire not to send
Yet more mere messengers;
They cannot tell me what I want told.

7. All those who pass by
Telling me of your thousand graces
They wound me more deeply, for
Stuttering utterances utterly beyond sense
They leave me, not knowing what, to die.

8. But how can you endure,
My life, not living where your life is?
They bring you close to death
The arrows you have felt
Fired by what the beloved has begot.

9. Why have you, who have wounded
This heart, not made it well again?
Why have you stolen it,
To leave it to lie,
Not taken your plunder with you?

10. End these sufferings of mine,
None but you may mend them;
And may my eyes behold you
For you are their light
And for only you would I open them.

11. Show your presence to me
And kill me with the sight of your beauty[6]
For see, the sickness
Of love is past relief
Save by your presence and likeness.

12. O spring of crystal water!
If shimmering on your silvery surface
You would in a flash form
The eyes for which I long
Whose look is etched deep in my heart!

13. Look away, then, my love
For I take wing.

Bridegroom

Turn back, my dove[7]
The wounded stag
Is climbing the hill
Cooled by the breeze of your flight.

Bride

14. My love on the mountains,
The lonely wooded valleys
The far islands unknown,
The deep-sounding rivers
The sigh of winds in love.

15. The stilled, hushed night,
When dawn winds draw close,
The soundless music,
The deep tones of solitude,
The feast that feeds and fills with love.

16. Catch the little foxes[8]
For the vineyard is now in flower.
So shall we make from roses
A bouquet bound like a cone,
And let no one show his face on the hillside.

17. Be still, dead wind of North,
Come South wind, awakening love,

Breathe through my garden
Let its fragrance flow
And my love will feed among flowers.[9]

18. O maidens of Judea
While amber gives forth its scent
Among the blooms and roses,
Await there at the gates
Make no move to cross our threshold.

19. Stay hidden, O dearest one,
Look, turn towards the mountains,
And dare not to speak.
Look rather to her companions,
She who journeys to the far islands.

Bridegroom

20. Birds light as air,
Lions, stags, leaping roes,
Hills, valleys and streams,
Waves and winds, bright burning things
And terrors in the wakeful night:

21. By the lilt of lyres
And the call of sirens, I command you,
Cease your angry calls,
Breach not her wall
That my bride may sleep more soundly.[10]

22. The bride has entered
The enchanting garden of her desire[11]
Has rested among its delights,
Laying her neck
On the arms of her gentle beloved.[12]

23. Beneath the apple tree
There you were betrothed to me
There I gave you my hand

And you were made new,
Where your mother was ravished.[13]

Bride

24. Our bed breaks into bloom[14]
Encircled by dens of lions[15]
Hung with fine purple
Resting secure upon peace,
Crowned with a thousand shields of gold.[16]

25. Tracing your tracks
Young girls hurry your way,
At the flash of a spark,
From the scent of spiced wine
Wafts balsam truly divine.[17]

26. Deep in the cellar within
I drank from my beloved,[18] and when I left
To wander through the valley,
I was conscious of nothing
And lost track of the flock I had followed.

27. There he gave me his breast
Taught me his knowledge tender
And I gave myself wholly to him
Nothing held back
And I bound myself over his bride.

28. My soul in his service,
Giving all, I have laid;
No herd do I tend
Nor other task take,
I lack nothing if only I love.

29. Henceforth, if now in the affairs
That press, I am not to be seen or found,
You must say I was lost

Wandering in love's daze,
I was lost and therefore was found.

30. Of flowers and emeralds green,
Gathered fresh from dawn's dews
We will weave garlands
From your love's blooms
Entwined with one hair of my head.

31. That one solitary hair
You looked upon fluttering at my neck,
You gazed at it on my neck
And it enchanted you,
And in one of my eyes I wounded you.[19]

32. When then you gazed on me
Your eyes so scored me with grace
That you fell for me;
Then could my eyes deserve
To worship what they beheld in you.

33. Do not despise me now,
For if first you found me dark,
You may well gaze on me now.[20]
For then when you looked on me
What grace and loveliness you left in me.

Bridegroom

34. The small white dove
Has brought back the branch to the Ark
And now the turtle-dove[21]
Has found the mate of her longing
On the river's green banks.

35. She lived alone
In solitude she made her nest,
In solitude he guided her,

His loved one, he alone,
He, too, wounded by a lonely love.

Bride

36. Rejoice with me, my love
Come, see us both one in your beauty,
Come to the mountain slope and hill,
Where pure waters flow,
With me wend deep in the woods.

37. Then on to the caverns we press,
Hidden high among the rocks[22]
So well concealed;
There we will enter in
And taste the pomegranate's juice.[23]

38. There you will let me see
What my soul has longed for,
There will you give me,
There, you, my life,
What you told me of that day.

39. The air's breathing,
The sweet nightingale's song,
The grove in its loveliness,
In the calm of night,
With a flame that fires without pain.

40. No one looked on any longer,
No Aminadab there to see;
The siege had ceased,
And the mounted hordes,
On sight of the waters, stood down.

NOTES

1. 'My beloved is like a gazelle or young stag', Sg 2:9.

2. 'My beloved had turned and gone . . . I sought him but found him not, I called him, but he gave no answer', Sg 5:6.

3. 'I adjure you, O daughters of Jerusalem, if you find my beloved, that you tell him I am sick with love', Sg 5:8.

4. 'I will hie me to the mountain . . .', Sg 4:6.

5. 'Have you seen him whom my soul loves?' Sg 3:3.

6. 'Turn away your eyes from me, for they disturb me', Sg 6:5.

7. 'Return, return O Shulamite', Sg 6:13.

8. 'Catch us the foxes, the little foxes that spoil the vineyards, for our vineyards are in blossom', Sg 2:15.

9. 'Awake O North wind, and come O South wind! Blow upon my garden, let its fragrance be wafted abroad. Let my beloved come to his garden and eat its choicest fruits'. Sg 4:16.

10. 'I adjure you . . . that you stir not nor awaken my love until she please', Sg 3:5.

11. 'My beloved has come into his garden', Sg 5:1; 'My beloved has gone down into his garden', Sg 6:2.

12. 'O that his left arm were under my head and that his right hand embraced me!', Sg 2:6.

13. 'Under the apple tree I awakened you. There your mother was in travail with you, there she who bore you was in travail', Sg 8:5.

14. 'Our couch is green', Sg 1:16.

15. 'from the dens of lions', Sg 4:8.

16. 'Whereon hang a thousand bucklers, all of them shields of warriors', Sg 4:4.

17. 'We will run in the fragrance of your ointments', Sg 1:4.

18. 'The king has brought me into his chambers', Sg 1:3.

19. 'You have wounded my heart, my sister, bride, you have wounded my heart in one of your eyes, in one hair of your head', Sg 4:9.

20. 'I am black but beautiful . . . Do not gaze upon me because I am swarthy . . .', Sg 1:5.

21. 'and the voice of the turtle-dove is heard in our land', Sg 2:12.

22. 'O my dove, in the clefts of the rock, in the covert of the cliff . . .' Sg 2:14.

23. 'Your shoots are an orchard of pomegranates', Sg 4:13.

Gregory the Great

Born *c.* 540 of a roman patrician family, Gregory would serve well as the patron saint of bureaucrats both in his earlier, secular life and later as abbot, papal diplomat and pope. He entered the roman civil service, becoming Prefect of the city of Rome in 570, though shortly afterwards, upon the death of his father, he entered monastic life. In 575 he turned the family home on the Coelian Hill into a monastery dedicated to Saint Andrew. It is thought that excessive fasting during this period contributed to the gastric disorder which troubled him for the rest of his life—on several occasions in his writings he complains of the disruption which it caused to his daily routine. It is quite possible that regret at his early over-enthusiasm is reflected in his later insistence upon ascetical moderation, as in the ensuing text, n. 25 below.

No doubt it was recognition of his administrative talents and experience which led to his appointment as *apocrisiarius* (papal representative) to the byzantine court in Constantinople. In spite of this opportunity for contact with greek theology and culture, Gregory appears not to have mastered Greek. Characteristically, he attempted to combine the duties of papal bureaucrat with his chosen (and preferred) monastic way of life, for he took monks of Saint Andrews with him. It was at their request that he wrote a commentary on Job which he later developed into his massive *Moralia in Job*.

In 586 he was recalled to Rome to be adviser to Pope Pelagius II, whom he succeeded in 590. Thereafter the administrative burdens of the papacy dominated his life, though by no means to the exclusion of writing. To this period we owe the surviving torso of what may have been a complete Commentary on the Song of Songs which, like the *Moralia*, had its origin in lectures given to his monastic community.

It is customary to disparage Gregory's latin prose and the relative dullness of his thought. This is not always fair. In any case, the Song Commentary is an unrevised text and, that fact notwithstanding, there is an appealing warmth and practical humanity about Gregory's writing and a judiciousness of thought which is a style in its own right.

The translation below contains all that we possess of his Commentary. I have translated from the critical text of P. Verbraken OSB in *Corpus Christianorum, Series Latina*, 144, Turnholt, 1963, but have had regard to R. Bélanger's edition and French translation for *Sources Chretiennes*, 314, Paris, 1984. I have adopted the paragraph divisions and numbers from Verbraken.

Gregory the Great

EXPOSITION OF THE SONG OF SONGS

In the name of the Lord here begins
the exposition of the Songs of Songs,[1]
reconstructed from the beginning of the notes[2]
of the Lord Gregory, Pope of the City of Rome.

1. When the human race was thrust out from the joys of paradise and had embarked upon the pilgrimage of this present life, it became blind of heart, lacking in spiritual insight. Had the divine voice spoken to this blind heart, saying, 'Seek God' or 'Love God'—as the Law has spoken to it—the heart once and for all sent into exile would not have grasped what it heard because of its slack indifference.[3] For that reason the divine Word speaks to the dull and lukewarm soul and, concerning those things which the soul knows, it secretly inspires a love of which it knows nothing.

2. For allegory supplies the soul separated far from God with a kind of mechanism[4] by which it is raised to God. By means of dark sayings in whose words a person can understand something of his own, he can understand what is not his to understand, and by earthly words he can be raised above the earth.[5] Therefore, through means which are not alien to our way of understanding, that which is beyond our understanding can be known. By that which we do know—out of such are allegories made—divine meanings are clothed and through our understanding of external speech we are brought to an inner understanding.

3. Thus it is that in this book, called *The Songs of Songs*, we find the words of a bodily love: so that the soul, its numbness caressed into warmth by familiar words, through the words of a lower love is excited to a higher. For in this book are described kisses, breasts, cheeks, limbs; and this holy language is not to be held in ridicule because of these words. Rather we are provoked to reflect on the

mercy of God; for by his naming of the parts of the body by which he calls us to love we must be made aware of how wonderfully and mercifully he works in us; for he goes so far as to use the language of our shameful loves in order to set our heart on fire with a holy love. Thus in humbling himself by the manner of his speech he raises us in understanding; we learn, from the words of this lower love, with what intensity we must burn with love of God.[6]

4. But we must be subtle enough to grasp this, lest when we hear the words of this external love we become fixed in the things of sense, and the instrument, which is given to lift us up, should instead weigh us down. We must seek out the more interior meaning in these bodily, exterior words and, though speaking of the body, ourselves be taken, as it were, out of the body. We must come to this sacred marriage-feast of bride and bridegroom dressed in a wedding gown, that is with the understanding which comes from interior charity; this is necessary:[7] for unless we come clothed in this wedding gown, this worthy understanding of charity, we will be cast out from the wedding-feast into the darkness outside—that is, into the blindness of ignorance (Mt 22:1–14). Through these words of passing desire we must cross to the safe ground of invulnerability.[8] The words and meanings of sacred Scripture are related as colours and objects are in a picture: and it would be particularly stupid were a person so to attend to the colours of a picture as to ignore what the picture depicts. For if we give ear to the words which are the external utterance and ignore the meaning, this is like attending only to the colours while ignoring the thing painted. It is written that *the letter kills, but the spirit gives life* (2 Cor 3:6). For the letter hides the spirit just as the chaff conceals the wheat. But it is beasts of burden who feed on the chaff; humans feed on the wheat. Using human reason, therefore, a person discards the chaff of beasts and hurries to eat the wheat of the spirit. To this end, therefore, it serves a purpose that the mysteries of the letter should be concealed under wraps

because the wisdom which has to be worked for is all the better to taste.[9] For this reason it is written: *The wise hide their knowledge* (Prov 10:14), because, of course, the spiritual meaning is hidden under the cover of the letter. Hence it is said again in the same book: *To conceal his word, this is the glory of God* (Prov 25:2). For God is the more gloriously revealed to the mind who seeks him the more he is sought with insight and interiority—as will be seen. But could it be that we are not to try to uncover what God hides in mysteries? Indeed we ought; for the text goes on: *to sift the meaning is the glory of kings* (Prov 25:2). For they are kings who have learned how to rule over and judge their bodies, that is, the promptings of the flesh. Consequently the glory of kings is to discern meaning; for it is the glory of those who live well to discern the secrets of God's commands. Therefore, on hearing the words of human discourse we must, as one might say, become more than human beings; for if otherwise we hear what is said in a human way we will not be able to sense the divine character of what we ought to hear. Paul wished his disciples to be no longer 'men' when he said to them: *Since there are jealousies and wranglings among you, are you not men?* (1 Cor 3:3–4). And the Lord considered his disciples not to be any longer mere humans when he asked: *Who do men say the Son of Man is?* (Mt 16:13). When they answered him in the words of human beings, he insisted: *But you, who do you say I am?* (Mt 16:15). For when he first said 'men' and then added 'but you', he was making a kind of distinction between 'men' and 'disciples': that is by inspiring them to things divine, he made them more than men. The Apostle says: *For anyone who is in Christ there is a new creation, the old creation has gone* (2 Cor 5:17). And we know that at our resurrection the body will be so united to the spirit that everything which was of changeable desire will be taken up into the power of the spirit. Therefore, the person who seeks God ought daily to imitate his resurrection: so that, just as there will then be nothing changeable in the body, so now he has nothing changeable in the heart; so that in the inner man there may be a new creature, he should trample down anything suggestive of the old man and seek out in the words of the old only that power of the new.[10]

5. For Sacred Scripture is like a mountain, and the Lord comes from that mountain to bring understanding into our hearts. It is about this mountain that it is said through the prophet: *God is coming from Lebanon and the Holy One from the mountain thick with cloud* (Hab 3:3). This mountain is thick with meanings and enshrouded with allegories.[11] But it should be understood that if we are to hasten up the mountain when the voice of the Lord calls, we are instructed first to wash our clothes and be cleansed of every stain of the flesh. To be sure it is written that if wild beasts set foot on the mountain they will be stoned (Heb 12:20). Wild beasts touch the mountain when they approach the heavenly heights of sacred Scripture while yet given over to irrational desires and fail to understand it as they should, but irrationally twist it to a fleshly interpretation.[12] For if anything which is without wit or is slow of wit is seen on this mountain, it is killed by harsh judgements—which are like stones. For this mountain is on fire: meaning, of course, sacred Scripture which he fills with the spirit, and he inflames it with the fire of love. Hence it is written: *Your promise is tried in the fire* (Ps 118:140). Hence, too, those who were travelling on a journey heard[13] the words of God and said: *Were not our hearts burning within us when he explained the Scriptures to us?* (Lk 24:32). Hence again it is said through Moses: *In his right hand the law is on fire* (Deut 33:2). On the left hand of God we find the wicked; they may not pass to the right hand. On the right hand are the chosen ones of God, who are set apart from those on the left. So on God's right hand the law is on fire: because in the hearts of the chosen, who are to be placed on the right hand, the divine commands are burning, aflame with the fervour of love. Hence this flame burns off all the external

rust of age so that he may offer our minds as a holocaust in the contemplation of God.

6. Moreover, it is not pedantic to note that this work is called not *The Song*, but *The Song of Songs*. Just as in the Old Testament some things are holy and others the Holy of Holies, some days are Sabbaths and others the Sabbaths of Sabbaths, so in sacred Scripture there are not only Songs but also the Songs of Songs. Holy things were found in the tent and carried outside it, the Sabbaths were the days celebrated each week; but the Holy of Holies were shrouded in a more hidden worship and the Sabbaths of Sabbaths were celebrated only on their feasts. So the Songs of Songs is a kind of mystery and is solemn in a more interior way; this mystery being discerned in hidden meanings: for, if attention is paid to the outer word, the mystery is lost.

7. Moreover you should know that in sacred Scripture there are songs of victory, songs of exhortation and battle, songs of rejoicing, songs seeking help and songs of union with God. An example of a song of victory is what Miriam sang after crossing the Red Sea: *Let us sing to the Lord, he has covered himself in glory, horse and rider he has thrown into the sea* (Ex 15:21); in illustration of a song of exhortation and battle there are the words Moses sang to the Israelites when they drew near to the Promised Land: *Listen, heavens, while I speak; earth, hear the words that I am saying* (Deut 32:1); an example of a song of rejoicing is what Hannah sang as she foresaw the fruitfulness of the Church itself: *My heart exults in the Lord* (1 Sam 2:1); and when she gives voice in the self-same image[14] to the fruitfulness of the children of the Church, she sings: *the barren woman bears sevenfold, but the mother of many is desolate* (1 Sam 2:5); there is also the song acknowledging help received, as when David, after battle, sings: *I love you, Lord, my strength* (Ps 18:1). But this song, the Song of Songs, is the song of union with God which is sung by the Bridegroom and Bride at their wedding. Which is of all the songs so much the

more sublime because of its being sung at a wedding feast of the most sublime solemnity. For by means of the other songs vices are spurned; but through this song each person is enriched with virtues; through the others the enemy is resisted, through this song the Lord is embraced with a more intimate love.

8. It should also be noted that sometimes in sacred Scripture the Lord calls himself 'Master', sometimes 'Father', sometimes 'Bridegroom'. When he wishes to be feared, he calls himself 'Master'; when he wishes to be honoured, 'Father'; when he wishes to be loved, 'Bridegroom'.[15] He says through the prophet: *If I am indeed master, where is my honour? If I am indeed father, where is my respect?* (Mal 1:6). And again he says: *I will betroth you to myself . . . with integrity and justice* (Hos 2:19–20). Or, most clearly of all: *I have remembered the day of your betrothal in the desert* (Jer 2:21). Of course there is no before and after in God: but because he wishes first to be feared so that he may be honoured and then to be honoured so that the love of him is attained, he also calls himself 'Master' on account of the fear, 'Father' on account of the honour, and 'Bridegroom' on account of the love. Thus, through fear we may come to honour and through honouring him to love. Therefore, as honour is more worthy than fear he is more pleased to be called 'Father' than 'Master'; and as love is dearer to him than honour, so God is more pleased to be called 'Bridegroom' than 'Father'. Thus, in this book the Lord and the Church are not called respectively, 'Master' and 'Servant', but 'Bridegroom' and 'Bride'; so that he may be served not only in fear, nor only in reverence, but also in love and by the exterior words an inner affection may be stirred.

When he calls himself 'Master', he shows that we are created; when he calls himself 'Father', that we are adopted children; when he calls himself 'Bridegroom', that we are betrothed. It is a greater thing to be betrothed[16] to God than to be created and adopted by him. In this book, where he is described as 'Bridegroom', something more sublime is suggested, since what is indicated is a treaty of marriage. And this language is frequently recalled in the New Testament (because the consummated marriage[17] of word and flesh and of Christ with the Church is celebrated). And so John says, when the Lord is approaching: *He who has the bride is a bridegroom* (Jn 3:29). And the Lord himself says, *The attendants of the Bridegroom do not fast while the Bridegroom is still with them* (Mt 9:15). And so it is told of the Church: *I have espoused you to Christ so as to give you away as a chaste virgin to this one husband* (2 Cor 11:2). And again: *so as to make her glorious, without stain or wrinkle* (Eph 5:27). And again, in the Apocalypse of John: *Blessed are those who are invited to the marriage supper of the Lamb* (Rev 19:9). And finally, in the same book, *I saw the bride, newly wed, coming down from heaven* (Rev 21:2).

9. It is not unrelated that, with its especially mystical character, this book is placed third in order among the works of Solomon. The ancient fathers spoke of three orders of life: the moral, the natural, and the contemplative—which the Greeks called the ethical, the physical, and the theoretical.[18] In *Proverbs* the moral life is referred to, where it is said: *Listen, my sons, to the wisdom [I offer] and pay attention to my [words of] prudence* (Prov 4:1). *Ecclesiastes* refers to the natural life in which all things are seen as tending towards their end, when it says: *Vanity of vanities and all is vanity* (Qo 1:2). But in the Songs of Songs the contemplative life is given voice, for in them is expressed a longing for the coming of the Lord and for the sight of him in person, as when in the words of the Bridegroom it is said: *I have come from Lebanon, I have come* (Sg 4:8).[19] The lives of the three Patriarchs, Abraham, Isaac, and Jacob, represent these orders. Abraham achieved the moral life by his obedience; Isaac represents the natural life by his digging of the well—for to dig wells to the depths is to examine diligently by natural reason all the things of this world below. But Jacob achieved the contemplative life

because he witnessed angels ascending and descending.[20] However, since natural reasoning does not lead to perfection without the observances of the moral life, Ecclesiastes is rightly placed after Proverbs. And because the highest contemplation is not achieved unless things lying here below are first despised, the Songs of Songs are rightly placed[21] in order after Ecclesiastes.[22] For the first thing to do is to establish virtue; thereafter, to come to see all things which are present as though they were absent; and in the third place, to look with a pure heart upon those things which are above and within. Out of the rungs of these books he therefore makes a sort of ladder reaching up to the contemplation of God;[23] so that while as a first step we carry out well the honest and worthy tasks of this world, next we despise even these honest and worthy tasks, and finally at the top we gaze upon the very intimate things of God. Thus, in general terms, in this work the Church speaks of its expectation of the coming of the Lord so that in turn individually each soul may look forward to the indwelling of God in his heart, as if awaiting the arrival of the Bridegroom in the bedchamber.[24]

10. Next, we should note that in this book four voices are given roles:[25] namely those of the Bridegroom, the Bride, the young maidens attending the Bride, and the circle of companions of the Bridegroom. The Bride is the Church in its perfection; the Bridegroom is the Lord; the young maidens attending the Bride are immature souls, adolescents in their new desire; the companions of the Bridegroom are either angels whom he often sends to appear to human beings, or else they are the saints of the Church who know how to proclaim the truth to humankind. Nonetheless, all these, who separately are handmaidens and companions, are, taken together, also the Bride, for taken together they are the Church. In any case, as appropriate, all three designations can be accepted. For anyone who already loves God perfectly is a Bride; he who preaches the Bridegroom

is his companion; and the person who as yet is a new traveller on the way of a good life is a handmaiden. We are invited therefore to become the Bride; if we are not yet capable of this, we are to be companions; if we are not yet even companions, we can at least attend as maids of the bedchamber.[26] Therefore, as we call the Bridegroom and Bride the Lord and the Church, so we hear the words of the Bridegroom and of the Bride in the role of handmaidens or of companions and from their words we learn the fire of love.

11. Therefore, the holy Church, waiting through the ages for the coming of the Lord, for so long thirsting for the spring of life, declares openly how much she wishes to see her Bridegroom in person, how she longs for him, and cries out:

12. *May he kiss me with the kisses of his mouth.* To her the Lord had sent angels, patriarchs and prophets, bringing gifts of the spirit; but she wishes to take those gifts not from the hands of the Bridegroom's servants but now from the Bridegroom himself. The whole human race, from the origins of the world to its end, that is to say, the whole Church, we now represent one single Bride, who in the Law had received a pledge of the spiritual gift; but now she seeks the presence of the Bridegroom himself and says, *May he kiss me with the kisses of his mouth.* For the holy Church, sighing for the coming of the Mediator between God and man, for the coming of its redeemer, addresses the words of its prayer to the Father, that he may send the Son, that he may illuminate her with his presence, that he may speak to this same Church no longer through prophets, but by his own mouth.[27] Hence, it is written of this same Bridegroom in the Gospel, when he was seated on the Mount and spoke the words of his most sublime precepts: *Jesus opened his mouth and said* (Mt 5:2); as if meaning, 'he who at one time, for the encouragement of

the Church, opened the mouths of prophets, then opened his own mouth'.[28]

13. But note, as she sighs, while she is seeking as if for one absent, suddenly[29] she is aware of his presence. For it happens by the grace of our Creator, that while we seekers are speaking of him we actually enjoy his presence.[30] Thus it is written in the gospel that while Cleopas and another were conversing about him on the journey, they were rewarded by seeing[31] him present with them. Therefore, as the holy Church desires the absent Bridegroom to be made flesh, of a sudden she is aware of his presence and adds: *for your breasts are more delightful than wine; and the fragrance of your ointments surpasses all fragrances*. Wine was the knowledge of the Law, the knowledge of the prophets. But with the coming of the Lord, because he willed to proclaim his wisdom through his flesh, he made that wisdom to be, in a manner of speaking, the breasts on which we may feed: for the wisdom which, in his divinity, we were scarcely able to grasp we can know in his Incarnation. And so it is right to praise his breasts: for by bringing his preaching down to earth, he can effect in our hearts what the teaching of the Law can hardly effect at all. For the preaching of the Incarnation nourishes in a way that the teaching of the Law cannot. And so it is said: *Your breasts are more delightful than wine*.

14. As if to reaffirm this, she adds, saying: *and the fragrance of your ointments surpasses all fragrances*. The ointments of the Lord are the virtues; his ointment was the Holy Spirit. Referring to this Spirit the prophet says: *God, your God, has anointed you, with the oil of gladness before your companions* (Ps 44:8). He was anointed with this oil when he became flesh: for he did not just become a human person and afterwards receive the Holy Spirit; but because he became incarnate by the power of the Holy Spirit, he was anointed by the same oil by which he was made man. The fragrance of his ointment, therefore, is the flaming forth[32] of the Holy Spirit and, proceeding from the one,

it rests upon the other. The fragrance of his ointments is the flourishing[33] of the virtues, which he has worked [within us]. But the Church inhales this fragrance: for she possesses many gifts of the Spirit, which, in the house of God, that is, in the community of the saints, give her the odour of good standing and proclaim the sweetness of the future Mediator. But *the fragrance of your ointments surpasses all fragrances*: because the brilliance of the Bridegroom's virtues, endowed through his Incarnation, overshadows the commands of the Law, which had been, as it were, earnest money paid in advance by the Bride. For the Church grows into a fuller understanding as it deserves to be endowed with the grace of a fuller vision. That fragrance of the Law was dispensed by angels; this oil was given by the very presence of the Bridegroom himself. Because by the brilliance of his presence the good things of the Law are surpassed, though they were believed then to be most sublime, it is rightly said: *the fragrance of your ointments surpasses all fragrances.*

15. But this, which we have said in a general way about the whole Church, we now experience as true in a special way of each and every soul. For next we turn our attention to the truth that a soul which perseveres in seeking the gifts [of the Holy Spirit], though its understanding perceive only by the light of another's preaching, a soul which had desired to be itself illuminated by divine grace, so that one day it will understand in its own light as well those things which it can understand [as yet] only through the words of preachers—this soul says: *May he kiss me with the kiss of his mouth.* 'May he touch me inwardly,[34] so that I may know by understanding and no longer delight only in the words of preachers but thrill to the touch of his grace'. The Lord, as it were, kissed Moses with the kiss of his mouth when because of his faithfulness he shared with him the grace of understanding. Thus it is written: *If any man among you is a prophet, I make myself known to him in a vision, I speak to him in a dream. Not so with my servant Moses . . . . I speak*

with him mouth to mouth (Num 12:6–8). To speak mouth to mouth is, in a way, to kiss, and to touch the mind with an interior understanding.

16. It goes on: *for your breasts are more delightful than wine.* The breasts of God, as we have said before, are the preaching[35] of his most humble Incarnation. The wisdom of the world, by contrast, is a kind of wine: it intoxicates the mind because it distracts it from that understanding which flows from humility. The philosophers are made drunk by this kind of wine and so, by reason of the wisdom of the world, they think themselves above common morality. The holy Church despises this wisdom; it desires the most humble preaching of the Lord's incarnation: in the weakness of its flesh, it prefers the taste of the food by which it is sustained, rather than that the world should be given the credit for an inflated and false wisdom; and so it says: *for your breasts are more delightful than wine.* That is, 'the most humble preaching of your Incarnation surpasses the proud wisdom of this world.' And so it is written: *For the foolishness of God is wiser than men, and the weakness of God is stronger than men* (1 Cor 1:25).

17. But sometimes the wise of this world do appear to aspire to some virtues—for you may see for yourself that many are charitable, are meek, practice honesty towards all, in an external way; but though they practice these virtues to please not God but men (and so they are hardly virtues, since they do not seek to please God) still, they smell good to the human nose for in the judgment of men they create a good impression. But when they are compared with the true fragrance of our Redeemer, when they are compared with the very truest virtues, it must be said that *the fragrance of your ointments surpasses all fragrances.* That is: 'the flaming forth[36] of your virtues prevails over every kind of virtue possessed by the wise of this world, for by their truth they surpass those empty fictions.'

18. But because we have said that in the second place all this can be applied to each soul, let us follow out this

same interpretation in more detail, if, with the help of the Lord,[37] we are able to do so. Each soul who fears God is already carrying his yoke, but since he walks in fear, only at a distance: for as a person makes progress towards God so he works out the sentence of fear and from him receives the grace of charity. Consider the soul of any one of the elect, who with constant desire burns with love to see her Bridegroom; for though in this life it is not possible to enjoy a perfect vision, she is able to contemplate his excellence and she is touched[38] by this self-same love. And this 'being touched', which is the work of love, which is the burning of desire, is a kind of kiss; whenever the soul kisses God, then it is touched by God. There are, of course, many who still [only] fear the Lord and receive the grace of good works; but they have not yet kissed him for they have scarcely at all been touched by the love of him. All this is well illustrated by the meal of the Pharisee who received the Lord in his house while despising the woman who was kissing the Lord's feet, and was told, *I entered your house . . . You gave me no kiss, but from the time I came in she has not ceased to kiss my feet* (Lk 7:44–45). A person who gives alms, who tries to do good works, has, as it were, received Christ at a feast: he feeds Christ because he has not failed to sustain him in his members. But if he is not yet touched by love, he has not yet kissed so much as his footprints. The woman who kisses, therefore, is preferred to the person who gives alms, because preferable to those who offer their external goods[39] is the person who is touched in the inner burning of the soul by the desire for the Lord. And so it is well said that *she has not ceased to kiss my feet*. For it is not enough to be touched just once in the love of God and then to rest easy; rather this touching must first happen and then increase in frequency. And so the woman is praised because she did not cease to kiss, that is, she hardly ceased at all being touched. In the same way it is said by the prophet: *Hold a solemn day in frequent assemblies, up to the horns of the altar* (Ps 117:27). A day solemn to the

Lord is the touching of our hearts. But a solemn feast is frequently held when the soul[40] is persistently moved to tears for love of him. And if we were to ask him: 'How often are we to do these things? How often are we to suffer trials?', he gives the limit to which we must go when he says: *up to the horns of the altar*. For the 'horns of the altar' are the transformation of interior sacrifice into glory: when we win through to that glory then it is no longer in any way necessary for us to hold a solemn feastday for the Lord with our sorrowings. The soul, therefore, which here wishes to be touched by love, which now aspires to the vision of the Bridegroom says: *May he kiss me with the kiss of his mouth.*

19. Alternatively, the kiss of his mouth is surely interior peace in its fulfilment: and when we achieve that peace, there is nothing besides it which we can want. And so it continues: *for your breasts are more delightful than wine.* That is, wine is the knowledge of God which we have received for as long as we remain in this life. But we will embrace the breasts of the Bridegroom when in the eternal kingdom we will contemplate him by embracing him in person. That is why it says: *your breasts are more delightful than wine,* which is as if to say: 'great is the knowledge which you have given me in this life, great is the wine of your knowledge, you have made me drunk on it; but *your breasts are more delightful than wine,* because then that which we know now by faith will be surpassed by sight and by the height of contemplation.'

20. *And the fragrance of your ointments surpasses all fragrances.* The holy Church here below has its fragrances for as long as it is strong in the power of its knowledge, of its purity, of its mercy, of its humility, and of its charity. If the life of the saints did not give off this fragrance of virtue, Paul would not have said: *For we are the aroma of Christ in every place* (2 Cor 2:15). But superior by far is that anointing contemplation of God to which one day we are to be called; by far superior to the fragrances of our virtues

is the fragrance of the oils of God. And however great are those things which we have already received, immensely more potent are those which we are to receive from the contemplation of our Creator. And that is why the soul sighs and exclaims: *The fragrance of your ointments surpasses all fragrances*, meaning, 'those gifts which you keep for us in your contemplation surpass all the rewards of virtue which you have given us in this life.'[41]

21. What we say of this Church we say also of this soul, so much in love, so consumed with love of her Bridegroom, from whom she has received so great a desire, in whom she has grasped a knowledge of his divinity. But see how she herself acknowledges the source when she says: *Your name is oil poured out*. Oil poured out is the Godhead made flesh. If oil is contained in a jar, little of its fragrance escapes; but if it is poured out, the aroma of spilled oil is pervasive. And so the name of God is oil poured out: for he has poured himself out from the greatness of his divinity into our nature and out of his invisible being he has made himself visible.[42] If he had not poured himself out, in no way would he have made himself known to us. He has poured himself out as an oil when, though preserving his divinity, he showed himself as a man. Paul speaks of this outpouring thus: *Who, though he was in the form of God, did not count equality with God a thing to be grasped, but emptied himself, taking the form of a servant* (Phil 2:6–7). Where Paul says 'emptied himself' Solomon says 'poured out'. And so, because the Lord has made himself known to the human race through the self-abasement of his incarnation, we can say to him: *Your name is oil poured out*.

22. Next it says: *therefore the maidens have loved you*. How are we to read 'maidens' at this point except as the souls of the elect renewed by baptism?[43] Clearly, the sinful life is the life of the old man, the just life is the life of the new. And so by pouring himself out like an oil he has filled the young maidens with a burning love for himself; for by renewing their souls he causes them to burn with his

love. Childhood is as yet unable to love; old age has ceased loving. A child is someone who has not yet begun the quest of the life of love; an old man is one who has begun, but has tired of, it. Since, therefore, neither those who have yet to begin, nor those who having once begun have gone cold, burn with love of the Lord, the book ignores the life of the child and of the old man and says of the maidens that they 'run', that is, that they are souls who are on fire with love.

23. All this we can read in another way. Adolescence can refer to weakness. The age of youth is the order of angels who suffer no form of weakness, are oppressed by no illness. So the text says: *Your name is oil poured out: therefore the maidens have loved you.* In other words: 'because by your incarnation you have spread abroad the knowledge of yourself, the weak souls of humankind are able to love you. But those exalted powers which are compared to youthfulness also love you even where you are not poured out: for they see you there where you retain the form of the Godhead. Therefore, even though, where you do not pour yourself out, you may nonetheless be seen by these high orders which are compared to the age of youth, still, for the sake of humankind, you do pour yourself out; and so it is that you may be loved by the young maidens as well, that is, by those who are weak in soul.'

24. Next it says: *Draw me.*[44] A person who is 'drawn' is brought to do something either because he lacks the power or because he lacks the will to do it. But if that person says *draw me*, then there is in him both a willingness and an inability. Human nature wants to seek God, but because of acquired weakness it cannot seek as it ought. Evidently, then, there is something in human nature by which it thrusts forward, something by which it is held back; hence the text rightly says: *Draw me.* Paul saw in himself that there was both something of will and something of inability when he said: *For I delight in the law of God in my inmost self . . . but there is a law of sin in my members*

(Rom 7:22–23) and: *I see in my members another law which is at war with the law of my mind* (Rom 7:23). And so, because there is a power in us which takes us on, another which weighs us down, we say: *Draw me.*

25. *We will run*[45] *behind you in the fragrance of your oils.*[46] We run amidst the fragrances of the oils of God when, filled with the gifts of the Spirit, we lovingly long for the sight of him. We should note, however, that people seek after God at a variety of different paces, sometimes at walking pace, sometimes running, sometimes at a sprint.[47] To walk after God is to follow him without enthusiasm; to run is to follow with energy; to run flat out[48] is to follow him through thick and thin. The time was when hearts could make no move towards God and would not willingly walk after him, that is, before the coming of the Lord into the world was made known and removed human souls[49] from their insensitive condition. For so it is written: *Their feet stood still while the earth was moved* (Hab 3:5–6).[50] Here, though, the reference is not to 'movement' but to 'running': for nothing less will do in our seeking than that we should run with desire. And because not any sort of running will do, but only running flat out, Paul says: *So run that you may win* (1 Cor 9:24). But then some people run too strenuously and are tripped up by their lack of judgment: they know all too much, more than they need, and they overtake him—that is, they choose their own virtues for themselves and leave behind them the commandments of him whom they once followed. Rightly, therefore, before it says *we run,* it says *behind you.* They run behind God who pay heed to his commandments, prefer his will to their own and strive to be with him by means of judicious action and good sense.[51] In this connection, the prophet, heeding the will of God and following it, says: *My soul clings to thee* (Ps 62:9). And Peter, who thought to give advice, is told: *Get behind me, Satan, for you know not the things of God but the things of men* (Mk 8:33). Therefore, because perfect souls observe the commandments of God with the greatest discretion,

and neither langorously fall short of them nor through ill-judged enthusiasm run ahead of them, it appropriately says: *We run behind you in the fragrance of your ointments.* That is, *we run behind you* in so far as we lovingly follow and, in awe of the judgments of God, do not run ahead.

26. *The king has brought me into his chambers. We will rejoice and be glad in you.* The Church of God is rather like the palace of a king. This palace has an entrance, stairs, a banqueting hall, and bedrooms. Anyone who belongs within the Church in faith has entered the gate of this palace. For as the door gives access to the rest of the palace, so faith is the gateway to the other virtues. A person who is within the Church in hope reaches the stairs of the house, for hope raises up the heart to desire higher things and to spurn the lower. A person who lives within this house in charity, walks within the banqueting hall, for charity is spacious and extends even to the love of enemies. A person who within the Church explores its sublime secrets, who is attentive to its secret precepts has, as it were, entered the bedroom. As someone has said of the entrance to this house: *Open the gates of righteousness that I may enter into them and give thanks to the Lord* (Ps 117:19). He says of the stairs of hope: *He has placed a way up in his heart* (Ps 83:6). And he says of the spacious banqueting halls of this house: *but thy commandment is exceedingly broad* (Ps 118:96). In a particular way this 'broad commandment' is charity. The king's bedroom is referred to when it is said, *My secret is mine* (Is 24:16) and elsewhere: *I have heard unspeakable words which no person may utter* (2 Cor 12:4). Immediate access to this house is therefore through the doorway of faith; next are the steps of the stairway of hope, then there is the great hall[52] of charity, finally there is the perfection of charity in the knowledge of the hidden things of God.[53] And, because the holy Church in its perfect members, in the holy doctors, in those who are already filled by and rooted in the mysteries of God, has thereby made its way to the highest secrets and even here on earth has entered into them,

therefore it says: *The king has brought me into his chambers.* For through the prophets, through the apostles, through the doctors who even in this life have broken through to the highest secrets, the Church has gained entrance to that king's bedchamber.

27. We should, however, be careful to note that the text does not say 'into the Bridegroom's chambers' but 'into the King's chambers'. By referring to the King it wishes to show respect for his mysteries: because the more distinguished the bedchamber, the greater the reverence due to the things we are admitted to. For this reason the person is said to enter 'the King's bedchamber'—as a safeguard against excess and against her falling into pride in her knowledge of the secrets of God and in her searching of the hidden commandments. In other words, the more the soul is led into the knowledge of his secrets, the greater the respect to be shown: so a person who has made progress, who has already been raised by grace and has come to the presence of the highest secrets, looks to herself and is the more humbled by that very achievement of progress. Thus it is that whenever Ezechiel is raised up to the contemplation of the highest things he is called 'the son of man'. It is as if he were being told: 'Look to what you are and do not make exaggerated claims for the things to which you have been raised.'

28. But it is the lot of few in the Church to break through to and to grasp these high and secret commandments. Nonetheless, by looking up to those strong men who have been able to achieve that great wisdom by which they contemplate the hidden things of God in their hearts, we little ones can gain confidence, because one day we will receive his pardon and then we will receive his grace. And so it goes on, in the words of the young maidens: *We will rejoice and be glad in you.* In the persons of those who are perfect, the Church enters the King's bedchamber and at the same time the young maidens promise themselves the hope of their own glorification: because as the strong men

achieve the contemplation of the highest things, the weak take heart that they will be forgiven their sins.

29. *The king has brought me into his bedchamber. We will rejoice and be glad in you, to think of your breasts surpasses wine. The righteous*[54] *love you*. This Bridegroom, who out of respect is also called 'King', has breasts. He has breasts, which are the holy men who cling to him[55] with their hearts. Breasts are placed on the cage of the chest: they bring nourishment from within to those who feed on them from without. The holy ones are the breasts of the Bridegroom: they draw upon interior food to feed those outside.[56] His breasts are the apostles, his breasts are all the Church's evangelisers. Wine, as we have said before,[57] is what the prophets and the Law had to offer; but because through the apostles more embracing commandments were given than were given through the prophets, *to think of your breasts surpasses wine*; for those who can keep the commandments which are laid down in the New Testament without doubt outstrip the knowledge of the Law.

30. Though we can understand this in another way. *To think of your breasts surpasses wine*. There are many who possess the wine of wisdom but lack that knowledge which comes with humility:[58] they are the ones whom knowledge 'puffs up', because charity does not 'build them up' (cf 1 Cor 8:1) But there are also many who have drunk so deep of the wine of knowledge that they know how to recognise the gifts of sound teaching, the gifts of spiritual grace: for the gifts of spiritual grace are like the breasts on the chest-cage which invisibly give their nourishment through hidden spiritual channels. *To think of your breasts surpasses wine*, therefore, because these people, who have learned how to seek out the gifts of your grace, who do not attribute to themselves the knowledge they have gained and do not exaggerate the degree of wisdom which they have been given; these people surpass those who do have an inflated opinion of their wisdom and are 'puffed up'. For it is a greater thing to know with humility than simply

to know; and they do not truly know who know without humility.[59] *To think of your breasts*, therefore, *surpasses wine*; because those who know, conscious of the gifts of spiritual grace, surpass those who possess a kind of knowledge but give no thought to those gifts. And so the text says quite openly: *to think of your breasts surpasses wine*; because humility is a greater thing than knowledge. Wine is the knowledge which makes men drunk; the thought of his breasts restores them to their senses, it recalls the mind to the knowledge of the gifts. Thus, *To think of your breasts surpasses wine*: for humility triumphs over any amount of knowledge.

31. *The righteous love you.*[60] This is as if to say, 'they are not yet righteous who fear you'. *The righteous love you*. A person who acts well out of fear may be right in deed but not in desire; for he wishes to avoid what he fears, and he would not act rightly could he avoid doing so. But a person who does good works out of love is right both in deed and in desire. On the other hand, the sweetness of love is hidden from those who fear.[61] Thus it is written: *Great is the number of your consolations, Lord, which you have hidden from those who live in fear of you but have brought to fulness in those who hope in you* (Ps 30:20). For the sweetness of God is hidden from those who fear God and is known to those who love him. Love is perfected, therefore, in a person who, out of love, earnestly strives to live well: he is not afraid of the judgment to come and so is unabashed whatever he may hear said about eternal punishments. It is for this reason too that Paul, making for the rewards of eternal life, had in mind the coming of the judge when he said: *God has prepared* [these rewards] *not only for me, but for all those who have loved his coming* (2 Tim 4:8). The eternal rewards are prepared by the judge for those who love, because anyone who knows that he does evil actions fears the coming judge; but a person who can have confidence in his actions welcomes the coming of the judge. The rewards are prepared for those who wait upon the coming of God

and for those who do so in love: for no one who is not sure of his case loves the approach of the judge. But any confidence in justice derives from love. For which reason it is very properly said: *The righteous love you.*

32. *I am black and beautiful, O daughters of Jerusalem, like the tents of Kedar, like Solomon's hides. Do not stare at me because I am swarthy; it is the sun which has burned me.* We know that in the early Church, when the grace of our Redeemer was preached, some of the Jews believed, others did not; but those who did believe were despised by the unbelievers, they suffered persecution, being condemned for having deserted to the ways of the gentiles. The Church, therefore, on their behalf, protests against those who were unconverted: *I am black but beautiful, O daughters of Jerusalem.* 'Black I am in your judgment, but beautiful by the illumination of grace'. In what way 'black'? *Like the tents of Kedar.* 'Kedar' means 'darkness'. Kedar was the second in line of descent from Ishmael (Gen 25:13) and the tents of Kedar belonged to Esau.[62] So in what way 'black'? *Like the tents of Kedar*: because in your view I am judged to be no different from the gentiles, in other words I am no better than the sinners. In what way, then, am I beautiful? *Like Solomon's hides*; for when Solomon was building the Temple he had all the precious vessels of the Temple covered with cured skins. But the skins which Solomon used must have been especially fine if they were worthy of his tent. Indeed, if they were made into his tent they must have been beautiful enough for the service of a king. But because 'Solomon' means 'peacemaker' we may by this name understand the true Solomon himself; for all those who cling to God are the skins of Solomon, they are cured to the point of being fit for the service of the king of peace. 'In your judgement', then, 'I am like the tents of Kedar, for I may be judged to be like one who has deserted to gentile ways; but in truth I am like Solomon's hides, because I am loyal in the service of the King.'

33. *Do not stare at me because I am swarthy; it is the sun which has burned me.* That part of Judaea which had not found faith in Christ turned its glare upon the sinful part which had. But this [faithful] part may say: *Do not stare at me because I am swarthy; it is the sun which has burned me.* The sun, the Lord himself, his coming has blackened me. By giving his own commandments he shows there to have been no beauty in the commandments of the Law. The sun blackens that on which it shines most intensely. In the same way, the Lord's approach blackens those he touches most closely by his grace: the nearer we come to grace, the more we know we are sinners. Witness Paul, leaving Judaea, scorched by the sun: *But if in our endeavour to be justified in Christ, we ourselves [are] found to be sinners* (Gal 2:17). People who in Christ discover themselves to be sinners are those who see themselves to have been scorched by the sun.

34. But note that that part which turned from Judaea to faith suffered persecution by the unbelieving Jews and was oppressed by the weight of many trials. And so the passage continues: *My mother's sons have fought against me*: for those children of the Synagogue, who have stayed fast in their unbelief, wage a war of persecution against the believing children of the Synagogue.

35. But when persecution befell those who had turned away from the Jews to the faith, they departed to preach to the gentiles; they abandoned Judaea and went to evangelise the gentiles.[63] Hence, the text continues, *they made me keeper of the vineyards; but my own vineyards I have not kept*: 'because, the Jewish people, by their persecution of me, made me a guardian of the churches'. *But my own vineyard I have not kept*: that is to say, I abandoned Judaea. And so Paul and the apostles who were with him said: . . . *to us has been sent the message of his salvation . . . but. .. since you judge yourselves unworthy, behold, we turn to the gentiles* (Acts 13:26, 46) In other words, 'We wanted to guard our

vineyard, but because you yourselves have spurned us, we have turned away to the custody of other vineyards.'

36. What we have said concerning the Synagogue converted[64] to faith we can now say of the Church called to faith: *I am black but beautiful, O daughters of Jerusalem.* The Church which emerged from among the gentiles looks on the souls of the faithful which it sees and calls them 'daughters of Jerusalem'. Jerusalem, in fact, means 'vision of peace'. She contemplates what has happened and what is now done: and, lest she should be proud, she confesses her past faults; lest she should be ungrateful, she acknowledges her present life; and she says: *I am black but beautiful.* 'Black' in merits, 'beautiful' in grace; 'black' on account of her past life, 'beautiful' on account of her subsequent record. In what way is she black? *Like the tents of Kedar.* The tents of Kedar belonged to the gentiles; they were tents of darkness. And the gentiles were told: *once you were darkness, now you are light in the Lord* (Eph 5:8). In what way is she beautiful? *Like Solomon's hides.* We were cured by penance. Our flesh was put to death through penance just as a hide is treated for the service of a king. Those who beat themselves in penance make themselves to be members of Christ. The members of Christ, therefore, who have punished themselves by penance are Solomon's hides, because their flesh has been done to death.

37. Notice, however, that there were some Jewish Christians who deemed the gentiles unworthy to be received into the faith. And so they complained to Peter when he received Cornelius.[65] In response to which, on behalf of the Church of the gentiles, it continues: *Do not gaze upon me because I am swarthy.* 'Do not despise me because of my gentile unbelief, do not despise my earlier sins, pay no attention to what I was'. Why? *It is the sun which has burned me.*[66] The sun scorches blacker what it burns, the more narrowly its rays are focussed and concentrated.[67] When God gives a rigorous[68] judgment, it is as if he were emphasising this concentration of focus; and he burns the

skin as he shines more intensely: because it is when he concentrates this focus[69] in penetrating detail that he is said to judge strictly.[70] When he looks upon our works mercifully he is like the sun witholding its rays; when he thinks of our actions rigorously it is as if he were showing his power in concentrated intensity.[71] For this reason the Church says: 'That is why I am swarthy and a sinner: it is the sun which has scorched me: for while my Creator left me to my own devices, I wandered into erroneous ways.'

38. But, O tortured and abandoned one, what have you deserved? What have you gained from your gift? *My mother's sons have fought against me.* The 'mother's sons' are the apostles. The mother of all is the heavenly Jerusalem. They themselves have fought against the Church because in bringing her by their preaching from unbelief to belief they stabbed her with their lances. Paul speaks like a fighter when he says: *We destroy arguments and every proud obstacle to the knowledge of God* (2 Cor 10:4–5).[72] A person who lays pride low is a fighter. These fighters, that is to say, these sons of mother Jerusalem, fought to rid the Church of error and to found it in justice. *My mother's sons have fought against me.* And what have these warriors done? *They made me keeper of the vineyards.* The vineyards of the Church are the virtues which bear fruit: for 'in fighting off the vices in me they set my evil works to flight. They made me rich in fruit and in desire for virtue. They made me guardian of the vineyards so that they would yield a good harvest'. And after the expulsion she can say with special emphasis: *My own vineyards I have not kept.* For the vineyard of the Church is its old habits of error; that is, when she is made guardian of the virtues, she abandons that vineyard which is its old habits of error.[73]

39. We have spoken of the Synagogue which turns to faith[74] and we have spoken of the converted gentiles; now we can speak of the whole Church at once and more particularly of what may be applied to each individual soul. There are mean-minded students who take no thought for

what their teachers are but only for what they were; on the other hand, there are honest-minded teachers who both admit what they once were and make known what they are: this, so that sinners may not hide themselves nor, on the other hand, ungratefully deny what gifts they have received. So the Church says in their name: *I am black but beautiful.* 'Black for my own part, made beautiful by what I have been given; black on account of my past, beautiful because of what I shall become in the future'. In what way black? In what way beautiful? 'Black' *like the tents of Kedar,* beautiful *like the curtains of Solomon.* It is an injustice to think of a person's past life; one ought to have regard not for what a person was, more for what he is. Consequently it goes on: *Do not gaze at me because I am swarthy; it is the sun which has burned me.* Sometimes in the sacred Scriptures the sun stands for the excessive burning of earthly desires. So we ask, Why swarthy? *It is the sun which has burned me,* because in the eyes of the Bridegroom I have been scorched by the heat of an earthly love: I have become ugly in the sight of the King.

40. *My mother's sons have fought against me.* In all of creation two natures have been created which are endowed with reason: the human and the angelic. The angel fell and seduced the man. But the mother of all creatures is the kindness and power of God. Both the angels and ourselves, because we were made rational creatures, share a sort of common brotherhood. But because the angels are created by the same power as we ourselves are, those angels who fell wage daily warfare against us, and so she[75] says: *My mother's sons have fought against me.* Take note, moreover, that when these rational spirits fight, these spirit children of their mother, when they wage war on the soul, they burden it with earthly things, causing it to be preoccupied with worldly business, to be anxious for matters of the moment.[76] For which reason it continues: *They have made me guardian of the vineyards, but my own vineyard I have not kept.* Vineyards stand for worldly affairs. It is like saying:

'They made me guardian of the business of this world'. And what then? 'My vineyard, that is, my soul, my life, my mind, I have neglected to care for: for while I was absorbed outside myself in the business of worldly affairs, I failed to keep watch over things within.' There are many who view themselves in the light of what is most immediate, not in accordance with what they are. What is most immediate to them is status or their roles in the world. And in the course of caring for the immediate, they neglect to watch over themselves. And so it says:[77] *They made me guardian of the vineyards, but my own vineyard I have not kept*. This means: 'While I was preoccupied with my behaviour in the world I neglected to keep watch within.'

41. Notice, however, that the soul, once restored to the grace of its Creator, would now wish to love, would now demand to know where its Redeemer is to be found. So it continues: *Tell me, you whom my soul loves, where you pasture*[78] *your flock, where you lie down at noon*. At noon the sun is at its hottest. A person who burns with faith burns with passionate love. This Bridegroom, who later on is called a 'young stag' (Sg 2:17), feeds the green grass of the virtues to their hearts, he lies down in the heart at noon, in the fire of charity.[79] *Tell me, you whom my soul loves, where you pasture your flock, where you lie down at noon*.

42. 'Why do you wish to know where he pastures, where he lies down?' She gives[80] the reason for her questions: *lest I begin to wander astray after the flocks of your companions*. The companions of God are his friends, members of his household, that is, all who lead a good life. But many have the appearance of being companions and are not so. For there are many teachers who offer misguided teachings, appearing to be companions though they turn out to be enemies. While they were still teachers, Arius, Sabellius, and Montanus seemed to be companions; but when they were carefully enquired into, they were seen to be enemies. There are too many faithful souls who, though they cling fast to the word of God, nonetheless in the course of

searching for what is profitable to them in their teachers do not know how to guard against the words of misguided teachers and are the losers by what they hear from them. How many are those peoples who came to the faith thanks to the companions, but, as they followed them, wandered into error among the flocks of those companions. Therefore it says: *Tell me where you will pasture, where you will lie down*[81] *at noon lest I begin to wander astray after the flocks of your companions*. Which is as if to say: 'Tell me, in whose hearts do you truly rest, so may I not begin to stray after the flocks of those who seem to be your companions, those who have the reputation of belonging to your household, but in truth do not.' All priests, all teachers are companions of God as far as appearances go; but in their lives many are not companions but enemies.

43. But what we have said of heretical teachers applies equally well to Catholics who fail in their lives. Many young people among the faithful of the Church desire to live well, they want to persevere in right-living ways, they look up to the lives of the priests who are held up before them; but because those priests themselves do not live good lives, because those who preside do not live well, those who follow them wander into false paths. As if in the name of these young and faithful ones, the Church says: *Tell me, you whom my soul loves, where you pasture*[82] *your flock, where you lie down at noon*. 'Show me which is the life of those who truly serve you; so that I may know where you pasture [your flocks] on the green grass of virtue, and that I may know where you lie down at noon—that is to say, where you bask in the fire of charity; for otherwise while watching the flocks of your companions I may myself begin to wander into error, not knowing whose words and doctrines to trust'. All who listen, all who are uncertain, ought to think carefully to whose words they give credence, whose teaching they should accept and whose example to follow.

44. Next, note the Bridegroom's words in response to the Bride:[83] *If you do not know yourself,*[84] *O fair among women, depart and follow in the tracks of the flock and pasture your kids beside the shepherds' tents.*[85] To know herself: that is all a soul need care for. To know yourself is to know that you are made in the image of God.[86] So if a person is made in the image of God he should not seek to become like the beasts of burden, which is to become dissipated in excessive or immediate desire. Elsewhere this ignorance is referred to in this way: *A man in the midst of his pomp cannot understand; he is like the dumb beasts of burden and his fate will be theirs* (Ps 48:12). The tracks of the flocks are like the to-ing and fro-ing of a crowd, which, the more it changes course, the more it finds its way blocked, the more it is led astray.[87] And so the Church says: *If you do not know yourself, O fair among women, depart and follow in the tracks of the flock and pasture your kids beside the shepherds' tents.* 'So are you, disfigured by ignorance, made fair by faith among other souls.' Clearly that is addressed to the Church of the elect. *If you do not know yourself,* that is, 'if you do not know this truth that you are made in my image, *depart,* that is, leave. But if what you do not know is by whom you are made, *depart and leave,* take to *the tracks of the flock,* follow not my example but the example of the crowd. *And pasture your kids beside the shepherds' tents.* Our 'kids' are the urgings of fleshly desire, they are our forbidden temptations. *Follow in the tracks of the flocks,* leave to follow the example of the herd. *And pasture your kids,* that is, feed your fleshly desires, no longer your spiritual senses but your fleshly desires.[88] Leave to be beside the shepherds' tents. If you pasture sheep, you feed them among the tents of the shepherds—that is, among the teachings of the masters, of the apostles and prophets. But if you pasture your kids, pasture them beside the shepherds' tents; so that you will have the name Christian by faith, rather than works, because you will be seen to be within by faith, and not within

by works. Yet look how you have complained, look how you have protested—(and what do you not say about your involvement in religious observance?)—Therefore, declare yourself!

45. In fact it goes on: *I compare you, my love, to the horses of Pharoah's chariots*. All those who are slaves to intemperance, to pride, to greed, to envy and falsehood have been to that extent harnessed to Pharoah's chariot; they are, as it were, horses in yoke to Pharoah's chariot and thus are in the power of the devil. But anyone who is alive in humility, in chastity, in sound teaching and in charity has become a horse of our Creator, harnessed to the chariot of God, with God as the charioteer. And so he was told, whom the Lord had already harnessed, *It hurts you to kick against the goads* (Acts 26:14), which is like saying: 'You are my horse: you cannot any longer resist the goad, for I am your master'. Elsewhere these horses are referred to thus: *Thou dost trample the sea with thy horses, the surging of mighty waters* (Hab 3:15). And so God has his chariots: for he is the master of the souls of the saints and he drives where he wills with these holy souls. Hence it is written: *Ten thousand are the chariots of God, many thousands are those who rejoice* (Ps 67:17). Pharoah has his chariots; but they were sunk beneath the Red Sea, because a great number of sinners were transformed by baptism.[89] Consequently, the Bridegroom says: *I compare you, my love, to the horses of Pharoah's chariots*, meaning: 'While you were still yoked to Pharoah's chariots, while you were enslaved to the devil's works, I compared you to my own team of horses. For I knew what I would work in you by predestination, and I have compared you to my own horses.' For God sees the many who are still slaves to intemperance and greed; but yet in his secret counsels he thinks of what he has already determined for them: for God has his horses, though he can see that many of them are as yet horses of Pharoah.

46. And because he knows in his mysterious ways that in his hidden foreordaining[90] they will be turned to good,

he thinks of them as already like his own horses: for he sees that they will be led to his own chariots who formerly were harnessed to Pharoah's. And so we must give thought to these hidden judgments: there are many who, because of their preaching and their wisdom, because of their charity, their generosity, and their patience in suffering seem to be horses of God; but yet in the hidden judgment of God they are compared to Pharoah's horses; and there are as many who, because of their greed and their pride, because of their envy and their intemperance, seem to be horses of Pharoah; but in the secret judgments of God are compared to God's horses: for he sees that the first will turn from good to evil, the others will be brought from evil to good things. Therefore, just as, in the strictness of his judgment,[91] many who seem to be the horses of God later fall into evil and become horses of Pharoah; so many seem to be horses of Pharoah who, through mercy are compared to the horses of God because they are his chosen ones on account of the holy life to which, in the end, they will devote themselves. And so the Bridegroom gives gentle encouragement and says: *I compare you, my love, to the horses of Pharoah's chariots.* That is: 'You were still enslaved, harnessed to Pharoah's chariots, you were running under the yoke of vice; but I have regard to what I have predestined for you. I compare you to my own cavalry; that is, I have had regard to your likeness to my chosen ones'.[92]

HERE ENDS THE BLESSED POPE GREGORY'S EXPLANATION OF THE SONGS OF SONGS.[93]

NOTES

1. Here the editor, as sometimes elsewhere in the text of Gregory, uses the plural form, consistently with the view of the text as containing a number of songs; see para. 6 below.

2. The title, as Verbraken comments, is obviously an editor's, since it explains the origin of the text. For an account of the MS tradition and the history of the text, see Verbraken's Introduction to *CCSL*. According to Bélanger, the 'notes' in question are those taken down by Claudius from Gregory's verbal exposition (SCh, 68, n. 2). An ambiguity: the Latin reads '. . . expositio in Canticis Canticorum a capite de exceda relevata . . .' which could be translated otherwise as 'a Commentary on the *Songs of Songs* beginning from the first verse, reconstructed from the notes . . . etc'. Thus Bélanger for his translation in SCh. But this seems unlikely, because hardly worth saying. On the other hand, the translation I have given, suggesting as it does that the editor had available to him only the torso we now possess, is also problematic. See P Verbraken, 'La Tradition Manuscrite du Commentaire de Saint Gregoire sur le Cantique des Cantiques', *Revue Bénédictine* 63 (1963) 277–288 and B. Capelle, 'Les Homelies de Saint Gregoire sur le Cantique', *Rev. Ben.* 41 (1929) 214–216, for a discussion of these issues.

3. Reading *insensibilitatis* as against the *infidelitatis* of CCL. See P. Meyvaert, 'A New Edition of Gregory the Great's Commentaries on the Canticle and I Kings', *JTS* 19 (1968) 217.

4. 'For the force of love is an engine (*machina*) of the soul', *Moralia*, VI.58.

5. *per terrenas verba separatur a terra*. Meyvaert prefers the *sperantur aeterna* which appears in two MSS.

6. By no means a theme original in Gregory, though as a general proposition on the possibility of naming the divine by means of metaphor it underlies the particular proposition that the love poetry of the *Song* may be read allegorically as the love of Christ and the Church. That the base language of human limbs may be so used is a common theme; see my discussion of Origen, pp. 127–128 above; and compare Ephrem the Syrian (c. 306–373): 'Let us give thanks to God who clothed himself in the names of the body's various parts . . . We should realise that, had he not put on the names of such things, it would not have been possible for him to speak to us humans. By means of what belongs to us did he draw close to us': *Hymn 31 On the Faith*, 1f, translated by Sebastian Brock, *The Luminous Eye*, (Rome, 1985–Kalamazoo, 1992) 43. The Pseudo-Denys speaks of what he calls 'dissimilar similarities', the likenesses of God derived from the things most unlike him, which, by virtue of their very dissimilarity, have little tendency to mislead us into mistaking the likeness for the reality—cf *CH* 141A, Luibheid, p. 150.

7. Accepting the reading of SCh as against CCL for the reasons given in SCh, 72, n. 9.

8. *ad virtutem impassibilitatis*.

9. Cf. Augustine: *De doctrina christiana* II.vi.8, quoted by Thomas Aquinas *Quaestio Quodlibet* 7, q. 6, a. 1, ad 2, p. 345 below.

10. Gregory emphasises the place of the body within our resurrection here as elsewhere: e.g. *Sitit anima mea ut Deum videat . . . caro quid sitit, nisi ut resurgat?*–'My soul thirsts to see God . . . and the body, what does it thirst for, but to be raised?" *In Ezechielem* II, Homilia 8.6.

11. Interestingly, Gregory uses the clouds surrounding Mount Sinai as an allegory of allegory itself.

12. Cp *Moralia*, VI.58: "And hence it is rightly said, *And if a beast touch the mountain it shall be stoned.* For 'a beast touches the mountain' when the mind, which is bowed down to irrational desires, lifts itself to the heights of contemplation. But it is 'smitten with stones', in that, being unable to bear the highest things, it is killed by the mere blows of the weight on high".

13. CCL omits *audirent* supplied here, as in SCh, to complete the sense.

14. Preferring CCL's *per semetipsam figuram* to the *figurate* of SCh and Meyvaert.

15. The passage which follows is the first of three in which Gregory discusses the relationship between fear of God and the love of God, the others being nn. 18 and 31 below. It should be noted that the three-stage progression outlined in this passage—from fear to honour to love of God—is meant to relate to the three-stage progression from the 'moral' to the 'natural' to the 'contemplative' lives outlined in n. 9. For a quite different account of fear as an obstacle to the progress of the soul, cf *Moralia* VI.58.

16. *coniunctos*, which I have translated as 'betrothed', 'since what is indicated is a treaty of marriage'—see next sentence.

17. *peracta coniunctio.*

18. Cp. Origen: 'There are three general disciplines by which one attains knowledge of the universe. The Greeks call them ethics, physics and enoptics; and we give them the terms moral, natural, and contemplative'; Greer, p. 231.

19. Origen: ' . . . he first taught in Proverbs the subject of morals . . . the second subject . . . the natural discipline in Ecclesiastes . . . he also handed down contemplation in the Song of Songs'. Greer, p. 232.

But see also Jerome: 'Solomon, a lover of peace and of the Lord, corrects morals, teaches nature, unites Christ and the Church, and sings a sweet marriage song to celebrate that holy bridal", *Letter* 53 (to Paulinus) in *A Select Library of Nicene and Post-Nicene Fathers of the Christian Church*, eds. Henry Wace and Philip Schaff, Vol VI, *St Jerome, Letters and Select Works* (Oxford 1893) 101.

20. Origen: 'Then too, I think this triple form of the divine philosophy was indicated beforehand in those holy and blessed men . . . Now Abraham expounds moral philosophy, through obedience . . . Isaac, natural philosophy . . . since he dug wells . . . Jacob receives the subject of

contemplation . . . for he gazed at the paths of angels, the ladders that stretched from earth to heaven', Greer, pp. 234–235.

21. The best MSS give the singular form *ponitur*, the majority of the rest, *ponuntur*, as translated here.

22. Origen: 'for this reason . . . he puts the book of Proverbs as the introduction to his work. In it . . . the subject of morals is handed down so that, when anyone has made progress in understanding and morals he may also come to the discipline of natural knowledge . . . And so after Proverbs he comes to Ecclesiastes, which teaches . . . that everything visible and corporeal is transitory and weak . . . And when a person who is eager for wisdom discovers that this is so, he will . . . press on to the invisible and eternal teachings that are given to the spiritual senses in the Song of Songs through certain veiled figures of loves'. Greer, p. 234.

23. This very influential metaphor of a 'ladder of ascent' to God is particularly appropriate here, since Jacob is represented as the highest rung, standing for the contemplative life, on account of his vision of the ladder reaching from earth to heaven (Gen 28:10–17).

24. A neat dovetailing of the allegorical and the moral senses of Scripture. The burden of this theological introduction to his commentary has been to show that the spiritual sense of the *Song* in its reference to the love of Christ and the Church can be grasped only by those who have themselves passed from the moral, through the natural to the contemplative in their personal lives. Levels of interpretation parallel and presuppose levels of progress in union with God.

25. Gregory's dependence on Origen is again very evident at this point. Origen described the *Song* as a 'wedding song, written . . . in the form of a play' (*Commentary on the Song of Songs, Prologue*, Greer, p. 217) and Gregory's assignment of roles is exactly that of Origen, cf. *Homiliae in Canticum*, 1.1.

26. Yet another three-stage account of the progress of the soul in the christian life, an adaptation of Origen's encouragement of the reader to identify with the Bride, 'to utter the words which the Bride utters, so that you may also hear what the bride hears. But if you are unable to speak with the bride her words so as to hear what is said to the bride, make haste to become one of the Bridegroom's companions. But if you are less even than they, at least join the young maidens, who delight in the pleasures of the Bride's company'. *Hom. in Cant.*, I.1.

27. Cp. *Moralia*, XXVII.: 'May he kiss me with the kiss of his mouth. The only-begotten Son of God can be referred to as the mouth of God, for he is like his arm, since the Father brings about through him all those things of which the prophet speaks'. The continuity of the mediaeval tradition of interpretation of the *Song* is nowhere better illustrated by the fact that at the end of the mediaeval period Denys the Carthusian quotes Gregory's words *verbatim*—see below n. 11.

28. Cp. *Moralia*, XIV. 51: ' . . . Matthew, when he was telling of the precepts being delivered by Him on the Mount, says, *And he opened his*

mouth and taught. As if he said in plain speech; "then he opened His own mouth, Who before had opened the mouths of the prophets"; it is hence too that it is said of Him by the Spouse longing for His presence, *Let him kiss me with the kisses of his mouth*; since for all the precepts which she had learned by His preaching, Holy Church, as it were, received so many "kisses of his mouth".'

29. This is characteristic gregorian teaching on the suddenness and brief duration of the soul's awareness of God's presence to it. See, e.g., 'Sometimes the soul is admitted to some unwonted sweetness of interior relish, and is suddenly in some way refreshed when breathed on by the glowing spirit . . .' (*Moralia*, XXIII.43). 'But forasmuch as the corruptible body still weighs down the soul, it is not able to cleave for long to the light which it sees in a momentary glimpse'. *Moralia*, VIII, 50. See also, Cuthbert Butler, *Western Mysticism*, 2nd Ed. (London, 1927) pp. 115–116, for a discussion of this teaching.

30. An augustinian dialectic of 'presence' and 'absence': to seek God (implying God's absence) *is* to find God. See, e.g., *Confessions*, I.1.

31. Meyvaert adds *subito*, 'suddenly'.

32. SCh translates *fragrantia* (*l'arôme*), but gives *flagrantia* in the latin text, as does CCL. I have followed the critical text and thus translate *flagrantia*.

33. Again, SCh translates *fragrantia*, again giving *flagrantia* in the latin text in accordance with CCL. Gregory is evidently enjoying the play on the words *flagrantia* and *fragrantia* which I have sought to reflect somewhat feebly by means of alliteration.

34. *Ipse me tangat intus*. See the discussion of *conpunctio* at n. 18 below.

35. SCh and Meyvaert restore *praedicationes*, 'preachings', which the critical edition omits. I have followed SCh, since the rest of the section supports the view that it is not the Incarnation itself but the *preaching* of the Incarnation which is compared to the divine breasts and is contrasted with the wisdom of the world.

36. Here, the most natural translation is 'fragrance', following SCh's *arôme*, but in all MSS but one the word is *flagrantia* and this is followed in the latin text by SCh and CCL.

37. *adiuvante domino*. Meyvaert prefers *adiuvante deo*.

38. *Conpungitur*. This word, and its cognate *conpunctio*, is a key-word in Gregory and pulls together a wide variety of meanings, untranslatable by any one word or phrase in English. The modern English 'compunction' will not do at all. I have translated the noun *conpunctio* by the gerundive form 'being touched by [love]', partly to convey the tactile metaphor, partly because Gregory's *conpunctio* conveys equally the sense of the soul's passivity to grace and the sense of being 'moved' (as by an emotion). For Gregory *conpunctio* refers to a new beginning, a conversion, as here, from fear to love, a new awareness of love, of sorrow and so a conversion of the *heart* to God. *Conpunctio* is therefore the basis of the mature life of the christian contemplative.

39. Reading *exteriora sua danti,* as in SCh, in preference to CCL's *suadenti.*

40. *mens.*

41. For Gregory, three things characterise the christian life: to feed the hungry, to preach the Gospel, and to be united with God in contemplation. Each finds its place within this Commentary: giving alms at n. 18 above; the preaching of the Gospel and its responsibilities at nn. 42 and 43 below; and here, the work of contemplation, which is the apex of the common christian life. The first two belong to what Gregory calls the 'active life', the life typified by Martha's active service to Jesus. The last, the contemplative life, is that of Mary, who sat at Jesus' feet conversing with him (Lk 10:38–42). But there is no suggestion in Gregory's account of this distinction that the contemplative life is the preserve of only a few privileged people, for all three belong inseparably to the common way of every Christian. See *Moralia,* VI. 59–64.

42. In later commentators, for example Alan of Lille (nn. 3–7 below) and Denys the Carthusian (n. 20), the 'kiss' is the type of the Incarnation and 'oil poured out' of the preaching of the Incarnation. For Gregory these typologies are reversed.

43. Cp. *Moralia,* XXIV.8.

44. *Trahe me,* which, unlike the mediaeval commentators, Gregory detaches from the next phrase, *post te.* In Gregory *post te* is attached to the *curremus* which follows; see n. 25.

45. Here Gregory uses the future tense, *curremus,* reverting to the present tense, *currimus,* at the end of this section.

46. This whole phrase is not found in the Hebrew or LXX. For Nicholas of Lyra's comment on how it found its way into the Vulgate, see n. 31 below.

47. *aliquando fortiter currunt.*

48. *perfecte.*

49. *mentes.*

50. This verse is found in the Vulgate, but not in the hebrew text.

51. *discretionis* as in SCh. CCL gives *discretione.*

52. *latitudo.*

53. Yet another gregorian account of the steps of the christian life towards perfection. The christian life is an ascent from the 'moral' virtues, the virtues, that is, of the 'active' life, to the theological virtues of faith, hope and charity; but it is completed in the 'contemplative' life, which is not distinct from but is the perfection of charity.

54. *recti.* In the Hebrew this is the adverb 'rightly'.

55. All MSS give the probably corrupt reading *adhaerentium.* I have accepted SCh's amendment to *adhaerentes.*

56. A repetition illustrating the unrevised state of the text.

57. See n. 16 above, where Gregory contrasts the breasts of God as the preaching of the Incarnation with wine as the 'wisdom of the philosophers'; and n. 19, where wine stands for the knowledge of God in this life as distinct from that of final vision.

58. Paraphrase for *cognitionem humilitatis.*

59. *Plus enim humiliter sapere quam sapere; neque enim vere sapere est, humiliter non sapere.*

60. There follows a further discussion of the relationship between fear and love. See note 15 above.

61. Cp. *Moralia* VI. 58: '. . . often at one and the same time love stimulates inactive souls to work, and fear keeps back restless souls in the exercise of contemplation. For a weight of fear is an anchor of the heart . . . Whence it is necessary that whoever eagerly prosecutes the exercise of contemplation, first questions himself with particularity, how much he loves'.

62. This reference is not found in *Samuel.*

63. Again the repetition indicates an unrevised text.

64. Reading *conversa* and *vocata* after SCh as against *conversam* and *vocatam* in CCL.

65. Cf. Acts 11:2.

66. The remainder of this paragraph is difficult to translate. The Latin depends upon the interplay between the *districtio* ('severity', 'searchingness') of the divine judgment and the *districtio* ('concentration') of the sun's rays.

67. *districtius.*

68. *districtum.*

69. *districtionem.*

70. *districte.*

71. *districte.*

72. Cp. Origen: 'We may take the Church's apostles to be the sons of the bride's mother, that is to say the sons of the heavenly Jerusalem', *In Canticum canticorum,* II, PG 13:115C.

73. A muddled passage, clearly in need of more careful editing than it got. At the beginning of the paragraph the 'vineyards of the Church' are the virtues; by the end the vineyards have become its "habits of error".

74. Reading *de synagoge ad fidem veniente* as in SCh and against CCL's *venientem.*

75. Gregory gives no subject for the verb. It could be either 'the soul' or 'the Bride', but in either case, 'she'.

76. A personal matter for Gregory, at once pope and by vocation and inclination, monk, who longed for the freedom from 'business' which the monastic vocation afforded him.

77. Reading *dicit* for CCL's *dicat.*

78. In accordance with the best MSS, CCL gives the present tense, *pascis,* 'where you pasture', the Vulgate the future, *pascas,* 'where you are going to pasture'; likewise *cubas,* 'where you lie down', as against the Vulgate *cubes,* 'where you will lie down'.

79. Bélanger points out that this reference to 'noon' (*meridies*) as 'the heat of charity' is unusual in Gregory, for whom the heat of noon usually

represents the heat of the passions (Cp. n. 39 above, but also *Moralia* XXX.79). Bélanger therefore suspects an interpolation by Claudius.

80. CCL gives *reddidit*. I have translated the variant, *reddit*.

81. *ubi pascas ubi cubes*, using the future tense of the Vulgate.

82. Gregory reverts to the present tense.

83. Here, for the first time, Gregory assigns words to the Bridegroom.

84. *si ignoras te*. The reflexive *te*, which is peculiar to the latin translations, allows Gregory to read here a reference to one of his favourite themes, self-knowledge, the *scito teipsum* of classical antiquity. On this, see Pierre Courcelle, *Connais-toi toi-même: de Socrate à St Bernard* I (Paris, 1974) 204–229.

85. For parallel commentaries on this verse found elsewhere in Gregory, cp. *Moralia* XVI.56 and XXX.56; and on the theme of self-knowledge, cp. in addition *Moralia* XI.58; XXIII.40; XXXV.6.

86. For Gregory, self-knowledge is not primarily a matter of knowing psychological facts about ourselves such as might be acquired by introspection or self-analysis. We 'know ourselves' when we know our place in the objective order of creation—that place is, as Augustine says, 'under him by whom [we] ought to be ruled, above those things which [we] ought to rule' (*De Trinitate*, X.v). We know ourselves truly when we see ourselves *in God*, in whose image we are made. Cf. also Origen: ' Know yourself . . . But Solomon says: if you do not know yourself, O fairest among women, and acknowledge that the source of your beauty comes to you from this, that you are made in the image of God'.

87. A paraphrase for *Vestigia gregum sunt actiones populorum: quae quanto multae sunt, tanto inpeditae, tanto perversae*.

88. The reduplication of *motus carnales* once again suggests an unrevised text.

89. Gregory here makes allusion to the christian symbolism of baptism as passing through water: as the sinking of his chariots beneath the Red Sea represents defeat for Pharoah, so the passing of so many through the waters of baptism represent defeat for the devil, of whom Pharoah is the 'type'.

90. *occulta praedestinatione*.

91. CCL and SCh and all MSS have *per discretionem*, but SCh translates a conjectural *per districtionem*, which gives a balanced contrast with the *per pietatem* of the second half of this sentence, in line with the contrasts of *districtio* and *clementia* of n. 37 above.

92. Throughout nn. 45 and 46 as also in nn. 42ff. Gregory persistently refuses to identify the Church with its visibly baptised members. The broad basis of Gregory's ecclesiology is set down earlier in n. 12 where the Church, the 'bride of Christ', is all the souls of the elect, indeed 'the whole human race'. Of course those who preceded Christ can be said to belong to his Church only insofar as they can be represented as desiring their redeemer (see n. 12) but Gregory nowhere goes so far as does Denys the Carthusian, who, while quoting Gregory's words of paragraph 12 with approval, assumes actual *foreknowledge* of Christ

as necessary to the salvation of pre-Christian peoples, see below, n. 3. The important point is to note that Gregory's 'Church' has not yet hardened into an institution with visible, hard and fast boundaries; many apparently within it do not belong and many apparently not belonging are within it. The membership of the Church is a mystery of divine predestination.

93. Various MSS give a variety of other, briefer, editorial explicits.

Alcuin of York

Alcuin was born in Northumbria, c. 730, was educated at the cathedral school in York and in 768 began teaching there. In 778 Aethelbehrt, archbishop of York and head of the cathedral school, resigned and handed over the headship of the school to Alcuin, who remained in this position until 782.

In 780 he was invited by Charlemagne to head the palace school at Aachen, a post which he accepted and occupied from 782–796. There Alcuin established a programme of study designed for the better approach to Scripture and it is evidence of the breadth of this approach that Alcuin brought with him from York a reputation for preferring Virgil to the Psalms—presumably for Latin style.

Alcuin was a lifelong deacon and was probably never a professed monk, though in 796, upon his resignation from his post at Aachen, he was entrusted with the abbey of Saint Martin at Tours. There he held responsibility for the spiritual care of the monks and wrote extensively, including scriptural commentaries, the lives of various saints, and hundreds of letters. He died on 19 May 804.

The extract from his *Compendium on the Song of Songs* is translated from Migne, *Patrologia Latina* 100:642–644.

ALCUIN OF YORK

A COMPENDIUM[1] ON THE SONG OF SONGS

CHAPTER ONE

1. Verse 1. *May he kiss me with the kiss of his mouth.* The Synagogue longs for God to be made flesh and runs to meet his arrival with holy charity. Her voice rings out for the first time in a song of love; at that time the holy prophets had over and again shown her how she should live and had revealed the coming of the one who, *like a bridegroom coming forth from his marriage bed* (Ps 18:6), brings a new blessing to the world; but then, the time for prophecy being past, she began to desire the presence of her King and Saviour himself, and said: *May he kiss me with the kiss of his mouth*; that is, may he not for ever appoint angels, not always prophets for my instruction, may he himself come at last,[2] who has for so long been promised, may the light of his presence shine upon me and, like a person offering a kiss, may he speak comfortingly to me in words of his mouth: may he not, that is to say, scorn to enlighten me as I question him about the way of salvation. We read that this was brought to fulfilment in the Gospel: *The disciples came to Jesus as he sat on the mount, and opening his mouth he taught them saying: Blessed are the poor in spirit, for theirs is the kingdom of heaven* (Mt 5:1).[3] Therefore it says: *May he kiss me with the kiss of his mouth*—may he delight me with the touch of his presence, he whom I have heard so often promised by the prophets.

2. *For your breasts are more delightful than wine.* The sweetness of the Gospels' teaching is preferable to the sour taste of the Law. *Wine* is the tartness of the knowledge which the Law gives.[4] Milk denotes a simple Gospel faith. Hence Paul says: *I have given you milk to drink* (1 Cor 3:2) and milk is food. The breasts of the Bridegroom are more delightful than wine for those to whom a simple Gospel faith has given new life by water and the Spirit[5] and they also lead through an open door to heavenly life: even prolonged

observance of the Law was not able to do that, as the Apostle makes plain when he says: *the Law can bring nothing to perfection* (Heb 7:19). The breasts are to be understood as referring to the teachers who give us the milk of knowledge to drink.[6]

3. Verse 2. *More fragrant than the finest oils*. Therefore the Holy Spirit is compared to ointments, because just as ointment heals a wound, so the Holy Spirit puts vices to flight, nurses souls and heals them. The ointments with which the prophets and priests of the Law were anointed were good, but better are those by which the Apostles and their successors were anointed invisibly. Paul speaks of them as *we whom God has anointed and whom God has marked with a sign* (2 Cor 1:21). And John: *May the anointing, which you have received from him, remain with you* (1 Jn 2:21).[7] *Your name is oil poured out*. This gives the explanation: for it is no strange thing if the members give off the perfume of this ointment when he himself took his name from 'ointment'. For 'Christ' comes from 'chrism'; that is, 'one anointed with oil', and this name is given to all the faithful by the Holy Spirit in baptism. And so Peter speaks of *how God has anointed him by the Holy Spirit and by power* (Acts 10:38). And in the Psalms we find: *God has anointed you with the oil of gladness before all your companions* (Ps 44:7). This oil, the text says, is not dispensed in drops, but *poured out*; for God does not give him the Spirit in measured amounts, for he is full of the Holy Spirit.[8] *Therefore the maidens have loved you*, they being the souls of the elect who have been made new by baptism.[9]

4. Verse 3. *Draw me after you*. The Synagogue first asked for God to come and then for the kiss of peace to be given her; now, knowing that he has come, knowing that he has returned to the heavens, she desires to follow him there. But since she cannot achieve this by her own powers, she begs him to draw her to him with whom she desires to be. *Draw me after you*; that is, because without you we can do nothing, we pray as we run towards you that you will

strengthen us, with the strong arm of your protection.[10] For to run, or at least to finish the course, is beyond our powers, unless we run with your guidance and help. So says Paul: I have worked harder than all these, though it was not I, rather the grace of Christ (1 Cor 15:10). *Together*[11] *we will run in the aroma of your ointments*. This means that working together with you and enriched by the gifts of the Holy Spirit we hurry to our place in the heavenly Jerusalem, following you in your ascent into heaven. *The King has brought me into his chambers*, that is, into the eternal joys of the heavenly fatherland. The chambers of the eternal King are the joys of the heavenly fatherland and the Church has been brought into them by faith, to be brought more fully into them in their reality.[12] *We will rejoice and be glad in you, mindful of your breasts which surpass wine*. It is not of ourselves, but in you that we recall how in all things the grace of faith is superior to the Law, which is to say, we do not extol ourselves for what we have received, but whenever we do anything well we rejoice in your mercy and remember with what compassion you restore us, and how you have been pleased to moderate the strictness of the Law by the grace of the Gospel faith.[13] *The righteous love you*. No one but the righteous love you; and no one who does not love you is righteous.

5. Verse 4. *I am black but beautiful, daughters of Jerusalem*. I am black because of the onslaughts of persecution, but beautiful in the adornment of virtues.[14] That is, I seem black in the eyes of the tormentors, but before God I shine with the dazzling raiment of virtue. *Like the tents of Kedar, like Solomon's hides*. Kedar was the son of Ishmael, which means 'darkness'. The Church says that she is black like Kedar, because she is so darkened by the attacks of the unbelievers as to have been made an enemy of the whole world. Solomon, by name and in his life, was the peacemaker, and he made tents for himself out of the hides of dead animals; so does the Lord create the Church from

those same animals by putting to death in her the desires of the flesh; thus is the Church *like Solomon's hides*.[15]

6. Verse 5. *Do not gaze upon me because I am swarthy, it is the sun which has burned me*. This means, do not wonder if I am ugly before men, for it is the heat of much persecution—or else it is the love of Christ[16]—which has burned me. *My mother's sons have fought against me, they put me in charge of the vineyards, but my own vineyards I have not kept*. The bitterness of persecution by the children of the Synagogue caused me to neglect the vineyard which is Jerusalem, but I am the guardian of many vineyards, that is churches, throughout the globe.[17] The Synagogue is the mother of the early Church, for it was foretold by the prophet: *Sion, you will be called the city, and the mother of cities* (Zach 8:3).

7. Verse 6. *Show me, you whom my soul loves, where you feed, where you lie down at noon, lest I should begin to wander after the flocks of your companions*. Show me, my shepherd, whom I love with all my soul, in whom is my strength and my rest, lest, confused by the fury of temptation, I should find myself looking for where the companions gather, that is, the heretics.[18]

8. Verse 7. *If you do not know yourself, O most beautiful among women, go out, depart, to the tracks of the flocks*: if, being in the grip of this kind of temptation, you do not know yourself to be betrothed to me, leave my company and take your lead from the behaviour of those who have lost their way. *And feed my kids by the tents of the shepherds*, that is, give nourishment to those lost ones who, because they have followed the teachings of foolish masters, will be made to stand on the left hand.[19]

9. Verse 8. *I have compared you, my love, to my team of horses, harnessed to Pharoah's chariots*. Just as I have set free the former people from their terror of Egypt, so you, my bride, if you will but trust me, will I free from the hands of your persecutors.

NOTES

1. Alcuin's commentary is indeed a 'compendium', being chiefly derived from Gregory and Bede. It is notable that although Bede was intimately acquainted with Gregory's other writings, he appears not to have known his *Commentary on the Song of Songs*, making no reference to it in his own. On the other hand, in Book VI of his commentary, Bede made a collection of glosses from Gregory on various verses of the Song, culled mainly from his *Moralia in Job*; most of these are referred to in the notes to my translation of Gregory. The ensuing notes to Alcuin's *Compendium* identify the main points of dependence on his two sources. References to Bede are to the edition of D. Hurst OSB for CCSL, 119B (Turnholt, 1983).

2. Gregory, n. 12; Bede, I.i, 1–33.

3. Gregory, n. 12; Bede, I.i, 37–40.

4. Gregory, n. 13; Bede, I.i, 50–51.

5. Gregory, n. 13; Bede, I.i, 54–58.

6. Gregory, n. 14.

7. These two sentences paraphrase Bede, I.i.86–97, who gives the same NT references.

8. Alcuin's commentary on this verse follows Bede closely (I.ii.99–106) but differs from Gregory's. For Gregory, the *pouring out* of the Bridegroom's name is the Incarnation, not, as for Bede and Alcuin, the bestowing of the Holy Spirit.

9. Gregory, n. 21.

10. Bede, I.iii, 152–155.

11. Alcuin adds *simul* to the Vulgate text.

12. Bede, I.iii, 164–166.

13. Bede, I.iii, 176–180.

14. Gregory, n. 32; Bede, I.iv, 202–203.

15. Gregory, n. 32.

16. For this alternative interpretation of the 'sun', see Gregory, n. 33.

17. Gregory, n. 35; Bede, I.v, 322–327.

18. Gregory, n. 42.

19. Bede, I.vii, 412–414.

Hugh of Saint Victor

Hugh was a Canon Regular of the abbey of Saint Victor in Paris. Only two dates appear to be determinable with any degree of certainty: he probably entered the Abbey before 1125, lived there for the rest of his life and died in 1141.

Hugh was the founder of the so-called 'Victorine' tradition of theology and spirituality. Remarkable for the great breadth of his learning, Hugh offered a systematic and unified programme of theological study combining, as Saint Bonaventure was later to remark, theology, biblical exegesis, and contemplation—and, one could add, the philosophical, rhetorical, and dialectical arts, historiography, textual criticism and the knowledge of the original biblical languages to boot.

In his biblical work, Hugh emphasised the relative importance of the literal sense not, like his disciple, Andrew of Saint Victor, to the virtual exclusion of interest in the allegorical, but as its foundation. He was critical of those exegetes who saw in every obscurity of the text of Scripture an excuse for postulating a hidden allegorical meaning, preferring to deploy the methods of text-criticism to achieve a clearer literal sense. He evidently had some knowledge of both Greek and Hebrew and was happy to consult jewish authorities, including contemporaries of the northern french school of interpretation, in an effort to determine the *sensus hebraicus* of the Scriptures.

The extract taken from his *Praenotiunculae de scripturis et scriptoribus sacris* is translated from the text of Migne, PL 175: cols. 9–28. The paragraph divisions and numbers are my own.

HUGH OF SAINT VICTOR

A SHORT PREFACE ON THE SCRIPTURES AND ON THE SCRIPTURAL WRITERS

Chapter Three: *On the threefold understanding of sacred Scriptures.*

1. Holy Writ is expounded by a threefold interpretation. The first is historical and in this interpretation we are concerned with the primary meaning of the words in terms of the events to which they refer. For the Sacred Word is of a kind which differs from other writings in this way, that in the first place the words uttered refer to events and objects, but then those events and objects are taken, in place of words, to signify other things. 'History' comes from the Greek word ἵστωρεο, (in Latin, *historeo*), which means 'I witness and report'. For this reason, among the ancients no one but an eye-witness was permitted to write of actual events, lest any falsehood should become mixed with the truth through the fault of the writer, either by exaggeration, by playing events down, or by misreporting the facts. This is how history in the proper and strict sense is defined; but it is also commonly understood in a broader way, as when history denotes the sense in which the meaning of the words refers to the states of affairs described by them.

2. The second interpretation is allegorical. You have allegory when that which is signified by the letter is held to signify something else, whether in the past, in the present or in the future. The word 'allegory' means 'speech about something other', for one thing is said, another signified; and it is subdivided into allegory proper and anagogy. Allegory in the strict sense is when through an observable deed something invisible is signified. Anagogy means 'a drawing up', when through something visible an invisible reality is shown forth.[1]

3. One example serves for this threefold interpretation. There was a man in the land of Hus, called Job, who at

first was rich but became reduced to such misery that he sat in a dung-heap and scraped the sores of his body with shards of clay. The historical sense is clear. As to allegory here, through the events and objects signified by the words, we take other things to be signified and one event to be referred to by another. Thus Job, a name which means 'man of sorrow', signifies Christ who from the first dwelt in the riches of the glory of the Father, coequal with him, then reached down to our misery and sat humbled in the dung-heap of this world, sharing with us all our weaknesses, excepting sin. We may ask, moreover, what this fact signifies about how we ought to be behave, or as to what would be a fitting response. Job can be taken to signify any just man or repentant soul, who piles up a dung-heap in his memory out of all the sins he has committed—and sits and contemplates and weeps, not just on the occasion, but rather unceasingly and of set determination.[2] And these literally recorded facts, which in this way represent spiritual realities, are called 'sacraments'.[3]

Chapter Five: *That the literal and historical interpretation is necessary.*

4. Since the mystical reading may be derived only from what the letter first sets down, I am amazed at how unblushingly some lay claim to be teachers of allegory though they yet ignore the primary sense of the letter. 'We', they say, read Scripture, but we do not read the letter. We care not for the letter, instead, we teach allegory'. How, then, will you read Scripture without reading the letter? If the letter is taken away, what is Scripture? 'We read the letter', they reply, 'but not in an literal way. For allegory is what we read and we explain the letter not according to the letter, but as allegory. For what is an explanation of the letter if not a demonstration of what the letter signifies? But the letter', they add, 'signifies one thing historically, another according to allegory. "Lion",[4] for example, signifies, in

the historical sense, a beast; allegorically it signifies Christ; and so the word "lion" signifies Christ'.

I, in my turn, will question you, who thus offer proof, how it is that 'lion' comes to signify Christ? Perhaps you will respond, as is customary in this matter, that it is on account of an appropriate likeness to the meaning of the thing mentioned; for a lion sleeps with its eyes open, or some such thing; for that reason 'lion' signifies Christ since it sleeps with its eyes open. Then it follows that what you have said is that 'lion', the word itself, signifies 'Christ', because it sleeps with its eyes open. But if that is the case, then either you must abandon the claim you have made [that 'lion' signifies 'Christ'] or else you must give a different argument from the one you have given. For either the claim is false that the utterance itself, 'lion', signifies 'Christ', or else the reason you give for holding that 'lion' signifies 'Christ' (namely that it sleeps with its eyes open) is beside the point. For it is not the word which sleeps with its eyes open, but the animal itself which the word signifies. You should be clear about this, therefore, that when saying that a lion signifies Christ, it is not the name of the animal but the animal itself which is meant. It is this which, as is said, sleeps with its eyes open and, by virtue of a kind of similarity, is a figure of the one who, in the sleep of death which he accepted, has slept in humanity, while remaining wide awake with his eyes open in divinity.[5]

5. Therefore, do not boast of your understanding of the Scriptures for as long as you neglect the letter. For to ignore the letter is to ignore what the letter signifies and why it is signified by the letter. And that which is signified by the first itself signifies a third thing. Since, therefore, those things which the letter signifies are signs of a spiritual significance, how can they be signs [of something else] for you if they were not themselves first signified to you? Therefore, refrain from leaping ahead lest you fall headlong over the cliff. He proceeds most surely who proceeds in due order. First of all, then, by careful reading, bring out

the comparison between those things which Holy Writ sets down and their mystical signification, so that you may derive from them a clear understanding; then, afterwards, you may reflect upon them and by means of similarity draw together what will either be constructive of faith or instructive of good behaviour.

6. 'But', they say, 'not everything may be read literally or be reasonably interpreted in that way. For when the prophet says that he has seen a river of fire streaming forth from beneath the throne of God and witnesses winged and many-eyed beasts flying around in circles and crying out (Dan 7:10; Ezek 1:5–14) and many other things in similar vein, no doubt some of those things which Holy Writ described may reasonably be interpreted according to the letter, but others may be understood only figuratively'. But they say this as if it were our view that everything said literally had therefore to be accepted entirely and only at face value; and as if nothing else could be meant by the utterance itself; further meaning is derived not from the letter itself, but is signified by means of what the letter refers to. For even in the case where an utterance is accepted figuratively, it cannot be denied that the letter has its own signification; for when we claim that what is said is not to be understood at face value, nonetheless we still insist that it is has some kind of *prima facie* meaning. Thus, something is said and signified literally, and this is so even when the words uttered are not to be understood at their face values, but signify something else through what they say. Therefore, taken all together, something is both said and signified literally and that is to be taken as the interpretation which is primarily signified by the letter; then, what is thus signified can be further interpreted.[6]

7. In this way we wish the reader to be warned not to despise this primary foundation for doctrine. Nor should he think worthy of contempt the knowledge of those things which Scripture lays down through the primary significance of the letter; for they are things which the holy

Spirit has shaped for the grasp of fleshly minds, which lack the power to grasp invisible realities except by means of visible, as, so to speak, simulacra of mystical meanings; and he constructs a clear revelation, by means of the likenesses he sets forth, of the things which are to be interpreted spiritually. But if, as these authors say, you might leap immediately from the letter to what needs a spiritual interpretation, then in vain would those figures and likenesses of events and objects,[7] by which the mind is brought to a knowledge of things spiritual, have been placed in holy Writ by the holy Spirit. For the Apostle is our witness that *what is of the flesh comes first, only then what is spiritual* (1 Cor 15:46). And the sight of the weak-eyed mind could never have been illumined for the spiritual contemplation of the wisdom of God itself, had that wisdom not first been known in a bodily fashion. Do not therefore scorn humility in approaching the word of God, because by means of humility you will be brought into the light of divinity. All this, which is the external covering of the Word of God, seems to you like clay, something which you might tread under foot, for it is low ground and you belittle the deed which the letter tells of in bodily and visible terms. But listen: it was by that clay which is trodden on by your feet that the eye of the blind man was given the light to see by (Jn 9:6–7). Therefore, read Scripture and learn diligently what it speaks of first in a bodily fashion. For if you zealously impress upon your mind the shape of those events in the narrative sequence in which they are set down, you will by reflection shortly take with you, as from a kind of honeycomb, the sweetness of a spiritual understanding.

Chapter Fourteen: *The nature of the fruit which sacred Scripture plucks—as distinct from other fruits—and why it excels other writings; and concerning the seven circumstances by which the events and objects which signify are to be determined.*

8. The diligent enquirer into holy Writ may on no account neglect the significances of events and objects. For just as knowledge of them is in the first instance acquired through their names, so an understanding, grasped and made fully manifest by spiritual teaching, is achieved through the signifying power of those selfsame events and objects. The philosopher gets to know, in other writings, the meaning of the words; but in the sacred page, greatly excelling the signification of the words is the signification of events and objects. For the first is a matter of convention; the second is determined by nature.[8] The first is the voice of men; the second of God to men. The signification of terms is the decision of human beings; the signification of events and objects is natural and is the work of the Creator deciding that certain things should be signified through others. Moreover, the power of events and objects to signify greatly exceeds in its variety that of words. For few words have more than two or three meanings; whereas any event or object has as varied a capacity to signify others as it has properties, visible or invisible, in common with other things . . . .[9]

NOTES

1. Hugh's threefold distinction of biblical senses is unusual in omitting the 'moral' or 'tropological' sense from his classification. Nonetheless, in the next paragraph Hugh gives a clear 'moral' interpretation of Job and, if anything, fails to give an illustration of the anagogical sense. In any case, it is hardly true to say, as is sometimes said, that Hugh's distinction of senses is exclusively 'threefold', the title of this chapter notwithstanding. It would be truer to say that he is not always very hard and fast in his distinction of senses and not always consistent or clear. In this connection it is noteworthy also that Hugh appears unable to make much of the distinction within allegory between allegory proper and anagogy. For some later writers, e.g., Thomas Aquinas, the distinction is clearer because set within a more sharply focussed eschatology, in which Israel's history is a type of Christ allegorically and christian history is a type of the final kingdom anagogically. See below, p. 348.

2. This is an unmistakable claim to a moral sense of Scripture.

3. But see the somewhat more qualified view of the *De sacramentis*, quoted on p. 124–125, n. 23 above.

4. Throughout this passage I have supplied quotation marks to indicate where Hugh and his imaginary opponents are referring to the *word* 'lion', as distinct from the real animal.

5. This apparently pedantic line of argument is very far from being otiose. Hugh is practising a *reductio ad absurdum* on his opponents' case; their position that allegory is the 'real' meaning of Scripture amounts to the proposition that the words of Scripture themselves have the properties of the objects they refer to and so that the *word* 'lion' sleeps with its eyes open. Since this is manifestly false, it follows that allegory cannot be derived from the *words* of Scripture as such and so cannot be part of the meaning of those words. It is, rather, derived from the significance of the events and objects described by those words, a point on which Thomas Aquinas was later to lay great stress. See pp. 103–107 above for a discussion of this argument.

6. A highly compressed and difficult passage. Hugh appears to be saying that his opponents have misunderstood his assertion of the primacy of the literal sense. It is not that the literal text always and only means what at face value it appears to mean. Of course the descriptions of visionary beasts in Ezekiel and Daniel need to be interpreted. But, Hugh insists, an understanding of the words of Ezekiel and Daniel is still an understanding of their literal meanings, even if those descriptions are metaphors for something other than what they mean at face value. It is what they are metaphors *for*, the things metaphorically referred to, which alone are capable of bearing a further, allegorical significance. It is this passage which suggests that, following Augustine's teaching in *De doctrina christiana*, III.29.41, Hugh regards metaphor as part of the literal meaning of Scripture.

7. Latin *res*, which I paraphrase, for Hugh is clearly thinking as much of the events recorded in the Old Testament as of natural objects.

8. Hugh does not mean that objects and events have their own natural power to signify allegorically, but only that power which the Holy Spirit, through his own choice as author of Scripture, gives them so to signify. The next sentence makes this plain.

9. See the similar comment of Thomas Aquinas, *Quodlibet* 7, q.6 a.1 ad 4, p. 345 below. Both reflect Augustine, *De doctrina christiana,* III.25.35.

William of Saint Thierry

It is now thought that the *Brevis Commentatio*, excerpted below, was written by William of Saint Thierry and not by Bernard of Clairvaux himself, though it is also believed that it was the product of conversations about the Song which the two friends had while convalescing together in Clairvaux; it is thought that these cannot have taken place later than 1124. Consequently they predate the composition of the earliest of Bernard's *Sermons on the Song of Songs*, the first of which dates from 1135, by some eleven years.

William was born in Liège, the date being disputed, but it was probably between 1075 and 1080. It is likely that he studied at Rheims, entered the Benedictine monastery of Saint Nicaise and was elected abbot of Saint Thierry near the same city in 1119 or 1120. William evidently found it increasingly difficult to combine a personal desire for contemplative solitude with the energetic public life of an abbot and theological controversialist and the tensions led, in 1135, to the resignation of his abbacy and retirement to the cistercian abbey of Signy. There he remained until his death in 1148.

William wrote his own *Exposition on the Song of Songs*, but the *Brevis Commentatio* provides the basic outline not only of his own work but of Bernard's *Sermons* as well. I have translated the excerpt from the *Brevis Commentatio* from the text of Migne, *Patrologia Latina*, 184:407–415.

WILLIAM OF SAINT THIERRY

A BRIEF COMMENTARY ON THE FIRST TWO CHAPTERS OF THE SONG OF SONGS, DRAWN FROM THE SERMONS OF SAINT BERNARD, IN WHICH AN ACCOUNT IS GIVEN OF THE THREEFOLD NATURE OF LOVE

1. The love of God in the christian soul has three stages. The first is sensual or animal; the second, rational; the third is spiritual or intellectual.[1] The Lord speaks of them in this way in the gospel: *You shall love the Lord your God with your whole heart, with your whole soul and with all your strength* (Mt 22:7). The first is signified by the word *heart*, that is, by a small organ of weak flesh, and it expresses itself in a loyal feeling of love for the humanity of the Saviour; the second by the word *soul*, by which that first love is given soul and life; for at this stage a person begins to seek out the mysteries of faith and the power of the sacraments with humble devotion; and the third by the words *all your strength*; for at this stage, however far you have advanced, you will still be able to say *And I said, Now have I begun* (Ps 76:11).

2. The first takes such pleasure in the contemplation and enjoyment of the humanity of Christ that Christ may with some reason say to those who are at it, *It is good for you that I go away* (Jn 16:17).[2] By now, at this second stage, a person's[3] heart is aflame, though, being still on the journey, her eyes are as yet prevented from seeing Christ as he speaks to her and explains the Scriptures to her (Lk 24:15–32). At the third stage, a person says, having gained full confidence, *And if once we knew Christ in a human way, that is no longer how we know him* (2 Cor 5:16), which the first person cannot say at all and the second hardly. For when the apostles were in the physical presence of the Lord, they experienced that presence in a sort of holy mental picture;[4] they retained the most pleasing memories of the

humanity of Christ, of what he said and of what he did, of his passion and resurrection and his ascension and of the benefits which have been given to us through them—all this inspired that feeling of love which led Peter, who loved God with the kind of affection with which a man does a man, to urge upon him, when he foretold the events of his passion: *God forbid, Lord, this shall never happen to you* (Mt 16:22). The third step is completely beyond human beings, above them; it is entirely in God and here a person loves God for God's sake, the just for the sake of the just and the good for the sake of the good; not because it is good for us, but because it is good in itself;[5] she is so much in love with God, with the good and the just that she would rather not be at all herself than that the good and the just should not be in God. This is the *love which is as strong as death* (Sg 8:6); this is the strength which came down upon the Apostles from on high (Lk 24:49). For the holy soul, made one spirit with God, can no more permit that she should in even the least degree fall from justice than justice can allow that it should itself fail in justice.

3. But reason's kind of love, falling on this scale between the higher and the lower orders, rules and enlightens the lower, while occasionally offering in service to the higher the hand of loyal desire; but soon it flees back to itself and, as David did, strikes its heart because it presumed to place its hand in Christ's. For *if any wild beast were to touch the mountain it would be stoned* (Heb 12:20); and when the voice calls from the firmament which hangs over the head of the animals, they stand still, do not go forward, and lower the wings of their strivings. For rational enquiry achieves nothing there where everything depends on the experience of love's understanding and feeling. And this highest level of love is like the heavenly firmament in which God lives, but it is not sustained by reason below it; all the same it does, sometimes, of its own accord, create reasons of its own and, returning from the hidden face of God to those its lesser companions,[6] holds them back in their due

place by the greater intensity of its light. But, as it is said in Revelations (8:1): *A great silence was made in heaven for half an hour*, and so, encouraging them in a brief moment of consolation, it seems to say to them: *So run as to win the prize* (1 Cor 9:25). But it is only in the daylight that this word breaks forth. These reasons, however, are not wrapped up in the paradoxes of reasoning but are pure and simple, derived from the pure and simple truth, glad with the oil of God's gladness, honey-sweet from the nectar of heaven; not puffing up the knower with knowledge, but building up with charity; nothing simpler for the poor in spirit, unintelligibly high stuff for the wise; on the one hand efficacious, for we read how it is said of them: *The Spirit looks into all things, even the deep things of God* (1 Cor 2:10); but on the other, firmly rooted in themselves and sufficient of themselves—hence we can understand this saying to refer to them: *the judgments of the Lord are true, they justify themselves* (Ps 18:10).

4. But all three loves, or levels of love, often run together and mutually support one another and in a sort of shared and friendly generosity with one another in which they each abound, give to and receive from one another: for the higher often takes pleasure in and enjoys the delights of the lower and sometimes the lower is filled with and moved by the joy of the higher, with the middle way running back and forth between either and rejoicing in both.[7]

5. But let us examine yet more closely the riches in which all three abound. The first resists temptations; the second resists heresies, while the third sings *I will lie down in him and rest in peace* (Ps 4:9). In the first is forgiveness of sins and the cleansing of vices; in the second, the practice of virtues; in the third the perfection of virtues and a clinging to and enjoyment of the highest good. In the first is the use of the sacraments; in the second, of the mysteries; in the third is the *res* of the sacraments or mysteries.[8] The first is humble with Mary the sinner, aflame with Peter's love, devout and gentle with John. The second is asleep to

the things of the world, awake to the spiritual, and suffers distress because the soul falls short of the salvation of God; it sees but does not discern and is sick with a love and desire to discern. The third hears words that cannot be uttered, silence, that peace of God which exceeds every sense (Ph 4:7). The first harry their sheep—that is, their diseased sensual desires—out into the desert, or, which is to say the same, into the inner depths of contemplation; there, they encounter the bramble bush which is on fire but is not burned—that is to say, the mysteries of the incarnation of the Lord and, wishing to approach nearer through their understanding, hear the Lord's words: *Do not approach this place, but take off the sandals from your feet: for the place where you stand is holy ground* (Ex 3:1–5). The second climbs the mountain and hears from the Lord: *But you, stand here with me, and I will teach you the laws and commandments which I will put before the children of Israel* (Deut 5:31); and she sees the exemplar of the everlasting tent which God and no man has made, and hears the Lord say: *See that you make all things to this model which you were shown on the mountain* (Ex 25:40). The third is buried by the Lord on the mountain, that is, is hidden in his hidden face and no man knows—that is, human wisdom knows not—the place of his burial to this day (Deut 34:6).

6. The first hears the word of humans who daily say to her *Where is your God?* (Ps 41:4); the second remembers those things and pours out her soul (Ps 41:5). The third goes to the place of the wonderful tent, ascending to the house of God (Ps 41:5). The first is in service to faith, the second to hope, the third to charity; and as faith births us in God, hope feeds us and charity completes our maturity, so the first step of love in us consecrates human feeling to God; the second throws off the old man in his actions and puts on the new man, created by God in the justice and holiness of truth (Eph 4:22, 24); the third brings us to maturity, brings us into conformity with God in both purity of mind and holiness of life. For all the gifts will cease, whether of

prophesy or tongues, or faith or hope: charity, however, never fails (1 Cor 13:8). Meanwhile, that highest step, as it were rewarding its teachers and guides and servants, sometimes pours out on them a kind of divine desire, a more than human desire, so that in a wonderful and unknown manner they are caught up above themselves in awe; and it leads them to him and feeds them so that that prayer of the Lord may be fulfilled in them: *Father, I pray that as you and I are one, so they may be one in us* (Jn 17:11–21).

7. Corresponding to these three steps of love, there are in the Song of Songs the young maidens, the companions and the Bride and Bridegroom, who all speak in their turn and in their own way. So the Bride speaks to the Bridegroom: *May he kiss me*, she exclaims, *with the kiss of his mouth*. But there is a language of angels and there is a human language. Human language is the way of speaking appropriate to human persons; and by means of it the holy Spirit reveals his mysteries to human beings in parables, for their weakness of mind would otherwise prevent them understanding.[9] And so the Lord too spoke in parables. What is more, it was for this reason that God himself was made man for all human beings, so that they, who did not know how to think of God, could, through the man they did know and through his teaching them little by little how to think of God and understand him, raise up their rational power of understanding. For this reason, not only did he speak to them in parables; his whole converse with them while on earth was a kind of brilliant parable, so that through what could be seen of him they could understand and grasp things unseen. Of all the kinds of fleshly love there are, there is none so attractive, none found more commonly desirable, than the union of Bride and Bridegroom; and so it is of the spiritual, of the [union of the] created spirit with the uncreated. In the one case the two become one flesh; in the other the two become one spirit.[10] And so, by means of the comparison drawn between the things of the body and those of the spiritual, between the human

and the divine, here are described the Bridegroom and Bride, Christ and the Church or the holy soul, which now, exercised for some time in the first two steps of love, longs to take the third and strives to pour herself out without restraint into the love and the sweetness of the Bridegroom; and out of desire for his embrace of love and for the kiss of his knowledge now says: *May he kiss me with the kiss of his mouth.* A kiss is a sign of peace. And if *our sins,* as Scripture puts it, *separate us from God* (Rom 5:10), when we make satisfaction for them, seeking reconciliation, this is like asking for a kiss of peace.

8. For, corresponding to the three steps of love, there are likewise three kisses of the lover.[11] The first is of those seeking forgiveness or reconciliation; the second of those who have gained some merit; the third of contemplatives. The first is to the feet, the second to the hand, the third to the mouth. The first is when, soiling herself in the dust of repentance and kissing the two feet of the Lord, she wins the mercy of sinners, as did the sinful woman. Now the two feet of the Lord are mercy and judgment, and he walks on them throughout the whole world and on the waves of the sea. On them he walks in justice, bestriding the souls of the spiritual, rejoicing like a giant at the course to be run (Ps 18:6); and if his feet may be described in this way, then aptly may she say of them: *And I will dwell in the midst of them and I will walk among them* (2 Cor 6:16).[12] She kisses those feet when she clings fast to them and sings to the Lord of his mercy and judgment.

9. Then she rises to his hand and offers him the second kiss, for now the faithful soul walks in newness of life and raises herself from the humility of repentence to the hand of the giver; she gives thanks for the gift of his love and for the effects of good works—these being designated by the hand. But it is not that she kisses the hand by right of her good works—for that, as Job says, *is the greatest crime and a denial of the most high God* (Job 31:27–28); rather, she kisses the hand of the giver, to whose gracious giving she

ascribes all that is, in a loving act of thanksgiving—which is what the kiss designates.[13]

10. The third is the kiss of contemplation or of contemplatives. The Bride is now overjoyed by the first two kisses, has gained in confidence; she longs to be noticed and to be made one with her Bridegroom in knowledge and love and in some measure to be made privy to his secrets. This is the kiss of his mouth and is vastly different from the previous kisses. *May he kiss me,* she says, *with the kiss of his mouth.* We must see what kind of kiss this is, what kind of mouth is his, what are the lips of the giver of this kiss, what are the lips of her who receives it.

11. In God, to exist and to know are not distinct things. Nor does the Father receive his knowing from the Son—for that would imply that he received his existence from the Son, which would be absurd. The Father has both his existence and his knowledge from himself; and so, if the Son exists from the Father, so too does his knowing. For the Son receives both existence and knowing from the Father in such a way that both are complete 'subsistences'—or, as the Greeks call them, 'hypostases'; nor does either depend on the other in his subsisting, so as to exist through the other, but they are, as we have said, (whether in the greek terminology) full hypostases subsisting in themselves, or (in the latin), persons (that is, *per se sonantes,* or 'self-expressive'), consistently with God's being one perfect Trinity. This vocabulary of 'substance' or 'subsistence' or 'persons', should confuse no one, it should not be a cause of even deeper obscurity, for it is the language of our insufficiency, it fails to express the essence of the godhead; rather, from its very inadequacy it bears witness to something beyond our understanding.[14] For the language of subsistences is an attempt to give expression to the nature of persons, while the language of substance to the simplicity and oneness of the highest essence.

12. Now there is a sort of 'turning' of the Father towards the Son and of the Son towards the Father; but the first of

these is the Father's turning towards the Son, for the Son is from the Father, not the Father from the Son (though this primacy is one not of time, but of a certain kind of relation, that of father to son). And this 'turning towards' is in a kiss and embrace. The kiss is a mutual recognition, the embrace a mutual love. That is why the Son says in the Gospel: *No one knows the Father except the Son and no one knows the Son except the Father*. And so the kiss and the embrace of Father and Son is the holy Spirit who proceeds from them both, the love of the Father for the Son and of the Son for the Father. Of the Spirit the passage goes on to say *and he to whom the Son chooses to reveal him* (Mt 11:27). Of course that 'choosing' is the holy Spirit himself, who is the will of the Father and Son, who reveals to us the unity of the Father and the Son, one God with the Father and Son. Naturally, therefore, it is the Father's role to reveal the Son, as it says in the Gospel: *it is not flesh and blood which has revealed this to you, but my Father who is in heaven* (Mt 16:17). It is the Son's role to give glory to the Father, for it is written: *I glorify*, he says, *my Father who is in heaven* (Jn 8:49). It is the role of the holy Spirit to reveal them both, as the Apostle says: *What eye has not seen, nor ear heard, nor heart conceived, that God has prepared for those who love him* [God] *has revealed through the Holy Spirit* (1 Cor 2:9–10). And so we say of him to whom the Son, through the holy Spirit, has made this revelation that God has kissed him not with his mouth, but with the kiss of his mouth. We do not touch his mouth: rather we are touched by his kiss.[15] We are touched by the kiss when we are filled with love and knowledge. We do not touch his mouth, for that would be to possess his self-understanding; we do not touch his mouth, because, as it is said, *No one knows the Son except the Father and no one knows the Father except the Son*; instead, we are touched by his kiss (which is what is referred to by *to whom the Son chooses to reveal him*). We do not touch the mouth, *because eye has not seen nor ear heard*. We are touched by the kiss, because God has made his revelation to us through the holy Spirit, for to whom does he reveal anything if not by the Holy Spirit? He, therefore, is the kiss; it is that kiss which touches us and it fills us with his twofold grace, that is with the knowledge and love of truth. And these are not exactly the lips of God, but the imprint of his lips—or, if it does not seem inappropriate to say so, the imprint of his lip: for what is twofold in us is simple in God in whom to know and to love are just one thing. In any case, this imprint is pressed in a holy kiss on the two lips of the Bride, namely, on her will and on her reason, love on the will, knowledge on her reason. But these two, knowledge and love, because, as we have said, they are one in God, are referred to in the well-judged singular *of his mouth* in the verse *May he kiss me with the kiss of his mouth*. And this can mean: 'May the Son kiss me with that kiss with which he kisses his own mouth', that is, the Father, who is said to be his mouth for the reason that the Son is the Word of the Father. And it says in Wisdom: *I came forth from the mouth of the most High* (Sir 24:3). Or it can mean: 'May God the Father *kiss me with the kiss of his mouth'*, the Father's mouth being the Son or the Word (for of course a word is articulate speech which comes forth from the mouth); that is, 'may he fill me with that converse in which the Father and the Son disclose themselves one to the other'. Or it can mean: 'may he send forth the Spirit of his Son into my heart so that we may love the Son as he himself loves him'.

13. But why does it say: *May he kiss me* . . . and not: *Kiss me*? A human bride and bridegroom will usually greet one another with a kind of mutual sensitivity and respect. And this case is like that of Rebecca who, when she met her new bridegroom, covered her face with a sort of veil of modesty (Gen 24:65); and she spoke in the language not of command, but in that of desire and wish: *'If only that, at some time eventually, he would kiss me with the kiss of his mouth'*.

14. There is also another kiss which, *in many and various ways speaking of old to our fathers through the prophets*, he had

promised to the Church and *in these last days he has spoken to us by a Son* (Heb 1:1–2).[16] Where it says *he has spoken to us in a Son*, this is the kiss. The meeting together of Word and hearer, of divinity and humanity, is a kind of kiss of charity. Isaiah foresaw this in his spirit and said: *There shall come forth a shoot from the root of Jesse and a flower will break forth from the root; and the Spirit of the Lord will rest upon him, a spirit of wisdom and understanding, of counsel and strength, a spirit of knowledge and piety and the Spirit will fill him with fear of the Lord* (Is 11:1–3). These are the seven gifts or charisms of the holy Spirit, which shone forth in a special way in the Lord Jesus, just as the holy Spirit rested upon him in a special way.

15. By fear is humility referred to; by piety, mercy; by knowledge, a sound judgment of earthly affairs; by strength, patience; by counsel, skill in shaping means to end; by understanding, union with the Godhead; by wisdom, the restraint of power. Through the first five, Christ binds a person to himself in the human nature which he assumed; through the last two, to the person who was eternally united with the divinity of Christ. For like a good doctor he has humbly bent down to the sick person, has mercifully treated his wounds, has recognised the symptoms, has patiently given comfort to the sick of mind, has precribed remedies for each sickness,[17] while all the while remaining inseparably one with the Father; and in a unique way he recognised God in the very truth of man, for *no one knows the Father except the Son*. Through that which he himself is, the wisdom of the Father, which powerfully extends its sway from end to end, he disposes all things in care and gentleness. And so this uniting of the divine and human nature is a kind of kiss, of the Bridegroom and Bride: and the Church longs for it and says: *May he kiss me with the kiss of his mouth.*

16. There are in addition three other kisses which unite the Bride with the Bridegroom: the kiss of nature; the kiss of teaching; and the kiss of grace. But at this point, having

dwelt at length on the kisses, they are left to the reader to reflect upon.

17. *For your breasts are more delightful than wine.* It is written, *The Lord has heard the desire of the poor, your ear has heard the preparation of their heart* (Ps 9:17). Because it is the way of things always for desire to precede trust, the Bridegroom replies and places his trust in the Bride who desires it, adding mention of the grounds for his trusting her; for, he says, *your breasts are more delightful than wine.* I seem to see the frightened Esther here, trembling as she approaches the throne of the king and hardly daring to lift her eyes to the splendour of his face; and I seem to see the king stretching forth his sceptre of mercy towards her and saying: *What is it you want, Esther, and what do you have to ask?* (Est 5:1–3). And in this same manner the Bridegroom speaks to the Bride: 'Why', he asks, 'are you afraid to request what you desire? You have already received much from me, and those gifts ought to give you the confidence to ask for more. From your experience of these past gifts, your hope of more in the future can receive strength. For you who desire contemplation have already been granted the perfection of the active life by my gift. *For your breasts are more delightful than wine.*'

18. A grape when crushed loses its juice once and for all; and so it is with the world's wisdom or with the knowledge of the law of the flesh; but the more the Bride's breasts are pressed the more they flow. By my grace your breasts are more delightful than wine—that is, they are more abundant than the love and wisdom of the world.[18] Both intoxicate: but your breasts are more abundant in good than [the love and wisdom of the world] are in evil. For the milk of Christian and apostolic teaching is simple: it dissolves all the argument of the logicians. But the new wine of the holy Spirit, which filled the apostles and made them drunk, also filled the blessed poor in spirit, the children of grace, the children of the New Testament, making them to embrace the love of God to the contempt of self; so as to think of

all things as dung and so as to gain Christ. For this reason the breasts of the Bride *are more delightful than wine.*

19. But the Bride has two breasts: one of compassion, the other of praise. From the breast of compassion may be sucked the milk of consolation; from the breast of praise, the milk of encouragement.[19] So as to make those breasts to be *more delightful than wine,* they are scented with the finest oils, for the finest oil—that is, a supreme charity—works its effect on them. And so the breasts of the Bride are anointed, they are smoothed with oil by the touch of the Bridegroom: the fragrance of good example, which is diffused far and wide like a fine scent mingles with the fragrance of the Bridegroom, through the sacrifice of a holy intention and holy desires.

NOTES

1. This manner of distinguishing between levels of the love of God is a favourite one of William's, cf, *The Golden Epistle*, trans. Theodore Berkeley OCSO (Kalamazoo: Cistercian Publications, 1980) I.xii, p. 25. But more especially see his own 'moral' reading of the Song, *Expositio super Cantica canticorum*, in SCh 82 (1962) nn. 12–24, where, however, what are distinguished as degrees of love in the *Brief Commentary* are distinguished as degrees of prayer. Paragraphs 1–6 of the *Brief Commentary* combine elements found in William's *Expositio* and Bernard's *Sermon* 20.5–9, the rest very largely anticipates Bernard's *Sermons* alone. William's *Exposition on the Song of Songs* is to be found in english translation by Columba Hart OSB in the Cistercian Fathers Series, no. 6 (Kalamazoo: Cistercian Publications) 1970.

2. William, *Cant*, 17: 'But . . . Jesus said to his disciples: *it is good for you that I go away* (Jn 16:17) that is, that your sight of my person in its humanity should be taken from you; for unless I leave you, the Paraclete will not come to you'.

3. William somewhat erratically switches between the description of the stages of love themselves and that of the persons who are at them. On the whole I have construed passages of either kind in the latter sense. Moreover, I have throughout feminised what are usually masculine personal pronouns since there is no reason in the Latin not to and some reason to maintain consistency with the interpretation of the soul as 'bride'.

4. William, Cant, n. 16: 'she [the soul] pictures him in a quite physical way and often, by virtue of the pleasure of this sensory act of imagination, deserves to be given instruction and to burn with desire for spiritual prayer or contemplation'.

5. William, Cant, n. 23: 'at this stage a person prays to God as God . . . she does not conform God to herself, but herself to God. She asks of him nothing but himself and what leads to him'.

6. William, Cant, n. 23: 'But just as the rational level always seeks to advance to the spiritual, so it is necessary for the spiritual, from time to tim, to return to the rational'.

7. This extension of the metaphor of erotic love to the relationships between the powers of the soul—sensual, rational and intellectual—and so to those between the different levels of love which correspond to those powers, may have its source in Augustine, who found inspiration in the language of the Song for the description of the mutual cooperation between them. So, too, in the fourteenth century did, Meister Eckhart, *The Book of the Parables of Genesis*, 3, 146, in *Meister Eckhart, Essential Sermons, Commentaries, Treatises and Defense*, trans. and introd. by Edmund Colledge and Bernard McGinn, Classics of Western Spirituality (New York: Paulist Press, 1981) p. 113; but Eckhart's source appears to have been Rabbi Moses (Maimonides).

8. A technical distinction made in a variety of ways within twelfth century sacramental theology, though it is not very clear how technically

William is intending to be understood. Broadly, however, William appears to be distinguishing between (i) the mere involvement in the external sacramental form (*usus sacramentorum*); (ii) the understanding of the 'mysteries' signified by the external sacramental form (*usus mysteriorum*); and (iii) the actual appropriation of the grace which is the mystery signified by the sacramental form (*res sacramentorum*).

9. William, *Cant*, 23: 'For, in view of the weakness of our eyes, not every involvement of the imagination is useless or harmful. Images are a sort of bodily means of transport, and perception and thought are familiarised by the body and its properties, so that the spirit who is given to prayer and contemplation is carried by them to the abode of truth . . .'

10. Cf Bernard, SC 8.9; 7.2.

11. Bernard, SC 3.

12. Bernard, SC 6.6.

13. Bernard, SC 28.8.

14. Whatever is to be said about William or Bernard's knowledge of greek sources, this is a distinctly dionysian statement of apophaticism—see *Celestial Hierarchy* 141A-B.

15. For this distinction between 'the kiss of his mouth' and 'the kiss of the kiss of his mouth', see SC 2.3 and 8.8.

16. Bernard, SC 2.5.

17. Bernard, SC 3.2.

18. Bernard, SC 9.7.

19. Bernard, SC 10.2.

ALAN OF LILLE

M.-Th. d'Alverny remarks that though Alan was one of the best known authors in the twelfth century we know virtually nothing about his life.[1] The only date which appears determinable with certainty is that of his death: 1203. As for the year of his birth, conjectures range from 1114 to 1128, a date nearer to the latter being the most likely. In any case he died an old man who, a few years previously had joined the cistercian community at Cîteaux, where his tomb was recently discovered.

For most of his life Alan was a teacher, being known universally as *Magister Alanus*, though he sometimes refers to himself as *dictus Magister*, 'called Master'. This may simply reflect a characteristic self-deprecation. It may just support the conjecture that on perhaps more than one occasion in his busy career as Master Alan retired to the monastic enclosure. The fact that he wrote his *Elucidatio* on the *Song of Songs* 'at the request of the prior of Cluny' does not by itself show that he was ever a Benedictine, though there is other evidence to suggest that he may at some stage have taken the habit of the Black Monks.

What is certain is that he taught at Paris and at Montpellier, and it was during his time in the latter city that he appears to have been impressed by the learning and simplicity of the Cistercians, who were engaged in preaching missions against the catharist heresy in Bas Languedoc. Alan commented on the superior ability of the Cistercians to communicate at once with learning and in the common speech of the people, in spite of having no formal mission in or training for preaching.

Poet, preacher, rhetorician, theologian, Master of the seven arts, but above all a teacher, Alan was admired for the extent of his learning. His epitaph claims that 'he knew everything to be known' and Alan certainly represents fully the expanding range of intellectual enthusiasms of the twelfth century, perhaps the most vital period in the whole Middle Ages.

I have translated the following extract from his *Elucidatio* on the Song of Songs from Migne, *Patrologia Latina*, 210, which is based upon the Paris edition of 1540.

NOTES

1. M.-Th. d'Alverny, *Alain de Lille, Textes Inédits* (Paris, 1965) 11.

ALAN OF LILLE

A CONCISE EXPLANATION OF THE SONGS OF SONGS, IN PRAISE OF THE VIRGIN MARY, MOTHER OF GOD.[1]

THE AUTHOR'S PROLOGUE

1. Many there are who make offerings of gold, silver, and precious stones, of blue and purple and scarlet stuff for the adornment of God's tent; but I, like those others mentioned, offer goat's hair (Ex 35:6–7). And while rich people out of their surplus put large sums of money into the Lord's treasury, I, with the poor little woman, put in but two mites (Mk 12:41–2). And if there are many who can pour out the wisdom of a Solomon or the eloquence of a Cicero in praise of the Virgin Mother[2]—she who is herself the tent of God, the palace of the heavenly King, the treasure house of virtues—and whereas they are themselves rich in virtue, are pure in chastity, fired with love, I too can offer praise of a sort in honour of the Virgin, poor man as I am as far as knowledge goes, cast low in life, a nobody in grace, made a tramp[3] by the cruel blow of sin.

2. And just as a spark is struck from a stone or honey extracted with a fragile reed; and inasmuch as the tongues of men and angels sing in praise of the Virgin, so too is her praise drawn forth from every creature capable of speech[4] and in all of Scripture the great worth of this mother is told. And so, although the song of love, Solomon's wedding song, refers particularly and according to its spiritual sense to the Church, in its most particular and spiritual reference it signifies the most glorious Virgin:[5] this, with divine help, we will explain as far as will be within our power.

3. So it is that in her eagerness for the presence of the Bridegroom, longing for that glorious conception of which she was told by the angel and out of her desire for the divine incarnation, the glorious Virgin speaks thus:

CHAPTER ONE

4. *May he kiss me with the kiss of his mouth.* This is but to say what is elsewhere said in these words: *Behold the handmaid of the Lord, be it done unto me according to your word* (Lk 1:38). For she had listened to the Archangel Gabriel who was sent to her as a heavenly proxy for her Bridegroom; and he honours the Virgin, filled as she is with extraordinary and spiritual blessing, and speaks a special and unheard of greeting: *Hail Mary, full of grace, the Lord is with you* (Lk 1:28). And when she heard that the Son of God would be born of her, she found no cause for self-congratulation in this news, she did not allow herself to be carried away by this word, nor did she take pride in herself because of her child; rather did she humble herself in and through all things before God; and, never doubting the prophetic word, she replied: *Behold the handmaid of the Lord* (Lk 1:38).

5. Which is the same as saying: *be it done unto me according to your word,* that is, at your word I will conceive the Word of God. And this is what is meant here by: *May he kiss me with the kiss of his mouth.*

6. For many reasons the Son is called the mouth of the Father.[6] For as one person speaks to another with his mouth, so the Father has spoken to the world by means of the Son. For the mouth is the same in nature as the rest of the body; so too is the Son of the same nature as the Father. And a kiss is offered to the mouth; so too does the Father offer the vessel of grace to the faithful soul.

7. The Virgin asks for three kisses. One kiss is the Incarnation. For as in one kiss two lips are pressed together, so in the Incarnation the divine nature is made one with the human. A second kiss is the Holy Spirit's by whom the Son kisses the Father, by whom the Father loves the Son. It is he who unites Father and Son, for his is the love of them both, their embrace and their kiss. The third kiss is

the gift of Christ's teaching, for it is not as Christ that the mouth should be interpreted; rather it is the teaching of Christ which is pre-figured by the mouth and the kiss of the mouth signifies the gift of his teaching.[7] So, she longs for the Incarnation to be wonderfully worked in her; and she longs for the Holy Spirit to come upon her and the power of the most High to overshadow her (Lk 1:35); and for the teaching of Christ to be given. These are the kisses by which the Father kisses the Son, or the Bridegroom the Bride, or the Lord his handmaiden, the son the mother, the pupil the teacher. But Christ, giving praise in return for her longing, responds to the Virgin's desire:

8. *For your breasts are more delightful than wine.* Which is as much as to say, 'You desire my kisses and I your breasts, *for your breasts are more delightful than wine.*' I can read this literally as referring to the Virgin's natural breasts, for the Gospel speaks of them in these terms: *Blessed is the womb that bore you and the breasts which you have sucked* (Lk 11:27).[8] Which breasts are more delightful, which better, than those which gave milk to Christ, milk drawn not by the foulness of lust, but from the rich store of virginity? Christ longed for those breasts, he longed to draw milk from them, so as to experience not the deceitful taste of the flesh, but rather the antidote of her virginity.

Those breasts were to Christ sweeter than wine, sweeter than the most pleasing of all drinks. For wine is the drink of drinks; it is what we mean when we speak of 'having a good drink'.

9. *More fragrant than the finest ointments*, that is, they may be compared in fragrance to the very best oils; for what oils emit by way of fragrance, the virginal breasts bestow in integrity. Because as the one attracts by its fragrance, the others nourish Christ on their aroma.

10. But this same passage may be read in its mystical sense,[9] so that when it is said *May he kiss me with the kiss of his mouth,* for the very reason that that prayer can be taken as addressed to Christ as Head, it follows that it may

also be read as spoken in the name of the body, that is, the faithful people.[10] Because just as the Virgin was the mother of Christ through conception, so she is the mother of the faithful through her teaching and by the instruction of her example.[11] Now the Virgin offers two kinds of example of how to live well: an example of chastity and an example of humility, and she offers them both for our instruction. By means of them, as by means of breasts, she nourishes the people of faith as a mother feeds her child. To the faithful, these breasts are sweeter than wine, sweeter, that is, than the delights of the flesh. For the example given by her chastity and by her humility is sweeter to the taste of the soul[12] than are the most refined savours to the palate of the belly.

11. Alternatively, the words *Your breasts are more delightful than wine,* can be understood in this way. The breasts of married women are fallen flesh, they are the inconstancy of lust,[13] they give the milk of the weak—children are fed on them, the sick refreshed by them. The breasts of widows are the strict discipline of self-control, the restraining of lusts which have already been experienced. Their breasts give not the honey[14] of sweetness, but the wine of harsh discipline. The breasts of the Virgin are the virginity of soul, they are flesh unsullied. They provide the wine of eternal delight, and the honey of joyful rest. Her breasts are better than any wine; they are, that is to say, better than the condition of wives and widows. *More fragrant than the finest ointments,* for the humility of the Virgin is beyond all words, so too is her purified virginity, and they stand out supreme in the company of the other spiritual gifts. For this reason the text continues:

12. *Your name is oil poured out.* For because of the exceptional nature of the gifts of the Holy Spirit which resound in the glorious Virgin, the fame and glory of her name echo throughout the whole world. For whose name but this Virgin's does the world proclaim? Whose praise but the Virgin mother's is honoured on the lips of the faithful?

Whose humility but the Virgin Mary's is set before us as a model? Whose virginity but the undefiled mother's is given us as a mirror?[15] So there is something very apt in comparing the fame and glory of her name to oil which is poured out. Oil restores the hungry, cures the sick, soothes aching limbs, gives off a fragrance, feeds the flame. So too, in praising the Virgin we are renewed, by her example persuaded to take the medicine of the virtues; exhausted by adversities we are restored by her patience; by the beauty of her life we are flooded with light. The prestige of her name is spread abroad, her name is compared not just with oil, but with oil *poured out*. Because as spilt oil gives off a more powerful aroma, so the more the name of the Virgin is spread abroad, the more her glory is increased. Therefore the text continues:

13. *And so the young maidens have loved you*. For the more her beauty is broadcast the more other virgins are encouraged to imitate and love her. And very properly are other virgins called *young maidens* in comparison with the Virgin mother, for she is mother, they daughters; she is queen, they handmaidens; she a great lady they but young girls; she the teacher, they disciples.

14. *Draw me after you*. These are the words of one pleading for the company of the heavenly Bridegroom, the words of the mother sighing for the presence of her Son. It is like saying: 'I have begged for your presence, I have been granted an audience; I have begged for your teaching and I have been comforted by it; but you have gone up into heaven by a miraculous ascension and so I am downcast at your absence and overwhelmed at the thought of the world's disastrous state and I cry out to you: *Draw me after you*.' Her use of the word *draw* is exactly right.[16] For it is not in the power of human nature to ascend to heaven of itself, unless this is something that divine grace miraculously makes possible. And note that just as the glorious Virgin desired the coming of Christ in the flesh, so her every prayer is a yearning to follow him after the

Ascension; and just as she was a pilgrim with her Son on earth, so she will reign with him in the heavens. For that selfsame sorrow which cut into Mary's soul at the Passion, when her Son died, wounds her again at the Ascension when she was separated from her Son. For this reason she pines for the presence of her Son and says, *Draw me after you*. With equal aptness she says *after you*, for the Virgin did ascend after her Son and with her Son's aid. In the meantime, before I will be drawn up, so that I may deserve to be so drawn,

15. *We will run in the fragrance of your oils*—that is, I and the young maidens who have been attracted by the fragrance of your oils, who, in other words, are suffused with the fragrance of the spiritual gifts with which you spiritually anoint us, gifts which are said to be yours because they have been given especially by you; *we will run*, we will not stand still delighting in the pleasures of the world's ways, in the darkness of our times, or dallying in the idle fantasies of worldly distractions, but *we will run*, working with real effort, rising from strength to strength.[17] We will run the course, so that we may attain the prize (1 Cor 9:24).

16. *He has brought me into his cellars*. After the King of kings and the Lord of those who rule had betaken himself into the cell of the virginal womb, he next, after his Ascension, brought the Virgin into the cell of paradise. The word 'cells' or 'cellars' is just the right word for it signifies what belongs to the 'celestial'.[18] For bearing in mind the overtones of the word, the wines which fill and inebriate and release the mind from the cares of the world are stored in cellars; in the same way celestial happiness inebriates the mind and as a result detaches it from company with and altogether removes from it the love of earthly things. Thus we read in the Psalm: *They will become drunk on the abundance of your house and thou givest them drink from the river of thy delights* (Ps 35:9). And just as a person who lives in a cell, as does the solitary hermit, is withdrawn from the

clamour of the times, so is a person in heaven withdrawn from the turmoil of the world.

17. Or else, we can take the word 'cellars' to mean the storehouse of the treasures of the wisdom and the knowledge of God.[19] For we store in cellars the things which we want to keep; in the same way the secrets of the wisdom and the knowledge of God are stored in the glorious Virgin (who is like a spiritual cellar). But when the young maidens—that is, the other virgins—hear the praise given to the glorious Virgin on account of her breasts, they pay their compliments to the Virgin and say:

18. *We will rejoice and be glad in you; the memory of your breasts surpasses wine. We will rejoice* in heart's devotion, *we will be glad* with clapping of hands.[20] *In you,* that is to say in our praise and imitation of you—*the memory of your breasts*—that is, the calling to mind of your breasts, namely your humility and your virginity, is what has drawn the young maidens to imitate you—*is better than wine*—that is, by this means, they are encouraged to be righteous and, leaving behind earthly pleasure, to imitate and love you. And in this vein it continues

19. *The righteous have loved you.* They are called righteous who advance straight ahead along the royal way, swerving neither to the right, as those do who are seduced by good fortune, nor to the left as those do who are broken by adversity, for they are not deflected towards worldly things by love of things here below, but are set on the path towards the things of heaven by love of heaven's rewards; they love God not because of the world, but because of God himself. Or else they are called 'righteous' who are not lame in one foot—as are those who fail in virginity either of body or of mind. These last do not *follow the Lamb wherever he goes* (Rev 14:4), nor the mother of the Lamb. But those who walk straight ahead on both feet, they in truth recall to mind the Virgin's breasts and rightly love her. But they are most particularly righteous who by loving and imitating suck from both breasts of the Virgin, from her

humility and from her virginity, for in this way, they recall her breasts with especial vividness. So Christ is brought into the cell of his mother's womb by his conception; but in the sight of men she seems to have been blackened and tanned by earthly lusts, which is why she says

20. *I am black but beautiful, O daughters of Jerusalem, like the tents of Kedar, like the curtains of Solomon. I am black,* that is, I am pregnant, and so it appears as if I have not kept my virginity intact; but *I am beautiful,* for I am a virgin in wholeness of mind and body. And so, addressing her words to the other jewish virgins, she says: '*Daughters of Jerusalem,* I may seem black in the eyes of men but nonetheless *I am beautiful,* I am a virgin in very truth. I am black,' she adds, '*like the tents of Kedar.*' The tents of Kedar represent the onset of trials to which the glorious Virgin was exposed; not only for herself, but also in the suffering of her Son. She calls her Son's trials her own and she does not distance herself from his sufferings. And so she was told: *And a sword will pierce your soul* (Lk 2:35). Quite appropriately, then, these trials are prefigured by the tents of Kedar. For we read that Kedar always lived in tents; hence his tents were exposed to every manner of storms and gales of wind and rain. And so the Virgin is suitably represented by Kedar's tents inasmuch as we read that she was exposed to trials both for herself and in and through her Son's.

21. *But beautiful like Solomon's curtains.* Solomon's curtains were made from the skins of dead animals dyed many colours. For this reason it is fitting to compare the Virgin to Solomon's curtains because of the variety of her virtue; in her flesh the true Peacemaker, Jesus Christ, was dressed. And because the Virgin's husband Joseph (Mt 1:19) was shocked when he saw she was pregnant and did not know how this had come about, she can be represented[21] as speaking to her spouse in this manner:

22. *Do not gaze upon me because I am swarthy; it is the sun which has burned me. Do not gaze upon me because I*

am swarthy—meaning 'swarthy I am because I seem to be pregnant; for it was not a man but the *sun of justice* which has burned me, burned me dark; so as to colour me not physically[22] but in a hue of soul. For the grace of the Holy Spirit is what has made me pregnant, but with no loss of my virginity; or else we can say that grace has made me pregnant so as to burn me but not as colours ordinarily do; it made me pregnant but not in the manner of an ordinary pregnancy. And truly it is because of my trials that I am black, for

23. *My mother's sons have fought against me; they put me in charge of my vineyards. My mother's sons,* that is, the jewish sons of the Synagogue *have fought against me* in my Son, as against my other self, insofar as they hounded my Son to death. And so *they put me in charge of the vineyards.'*

24. *But my own vineyards I have not kept.* For the Virgin, who was once the type of the Synagogue representing true belief and the good life, later forsook that faith; she abandoned her guardianship and went over to the Gentiles, instructing them with her example and sustaining them by her protection. And so she becomes the wardress of other vineyards—of the gentile churches—having abandoned her own vineyard, namely the Synagogue. Moreover, since we know that in this Song whatever is said of the blessed Virgin herself can also refer to her actions, whether bodily or spiritual, the text goes on:

25. *Show me, you whom my soul loves.* This refers to the time of the Passion and they are the words of the Virgin to Jesus: for at the time of the Passion the disciples failed in faith, though the Virgin did not waver. She is in doubt which of them she can rely on for faith, whom she can take to herself spiritually. For we read that only the thief was freed from slavery, that is, had been incorporated into the Church. And so she is represented as asking: *Tell me, you whom my soul loves,* for I see your own people raging against you; I see the apostles in flight, and so I do not know in whom you live in faith. Therefore, tell me you

whom my soul loves, that is, show me in whom I may be certain you dwell in faith. More openly, however, she says, *You whom my soul loves*, as if to say to you, as one giving voice to her inexpressible love for her Son, that she will not desert him at the moment of his suffering though in the apostles the fire of love should flicker and fail. For she loved Christ with all her heart, she who fed and nurtured the body of Christ and did so in such a way that, for love of his body she cared not for the love of her own and poured all her heart's affection into his needs of birth and feeding, his child's crying, and his growth. To the same degree she loved Christ with all her soul, for such was the strength with which the Holy Spirit sustained her that he set her on fire with the love of Christ, strengthening her in every kind of life-giving and most holy deed. She loved Christ in completeness and power of virtue; it was enough to gain her a title of praise that she was so possessed with the power of love, and though the disciples fled, she, forgetful of her weak sex, stood in tears by the Cross, comforting her dying Son; there in her passion she gave her soul for her Son; yet more, she bared her soul in compassion.

26. *Where you feed, there you lie down at noon*. Therefore, *show me where*—meaning, in whose soul you give the food of faith; *where you lie down*—that is, in whose spirit you rest in charity, you who work in the world through your suffering. And all this *at noon*, for that was the time of your passion. Appropriately noon is given as the time of your passion because, as John says, Christ was crucified at the sixth hour (Jn 19:14). And just as the heat of the sun is at its peak at noon, so the fire of suffering consumed Christ at the time of his passion. This, I say, I ask

27. *That I may no more stray after the flocks of your companions*. The companions stand as a figure of the disciples of Christ; and they, when the shepherd is struck down, are scattered like the sheep of the flock (Mt 26:31). Then would the Virgin have wavered as the disciples did had she remained in doubt, had she felt her faith altogether

to have fallen away. Christ replies to these words and is brought into the dialogue thus:

28. *If you do not know yourself, O fair among women, be gone and follow in the tracks of the flock.* Who can be fair among women if not the Virgin mother who is privileged above all others in spiritual gifts, she, the Mother of God, the shrine of the Holy Spirit, the seal of virginity, the mirror of humility? And so Christ speaks to her: *If you do not know yourself,* as if to say: 'For as long as you love me you know yourself and you will experience my resting in you in love. But if you do not know yourself as the Mother of God, if you do not love me as a mother her son, you will abandon me through ignorance and unfaithfulness and go out after the tracks of the flock: in other words you will be no different from the apostles, not to be trusted in their ignorance and lack of faith. And you who are now a model for others through your faith will, by your example of faithlessness, corrupt the apostles', who, on account of their lack of trust, may be compared with kids. That is why he says: *be gone and follow in the tracks of the flock.*

29. *And pasture your kids beside the shepherds' tents.* They are called the 'kids' of the Church of God whom the Church's shepherds rule. But the apostles, whose faith failed, were as a result neither in the Church nor of it, but through faithlessness were wandering alongside the Church—and this, though their predestination was assured: Therefore I say: 'If you do not know yourself, these things will happen. But you are not without knowledge; I have taken my seat within you in faith, I rest in you through charity. And therefore:

30. *I have compared you, my love, to my horses harnessed to Pharoah's chariots.'* Who is God's team of horses but the Church which takes the bridle of his discipline and carries the yoke of his sweetness, who acknowledges the Spirit of God and is in this saved? And so we read: *Your salvation is in chariots* (Hab 3:8). And this means: *I have compared you to my horses harnessed to Pharoah's chariots.* By contrast,

Pharoah's chariots are those who are subject to the spiritual pharoah, subject, that is to say, to the devil, and are his teams of four; and he works on them and drives them to persecute the people of God and to oppress Israel. But those who are converted to the faith become the horses of God, they bend their backs—that is, their free wills—under the weight of Christ their rider, they submit themselves to the harness and yield to whatever he wills. And *my love* refers to the Virgin Mary, my beloved one, my Bride, special and unique; I have likened you—that is, I have made you to be like—to my mares, that is, to be like my Church, which was once harnessed to Pharoah's chariots, when it was under the whip of spiritual wantonness.

31. For the Virgin is like the Church in many ways.[23] For as the Church of God is the Mother of Christ present in her members by grace, so the Virgin is the Mother of Christ, the head of the Church by virtue of his human nature. And as the Church is without stain or wrinkle, so also is the Virgin glorious. And as the Church possesses the whole range of gifts distributed among different persons, so the Virgin possesses the whole range of graces in herself. That is why we have seen Christ insist with the Virgin that if she did not know herself, she was to be gone and follow in the tracks of the flocks, so to feed not sheep, but goats. It is as if the Virgin should blush at this harsh threat, and because her face reddens with shame her cheeks light up with beauty; and the Bridegroom says to her:

Your cheeks are beautiful like doves.[24]

NOTES

1. Alan is unusual, but by no means unique, in reading the *Song* as an allegory of the Virgin Mary. The first known systematic interpretation of this kind is by Rupert of Deutz, who died sometime between 1129 and 1135 and so contemporaneously with Alan's birth. No doubt mariological interpretations were encouraged by—if they are also presupposed to—the practice, originating at least four centuries earlier, of including readings from the *Song* in the offices of the feast of the Assumption (and later on the feast of the Nativity of the Virgin Mary). See J.-M. Salgado, 'Les Considerations Mariales de Rupert de Deutz (†1129–1135) dans ses *Commentaria in Canticum Canticorum*', *Divinitas* 32 33 (1988) 692–709.

2. In fact Alan, philosopher and theologian, but also poet and preacher, was himself famous for his eloquence and for a sophistication of style and vocabulary which we might see as artificial and overelaborated. G. R. Evans, however, emphasises Alan's 'common sense as a teacher' and his relative simplicity of style in his preaching. This *Elucidatio* is at times almost conversational in tone, 'as though Alan leans over the edge of his (lectern) to take his readers into his confidence'. (Evans, [1983] *Alan of Lille*, 167). Alan himself, commenting on the art of preaching remarks that 'true simplicity is better than a superfluity of words; better a holy plainness than a sinful eloquence' (*Melior est vera simplicitas quam abundans loquacitas: melior est sancta rusticitas quam peccatrix eloquentia*), *Summa de arte praedicatoria*, PL 210:163D. This is a thoroughly cistercian sentiment.

3. *hispidus*, lit., 'hairy', 'unkempt'.

4. *ex omni creaturae significante.*

5. In addition to this *Elucidatio* Alan also wrote *Glosatura* on all the songs of the Old and New Testaments. In his *Glosatura* he reads the Song of Songs exclusively as an allegory of Christ and the Church, referring to it as 'that wedding song, compiled by Solomon, to describe the marriage of Christ with the Church . . .' (d'Alverny [1965] 78). Likewise, in his *Distinctiones* he calls the Song 'a wedding song of Solomon's, which sings of the indescribable union of Christ with the Church', (PL 210:730). However, in this *Elucidatio*, Alan's reading of the Song as an allegory of Mary and Christ is not meant to displace its reference to Christ and the Church. Far from it. The two interpretations are meant to 'read' each other. d'Alverny notes that Alan follows 'une tradition vénérable de la typologie patristique et médiévale: Marie est le "type" de l'Église.' (d'Alverny [1965] 74). See also no. 31 below. For this reason Alan's mariological reading of the *Song* does not add a further 'sense' to the conventional four; it is but a special case of the allegorical-typological sense.

6. Cp this passage with William of Saint Thierry, *Brief Commentary*, nn. 11–12.

7. Cp. Gregory, n. 12 and Thomas of Perseigne, n. 1.

8. This passage illustrates what Nicholas of Lyra was later to call the 'double-literal' sense of Scripture. The Old Testament literally refers to

the Bride's breasts and this is read in terms of the New Testament's literal reference to Mary's breasts. See Nicholas, n. 14.

9. Alan appears to be using the term 'mystical' in a relatively loose way, as equivalent to 'non-literal', not in the strict meaning of 'mystical' or 'anagogical'. In fact the passage which follows illustrates the 'moral' or 'tropological' sense of Scripture.

10. Cf, Thomas Aquinas, '. . . what can be said literally of Christ the Head can be explained allegorically referring to his mystical body'—see *Quodlibet* 7, q. 6 a. 2 ad 5 and Nicholas of Lyra, n. 11. Alan is following the first of the rules of interpretation of Tychonius the Donatist.

11. See note 5 above.

12. *mentis.*

13. *discursus concupiscentiae.*

14. *mel.* PL gives the variant *lac,* 'milk'.

15. Alan's praise of the Virgin elsewhere borrows imagery from the Song, as in his *Anticlaudianus*: 'She is . . . a walled garden, a sealed fountain, an olive bearing fruit, a sweet smelling Cedar . . .' (V.471 ff., Bossuat, 138).

16. *eleganter*, one of Alan the rhetorician's favourite words of literary approval.

17. or, 'from virtue to virtue', *de virtute ad virtutem.*

18. The play on words between 'cell' (*cella*), 'cellar' (*cellarium*) and 'celestial' (*coelestis*) is typically monastic. Whatever may be the truth concerning Alan's relationship with the Benedictine Order (see Biographical Note), the origin of this work in a commission of the 'Prior of Cluny' is sufficient to explain the presence of this motif.

19. Cp. Peter of Celle, 'The cloister is also the treasure room, where gold, silver and precious stones are stored away', *The School of the Cloister*, XIII.1, p. 92, in Peter of Celle, *Selected Works*, trans. Hugh Feiss OSB (Kalamazoo: Cistercian Publications, 1987).

20. *corporali applausione.*

21. The Latin is ambiguous, suggesting that, if anyone, it is Joseph who is introduced as speaking to the Bridegroom in the words which follow. But this hardly makes sense, for the verse 'Do not gaze on me . . .' is put in the mouth of Mary in no. 22 below. It is more natural, therefore, to understand Mary's protestation of innocence as addressed to Joseph, her natural *sponsus*, rather than to Christ, her spiritual Bridegroom.

22. *non colori materiali.* This is a variant given by PL, though the editor prefers *non colori mali*, 'not in the hue of evil'.

23. See note 5 above.

24. The MS concludes with these words: THE END OF THE EXPOSITION ON THE SONG OF SONGS OF ALAN OF LILLE, WRITTEN IN PRAISE OF THE GOD-BEARING VIRGIN MARY, AT THE REQUEST OF THE PRIOR OF CLUNY.

Thomas of Perseigne

Very little can be established about Thomas of Perseigne. It is uncertain whether he is to be identified with Thomas the Cistercian and with Thomas of Vaucelles—though it is now generally agreed that he is to be so identified. His dates of birth and death are unknown, though we know through the dedications of his works that he was writing in the final third of the twelfth century. Nor is it certain to which community of Cistercians he belonged: it is likely that at some time he was a monk of Vaucelles and perhaps also at Cîteaux, Clairvaux or Perseigne.

Two works seem certainly attributable to Thomas, the *De preparatione cordis*, a rambling ascetical treatise, and his vast *Commentary on the Song of Songs*. In spite of its great length (some 845 columns of Migne) and rather loose structure, the survival of some sixty manuscripts suggests that this latter work achieved considerable popularity in the Middle Ages. His writing exhibits a wide range of christian and pagan sources and his habit of quoting pagan, particularly roman, poets appears to have been influential.

The following brief extract from Thomas' *Commentary on the Song of Songs* is translated from the text in Migne, PL 206, which is a reprint of the 1521 Paris edition of Josse Badius Ascentius.

THE FIRST BOOK OF THE MOST LEARNED COMMENTARY OF THE CISTERCIAN MONK, THE REVEREND FATHER THOMAS, ON THE SONGS OF SONGS

CHAPTER ONE

May he kiss me with the kiss of his mouth

1. Thus speaks the voice of the Synagogue which had learned from the angels of the coming of Christ into the world, had heard tell of it from the prophets. And thus inflamed by her desire, she exclaims: *May he kiss me with the kiss of his mouth* for my instruction and my salvation: no longer does he send angels, patriarchs and prophets; for he who is to come will come in his own person.[1] His kiss is teaching from his own lips. So he will come and teach me also with those selfsame lips. But in turn he will patiently receive the touch of my mouth, that is to say, he will not scorn to hear me out as I question him about the way of salvation. It is our faith that this desire is fulfilled when, seated on the Mount, he taught his disciples and said: *Blessed are the poor in spirit, for theirs is the kingdom of heaven* (Mt 5:3). There he gave his kiss, because there he opened his mouth and promised the joy of the heavenly kingdom to his apostles.[2]

2. There are, however, four kinds of kiss: the kiss of the flesh; the kiss of the devil; the kiss of man; and the kiss of the beloved. From the flesh we receive the kiss of dissolute pleasure; from the devil a poisoned kiss; from man the kiss of kith and kin;[3] and from the beloved a holy kiss. The first is attributed in Proverbs to the vain woman: *She seized the young man and kissed him* (Prov 7:13). The second is the kiss which Joab gave to Amasa when he seized his chin and kissed him, saying: *Welcome, brother* and killed him (2 Sam 20:9)[4] and the kiss which Judas gave when he said *Hail, Rabbi* and betrayed him (Mt 26:49). The third is the

kiss which Isaac gave to Jacob his son, saying: *Give me a kiss, my son* (Gen 27:26). The Apostle refers to the fourth when he says: *Greet one another with a holy kiss* (Rom 16:6). The first is evil, the second worse, the third is good, the fourth best of all. But since the first is unchaste, the second evil, the third natural within the family, and the fourth religious, the holy soul chooses this last above all the rest. She scorns the first, she flees from the second, she ignores the third, and longs for the fourth. That is why she cries out: *Let him kiss me with the kiss of his mouth.*

3. There are three characteristics of the kiss which should come to mind, namely, that the lips of those who kiss are joined; that they draw one breath together; and that their bodies are brought close. In the first is the joining of natures; in the second is the uniting of two spirits; in the third is a sharing of things suffered. The natures joined are those of the man and of the Word; the spirits which breathe together are the divine and the human; the things suffered are shared by Christ and the Christian. It is said of the first that *The Word became flesh* (Jn 1:14); of the second that *he who is united with God is one spirit with him* (1 Cor 6:17); of the third: *If we have been united with him in a death of this kind, we will be raised as he was too* (Rom 6:5); also: *if we endure we shall also reign with him* (2 Tim 2:12).

4. Again, in its moral sense, lips are the instrument of speech, and so their being pressed together signifies the mutual coming together of brotherly prayers; the drawing of a single breath signifies a singleness of will; the joining of bodies signifies the sharing of burdens. James the Apostle speaks of the first: *Pray for one another that you may be saved* (Jam 5:16). In the *Acts of the Apostles* we read concerning the second: *The whole body of the believers was of one heart and one soul* (Acts 4:32). Again we read how there was *One spirit and one faith* (Eph 4:4–5) among them. About the third it is written: *Bear one another's burdens, thus will you fulfil the law of Christ* (Gal 6:2). And the Apostle speaks of all three when he says: *May God the Father grant that you may know him in*

one another, so that you may with one soul and voice give glory to God, the Father of Our Lord Jesus Christ (Rom 15:5). They know him in another, who bear one another's sufferings in their hearts and suffer them in the body, and so make those sufferings of others their own by suffering with them. But in the longing for this kiss are found together the Word who gives the kiss, the flesh which is kissed, and the God-man who is the kiss itself.

5. Again, there is the kissing of the feet for the forgiveness of sins; there is the kiss to the hands, in gratitude; there is the kiss mouth to mouth, in love.[5] In the first are the initial steps in our conversion; the second is bestowed upon those who have progressed; the third is experienced only in the perfection of reason. Or again, the first is the kiss of repentance, the second is the kiss of devotion, the third is the kiss of contemplation. Yet again, they are the Father who kisses, the Son who is kissed, and the kiss itself, the Holy Spirit.[6] This third kiss is at once sweeter to the taste, more delicate and the hardest for our minds to comprehend. The Bride seeks, not the seductive kiss[7] of unchaste women, or the natural kiss of married people, but the kiss of friends, the kiss which the Bridegroom offers the Bride, which Christ gives to the Church, God gives to the soul. The lips of the Bridegroom are mercy and truth; the lips of the Bride[8] are fear and love. She[9] who asks for the kiss must be well-disposed in three ways: in repentance, in purity and in spiritual fervour. The first of these achieves forgiveness; the second, clarity of vision; the third an increase of virtue. She must be repentant, so as to be ashamed of her past evil deeds. She must have purity, for it is in a clear conscience that she can present herself in the sight of the Creator in confidence. She must be fervent in spirit, for by means of it she burns constantly with a higher longing[10] for virtue. This fervour combines elements of love[11] and elements of desire;[12] love, for by reason of love she sets her heart[13] with intensity on the good things which God gives her; desire, for on account

of this desire she hurries eagerly forward to those things which, as yet, are beyond her grasp. And so we can think of three kisses: the kiss of reconciliation; the kiss of reward; and the kiss of contemplation. The first to the feet, the second to the hands, the third to the mouth. In the first we receive the remission of sins, in the second the reward of virtue, in the third, the knowledge of mysteries.

NOTES

1. Gregory, n. 11; *Brief Commentary*, n. 14.
2. Gregory, n. 12; Alan of Lille, n. 7.
3. [*osculum*] *domesticum*.
4. Vulgate: 2 Kings.
5. A passage clearly derived from Bernard, see SC 3 and 4; and *Brief Commentary*, nn. 8–10.
6. Bernard, SC 8, and *Brief Commentary*, n. 12.
7. Thomas contrasts the *suauium . . . impudicarum mulierem*, the *basium...coniugatorum* and the *osculum amicorum*.
8. The Latin text of PL has *labia sponsi*, which I have amended to *sponsae*.
9. PL has *eam*, but as the subject of the sentence, this should be *ea*.
10. *fervor*.
11. *amor*.
12. *desiderium*.
13. *diligat*. Thomas effectively identifies *amor* and *dilectio* which combine with *desiderium* within *fervor*.

Thomas Gallus

Thomas Gallus was born probably in France, and certainly before 1200. He was known to be teaching and writing in Paris by about 1218 where he was an augustinian canon of the abbey of Saint Victor. He was recruited in that year by Cardinal Guala Bicchieri to help found the victorine abbey of Saint Andrew at Vercelli in the Piedmont. First prior and then abbot of Saint Andrew's, his reputation spread sufficiently that, largely on his account, the Franciscans transferred their *studium generale* from Padua to Vercelli in 1228.

The political vicissitudes of his patron's family affected Gallus' own fortunes by association and he was excommunicated and exiled to Ivrea, where he continued writing until his death, either in Ivrea or in Vercelli, on 5 December 1246.

Gallus was an ardent dionysian. As he puts it in the Introduction to his second Commentary on the Song, the divine wisdom of the pseudo-Denys gives the speculative theology of the christian life, the Song of Songs the practice. He wrote commentaries on the pseudo-Denys' *corpus* and *extractiones*, or paraphrases, of his main writings; both genres had a considerable influence on the mystical writers of the later Middle Ages, notably on the *Cloud* Author, who translated Gallus' *extractio* of the *Mystical Theology* into Middle English. Gallus' reading of the pseudo-Denys is, if enthusiastic, also revisionary. His tendency was to ameliorate the intellectualism of his mentor's conception of contemplative activity in favour of a more 'affective' or 'voluntarist' interpretation.

The following extract from the second of the three 'dionysian' commentaries on the Song is translated from the edition of Jeanne Barbet, *Thomas Gualterius, Abbas Vercellensis, Commentaires du Cantique des Cantiques*, Textes Philosophiques du Moyen Age n. 14, Paris, 1967. I have not adhered to Barbet's paragraph divisions and I have supplied paragraph numbers of my own. The extensive quotations from the works of pseudo-Denys are usually given in Luibheid's translation, but I have occasionally amended Luibheid where the Latin translation of Scottus Eriugena, used by Gallus, departs significantly from the Greek. Such amendments are contained in triangular brackets (< >).

THOMAS GALLUS

HERE BEGINS THE PREFACE TO THE SONGS OF SONGS EXPLAINED IN TERMS OF HIERARCHY, BY THOMAS, THE LORD ABBOT OF VERCELLI.

1. Jeremiah 9:24: *Let him who glories glory in this, that he understands and knows me.*[1] Thus is the knowledge of God described as being of two kinds; the first is intellectual, this being acquired by the contemplation of the created order, as is explained in Ecclesiasticus in the gloss of the venerable doctor, Master Hugh,[2] sometime canon of our church of Saint Victor at Paris. Concerning this kind of knowledge, see Romans 1:20: *Ever since the creation of the world his invisible nature . . . has been clearly perceived in the things that have been made*; and in Wisdom 13:1: *For all men who were ignorant of God were foolish by nature; and they were unable from the good things that were seen to know him who exists*; and 13:3: *for the author of beauty created them.* Denys, in his *Letter to Titus*, says: *The ordered arrangement of the whole visible realm makes known the invisible things of God;*[3] and in the *Divine Names* he says: *It might be more accurate to say that we cannot know God in his nature, since this is unknowable and is beyond the reach of mind or of reason. But we know him from the arrangement of everything, because everything is, in a sense, projected out from him, and this order possesses certain images and semblances of his divine paradigms. We therefore approach that which is beyond all as far as our capacities allow us. . . .*[4] This knowledge of God is a kind of abstract reflection[5] and is dark and obscure, is spoken of and taught to all and sundry, through meditation, hearing and reading. The pagan philosophers are able to achieve only [knowledge] of this kind. That is why the Apostle says in Romans 1:19, *what is known of God is plain to them.* That is known which may be gleaned from prior knowledge of the things of the sensible world.

2. But the other is the knowledge of God which exceeds the first beyond all possibility of comparison, and the great Denys describes it in *Divine Names*, 7, as *the most divine knowledge of God . . . which comes through unknowing, . . . [it] is achieved in a union far beyond mind, when mind turns away from all things, even from itself, and . . . is made one with the dazzling rays, being then and there enlightened by the inscrutable depth of Wisdom;*[6] *This is the wisdom of Christians which is from above* (Jam 3:17), *and it descends from the Father of lights* (Jam 1:17), for this wisdom exceeds what is in the heart of humans, and so it is said, *the heart of man does not reach up to it* (1 Cor 2:9). The intellectual wisdom first referred to does reach up from the level of sense to the intellect. But this higher than intellectual [wisdom] is a *maidservant of the thrones of God* (Wis 9:4). It is said by the Apostle to belong to the mature (1 Cor 2:6). And, drawing on the teaching of the Apostle, the great Denys the Areopagite has written his account of this more than intellectual wisdom, insofar as it is possible to write one down, in his book on *Mystical Theology*; ten years ago I wrote a careful exposition of this work.

3. But in this book [the Song of Songs] Solomon gives us the practice of this same mystical theology, as is clear at every point of the whole book. And if [the reader] is to understand [my] explanation of it, it is necessary to set out first the meaning of the statement in the *Angelic Hierarchy*[7] that: *<it is not out of place to add that> each intelligent being, heavenly or human, has its own set of primary, middle, and lower orders and powers, and in accordance with his capacities these indicate the aformentioned upliftings, directly relative to the hierarchic enlightenment available to every being.*[8] Denys says this by way of recapitulation and summary of the Angelic Order, having in chapters 7, 8, and 9 given in turn an extended account of the three hierarchies and of the threefold ranks within each.[9]

4. Now seventeen years ago, when in the monastery of Saint Victor at Paris, I dealt explicitly with the question of the manner in which is established the three hierarchies in

the ordering of angels, and of how, within each of them, the three orders or ranks[10] are duplicated in the hierarchies of every individual mind; and these ranks of angel are, at the lowest hierarchy, the Angels, Archangels, and Principalities; at the middle level, the Powers, Virtues, and Dominions; on the highest, the Thrones, Cherubim, and Seraphim.[11] I [explained these things] commenting on the text of Isaiah 6:1 in the passage which begins: *I saw the Lord sitting upon a throne*; and for the most part I repeated this exposition in my commentary upon Chapter 10 of the *Angelic Hierarchy* to the end. On this occasion, however, I set out briefly whatever seems necessary by way of introduction to this work, since the Bride is described first as being in one hierarchy of her mind, then in another, now in one rank, next in another.

5. The lowest hierarchy of mind consists in its very own nature; the middle in what it can do by effort, which incomparably exceeds nature; the highest in ecstasy.[12] At the lowest, only nature is at work; at the highest, only grace; at the middle, both grace and effort work together. The lowest rank of the lowest hierarchy, called the 'angelic', includes the basic and simple natural modes of apprehension, both of knowledge and love, without any judgment of the appropriate and inappropriate,[13] which is just like the angels, that is, the 'announcers', who, in the simplest sense, bring news to the soul. The middle order includes the natural judgments about things apprehended, judging them to be fitting or not,[14] and to it therefore belongs a power of communication which is closer to its source[15] than the first.[16] The third includes the desires for and aversions from things apprehended in affirmative and negative judgments; aversion is from evil and desire is of the good and so this rank gives leadership to lower things, leading them to the divine; this is signified by the name 'Principalities'.[17]

6. The fourth rank, which is the lowest in the second hierarchy of the mind, includes the voluntary acts both of intellect and of love which proceed at this stage from free will;[18] they search out by rational scrutiny an appropriate

relation with good and evil, and set the mind in order insofar as they can, through a definitive commitment to desire and seek the highest good with all the powers of love and knowledge and to the rejection of all obstacles to it; and the name of 'Powers' signifies this ordering, according to Denys.

7. The fifth, which is the middle rank of the middle hierarchy, contains the powerful energies of mind, those of the natural and supernatural virtues, which enable the effective achievement of what has been properly ordained by the 'Powers', and these are indicated by the name 'Virtues'.

8. The sixth, the highest rank of the middle hierarchy, contains the authentic commands of free will by which the desire and understanding at their highest points[19] are raised in all their power to receive the divine inpourings, insofar as this is possible for free will aided by grace, and the exalted character of this elevation and mastery and freedom is designated by the name of 'Dominions'. In this rank, the mind which is still contained within itself[20] is extended and stretched out towards the higher rays, up to the very limits of its nature.

8. The seventh rank, through an ecstasy of mind, is receptive to the overflowing inpouring of the divine; and so it is known by the name of 'Thrones'; and there are as many 'Thrones' as there are hidden powers of the mind which flow from that supersubstantial ray, which is utterly simple in its essence, manifold in its effects.

9. The eighth rank contains every kind of knowledge of the intellect which is drawn towards the divine heights, although it is not able to reach them, and of desire similarly drawn, though it may not transcend the height to which intellect is drawn. For they are drawn together, and desire and intellect, as it were, walk hand in hand up to the point at which intellect finally fails—this, at the supreme apex of this rank, is the 'Cherub'; and intellect, though drawn up to it, can go no further but there achieves the fulfilment

of its knowledge and light; hence this rank is called the 'Cherubim'.

10. The ninth contains the highest aspirations for God, the excesses and inflowings which go beyond understanding, burning brilliance and brilliant burnings; understanding cannot be drawn into the sublime ecstasies and excesses of all these lights, but only the supreme love which can unite.[21] It is on this rank that are offered *the most pure prayers* by which we are taken into God.[22] This rank embraces God and is wrapped in the embraces of the Bridegroom, this is no knowledge in a mirror,[23] it takes *Mary's part, which will not be taken away* (Lk 10:42). In this order the bed is laid for the Bridegroom and Bride. It is from this order that the torrent of divine light pours down in stages to the lower orders.[24]

11. We have set out the names of the nine orders or ranks referred to above according to Denys' exposition, which may be found as follows: on the Seraphim: the *Angelic Hierarchy*, c. 7; on the Cherubim, c. 7; on the Thrones, c. 7; on the Dominions, c. 8; on the Virtues, c. 8; on the Powers, c. 8; on the Principalities, c. 9; on the Archangels, c. 9 and on the Angels, c. 9; we have shown this in a careful study of the *Angelic Hierarchy*. Therefore, anyone who will read these glosses with attention may, when need arises, refer freely to those ranks, but especially to the higher ones. A frequent and clearly thought-out reflection on these rankings is more useful than any other means, for it is through them that the ninefold [structure of] both the angelic and ecclesiastical hierarchies is summarised in the divine Oneness and it is from this summary that they give birth to the Holy and Unique Trinity in her too; as it says in chapter 4 of the same work: *In this divine yearning shows especially its unbeginning and unending nature traveling in an endless circle through the Good, from the Good, in the Good and to the Good, unerringly turning, ever on the same centre, ever in the same direction, always proceeding, always remaining, always being restored to itself.*[25]

AN EXPLANATION OF THE SONGS OF SONGS ACCORDING TO THOMAS, ABBOT OF VERCELLI

[Chapter One]

12. *May he kiss me with the kiss of his mouth.* Thus should you understand that the Bride, insofar as it in her to do so, insistently *chooses to be lifted above* herself, as it is put in Job, 7[26] and there she receives the means by which, through her effort, she may ascend further, that is, to the Dominions, neither lapsing through neglect to the levels below her, nor elevating herself through pride beyond what is granted to her (*DN*, 1, 589A). Therefore, taking her place among the Dominions, to the extent possible in a mirror, she gazes upon the beauty of the divine brilliance, as it says in 2 Corinthians 3, *and we all, with unveiled face,*[27] and she longs to be united to the primary beauty beyond all beauty; and so is the beginning of union set in train. And because she has *wandered* from his face (2 Cor 5),[28] she prays as if set at a distance from him: *May he kiss me with the kiss of his mouth*, that is, may the Father be united with me in a *kiss*, in the intimate touch[29] of his mouth, in a spiritual union with the Word—as it says: . . . *he who is united to the Lord is one spirit* [with him] (1 Cor 6:17).

13. But the Bridegroom, who is more loving than loved, without any delay responds to these spiritual, burning desires and, as it were, extends his hand—which is to say, by means alone of his grace (Ezek 8)[30]—raises her up to the order of the Thrones. And so, as though brought into his presence by means of her oneness with him, she speaks to him from among the Thrones in the second person: *for your breasts are more delightful than wine.* Wine is extracted from the fullness of harvest; the fullness of breasts flows from the bosom. The word 'wine' signifies the intellectual knowledge of God which is gathered together from the community of creatures into the knowledge of the universal cause, as it says in Romans 1: *the invisible things of God;*[31] see also Wisdom 13.[32] The word 'breasts' stands for

the loving and uniting knowledge, bursting forth from the very spring and, as you might say, 'breast' of wisdom: this is what the *Divine Names* refers to where it says: *the most divine knowledge of God, that which comes through unknowing, is achieved in a union far beyond mind . . .* (7, 872A). On the difference between these two forms of knowledge, see Psalm 103: *From thy lofty abode thou waterest the mountains; the earth is satisfied with the fruit of thy work* (v. 13). For a mountain both rests upon the earth and rises above it and it signifies the mind which transcends its own nature and strives towards the divine ideas:[33] as the *Divine Names* puts it: . . . . *mind turns away from all things, even from itself, and . . . is made one with the dazzling rays* (7, 872A); and the *Mystical Theology*: *by an undivided and absolute transcendence of mind above yourself and all other things, shedding all and freed from all, you will ascend to the ray of divine darkness which is above all that is* (1000A);[34] and it says in 2 Corinthians 5: *for if we are beside ourselves it is for God;*[35] and in Lamentations 3: *he has lifted himself up.*[36] This mind God waters from the higher insights[37] of the eternal wisdom—[those insights] do not rise up in the human heart, as do intellectual ideas which begin from the senses, but come down from the *Father of lights* into the heart of man (Jam 1:17); see the *Mystical Theology*: *Amid the wholly unsensed and unseen they completely fill our sightless minds with treasures beyond all beauty* (997B). [These insights] do not have mental sight, they are blind, they lack reason and understanding, just as the sun throws its rays down upon the mountains and dazzles the eyes (see Ecclesiasticus 43:4).[38] This blinding is spoken of at that place in Deuteronomy (11:11) where it says: *awaiting the rain from heaven*, which refers to the watering of the mountains from on high. The earth is likened to those for whom that wisdom suffices which comes from the objects of the senses and is obtained by means of an investigation which works up from below; Baruch 3:23 refers to *the wisdom which is won from the world*; such people are described in the *Mystical Theology* (1000A) as *uninformed*. These people, then, drain off [the juice] from the grapes of their own work as one does wine; they do not yearn for the wisdom which is beyond understanding and so, for sure, they have not tasted the true wisdom which says: *They who eat me will hunger for more, they who drink me will thirst for more* (Ecclesiasticus 24:29).

14. *More fragrant than the finest ointments*. Notice here that understanding sees and hears and perceives external things and that the external senses are models of the inner and mental powers;[39] they are in this way models of love because love meets its objects by touching, smelling, and tasting;[40] the ointments are the priceless consolations of the divine sweetness, at once countless in number and contained in a single, simple, substance: as Wisdom says: *And the substance you gave showed your sweetness to your children, for pleasing the taste of each, it became what each desired* (16:21); and it gave forth every fragrance although it was supremely undivided, and only love may smell the sweetness of these ointments, see *Ecclesiastical Hierarchy* (476D):[41] *. . . the hierarch . . . spreads the lovely fragrance to even the least sacred areas* [of the Church], *returns to his starting point and teaches thereby that the gifts of God are shared according to merit by all the sacred people without, however, undergoing either diminution or change and preserving all the time those abundant attributes which are characteristically theirs at the heart of the divine unchangeability*. A truly loving wisdom therefore suffuses the contemplative soul with these fragrances, which exceed understanding and the powers of any substance; see Ecclesiasticus, which says: *the love of the Lord is a wisdom worth honouring* (1:14). Notice how wisdom is the love of God.[42]

15. *Your name is oil poured out*: that is to say, the knowledge of you which I have been able to extract by means of experience from your hiddenness, is like *oil poured out*, oil which cleanses, enlightens and heals all my height and depth:[43] *it spreads itself generously towards us, and, in its power to unify, it stirs us by lifting us up* (*CH*, 120B). At

the level of the Thrones, the Bride says *Your breasts [are more delightful than wine]*, receiving wisdom, as it were, from the breast, the Thrones being the royal precursors; at the level of the Cherubim she says: *more fragrant than the finest ointments*, for theirs is an ascent to a higher place than the Thrones and theirs is a richer experience. At the level of the Seraphim she says: *Your name is oil poured out*; for that order learns promptly[44] through experience what is unknown of God, as it says in Psalm 50:8: *the uncertain and hidden things of your wisdom you have made clear to me*; and in 1 Corinthians 2:10: *the Spirit searches to the depths of everything, even the depths of God*; likewise Job says: *he shows forth the depths in their darkness* (12:22) and: *the thing that is hid he brings forth to light* (28:11). And in the *Mystical Theology* it says: *Lead us up beyond unknowing and light, up to the farthest, highest peak of mystic scripture, where the mysteries of God's Word lie simple, absolute and unchangeable in the brilliant darkness of a hidden silence* (997A); and Job again: *He has searched the depths of the rivers and hidden things he has brought to light* (28:11). This is what the rank of the Seraphim says: *Your name is oil poured out*. For it draws sustenance for itself and then pours into and overflows upon the lower ranks, to each according to its capacity, as it says in the *Angelic Hierarchy*: *they are on fire* (205C), for they draw their sustenance from God, that is, from his overflowing.

16. *The young maidens*, the proper activity of the Dominions, are weak, though they are of child-bearing age,[45] and though they have some share in the ancient eternity, they are not yet one with it in intimate union and nothing is made eternal except by union; *have loved you* greatly, for having tasted the inflowing, they long to be raised definitively to a fuller draught. Notice that in some degree he makes known the name of the Bridegroom—that is, what is known of God—to the great philosophers of the world, but what is unknown he altogether hides from them; hence, the Apostle reproves their pride and says (Rom 1:19): *For what*

can be known about God is plain to them, because God has shown it to them; and this implies that they have altogether failed to reach his unknowableness. And so it is clear that the wisdom of Christians, which Denys explains in the *Mystical Theology* (997A) goes incomparably beyond every kind of pagan wisdom.[46] For wherever that wisdom reaches its height, it does not reach up to (christian wisdom) with which it cannot compare, for christian wisdom starts where the wisdom of the pagans ends. For this reason Denys says first: *leave behind you everything perceived and understood, everything perceptible and understandable, all that is not and all that is* and then at the end says: *strive upwards as much as you can towards union with him who is beyond all being and knowledge* (997B); and in the *Divine Names* he says: *we must learn about wisdom from all things* (872B). But note that they[47] have seen the light of the moon, not of the sun; they are set upon the clarity of light, not the fire of charity, see Baruch 3:20: *the young men have not seen the light*.

17. *Draw me*, that is, pour into me those rays by which you lead me to you. The *Divine Names*, 4, says: *he is the one who draws and moves his own into his very self* (700B) for the love of God draws itself in and attracts itself to the minds and the minds to itself. *Draw*: this is the yearning of the young maidens. The Bride, raised to the level of the Dominions, but unable to mount higher, asks to be drawn up; *no one comes to the Father unless the Father draw him* (Jn 6:24); and if you are to draw us up, me and my desires, since we are unable at this stage to struggle further, *we will run*, that is, we will be ravished by a burning desire *in the fragrance*, that is, by a sweet longing, *of your ointments*, as explained above.

18. He hastens to hear me and *he has brought me* within. It has been said, however, that those who do not make their requests in a prayer which is pure are not heard; but she makes her request in a prayer so pure that it is without any kind of frivolous distraction, and so she is always heard; for a person who asks the King for dung is disgraced. On

the prayer which is pure, see the *Divine Names* 3 (680B–D). She who prays for temporal goods is pure; more pure is she who asks for spiritual goods, or to be freed from spiritual evils; but she is most pure of all who prays not for what the Bridegroom can give, but for the Bridegroom himself alone, as in *Draw me after you* and *May he kiss me,* and in similar prayers. See 1 Timothy 2:1 on prayer of this kind and, on the most pure prayer of all, see Wis 9:4: *Grant me wisdom, consort of your throne* and *Who will give you to me as my brother?* (Sg 8:1).

19. She has been heard, therefore, and she speaks from among the Thrones: *he has brought me within,* she says. The contemplative mind has made its way one by one up the six steps of contemplation and at the top of the sixth she fixes the gaze of her mind upon the order of Dominions and strives for the ecstasies of contemplation,[48] longing to be taken up into the rank of the Thrones of the mind so as thereby to be made present to the Godhead as it is present to all things; for it says in the *Divine Names*: *The Trinity is present to all things, though all things are not present to it* (680B). In that book three strategems are described, namely *the most [pure] prayers, revelations of the mind, and a disposition to oneness* (680B). On the first, see above (n. 18). The *revelations of the mind* consist in detachment from all things exterior and from every obstacle, however small—see *Mystical Theology* 1 (997B). The *disposition for union* is obtained by means of an overflowing devotion and melting of soul, for liquids are quickly and easily commingled; as it says, *my soul has melted* (Sg 5:6). For this reason, Gregory, in Homily 10 *on Ezeckiel,* says: *if iron is to be joined to iron it is first melted so that then it holds by its own strength. But if it is softened only a little then it is not able to make a firm joint.*[49] At Job 7:15 it says: *my soul chooses to be raised up and my bones choose death.* This 'being raised up' is the stretching of the mind out to the overflowing brilliance of the insights[50] up to the highest point of the order of the Dominions of the mind—see *Divine Names* 1, where it says that [*minds*] *are*

raised firmly and unswervingly upward in the direction of the ray which enlightens them (589A). 'Bones' are the strongest capacities of mind, namely, its contemplative insight[51] and its ultimate source of desire,[52] than which nothing is as strong in things divine. Two observations may be made about death: it is a failure, for as Daniel [8:27] puts it: *Lord, in your vision my joints are loosened and all my powers are wasted away*; and it is a separation; the *Divine Names* refers to this in the passage which begins: *when mind turns away from all things, even from itself . . .* (872A). When, therefore, the mind receives him from himself it is, rather, received and absorbed by him who properly speaking contains but is not himself contained. Hence, the Lord says to Augustine in *Confessions* VII.10: *you will be changed into me, not I into you*;[53] hence, in my being consumed I consume. *The king*, so called because he rules over me: I am acted upon, it is not I who act; *into his cellars*[54]—by these words is to be understood the plenitude of God's invisible graces, from which fullness we have all received and have received all things, in the same way as all the other offices, the refectory and so on are served in full measure from the storehouse.

20. *We will rejoice*: she speaks thus from among the Cherubim. Rejoicing is, in a certain way, the external expression of the highest part of the understanding, expressive of its capacity for love, for there there is a permanent interior joy; *in you*, that is to say, not in your gifts; and this is the mark of the Cherubim; *thoughts of your breasts*, that is, the recollection of the wonders experienced in the highest point of understanding, wonders which are the gleaming whiteness of milk and the burning ardor of love; these are present together in that highest point of understanding and are the sweet taste of milk; *surpass wine*, as explained above. *The righteous love you*. In the order of the Seraphim, with all her powers she directs all the desires which belong to that order up, where they are refused entry to that highest point unless her impetus is that of the holy and supreme love of the lover.

21. *I am black,* and she says this from among the Seraphim: she fixes her gaze more steadily, more intently than before. Held in the Bridegroom's embraces and entering upon the cloud which is resplendent beyond all radiances, she speaks out of her experience and says: *I am black,* I am enclosed by the cloud, my powers of understanding are denied, but I am not made unsightly by this cloud, only more beautiful. For it is beautifying and brilliant beyond all brilliance, as it says in *Mystical Theology,* 2: *I pray we could come to this darkness so far above light* (1025A). And so it goes on: *but beautiful, O daughters of Jerusalem.* These whom it had previously called *young maidens,* they have been reborn from the abundant inflowing of the light which comes down from the Father, and this is Jerusalem, that is, the 'vision of peace'; for by these lights the Bride is no longer inwardly darkened;[55] *like the tents of Kedar,* stretched out to the East to receive the sun's rays, she likewise remains open to receive the divine ray of light and perseveres at the level of Seraphim and does not come down from it; Job first described this when he says: *he spreads his wings to the South* (39:26); and by means of frequent and persistent fanning of the fiery flames (Qo 43:4) produces a supremely intense, brilliant and red-hot furnace; *like the* red *hides of Solomon*—see Job: *the home of the wild ass is in a land of salt,* which suffers from excessive heat and the presence of so much salt intensifies the thirst [cf Jb 39:5]; see Psalm 41:1–2: *As a hart longs for flowing streams, so longs my soul for thee, O God, my soul thirsts for God.*

22. *Do not gaze upon me*: that is, it is hard for you to see me, for I am wrapped in a cloud; and this is to say that *I am swarthy, for the sun has burned me,* it has drained me of all colour and so has made me invisible, since what lacks colour cannot be seen, and, for the sake of these priceless pleasures, I would forever stop here, if for ever I might. But *my mother's sons*—this refers to the particular works of the virtues, which are the sons of the mother (that is, of understanding); she, through steady application, gives

birth to love, in the same way that knowledge precedes and begets love (although, in fact, it is excelled by love). Or else *the mother's sons* are beings of the heavenly city who flood burning and deeply penetrating lights upon contemplative minds and both arouse them to ecstasy (as to a spiritual death) and, like soldiers, aim their sharp and burning darts of desire first upon the Bridegroom's companions and then upon the Bridegroom—*have fought against me,* which means, they have effectively and insistently distracted me from my commitment to contemplation: these *sons* are the works of the virtues of the middle hierarchy.[56]

23. *They have put me in charge of the vineyards,* that is, they have appointed me to defend and care for the ranks of the middle hierarchy, where there is a proliferation of acts of meditation, of desires, of intentions, of judgments, of thoughts and of other various activities, and they are the *vineyards* in the plural. And while I am preoccupied with these, *my own vineyard,* in the singular—the order of the Seraphim—*I have not kept,* I have not cultivated that single act of worship, which is *the one thing necessary* (Lk 10:42); and *one of your eyes wounds me,*[57] that is to say, the one loving knowledge[58] which alone cuts and wounds deeply; for the eye of the understanding looks at what is around it externally and does not penetrate within, as taste does, but sees only the external colour;[59] but it is with the other single eye that the one vineyard is kept.

24. *Show me*: the Bride reflects how sometimes she has dwelt in delight with her Bridegroom, though she has not been able to rest with him as often as she has wished, and so she brings herself back to the order of the Dominions[60] and now urgently demands to know where she may find him, where she may dwell more restfully with him in accordance with her desire; and so she says: *Show me, you whom my soul loves,* that is, he who is without name and above every name by which things are named, whether in heaven or on earth, known to me only by my love for him; this is *he whom* [my soul] *loves. Where you feed at noon*:

lead me to you so that I may be restored by your most reviving nourishment, such as we read of in Tobit 12:19: *but I was using an invisible food and drink, which cannot be seen by humans*; see also the *Angelic Hierarchy*, 7:[61] and in this untroubled grazing she tarries the longer and more companionably—hence, *where you lie down*; and note that it says *where you feed*, not, *where you are fed*.[62] *At noon*, that is, in the full glare of brilliant light and heat, referring thus to the knowledge of truth and the ardent desire for good in the ray of the *sun of understanding* (Wis 5:6)—see also Malachy 4:2 for the *sun of justice*. The first of these refers to the brilliant light of understanding, the second to the burning desire for justice, that is, the love of goodness; and these are the shaft of fire at noon and the fires of burning love—see Ecclesiasticus 43:3,[63] and the reference to the heat of the day when Abraham sat down, in Genesis 18:1.

25. *Lest I should begin to wander*, that is, lest I should fall back upon myself and should begin little by little to *wander*, away from you into whom I ever long to enter so that *you will not cease to follow me* (Jer 3:19) *in the flocks of the companions*—'flocks' corresponding to the vineyards, 'flock' to the vineyard; [the former] signify holy and honest actions.[64] And it is of some significance that it says: *lest I should begin*, because the first steps lead to widespread breakdown, as Isaiah 22:18 says: *he will toss you like a spear into a wide and spacious land*; and this is the same as what is said in Micah 1:13: *inhabitants of Lachish, you were the beginning of sin*; and Isaiah 57:14: *remove every little obstacle from my people's way*; and Ecclesiasticus: *pray in* [the Lord's] *presence and lessen your offences*. *The companions* are the active virtues and they are given birth and sustained by the nourishment of the Scriptures, as by a heavenly banquet; for *man does not live by bread alone* (Deut 8:3). The manifold works of mercy come in flocks and all are fed from the heavenly table of the Scriptures. For contemplatives, the wisdom of God is a mistress; for actives, the chooser of [right] action, and these are the birds and the beasts of Daniel 4:18,[65] and all

feed from the tree (v. 17);[66] and in reference to this action and contemplation, Scripture is said in Deuteronomy 11:11 to be a *land of hills and valleys which drinks water by rain from heaven*; this passage compares true wisdom with the wisdom of the pagans, the latter being like the land of Egypt where seed is sown and it is watered by canals.

26. *If you do not know*. For, we might say, nothing is more present to you than yourself and you are the place of my rest (Is 66:1)—for *heaven* is my *throne*, but this [Bride] is my rest on earth, for *my delight is to be with the sons of men* (Prov 8:31). In 4 [2] Kings 4:10 it says: *let us make a small chamber and put there for him a bed, a table, a chair, and a lamp, so that whenever he comes he can go in there*: a *small chamber* is our own will and, in the Passion narrative (Lk 22:12) a large chamber is mentioned, large on account of the love of the majesty who used it; Augustine, in his *Confessions* says: *small is the house of my soul to contain you, to be enlarged by your presence* (I. 5).[67] Likewise, in 3 [1] Kings 8:27 it says: *Behold, heaven and the highest heaven cannot contain you*; and: *God gave Solomon wisdom and understanding beyond measure, and largeness of mind like the sand on the seashore* (3 [1] Kings 4:29); clearly, in either case, she is in herself small, but she is magnified by the gift of God. Therefore, if you know yourself, you know where I feed and where I lie down; but if, and may it not be so, you were through negligence not to know yourself, then *depart*—that is, leave both me and yourself—and *go out*—that is, you will leave me by abandoning yourself—*and feed*—that is, you will feed, the *goats*, not to say sheep or flocks, for you will feed the lustful and unclean passions which are *beside*, not within, the *shepherds' tents*; and this happens when, with the appearance of virtue, dissolute and pleasure-seeking acts are performed. Ecclesiasticus 18:30 forbids us to follow after these goats: *Do not follow these base desires, but restrain your appetites*;[68] so too 2 Esdras [Nehemiah] 6:3 says: *I am doing a great work and cannot come down. Why should the work stop while I leave it and come down to you?* And there is

an example in the dead man Eutychus, who fell from the upper chamber (Acts 20:9)[69] and in the departure of Shimei from Jerusalem in 3 [I] Kings 2:41. Alternatively, the goats are the inclinations and desires of the seraphic mind, the tents of the shepherds are the uniting acts of contemplating the Trinity which are proper to the highest orders, who rule over the others and feed them with the food of heaven.

27. [*I compare you, my love*] *to my team of horses, harnessed to Pharoah's chariots*. He has already given her a warning and so many obstacles are there to a person's coming [to him] that she can say: 'I cannot venture it on my own account'. To which he replies: 'I take on your enemies, as I did in Exodus 15'; for the water yielded a crossing to the Jews and sucked the Egyptians in; this is the water of saving wisdom, as Ecclesiasticus 15:3 puts it: *She will give him the water of wisdom to drink*; and *I* [*wisdom*] *flowed forth like a river* (24:40); and Daniel 7:10: *A stream of fire issued and came forth before him*; and Genesis 36:24: *he is Anah who found the hot springs in the wilderness*. And note that God's forces are of two kinds: the infantry are the cardinal virtues who, it is said below,[70] stand round Solomon's bed; and in Wis 8:7: *if anyone loves justice, her labours are great virtues*; the cavalry are the contemplative virtues[71] (1 Cor 13:13). *My beloved,* that is, she whom I love, so that you may trust in me more confidently, that you may understand how I love that oneness which you have already achieved with me. For there is this comparison to be made: just as the abundance of the Red Sea opened a way through to the holy land for my people, and then fell back, so the abundance of the wisdom of Christians which shines red with heat, like molten gold, opens up a way for the solid ground of holiness, once the obstacles to the contemplative ascent have been removed. Genesis 49:55 speaks of this solid ground when it says: *Issachar . . . saw a resting place that was good and a land that was best*; it praises the land more than the resting place, for a resting place on solid ground is best, even if a resting place is good.

NOTES

1. Gallus' Commentary is a pastiche of quotations and references from Scripture and from the writings of the pseudo-Denys. Generally in the MSS and in Barbet's edition these are indicated only by their opening and closing words and sometimes only by chapter references. I have supplied the full quotations either in the text or, occasionally, in footnotes.

2. Hugh of Saint Victor, PL 175:113–256.

3. 1108B, Luibheid, p. 284.

4. 869C–869D, Luibheid, p. 108.

5. *speculativa.*

6. 872A–B, Luibheid, p. 109.

7. As the *Celestial Hierarchy* was commonly known in the Middle Ages.

8. 273C, Luibheid, p. 174.

9. That is, having dealt with the three main hierachies of angelic beings and with their subdivisions, Denys discusses their microcosmic reflections within the minds of each, particularly within the human soul. The structure of Gallus' Commentary is determined by this parallel between the macrocosmic and microcosmic manifestations of hierarchy.

10. I have translated Gallus' *ordo* as 'order' or 'rank', as seems appropriate, to designate the subdivisions within the 'hierarchies' of angels.

11. I have preserved the traditional names of the angelic orders in preference to Luibheid's modernisations.

12. *in excessu mentis.*

13. *commodi vel incommodi.* One could paraphrase: 'of the true and the false and of good and evil': for knowledge 'judges' of the true and the false, love of good and evil. See also note 14.

14. The distinction between the 'basic and simple modes of apprehension' (*primas et simplices apprehensiones*) of the lowest order of the lowest hierarchy and these 'judgments of things apprehended' (*dictationes apprehensorum*) of the middle order of the lowest hierarchy appears to be that between the simplest possible grasp of an object and the ability to relate the apprehensions of two or more such objects in affirmative or negative judgments (*dictationes commodi vel incommodi*).

15. *principalior.*

16. Gallus does not say so, but this second order of the first hierarchy is the order of Archangels.

17. In accordance with his 'voluntarist' inclinations, Gallus ranks the Principalities above the Archangels on the grounds that the powers of the former are those of love and of the latter those of intellect. A similar ranking of love above intellect is found in the eighth and ninth orders, see nn. 9 and 10 below.

18. i.e., are not, as in the case of all the acts of the first hierarchy, merely 'natural'.

19. *apices affectus et intellectus.*

20. *adhuc sobria*, literally, 'as yet still sober'. The contrast is with the *excessus mentis* of the next rank, at which the mind overflows its own limits in ecstasy.

21. *sed sola principalis affectio unibilis.*

22. *DN*, 680B, Luibheid, p. 68.

23. A reference, no doubt, to Paul's *per speculum in aenigmate*, 1 Cor 13:12.

24. As noted, the distinction between the Cherubim and Seraphim is between that contemplation at which knowledge and love walk hand in hand to the very limits of knowledge, but not beyond them and that higher, seraphic, contemplation at which love's *excessus* reaches beyond the limits of knowledge. Gallus 'cloud of unknowing' is not, therefore, the darkness into which intellect is drawn by its own *excessus*, but rather the dark knowing of love which has left intellect behind. There is no *excessus* of intellect in Gallus, as there is in the pseudo-Denys; the Middle English *Cloud* Author clearly follows Gallus more closely here than he does the pseudo-Denys. See my comment on John of the Cross, p. 179 above.

25. *DN*, 712D, Luibheid, p. 83.

26. An exceptionally forced exegesis even of the Vulgate *elegit suspendium anima mea* (Job 7:15), never mind of the Hebrew, which represents Job as preferring to be 'strangled' (RSV and JB) or, as the Vulgate has it, 'hanged', rather than continue with his miserable existence!

27 . . . . *beholding the glory of the Lord, are being changed into his likeness from one degree of glory to another* . . . (v. 18).

28. *we know that while we are at home in the body we are away from the Lord, for we walk by faith not by sight* (vv. 6–7).

29. A rather free translation of *coniunctione oris sui.*

30. *He put forth the form of a hand, and took me by a lock of my head; and the Spirit lifted me up between earth and heaven, and brought me in visions of God to Jerusalem* . . . (v. 3).

31 . . . . *namely his eternal power and deity* [*have*] *been clearly perceived in the things that have been made* (v. 20).

32. *For all men who were ignorant of God were foolish by nature; and they were unable from the good things that are seen to know him who exists, nor did they recognise the craftsman while paying heed to his work* . . . (v. 1).

33. *theoriis.*

34. I have translated this passage from the Latin of John Scottus, *De mystica Theologia* (PL 122:1174C), rather than from Gallus' own paraphrase, since the fragment of the passage given in the text is nearer to Scottus' translation than to Gallus'.

35. v. 13.

36. *levavit se.* The verse in the Vulgate reads: *Sedebit solitarius, et tacebit, quia levavit super se*: 'He sat down alone and was silent, for he lifted him above himself'.

37. *theoriis.*

38. *the sun burns the mountains . . . and with bright beams it blinds the eyes.*

39. See pp. 127ff above for a discussion of this view of the external senses as models for the 'inner' mind, a view inherited from Origen.

40. See Giles of Rome, n. 16.

41. Barbet gives a reference to *CH* where nothing *a propos* is to be found. The passage quoted from *EH* seems at least relevant.

42. Again, Gallus here takes the opportunity to emphasise the affective nature of 'wisdom', by contrast with the intellectualisation of his mentor, the pseudo-Denys.

43. *totam hierarchiam meam.*

44. *immediate*; this could be translated with greater force in conjunction with *per experientiam* to read 'through the immediacy of experience'.

45. *ad fecunditatem apte.*

46. Here, as in n. 1 above, Gallus identifies the affirmative way, which knows 'what is to be known' of God, with the natural knowledge of the philosophers and the negative way, which enters into the divine 'unknowableness', with the mystical knowledge of the Christian. The pseudo-Denys did not, and probably could not, have accepted such identifications, see p. 69, note 2 above.

47. *ipsi*: Gallus is therefore presumably referring to the 'pagan philosophers', not to the 'young maidens'.

48. *in theoricos excessus.*

49. PL 76:906C.

50. *theorias.*

51. *intellectus theoricus.*

52. *principalis affectus*, a difficult phrase to translate and a crucial one, since for Gallus the *principalis affectus* is at once the highest point of the human mind (the *apex mentis*) and the deepest source of its spiritual capacity, especially of love. It corresponds with the 'nakyd entente' of *The Cloud of Unknowing*, indeed, very probably this was the Middle English author's translation of Gallus' phrase.

53. The full quotation is: *Nec me in te mutabis sicut cibum carnis tuae, sed tu mutaberis in me*, PL 32:742.

54. Gallus, like Alan (n. 16), gives a distinctly 'monastic' reading of the Vulgate's *cellaria.*

55. *penitus incontemplabilis.*

56. A rather confused line of thought. Gallus alternates between two interpretations of the *mother's sons*; the first, to which the last sentence of this paragraph returns after interruption, reads the *mother's sons* as the works of the virtues, preoccupation with which calls the contemplative soul back from its 'Seraphic' levels of contemplation to the middle hierarchy; the second, which he throws in half way through this explanation, being the 'Seraphic' outpourings which the soul directs upon the Bridegroom.

57. Presumably a reference to Sg 4:9.

58. *affectiva cognitio.*

59. See Giles, nn. 15–16.

60. i.e., she raises herself from the order of Virtues, where she was distracted by the concerns of Martha mentioned in the previous paragraph.

61. 212A: where, in reference to the order of the Seraphim, it says: *It is filled with divine nourishment which is abundant.*

62. The significance of this comment is not entirely obvious.

63. *At noon [the sun] parches the land, and who can withstand its burning heat?*

64. This refers to n. 23 above: as these 'vineyards' stand for the multifarious 'acts of mediation, desires, inclinations, judgments and thoughts', the 'vineyard' to the *unum necessarium* of contemplation, so here 'flocks' stand for the holy and honest actions of virtue (the active life), the 'flock' to the Bridegroom of the contemplative life.

65. In the Vulgate; 4:12 in RSV.

66. In the Vulgate; 12 in RSV.

67. PL 32:663.

68. The text adds: *unde de Div. nom. 1 et 2.* But I can find no reference in either chapter of the *Divine Names* which seems appropriate.

69. Barbet mistakenly gives the reference as Acts 9:14, the text as Acts 10.

70. Sg 3:7.

71. *virtutum theoricarum*, or, in another reading, *theologicarum*.

Thomas Aquinas

Undoubtedly one of the greatest thinkers of the Middle Ages and a towering figure in any age, Thomas Aquinas was born in 1224 or 1225 in Aquino near Naples. Against determined opposition from his family, in 1244 he entered the Order of Preachers founded some thirty years earlier by Saint Dominic. After his novitiate in Naples he studied in Cologne under Albert the Great and was ordained priest in 1250 or 1251.

Thereafter, Thomas' life was exclusively that of student, scholar, teacher, and writer. In 1256, after a long and bitter struggle by the secular Masters to prevent it, he and the Franciscan Saint Bonaventure were elected Regent Masters in Theology at the University of Paris, Thomas' inception taking place between March and June of that year. Periods of teaching duty in Italy followed this Paris Regency, and from 1269–72 Thomas was back in Paris for his second Regency, thereafter returning to Naples.

In December 1273, Thomas announced his intention to cease writing. Thomas' literary output during the previous two years had been prodigious, and overwork and nervous exhaustion would be explanation enough for this decision. He, on the other hand, related to his amanuensis, Reginald of Piperno, that he had experienced a vision, in comparison with which his own writing was but 'as straw'. In any case Thomas wrote nothing more before his death on 7 March 1274.

Early lists of Thomas' works include a commentary on the *Song of Songs*. He is also said to have dictated a second brief commentary on his deathbed. Unfortunately neither commentary survives.

Included in this anthology is the whole of Question 6 of the *Quodlibetal Question* 7 in its present form. James Weisheipl OP considered that Question 6 does not belong in *Quodlibet* 7 and that it was an independent *Quaestio Disputata* debated by Thomas as one of four such disputes in fulfilment of the requirements of his inception in the second quarter of 1256.

If Weisheipl is right this may have some significance. In a Quodlibetal Question the Master was required to debate a topic chosen for him by a student. The topic of a Disputed Question was decided by a Master and the fact that Thomas chose to dispute the topic of the senses of Scripture on the occasion of his inception may suggest the importance he attached to this topic within his conception of theology.

In this Question Thomas presents views on the interpretation of Scripture which are in every way as mature and in some respects even fuller than in the later discussion in the *Summa Theologiae*, I, q.1, aa. 9–10. I have translated from a not entirely satisfactory Spiazzi edition, in the absence of a critical edition.

THOMAS AQUINAS

QUODLIBET 7, QUESTION 6: *ON THE SENSES OF SACRED SCRIPTURE*

Article 1. In addition to the literal sense may there be other senses hidden in the words of sacred Scripture?

As regards the first question: It seems that there may not be many senses hidden in the same words of sacred Scripture.

1. For it is not proper to use words at any one time in unrelated or different ways. But many senses give many different utterances.[1] So there cannot be many senses implicit in any one utterance of sacred Scripture.

2. Moreover, sacred Scripture is meant for our enlightenment; as Psalm 118:130 says: *The utterance of your judgments . . . gives understanding*. But a multiplicity of senses clouds the understanding. So there ought not to be many senses of sacred Scripture.

3. Again, everything ought to be avoided in sacred Scripture which could be an occasion of error. But to suppose senses of Scripture other than the literal can be an occasion of error, because then anybody would be able to interpret sacred Scripture just as he pleased, as evidence for his own opinion.[2] So there ought not to be many senses in sacred Scripture.

4. Again, Augustine says in Book 2 of his *Literal Commentary on Genesis*[3] that the authority of sacred Scripture is greater than the insight of any human power of mind. Consequently any sense which lacks the authority to substantiate anything is not an appropriate sense of sacred Scripture. But no sense other than the literal has the power to substantiate anything, as is clear from Denys' *Letter to Titus*[4] for he says that *symbolic theology*, that is, the kind of theology which works with images, *has no probative power*.[5]

Hence, sacred Scripture contains no senses other than the literal.

5. Again, any sense extracted from the words of any writing which the author does not intend is not a proper sense, for an author cannot understand more than one thing in any one piece of writing; as the Philosopher[6] says, it is impossible for a person to understand many things at once. So there cannot be more than one proper sense of sacred Scripture.

As against this, 1. There is what is written in Daniel 12:4: *Many will pass through and knowledge will be manifold.*

2. Also, Jerome says, in his *Prologue to the Bible*, speaking of the book of *Revelation*: *in each word many meanings are found.*[7]

My own reply is this: sacred Scripture is divinely ordained to the end that through it the truth necessary for salvation should be made plain.

But the revelation or expression of a truth about something is possible by means both of things and of words, inasmuch as words signify things and one thing can be a figure of another.[8] But the author of things not only can make use of words to signify something, but also can arrange for things to be a figure of another. Because of this the truth is made plain in sacred Scripture in two ways. In one way insofar as things are signified by the words: and this is the literal sense. In another way by virtue of the fact that things are figures of other things: and this is what the spiritual sense consists in. In this way more than one sense is proper to sacred Scripture.

In reply to the first objection, when there is a variety of senses such that one does not follow from[9] the other, then a plurality of utterances results; but the spiritual sense is always based upon the literal and follows from it; hence, from the fact that sacred Scripture is interpreted both literally and in a spiritual way, no such plurality results.

In reply to the second, as Augustine says in *On Christian Doctrine*[10] there is value in the fact that God has in this way arranged for the truth in sacred Scripture to emerge only with difficulty. It has this advantage: that it reduces scope for contempt; for the mind is drawn the more attentively to what is problematic and that relieves boredom. For just the same reason, the opportunity for arrogance is removed when a man can grasp the truth of sacred Scripture only with difficulty. Again, in the same way, the truth of the faith is protected from the mockery of unbelievers; which is why the Lord said *Do not give what is holy to the dogs* (Mt 7:6); and Denys warns Timothy to preserve what is holy uncontaminated by the unclean.[11] Thus it is clear that it does service to the truth of the faith that it should be communicated in a variety of senses.

In reply to the third, as Augustine says in *On Christian Doctrine*,[12] there is nothing obscurely communicated in any place in sacred Scripture which is not explained clearly elsewhere. Consequently, a spiritual explanation must always have support in some literal reading of sacred Scripture; in this way all occasion of error is removed.

In reply to the fourth, it is not on account of any lack of authority that conclusive argument cannot be derived from the spiritual sense, but because of what a likeness is; for the spiritual sense is constructed out of likenesses.[13] One thing can be like many other things; and so it is not possible, when sacred Scripture sets out one such, to argue from it to any one of the alternatives without ambiguity; for that would be the fallacy of the consequent.[14] For example, by virtue of a certain likeness, a lion signifies both Christ and the devil; and so when a lion is referred to in sacred Scripture, a conclusion can be drawn about neither in the course of arguing from sacred Scripture.[15]

In reply to the fifth, the principal author of sacred Scripture is the Holy Spirit who in one word of sacred Scripture has understood many more things than the commentators of sacred Scripture explain or see. Nor, for that matter, is it unreasonable that a man, who was the instrumental author of sacred Scripture, should understand many things in one word: for the prophets, as Jerome says on Hosea,[16] spoke of things present as also intending to signify things future.[17] Hence, it is not impossible at one and the same time to understand many things, because one thing can be a figure of another.

Article 2. Can four senses of sacred Scripture be distinguished?

As regards the second question: It seems that we ought not to distinguish four senses of sacred Scripture, these being the historical or literal, the allegorical, the moral, and the anagogical.

1. For just as in sacred Scripture things are said figuratively of Christ, so also they are said figuratively of many other men; as (in Daniel 8:5) the king of the Greeks is signified by the he-goat of the she-goats. But such figurative expressions do not amount to a sense distinct from the literal sense of sacred Scripture. And so neither should the allegorical sense—by means of which things which preceded Christ in figure are explained in reference to him—be proposed as different from the historical sense.

2. Moreover, the head of the Church and its members form just one Church. But the allegorical sense evidently refers to the head of the Church, which is Christ, while the moral sense refers to his members, the faithful. Therefore the moral sense should not be distinguished from the allegorical.

3. Again, the moral sense has to do with moral instruction. But in many places sacred Scripture gives moral instruction in a quite literal way. So it is wrong to distinguish a moral from a literal sense.

4. Again, Christ is the head of the Church militant and of the Church triumphant too; there are not two Christs. No more, therefore, can an anagogical sense—in accordance with which some things are explained as referring to the Church triumphant—be distinguished from the allegorical sense—in accordance with which some things are explained as referring to the Church militant.

5. Again, if these four senses are intrinsic to the text of sacred Scripture, then every passage of sacred Scripture should bear these four senses. But it is not true to say this; for Augustine himself says in his *Literal Commentary on Genesis*:[18] *in some passages only a literal sense is to be expected*. Consequently, the four senses are not intrinsic to the interpretation of sacred Scripture.

As against this: 1. there is what Augustine says in Book I of the *Literal Commentary on Genesis*:[19] *in each of the sacred books one ought to consider what things in them refer to eternal truths, what deeds are there recorded, which future events are foretold and what things are laid down concerning what is to be done*. The first of these refers to the anagogical sense, the second to the historical sense, the third to the allegorical, and the fourth to the moral. Therefore there are four senses of sacred Scripture.

2. Moreover, Bede, in his Commentary *on Genesis*[20] says: *There are four senses of sacred Scripture; history, which describes events now completed; allegory, in which one thing is understood by means of another; tropology,* that is, moral discourse, *which deals with the moral norms which are laid down; and anagogy, by which we will be drawn towards the highest and heavenly things and so be led back to those things which are above us.*

My reply is that the distinction between these four senses ought to be made in the following manner. As we have said, sacred Scripture reveals the truth which it hands down in two ways: through words and through the types of things. The disclosure which is made through words yields the historical or literal sense; and so all this is part of the literal sense which can genuinely be got from the meaning of the words.[21] But as has been said, the spiritual sense is got from, or consists in, the fact that some things are expressed through the types of other things, for it is normal for visible things to be figures of invisible things, as Denys says.[22] Thus it is that the sense which is derived from types is called the spiritual sense.

But the truth which sacred Scripture hands down through the figures of things is directed to two goals: to right belief and to right action.

As directed towards right action, there is the moral sense, whose other name is the tropological. As directed towards right belief, a distinction should be made in accordance with the hierarchy of things to be believed; for as Denys says in Chapter 4 of the *Celestial Hierarchy*,[23] the Church stands midway between the Synagogue and its status as Church triumphant. So the Old Testament was a type of the New; but the Old and the New together are a type of the things of heaven.

So the spiritual sense, ordered to right belief, can be based in that way of typifying in which the Old Testament typifies the New; and this is the allegorical or typical sense; in accordance with which, things referred to in the Old Testament are interpreted as of Christ and of the Church; or it may be based in that way of typifying in which the Old and the New together both signify the Church triumphant; and this is the anagogical sense.

In reply to the first objection: a he-goat, or other such descriptions, by means of which persons other than Christ are referred to in the Scriptures, were themselves not actual things, but metaphors,[24] contrived solely for the purpose of signifying those persons; and so the meaning by which those persons or kingdoms are referred to in those metaphors is historical only.[25] But in addition those things which are referred to in actual fact so as to signify Christ are related as shadow to truth; and so that meaning, by means of which Christ and his members are referred to, gives rise to another sense than the historical, namely the allegorical. But if it happens in any text that Christ is referred to by means of a metaphor, that meaning adds nothing over and above the literal sense; in this way Christ is referred to as a stone cut from the mountain, but not by human hands (Dan 2:24).

In reply to the second: the allegorical sense refers to Christ not only as head, but also in his members; for example, the twelve apostles are referred to by the twelve stones chosen from the Jordan (Josh 4:3). But the moral sense refers to the members of Christ in respect of what they do, not strictly as members.

In reply to the third: not every sense in which moral instruction is given is called a moral sense, but only in the case when moral instruction is given through a representation[26] of some action done; for in this way the moral sense is one kind of spiritual sense, so that the moral and the literal sense are never the same.

In reply to the fourth: in the same way that the allegorical sense refers to Christ as head of the Church militant in his role as justifying her and filling her with grace; so the anagogical sense refers to him as head of the Church triumphant, in his role as glorifying her.

In reply to the fifth: these four senses are not ascribed to sacred Scripture as if implying that they are all to be explained of each part of it; but sometimes all four, sometimes three, sometimes two and sometimes just one.[27]

For in sacred Scripture especially, later events are signified by earlier events; and so, sometimes in sacred Scripture an earlier event is signified literally and can be explained in a spiritual sense of later events, but not vice-versa.

Now of all the things which are described in sacred Scripture, the first are those contained in the Old

Testament; and so whatever in its literal sense bears on Old Testament events can be explained in the four senses.

But secondly, there are those things which have to do with the Church in its present status[28] in which those things which refer to its Head are prior, relative to those things which refer to its members; for the actual body of Christ himself and everything which happened to it are types of the mystical body of Christ and of those things which happen to it; and so we ought to derive a pattern of how to live from Christ himself. But also, in Christ the future glory is shown forth to us in advance; hence, what can be said literally of Christ the Head can be explained allegorically, referring to his mystical body; morally as relating to our actions, which must be amended so as to conform to him; and anagogically, insofar as in Christ is revealed to us as the way to glory.

But when something is said literally of the Church it cannot be explained allegorically; except, perhaps that things said of the early Church can be explained in reference to the future state of the present Church; but such things may be explained morally and anagogically.

Anything of a moral character which is said literally is normally read only in an allegorical fashion.

But nothing which literally refers to the state of glory is usually explained in any other way; for nothing of this kind is a type of anything else; rather, all other things are types of it.

Article 3. Are these senses found in other writings?

As regards the third question: it seems that the aforementioned four senses must be distinguished in other writings.

1. The spiritual senses of sacred Scripture are derived from images of a certain kind. But other branches of knowledge are constructed upon images of one sort or another. And so in the works of other sciences many senses can be found.

2. Moreover, the art of poetry works by showing the truth through the construction of images. And so it would seem that the spiritual senses are found in the sayings of the poets and not in sacred Scripture alone.

3. Again, the Philosopher says that to say one thing is in a certain way to say many.[29] And so it seems that in other branches of knowledge it is possible through one sense to designate many things; and so it is not only sacred Scripture which contains these spiritual senses.

As against this there is what Gregory says in Book 12[30] of the *Morals*: *Sacred Scripture surpasses all sciences and forms of teaching even in its very manner of speech; for in one and the same utterance, in the course of telling of some deed done, it discloses a mystery.*

My reply is that the spiritual sense of sacred Scripture is derived from the fact that events working out their course signify something else and that is what the spiritual sense lays hold of.

Now events are so arranged in their course that the [spiritual] sense can be understood in them; though it is for him who governs events in his providence to do this, namely, for God alone. For just as a human person can use words or construct images in order to signify something, so God uses the actual course of events which are subject to his providence in order to signify something.[31]

But to signify something by words, or merely by the construction of images designed to signify, yields nothing but the literal sense, as is clear from what has already been said.

Hence, in no form of knowledge which is the product of human powers, is any but the literal sense to be found but only in those Scriptures of which the Holy Spirit is the author, man but the instrument; as the Psalm says: *My tongue is a pen of a scribe, writing quickly* (Ps 44:2).

In reply to the first, the other branches of knowledge work by argument from similitudes; not because by means of the words which signify one thing something else is also signified.

In reply to the second, poetic images refer to something else only so as to signify them; and so a signification of that sort goes no way beyond the manner in which the literal sense signifies.

In reply to the third, to say one thing is in a way to say many, namely potentially, insofar as conclusions are contained potentially in the principles; for many conclusions follow from one principle; it is not that in the other branches of knowledge what is said of one thing is simultaneously and by its manner of signifying understood as signified of other things, although it might be derived from it by argumentation and other means.[32]

NOTES

1. Thomas' objection is that the piling up of unrelated meanings upon just one utterance results in a pile-up of unrelated utterances; for an utterance with more than one meaning says more than one thing. And this leads to the problem stated in the second and third objections below.

2. For Thomas the potentiality for arbitrariness in the patristic and mediaeval practice of exegesis has implications for the method of theology as a whole. Thomas' approach to theology is rooted in the Scriptures. Arbitrariness in the interpretation of the latter threatens the claim of theology (*sacra doctrina*) to provide genuine knowledge (*scientia*). There is no doubt that the objections put forward in this article as elsewhere are taken with the utmost seriousness and express anxieties every bit as real as those entertained by Nicholas of Lyra on the same score of allegorical fancifulness. See Nicholas, n. 4 and Hugh of Saint Victor, n. 4.

3. A paraphrase of *De Genesi ad litteram* II.ix.21 (PL 34:271).

4. This reference is not to be found in so many words in Denys' *Letter to Titus*, though a stricture against arbitrariness in 'Symbolic Theology' is offered: 'For of course one cannot use sacred symbols haphazardly' (1108 D, Luibheid, p. 285).

5. Again, the force of this objection is that an apparent argument from scriptural authority has to be a real argument from unambiguous claims to authority; which arbitrary deductions from merely fanciful accommodations of scriptural texts would, in his view, entirely lack.

6. Aristotle, known to Thomas simply as '*the* Philosopher'.

7. *Epistola ad Paulinam*, PL 28:178.

8. The distinction, but also the interplay, between the signifying power of words (*verba*) and things (*res*) is crucial in many aspects of Thomas' theology, perhaps especially in his sacramental theology, where the words of the sacrament play their part in the divine action of using things (actions, objects) to signify and realise divine realities. Thomas' sacramental theology is based upon the same proposition as that which underpins the theology of biblical interpretation here, namely, that through Christ all things—but particularly the historical events which the literal sense of Scripture relates—are given the power to signify divine realities beyond what human agents have the power, by convention alone, to make them signify; for all creation is sacramental. See also, Hugh of Saint Victor, n. 3.

9. . . . *quorum unus ab alio non procedit*, lit. 'of which one does not proceed from the other'. The force of the *procedit* is evidently less than that of strict logical entailment, though it is characteristic of Thomas' exegesis to allow that what can be established by inference as following from a text of Scripture is part of the meaning of that text—if only of its literal meaning (see article 3 ad 3 below). As for the spiritual senses, Thomas is emphatic that they are 'based on' the literal sense (*fundatur super litteram*) but he is never very clear about the precise form of this dependency, nor about how this dependency functions to

preclude fanciful accommodations. Like Augustine, however, he will allow only such spiritual senses as are confirmed elsewhere in Scripture by an unambiguous literal sense, see below, ad 3.

10. *On Christian Doctrine*, II.vi.8, Robertson, p. 38.

11. See, e.g. *The Celestial Hierarchy*, ch. 3, 145 C: 'Keep these holy truths a secret in your hidden mind. Guard their unity safe from the multiplicity of what is profane, for, as Scripture says, you must not throw before swine that pure, shining and splendid harmony of the conceptual pearls.' (Luibheid, p. 153).

12.*On Christian Doctrine*, II.vi.8, Robertson, p. 38.

13. *similitudines*. In this context and below, *similitudo* probably refers to the kinds of likenesses on which metaphors are based. Note that Thomas does not say that spiritual senses *are* metaphors, but 'constructed out of' (*fundatur in*) metaphors. Metaphors are, for Thomas, part of the literal sense. When the Old Testament speaks of 'the Lion of Juda', therefore, this refers metaphorically, *and so literally*, to a person who is, allegorically, a type of Christ.

14. The 'fallacy of the consequent', more precisely, the fallacy of affirming the consequent, has the following schematic form: if p then q, and q therefore p. Thus: 'If Box is Cox's brother, then Box will have no strawberry birthmark on his right arm; but Box has no strawberry birthmark on his right arm. Therefore Box is Cox's brother.' As Thomas says, just because in Scripture Jesus is typified by a lion it does not follow that mention of a lion signifies Jesus. The point is that you can tell only from the literal meaning what a type typifies i.e. from the actual historical, factual context in which it occurs. For a similar discussion, see Hugh of Saint Victor, n. 4.

15. Cf Hugh of Saint Victor, n. 4 above.

16. *Epistola ad Paulinam*, PL 28:174.

17. Of the five objections discussed in this article this is the only one in which, in reply, Thomas rejects the premise. It is not true that an author can intend only one meaning, first, because the Holy Spirit is the principal author of all Scripture and can bring multiple significance to historical events; secondly, because in any case a human author can intend more than one meaning in his or her account of those events. As for the hermeneutical theory of intended meanings, it is clear that, for Thomas, at least as far as Scripture is concerned, the *human* author's intentions are not decisive in the determination of the meaning of the text.

18. *De Genesi ad litteram*, VIII.1, PL 34:371–373.

19. *De Genesi ad litteram*, I.1, PL 34:247.

20. Glorieux, 'Pour revaloriser Migne', *Mélanges de science religieuse* 9 (1952) identifies Bede, *In Genesim expositio* (PL 91:189–280) as inauthentic. On Tropology, see Bede, *In Tabernaculo* 1 (CCSL 119A: p. 25, 1.783).

21. Here, as later in reply to the first objection, Thomas makes it plain that the spiritual senses of Scripture are not simply figures of speech,

nor are they in any way part of the meaning of the words of Scripture, as metaphors are.

22. Cf. *Letter to Titus*: 'As Paul said (Rom 1:20) and as true reason has said, the ordered arrangement of the whole visible realm makes known the invisible things of God'. (1108 B, Luibheid, p. 284).

23. There is no obvious source for this reference in *CH*, ch.4.

24. *Similitudines imaginariae*. See note 13 above.

25. This exactly describes the method of interpreting the Song adopted by Nicholas of Lyra. Nicholas sees the first six chapters of the Song as a parable, that is, as an extended series of metaphors for Jewish history. In his sense and in Thomas', Nicholas' interpretation of these chapters of the Song is strictly 'literal' or 'historical'.

26. *similitudo*.

27. Where Scripture has only one sense, this must always be its literal sense, for any other sense is always based upon the literal, see a 1 ad 1 above. When, therefore, Denys the Carthusian argues that the Song has no literal reference to Solomon or to Pharoah's daughter, but only an allegorical sense (or, alternatively, that the literal meaning *is* the allegorical meaning) he is clearly departing from Thomas' position, though possibly more consciously in reaction to Nicholas of Lyra's 'literalism' than to Thomas'.

28. That is, the 'Church militant', the Church which is 'midway between the Synagogue and the Church triumphant', see a. 2 corp. above.

29. *Categories*, c. 1, 1a, 1–15.

30. Thus Spiazzi: in fact the reference is to *Moralia* XX.i.

31. It is clear from this that Thomas believes 'history' to have a real significance of its own, objectively made manifest in Scripture. The spiritual sense is no subjective interpretation of 'ours'. History and Providence are one and the same, or at any rate, the providential meaning of history is to be found only within actual historical events themselves and Scripture is the key to our reading of that significance from historical events.

32. Thus, for example, in the field of morality, Thomas believes that all moral judgments can be derived by inference or by 'other means' from its most general principle, which is 'the good is to be done and evil avoided' (*ST* 1–2ae q.94 a.2 corp.). The manner in which many conclusions may be drawn from the general principles of any field of knowledge is quite different from that in which a text of Scripture makes available multiple layers of meaning. One such difference has been a central preoccupation of this Question: in the other fields of knowledge multiple conclusions are drawn by inference and inference is valid only if ambiguity and multiplicity of senses is excluded. Hence, as Thomas has insisted at a. 1 ad 4 above, no argument from Scripture may be legitimately constructed except from its literal sense.

GILES OF ROME

Giles was born c. 1247 at Rome and at an early age entered the community of the Hermits of Saint Augustine in Paris. He studied theology at the University of Paris and very probably attended the lectures of Thomas Aquinas during his second regency, 1269–71. He clearly regarded himself as a disciple of Thomas, though in some very fundamental respects of philosophy he either differed from or misconstrued the thought of his master. In any case his firm defence of Thomas' doctrine of the unity of substantial forms earned him inclusion in the condemnation of some of Thomas' doctrines in Paris in 1277. Refusing to recant, he was expelled from the city by the archbishop of Paris, retreated to Bayeux, and returned to Rome to become Vicar General of his Order in 1285. Thereafter he was reinstated in Paris where he took up the first Augustinian chair in theology.

Having progressed through the Augustinian hierarchy to become Prior General in 1292, he was appointed Archbishop of Bourges in 1295. He died in Avignon in 1316.

A highly inconsistent 'Thomist' and an 'Aristotelian' only within strict limits, it is hard to explain how at least two of his works, the *De regimine principum* and the *Expositio in Canticum canticorum*, excerpted here, came to be attributed to Thomas. The extract from the latter work is translated from the Venice Edition of the *Opera* of Thomas Aquinas, Vol. I (1745), where it is found in the company of a shorter *Expositio* on the Song, also attributed to Thomas, in fact, the work of Haimo of Auxerre (d. 875).

GILES OF ROME

EXPOSITION ON THE SONG OF SONGS

1. *May he kiss me with the kiss of his mouth.* The main purpose of this work is to give expression to the kinds of desire by which the Bridegroom and Bride—that is, Christ and the Church—long for one another; and because these kinds of desire differ as the Church differs in its status, so accordingly we ought to divide the book.

2. Now the Church may be considered as having existed in three states.[1] First, in its primitive state, when it is like a 'severed branch'; for the Jews were made blind and the Gentiles were received—as is explained in Romans 11:17: *But you [Gentiles], a wild olive shoot, were grafted in place of them (that is, of the branches of the good olive tree)* onto the stock and share in the fruitfulness of the good olive tree. Secondly, it can also be considered from the standpoint of its final state, when all the Jews will be saved; for in that time, *Though the number of the sons of Israel be as the sand of the sea, only a remnant of them will be saved* (Rom 9:27). And because there are no extremes without a mid-point, so, in addition to the first and last state, there is a state between them. The Apostle makes some reference to all three states in Romans 11:25, when he says: *A blindness has befallen part of Israel*—(referring to its primitive state)—*until the full number of the Gentiles come in*—this being a reference to the interim state in which the Church flourishes and almost all the Gentile people are converted. He adds that *then all Israel will be saved* (v. 26), referring to the final state when the jewish people will be as a whole converted to Christ, which will be at the end of time.

3. In accordance with these three states [of the Church] this book is divided into three parts.[2] For the first gives an account of the ways in which Christ and the Church long for one another in its primitive state; the second tells of these mutual desires in the interim state, and the third in

its final state. The second part begins, *Behold, sixty strong men drawn from Israel's strongest surround Solomon's bed* just after the middle of Chapter Three (v. 7). The third part begins, *I have gone down to my garden*, towards the end of Chapter Six (v. 11).[3]

4. The first part is in turn divided into two subdivisions, because of the distinction which can be made between two kinds of desire found in the early Church—distinguished in terms of the achievement of good and the flight from evil. And so Solomon gives an account of these different desires by which the Bride (the Church or the holy soul) desires—desires by which she longs to taste the pleasing favours of God and the savours of Christ her Bridegroom. Secondly, then, he tells of those desires by which she longs to be rid of external trials. This second is referred to at, *I am black but beautiful* (1:5).

5. Of these, the first is divided into two, and the first describes the longings of the Bride; in the second she pleads for divine help, for of herself the Bride lacks the power to obtain what she longs for. The second is found at *Draw me after you* (1:4). And the first has three sections: the first tells of the Bride's desire; the second adds the cause or reason for this desire; the third draws the conclusion from the reason given, that her Bridegroom is indeed her beloved one. The second is found at *For your breasts* (1:1) and the third at *Therefore the maidens . . .* (1:2).

6. For the Church's desire is such that she longs to be kissed by the kiss of God's mouth, that is to say, she longs to obtain from him sweetness and grace. The words ought to be read therefore in the optative mood. *May he kiss* means 'Would that God the Father kiss me with the kiss of his mouth'; for God the Father is the one who kisses, the Son is the mouth and the Holy Spirit is the kiss.[4] Now the Son is called the 'mouth of the Father' because he is his Word and so reveals him. And the Holy Spirit is called 'the kiss', because just as in a kiss the physical breath is drawn through the mouth from the one who kisses, so the

Holy Spirit proceeds also from the Father through the Son's procession, for it is from the Father that the Son is such as to breathe forth the Spirit.[5] For this reason Augustine says in Book 16 of *On the Trinity* that the Holy Spirit proceeds principally from the Father.[6] She therefore longs to taste the sweetness of grace, which is an appropriation of the Holy Spirit, by sharing in his gifts and his grace.

7. Then when she says: *For your breasts are more delightful than wine*, she gives the cause and reason of her longing. But before we give an interpretation of this text there are three doubtful points which occur to us about its literal meaning.

8. The first is that the text seems here to be defective,[7] for the Church began by speaking in the third person, saying *May he kiss me with the kiss of his mouth*; but then, when giving the reason, she spoke to God in the second person, adding: *For your breasts are more delightful than wine*. But also, there is a second reason for supposing that the text is corrupt, and its apparent meaning unlikely;[8] it is that since what the Bride longed for was a kiss, in wanting to give the reason for her desire, she should have praised the lips, which are what you kiss with, not breasts. And the third reason why such a form of words seems out of place is that it is the Bride who has breasts, not the Bridegroom. Since, therefore, it is the Bride who addresses the Bridegroom in this manner, it does not seem very appropriate to praise his breasts.[9]

9. In reply, I should point out that the *Gloss*[10] solves the first difficulty, noting that the Bride speaks in the manner of a lover and that because of the intensity of her love she is not able to control her speech; and so she sometimes speaks in the third person, sometimes in the second. But, in a similar spirit, we can explain it thus: at the beginning of her speech she addresses [the Bridegroom] in the third person because she has not the courage at first to speak to so great a Lord in the second person; but once she has made her plea, she recognises that she cannot desire

such things without the grace of God—as it says in 2 Cor 3:5: *Not that we are able of ourselves to think anything as coming from ourselves; our sufficiency comes from God.* And so, having entrusted herself to the divine aid, where she had first placed her longing before God in the third person, saying: *May he kiss me with the kiss of his mouth,* now, when giving the reason for her desire, she speaks to him in the second person, and says: *For your breasts are more delightful than wine.*

10. The second difficulty may also be solved by reference to what Denys says in Chapter 1 of *The Divine Names,* where he says that things of the intelligible realm are beyond the grasp of the senses;[11] and so an intelligible reality is not revealed in its fullness by any one sensible thing; rather, many sensible realities are required in order to show forth more fully an intelligible reality.[12] Consequently, in order to make it understood that the kiss which the Bride sought was not a bodily, but a spiritual kiss, in which there is delight not only of lips but also of breasts and of many other senses, thereby enriching our grasp of it, the Bride praises this kiss by praising breasts, not lips.

11. The third difficulty is overcome in the way the *Gloss* resolves it: the Bride ascribes breasts to the Bridegroom so as to make it clear that she is speaking figuratively.[13] But [the difficulty] can also be solved in another way: for the marriage of the flesh and spiritual marriage have different properties. In a marriage of the flesh the Bride gives a dowry to the Bridegroom, but in a spiritual marriage it is the other way round, for the Bridegroom endows the soul with spiritual gifts; likewise therefore, in the marriage in question here, it is the Bridegroom who in the most important sense has breasts.[14]

12. Granted these things, we should note that, to give the reason or cause why anything is desired is to show in what way it is good; for, as the Philosopher[15] says in Book 1 of the *Ethics*[16] and in Book 1 of the *Rhetoric,*[17] 'the good is what all things desire'. And because things

spiritual become known to us through bodily things, the Bride, in proclaiming the excellence of the Bridegroom's kiss, praises the goodness of the divine delights through images of three kinds. First, because it refreshes the palate; this is referred to when she goes on to say: *For your breasts are more delightful than wine*; secondly, because it pleases the sense of smell, this being referred to at: *more fragrant than the finest ointments*; thirdly, because it gives pleasure to the sense of touch; and this is referred to when she says: *Your name is oil poured out.*

13. In explanation of these points we should remark that the sweetness which the Church, the Bride of Christ, longs to taste is a draught drawn by means of the contemplative life. Now the contemplative life is something which the philosophers and the saints speak of in different ways. For the philosophers place the goal of the contemplative life in knowing wisely. And so in Book 10 of the *Ethics*, where the subjects of contemplation and happiness are discussed, it is shown that happiness is perfect activity in accordance with intellectual contemplation.[18] For to gaze in wonder in the way of wisdom[19] or—which is to say the same—in the way of metaphysics, is the highest form of happiness the philosophers have advocated. Consequently, in Book 4 of his *Ethics*, when the Philosopher wishes to give the highest praise to such happiness, he shows it to be the most pleasurable, saying that evidently Philosophy brings pleasures marvellous in their refinement and strength.[20]

14. But contemplation as the theologians speak of it is more a matter of experience than of wisdom's expertise;[21] and consists more in loving and sweetness than in philosophical contemplation.[22] And if, according to the theologians, some study of the Arts does turn out to belong to the contemplative life, this is only insofar as we are led by this study to the love of God. Therefore, the person who studies in order to know, not to build up and make progress in the love of God, should recognize that he leads the contemplative life as the philosophers, not as

the theologians, describe it. Hence, if we wish to speak of the contemplative life in terms drawn from the senses, we could, in a manner of speaking, adapt the metaphor and say that the contemplation of the philosophers gives delight to hearing and sight; whereas the spiritual contemplation of the theologians gives delight to taste, smell, and touch.[23]

15. For although all the senses serve the end of our knowing, nonetheless hearing and sight are the ones most powerful in the service of knowledge. As Aristotle says, whatever a person knows he knows either as one who learns or as one who discovers.[24] Hearing, which is the trainable[25] sense, is a means to knowledge of that sort which, as is said in Book 1 of the *Metaphysics*,[26] we acquire by being taught, and so as students. But sight, which reveals to us the many differences between things, as is also shown in Book 1 of the *Metaphysics*,[27] is a means to that kind of knowledge which we acquire by discovery—so we know it as enquirers. Therefore, philosophical contemplation, which consists in knowing wisely, seems, in view of the considerations just mentioned, to give pleasure to hearing and sight.

16. But spiritual contemplation, which consists in tasting—and as such is a more vital activity—has the character rather of pleasing taste, smell, and touch, which do more to provide for the needs of life. And so, while the happiness of the philosophers is a matter of the intellect, spiritual happiness resides in its fullness and in its highest form in the will, as it will be possible to make clear in its due place.[28] For the thoughts of the mind are called its 'utterances' and its 'seeings', as Augustine clearly states in Book 9, chapter 11 of *On the Trinity*. But tasting, smelling, and touching cannot rightly be so called, for these seem rather to stand on the side of will. It seems sufficiently clear from all this that what we have argued was well justified, namely that philosophical contemplation pleases hearing and sight and spiritual contemplation taste, smell

and touch. This is why the Bride, by way of praising not philosophical but spiritual contemplation, says: *Your breasts are more delightful than wine, more fragrant than the finest oils.*

17. In these words she refers to three kinds of people in the Church to whom in one way or another the divine sweetness gives delight. For in saying of the breasts of the Bridegroom (referring thus to the desire for his sweetness) that they are more delightful than wine (and so that they are more delightful than any physical taste) she says that they feed the perfect, who eagerly seek the taste of that sweetness; but insofar as they *are more fragrant than the finest oils* (and so are more fragrant than any physical fragrance) these breasts sustain the proficient, who are attracted to this sweetness through its smell. And as the name of Christ is *oil poured out*—and oil, because of its rich, soothing properties gives pleasure above all to touch—so those breasts give refreshment to beginners; for beginners in the spiritual life are like those who enjoy only the sense of touch. For in the same way that in a sick person sensation is limited to touch (and Aristotle says in this connection that different kinds of life correspond with the different senses[29]); and as that kind of life cannot exist without touch; so beginners possess a life of the spirit in sickness and are capable only of a life of touch.

18. But when they have progressed, that is to say, have acquired the power of reason, they acquire a sense of smell and so they are attracted by delicate perfumes. Then, when they are perfect, they take their pleasure fully in Christ and taste his delights. Hence, when it says *Therefore the young maidens . . .*, it implies by these words that Christ the Bridegroom is loved throughout the whole Church, and the text continues in this vein: 'O Lord Jesus Christ, who are all in all, you bring all men into your likeness, *therefore the young maidens*, that is, the beginners, have loved you'. For the Bride wishes to argue from the standpoint of the weaker; if, then, the young maidens—the beginners—love

Christ, and they are clearly the least, it follows that Christ is loved throughout the whole Church.

19. We should note, furthermore, that this conclusion, *therefore the maidens love you*, can be drawn in two ways. First, in that it follows from all that has just been said by way of exposition and secondly in that it follows immediately and without gloss from the preceding words of the text. In this latter connection, because the name of Christ is *oil poured out*, and so sustains beginners, as was explained, *therefore the young maidens*, namely, 'beginners', *have loved you*. Beginners are called *young maidens* for the reason which the *Gloss* gives, that 'young maidens are not old women through guilt, but novices in grace'. Either way, arguing from the standpoint of the weakest case, it shows that Christ is loved throughout the Church.

20. *Draw me after you*. When the Bride has given voice to her longing to partake of the sweetness of Christ, but seeing that she cannot obtain her desire through herself, therefore in this verse she pleads for divine aid. This section is in two parts, for in asking for this assistance first the Bride's request is presented and secondly we have the Bridegroom's reception of it, at *The King has brought me*. As far as the first is concerned [the text] does two things: first the Bride makes her plea for divine help; secondly, she says how gentle and strong he is. The first of these is at, *Draw me after you*; the second when she adds, *We will run in the fragrance of your ointments*.

21. And so she goes on in this vein: 'Lord Jesus Christ, I see that I cannot by my own power reach you, nor taste your sweetness; and so, imploring your help, I ask: *Draw me after you*. For, in accordance with what Christ said in John 6, *No one can come to me unless the Father who sent me draw him*' (v. 44). 'And because the works of the Trinity are undivided'—as Augustine says in *On the Trinity*, Book I, Chapter 3; and Damascene in Book 3,[30] Chapter 18—therefore, no one reaches Christ the Bridegroom unless the Father draw him. And so the Bride, that is, the

Church, does well to say to Christ her Bridegroom: *Draw me after you.*

22. Then, when she says, we will run in the fragrance . . . , the Bride declares that Christ's help is gentle and powerful. And then it goes on in this manner: 'I do not say idly, *Draw me after you,* because your drawing is gentle and strong. For if you draw me I will not move in just any fashion; rather will I run *in the fragrance of your ointments*; I will, in other words, move swiftly for as long as I can sweetly catch the smell of your power and your gifts'. But we should note that when the Bride says that she will be running in response to Christ's drawing, she declares that this Christ's drawing is not a violent dragging, but is gentle: for to run is a form of voluntary movement.

23. On the other hand, she says that this drawing is strong, for running is movement at speed, brought about only by great exertion. And it should not be a cause of wonder that Christ draws gently and powerfully for, as the Apostle says (1 Cor 1:25): *Christ is the power and wisdom of God*; and *wisdom* (as we read in Wisdom 8:1) *exerts her power from one end of the earth to the other and gently disposes all things.*

24. And we should also note that when the Bride asks to be drawn, she speaks of herself in the singular, saying, *Draw me after you.* But when she speaks of herself responding to this drawing, she speaks of herself in the plural, saying, *we will run in the fragrance of your ointments.* The reason for this is that, when we consider God as he is in himself, God draws in just one way; for as Denys says (in Chapter 4 of *The Divine Names*): 'just as the sun, without calculation and without exercising rational choice, sends out its sensible rays, so God sends out his intelligible rays'.[31] But we are not all drawn in the same way, because although there is just one way in which God relates to everything, there is not just one way in which everything relates to God, for the same causal influence is received in different ways by different creatures. Elsewhere we have

explained how Denys' remark is to be understood and how God is related to all things in the same way.[32]

25. Then, when he says, *the King has brought me,* we are told how the Bridegroom receives the requests of his Bride. And the Bride shows three things concerning this: first, that she has been led to the sweetness which she had sought for; secondly, that the good she had desired she rejoices to have achieved; thirdly, she says that she has not been deceived about that good.

26. The first of these is referred to where it says: *The King has brought me into his chambers*; the second, where it adds: *we will rejoice and be glad in you*; the third, where it goes on further, *to remember your breasts is beyond wine; the righteous love you.*

27. So, then, it continues: 'Not in vain have I called upon the divine help, because my Bridegroom, who is Christ, *the King of kings, the Lord of those who rule* (Rev 19:16), looks upon my humble request and *has brought me into his chambers,* so to say, into his sweetness, has given me his grace'. Grace is called *chambers* in the plural because each of the spiritual virtues flow and are derived from it, perfecting each of our several powers; and the different virtues of our several powers are so many different ways in which we rejoice and are glad in the Lord; and thus perfected by such virtues flowing from grace we in a certain manner drink the wines of spiritual joy from different cellars.

28. Then when it says *we will rejoice and be glad in you,* it tells us that the Bride has achieved the good which she had desired, which is God himself. For according to our way of understanding we are first perfected by divine grace and then, when perfected by grace, we reach him to whom grace directs us; and so brought by grace into spiritual joy, *we rejoice and are glad in him.*

29. But we should note that all men without exception desire happiness; but they differ in particular, for some put for happiness sexual pleasure, some riches and in the same way other things; in none of these is true happiness,

for they are not enjoyed in the highest and true good itself, but in a degree of participation in it, since all things share in the complete good. But divine grace causes us to place our happiness in the highest and true good and not in anything else; which is why it says, with emphasis, *we will rejoice and be glad in you*, who is the highest and true good.

30. Then, when it says, *the thought of your breasts surpasses wine*, it shows that she has not been deceived in the good which she has desired. In support of this we should note that the difference between goods of the senses and goods of the mind lies in this: that before they are possessed, the goods of the senses are thought to be great, but once had, they diminish—as can be read in Augustine in his book *On Christian Doctrine*[33] and in Aristotle in Book I of the *Ethics*.[34] For this reason a person discovers he has been deceived when he obtains goods of the senses, for he thinks them not so fine when he possesses them as he had thought.

31. But with the goods of the mind things are otherwise, for when they are possessed they are thought to be finer, most potent, and above all the highest of goods, which is what God is. The reason why the goods of the senses give pleasure only briefly and turn out to be not such great goods as they were thought is easy to give: it is because this kind of good is not desirable in itself, and they give pleasure only to a corrupted desire; for as a man is, so does his end seem to him, as is said in the *Ethics* Book 3.[35] And because a desire of this sort follows nature in its changeableness, when nature changes, what were at first delightful subsequently cease to be so. And so the Philosopher says in Book I of the *Rhetoric*,[36] in the discussion of deception, that to change gives pleasure, because change is in our nature. But with the good things of God, divine things, it is different: for goods of this sort are desirable in themselves and so are delightful in their own right, and this is because we desire them out of that in us which is highest and best. This is why, also, when we desire them, we are removed from this kind of changeableness; and so

when we have attained them they are never a source of boredom, on the contrary, they constantly turn out to be better than we thought they would be beforehand.

32. Therefore the text continues: we retain *the memory of your breasts*, that is, mindful of what we have said about the breasts, which are *more delightful than wine*, we are not deceived in our judgment, because the *right minded*, those who rightly know, *love you more than wine*. Well could that Bride have said, when the Bridegroom had brought her into his chambers and she had tasted his sweetness, what the Queen of Sheba said to King Solomon: when she heard of Solomon's fame, it tells us in 2 Chronicles 9:1–5, she came to test him, and she laid before him everything that was in her heart; and Solomon explained to her everything that she had told him of and nothing she said was too deep for the King; and, acknowledging his wisdom, she was breathless with wonder and said to the King: *The talk which I have heard in my own country about your powers was true* (v. 5).

33. But we should note that the Bride first speaks in the singular and says, *he has brought me*; then in the plural when she says, *We will rejoice and be glad in you, remembering your breasts*. And the reason for this is the same as we gave before. Though another reason may be suggested, namely that the Bride, who seeks just one thing, discovers that it is given and is to be given in many ways and in many forms; and so she is made happy and on account of these many gifts says: *We will rejoice and be glad in you*.

34. *I am black but beautiful*. Now that account has been given of the Bride's desires, those which drive her to seek the divine sweetness—that is, the good things of God—next are set out the desires by which she flees from trials and evil things. By way of explanation of what is to be said, we should note that the Bride of Christ is the Church. But the Church can be taken in two ways. First as the whole assembly of the faithful; secondly, as the bishops themselves—for when a name is predicated of a whole

gathering it may be given to its highest part—we may see this in the case of man which is the name of the whole composite; but because the intellectual part of a man is the highest, we may also call by the name 'man' that highest, intellectual, part; for what constitutes man in his intellectual part makes a man as such. Thus the Philosopher says in Book 9 of the *Ethics*, 'man is more intellect than sense'.[37]

35. In the same way, because the name 'Church' is given to the whole assembly of the faithful, the bishops, who occupy the highest position in the Church, are called 'the Church'; and what the bishops do the Church is said to do. And the Lord, referring to those who refuse to listen to one or two or three, says, *report it to the Church* (Mt 18:17)—that is, on one view of how it should be interpreted, 'to the bishop'. If we read for 'the Church', 'the bishops', we are better able to follow the flow of the text. So, granted this, we should recognise that bishops, because of the pastoral care with which they are charged, can be troubled by two kinds of difficulty: the first by the onset of trials from without; the second by troubles within, because interior difficulties can cause such distraction of mind that if, after facing them, a person wants to return to himself, he finds that he can no longer experience that consolation which he once knew.

36. And so when Solomon at this point describes the trials of the Church (that is, of the bishops), he does two things: first, he gives an account of the external trials, secondly, of the interior distractions—this at: *on my bed I sought him whom my soul loves* (Sg 3:1). As for the first, we should note that the early Church—which, as the text makes clear, is what we are concerned with—suffered four kinds of trial; two of these apply to the contemporary Church, the other two do not. For there are two ways in which the contemporary Church, that is, the bishops of our time, are beset: first, in their government of their own, for there is no government without trouble, as is written in 2 Roman 11. But they are also perturbed by the betrayal of heretics, for

even today many false Christians hold positions of power. But these two kinds of trouble afflicted the early Church; for the bishops of that time had the care of those under them and heretics betrayed them [too]. But that Church had in addition two kinds of difficulty which the Church today does not have: because in those times Christians in general and particularly the bishops, were subjected to the hostility of the Jews and of the Gentiles, who no longer now attack them, for they are not attacked by the Gentiles, since all the peoples of the world have now entered the Church; nor are they attacked by the Jews, for they are not in the position of authority over the Christians in which they were then.

37. So Solomon does two things: first he describes those troubles of the early Church which differ from those of today; secondly, those which are common to our Church, these latter at the beginning of Chapter 2, *I am a flower of the field* (v. 1). The first part is divided into two subdivisions. In the first the Bride tells of problems of the kind mentioned; in the second she seeks Christ's assistance, this at *Show me, you whom my soul loves* (Sg 1:6). The troubles which afflicted the early Church, though not the modern Church, were the provocation of the Gentiles and the hostility of the Jews; and so, in connection with the first he does two things: first he tells the Church of how it would be subjected to the provocation of the Gentiles; secondly, how it would be beset by ill-treatment from the Jews, namely at *My mother's sons* (Sg 1:5). Then again, the first part is divided into two; first it presents the Gentiles' hostility; then it further adds advice to the children of the Church at *Do not gaze upon me* (Sg 1:5). In connection with the first of these two it says that the assault on the Church is provoked by its beauty; and so, in the course of telling of the trouble it suffered at the hands of the Gentiles, the Church also describes its own beauty.

38. And so the text continues: 'O daughters of Jerusalem, I am responsible for your care, *I*, your mother the Church,

am black like the tents of Kedar; but *I am beautiful like Solomon's hides*'. Kedar was the second son of Ishmael, we are told in Genesis 25 (v. 13), and was a fugitive in the land as was his father Ishmael, who was told: *Your hand is set against everyone and everyone's hand is set against you* (Gen 16:12). And so Kedar was held in contempt by all the people and did not live among them, but apart from them in tents which had become discoloured by rain. So too is the Church despised by the Gentiles and cannot dwell among them without harassment, as the *Gloss* clearly states where it tells of the troubles which the Church suffered at the hands of the Gentiles. 'And even if I may be black on account of the persecution to which I am subjected externally, nonetheless within I am beautiful *like Solomon's hides*'—which were dyed red and made into tents, as the *Gloss* says; alternatively, they were what he used to adorn the Ark of the Lord with; thereby, reference is made to the beauty which comes from charity.

39. Then when she says: *Do not gaze upon me because I am swarthy, for it is the sun which has scorched me*, having given an account of its difficulties, the Church turns from the trials to which she is subjected and instructs her children: 'O daughters of Jerusalem, *Do not gaze upon me because I am swarthy, for it is the sun*, that is, Christ, *which has scorched me*, that is, has turned me black'. For Christ is said to have 'blackened' the Church, in the sense that he was the ultimate reason for this darkening: it was for Christ's sake that she was darkened in experiencing the hardships brought upon her by the Gentiles. And so the Church means to instruct her children in this explanation: for our intention and our mind ought not to be fixed upon the means to the end but upon the end itself. But the hardships of the world are the means by which we come to Christ; and, Christ being our goal, when we suffer adversity for Christ's sake, we ought not to give thought to or be preoccupied by these troubles themselves, rather, all our attention ought to be on Christ, for whose sake we undergo such things.

40. Then, when it says, *My mother's sons have fought against me, they have put me in charge of the vineyards,* it takes up that section in which, having told of the hardships caused by the Gentiles, the Church tells of the provocations of the Jews. In this connection we should note that by persecuting the Apostles and the Christians who were in Jerusalem, the Jews caused these Christians to turn to the Gentiles, as Acts 13:47 tells: *Therefore we will turn to the Gentiles;* and in turning to the Gentiles they were made guardians of the vineyards, that is, of the Gentiles: and so the Jews were at the least the occasion of the early Church being made guardian of the Gentiles' vineyards, by expelling them from Jerusalem: thus it is that by taking guard over the Gentiles the Apostles ceased to be the guardians of Jerusalem, which had been, so to speak, their own vineyards.

41. Therefore, in the enumeration of the hardships caused to the Church by the Jews, it lists three things. First, it describes the people who attacked her, where it says: *My mother's sons*—that is, the Jews—*have fought against me*; for the Synagogue was like our mother since, in a way, the Church was born of her. And since the Jews were the sons of the Synagogue, the Church calls them 'the sons of her mother'. Secondly, it gives account of the extreme degree of the hardships when it says: *They put me in charge of the vineyards;* for such was the extent of the hardships caused that the Christians were unable to remain in Jerusalem and they turned to the Gentiles, and so became their guardians. Thirdly, it describes the effects of this persecution, where it goes on to say: *My own vineyards I have not kept*; for the result was that they left Jerusalem.

42. Then, when it says, *Show me, you whom my soul loves, where you feed, where you lie down at noon,* the Church, in view of the great number of the hardships it was experiencing, calls for Christ's aid and support. This is divided into two sections, in the first of which we have the Bride's request in the form of a question, while in the second we

are given the reason for the request, at *Lest I should wander among the flocks of your companions.*

43. And so it goes on: 'O my Bridegroom, Lord Jesus Christ, *whom my soul loves,* you see me surrounded by so many difficulties; and because I cannot escape them without you, therefore, *show me where you feed, where you lie down at noon.* For the Church wished to know where Christ lives, for his home is where we find food and rest; and she knew that Christ was no tramp; on the contrary, anyone who would go to his house to find him and seek his help in his troubles, knew that he would always find him ready and eager to respond. And so it says, *Show me where you lie down at noon . . . .* Human beings lie down at night; Christ lies down at noon, in the full light of day, because he is true God and the true *light and in him there is no darkness* (1 Jn 1:5).

44. Then, when it says, *Lest I should wander* among the flocks of the companions, it gives the reason for the request: that is, the Church has recourse to Christ in her difficulties lest she should begin to go astray. And it mentions the companions of Christ. Heretics are called 'the companions of Christ' for they do not care to be imitators, but his colleagues and equal companions, inasmuch as they want to teach their own doctrines and to be teachers, as Christ was.

45. Next, when it says, *if you do not know yourself, O most beautiful among women,* it gives Christ's response. In which connection we should know that there are two grounds for complaint against the Bride: first, on account of the question she addressed when she said, *Show me . . . where you feed*: for this showed that she was trying to find a God who is far away, whereas she should have sought him in herself; and so the question she addressed to him gave grounds for complaint of her ignorance; and as far as concerns the reason for her request, grounds for complaint arose from her lack of trust; for she seemed to doubt whether Christ would ever be present and come to her aid when she said, *Lest I should begin to wander* astray.

46. Therefore, this part is divided into two, for first Christ complains of the Bride's ignorance; secondly, lest she mistrust, he tells of the evils which will befall her on account of her ignorance. *Depart and go out*. And so he says, *O most beautiful among all women,* you seek me as if I were far away because *you do not know yourself.* For if you knew yourself you would look for me within yourself. Note that he calls the Church *most beautiful* because God is to be sought in the soul, for the soul is his image. And in the course of complaining to her of her ignorance he therefore calls her *most beautiful,* because insofar as she is the image of God she is *most beautiful.* Therefore, when it says, *depart and go out,* he is describing the evil results which will befall her because of her ignorance and mentions two. The first is blindness of understanding, the second is perversity of feeling. It continues thus: 'Because you, *most beautiful among women* in this way *do not know yourself, go out and depart,* that is, you will go out and will depart *in the tracks of the flocks,* that is, in the teachings and example of the heretics, for these *flocks* are referred to here as they were above at *Lest I should begin to wander after the flocks of your companions,* that is, after heretics, as was said: here what is referred to is the ignorance of the heretics. *And feed,* that is, you will feed, *your goats,* that is, you will sate your carnal lusts. For the goat is a filthy animal; its carnal desires are there for all to see. And this [you will do] *beside the tents of the shepherds*: for you will go out in the ways of carnal lust as other carnal people do, who are referred to as 'goat-herds'.

47. Then it says, *I have compared you, my love, to my team of horses harnessed to Pharoah's chariots,* for the Bride had seemed to fail in trust; and so that she will not mistrust but place her confidence fully in Christ, he tells of the good things he has given her. And in this connection he says two things. First, he describes the benefits which he has conferred by throwing down her enemies; secondly, the benefits given her by way of the greater goods which she has acquired, this last at *Beautiful are your cheeks.* And

so it continues, 'O my beloved, do not mistrust, for *I have compared you to my team of horses,* that is, to the people of Israel, who were my special people whom I owned and trained like a horse. And so I have compared you to that people *harnessed to Pharoah's chariots;* for as Pharoah's chariots were sunk in the Red Sea, as is told in Exodus 14:28, so will I tread down and oppress the demons which infest you—for that is what *Pharoah's chariots* refers to.

NOTES

1. Uniquely among the commentators of our anthology, Giles' historical ecclesiology is limited to the history of the Christian Church. He thus lays himself open to Nicholas' accusation that 'Catholic interpreters commonly say that the book speaks of the love of Christ and the Church, meaning the Church in its distinction from the Synagogue' (n. 4 below) allowing the Song no significance for Jewish history or faith.

2. This detailed division of the text is typical of the scholastic style of commentary and marks it off from the less formalised divisions of the monastic commentary. It is possible that the scholastic enthusiasm for divisions owes less to pedantry than to the desire to construe the text in a less piece-meal and fragmentary way than results from the monastic, verse by verse, even word by word, exegesis.

3. Again, Giles' division of the text of the Song invites comparison with Nicolas of Lyra's. Nicholas considers that all of Chapters 1–6 are a parable of Jewish history, only Chapters 7–8 an allegory of the Christian Church 'in its distinction from the Synagogue'. This is in accordance with his broader historical ecclesiology for which the history of the people of Israel forms a part of a single history of the Church's love for God in which one can distinguish only different degrees of explicitness in its expression, n. 6.

4. Giles gives the, by now, conventional Trinitarian reading of the 'kiss', cp. *Brief Commentary*, nn. 11–12 and Alan of Lille, n. 6.

5. Cp. Thomas of Perseigne, nn. 3 & 4.

6. *De Trinitate*, XV.xxvi.47 (PL 42:1094). A notably moderate and in western terms notably orthodox reading of the so-called *filioque* clause, a formula equally to be found in his Master, Thomas Aquinas: *Filius habet a Patre quod ab eo procedat Spiritus Sanctus* ('it is from the Father that the Son is such that the Holy Spirit proceeds from him')—*Summa Theologiae*, 1a q.36 a.3 corp.

7. *Dissutus*, literally, 'unstitched'.

8. *Inconveniens*.

9. Cp. Nicholas of Lyra, n.10.

10. *Glossa Ordinaria*, the standard commentary on Scripture compiled in the twelfth century out of the commentaries of earlier and contemporary authorities and frequently set alongside the text of Scripture in MSS and, in the fifteenth century, some printed editions.

11. *DN*, 1, 588B.

12. *DN*, 1, 596D–597A.

13. The *Gloss* comments: 'breasts are mentioned as of the bridegroom, though they are attributes of women, so as to make clear from the very beginning of the Song, that he speaks of himself in figures'.

14. See the discussion of this passage on pp. 112ff. above. Not until Nicholas of Lyra is the simpler solution offered, namely that the Vulgate mistranslates a hebrew text which makes perfectly good literal sense: see Nicholas of Lyra, n.10.

15. i.e. Aristotle, known from the thirteenth century on as 'the Philosopher'.

16. *Nicomachean Ethics*, Bk.I, ch.1, Bekker, *Aristotlis Opera* 1 (Berlin, 1831) (ET *The Works of Aristotle*, ed. W.D. Ross, *IX: Ethica Nicomachea*, trans. W.D. Ross [Oxford: Clarendon, 1925]. 1094a 3.

17. *Rhetoric*; I.6, 1362a 24 (Ross, *XI: Rhetoric*, trans. W. Rhys Roberts [1971]).

18. Aristotle, *Nicomachean Ethics*, 10.vii, 1177a 16–19.

19. *speculari secundum sapientiam*. The English 'speculate' with its suggestions of idle curiosity and restless uncertainty can do no justice to either Aristotle's or Giles' view of contemplation, even of the 'philosophical' sort. For Aristotle and for Giles philosophical contemplation is a combination of an intellectual restfulness in ultimate truths with amazement and awe at the truths contemplated. Giles has his own contrasts to make between the contemplation of the philosophers and that of the theologians but they are misconstrued if read in the light of later mediaeval (and in some degree twentieth century) forms of anti-intellectualism.

20. In fact, *EN*, 10.7, 1177a, 25–28.

21. *magis consistit in sapore quam sapere*.

22. *contemplatione*. An alternative reading gives *sermone*, 'than in speech'.

23. Giles here is following the dionysian principle that the higher a reality on the scale of excellence the more appropriate it is to use images of lower things to describe it, see pp. 56–57 above. The three stages of the 'higher', theological, kind of contemplation are represented by the three 'lower' senses, taste, smell and touch, and the 'lower', philosophical, contemplation by the 'higher' senses, sight and hearing. See, *CH*, 137C-D and cp Gallus, n. 23, who likewise contrasts the rational knowledge of the philosophers with affective, mystical knowledge as sight contrasts with taste.

24. Aristotle, *Metaphysics*, I.1, 980a–981b (Ross, vol. VIII: *Metaphysica*, trans. W.D. Ross [1972]).

25. *disciplinabilis*.

26. Aristotle, *Metaphysics*, I.1, 980b 23.

27. *Metaphysics*, I.1, 980a 25.

28. This passage so very clearly could not have been written by Thomas Aquinas as to make the attribution of the Commentary to him incredible. Aquinas could never have construed the distinction between philosophical and theological contemplation in these voluntarist terms; he consistently took the view that all contemplation as such is an intellectual activity—see, *Summa Theologiae*, 2–2ae, q. 180, a. 1, corp.

29. Perhaps Aristotle, *De anima* II.3, 414a29–414b5.

30. The reference is presumably to John Damascene, *De fide orthodoxa*, III. xviii, PG 94:1071–1078) where, however, nothing very relevant is to be found.

31. *DN*, 693B.

32. Consistently with his belief in the Thomistic authorship of the Commentary, the editor gives the reference to *Summa Theologiae,* 1a q.47 a.1 corp. where Thomas says: 'for that goodness which in God is possessed absolutely and uniformly, is manifold and divided in creatures'.

33. *On Christian Doctrine,* I.xxxviii.42 (Robertson, p. 32)

34. *EN,* 1.8, 1098b 13–17.

35. *EN,* 3.5, 1114a 30–1114b 2.

36. *Rhetoric,* 1.11, 1371a 26.

37. Perhaps *EN,* 9.9 1170a 16–18.

Nicholas of Lyra

Written late in the Middle Ages, Nicholas of Lyra's *Postillae* on the whole of the Bible thereafter rivalled all others in popularity; his were the first commentaries on Scripture to receive a printed edition—at Rome in 1471. The glosses to the Wycliffite vernacular Bible included much material from Nicholas' *Postillae* and they were particularly favoured by Martin Luther.

Nicholas was born in Lyre in Normandy, c. 1270. He joined the Franciscans at Verneuille about 1300, studied at Paris and became Master there in 1309. Unusually in his time he was well acquainted with Hebrew and he much regretted what he regarded as the lamentable state of contemporary biblical scholarship, in particular its failures of textual criticism and its excessive proliferation of 'mystical' readings, which, he said, served only to 'smother' the literal sense of scripture. Though by no means himself averse to the allegorical, he favoured a plainer, more literal, and more textually responsible approach to exegesis. In his detailed exegesis he was much influenced by the eleventh century jewish scholar, Rashi, and in theoretical hermeneutics by Thomas Aquinas. The substance of the case which

Nicholas presents for the primacy of the true literal sense is derived, almost *verbatim*, from Thomas.

Nicholas died in 1349. The *explicit* of his *Postillae Morales seu Mystice* states that the work was completed on the feast of Saint George in 1339.

The extracts from his *Postillae Litterales* on the Song of Songs have been translated from the Rome edition of 1471, as also have those from the General Prologues; that from the *Postillae Morales seu Mystice* comes from the Strasbourg edition of c. 1475. Headings other than those supplied in these editions are contained in square brackets. Paragraph divisions and numbers are mine.

NICHOLAS OF LYRA

1. THE FIRST PROLOGUE OF NICHOLAS OF LYRA TO THE *POSTILLA LITTERALIS*:[1]

ON THE COMMENDATION OF SACRED SCRIPTURE IN GENERAL

1. . . . There is something special about this book [Sacred Scripture], namely, that in it any one text contains many senses. The reason is that the principal author of the book is God himself and it is in his power not only to use words to signify something, which men are able to do as well and in fact do; but also he uses the things signified by the words to refer to other things. Thus any book uses words to signify something, but it is peculiar to this book that the things signified by the words signify something else. By means of the first signification—that is, by words—we get the 'literal' or 'historical' sense; and by means of the other signification—that is, by the things themselves—we get the 'mystical' or 'spiritual' sense—which, speaking generally, is of three kinds. For if the things signified by the words refer in what they signify to those matters of belief which belong to the New Law, then we have the allegorical sense. If they refer in what they signify to those actions which we are to perform, then that is the moral or tropological sense. But if they refer in what they signify to those things which we are to hope for in future bliss, then that is the anagogical sense[2]—so called from *ana*, which means 'above' and *goge*, which means 'being led'.

> The letter tells of deeds done, allegory of what to believe,
> The moral, of what to do, anagogy, the goal of our striving.[3]

2. And these four senses may be explained by way of illustration by the word 'Jerusalem'.[4] In its literal sense it refers to a certain city which was once the capital of the kingdom of Judea, founded in the first instance by

Melchisedech and later expanded and fortified by Solomon. But in its moral sense it refers to the faithful soul; it is in this sense that Isaiah says: *Rise up, Jerusalem, take your seat* (52:2). But in its allegorical sense it refers to the Church militant, as when it says in Revelation 21:2: *I saw the holy city, the new Jerusalem, coming down from heaven, like a bride dressed for her husband*. In its anagogical sense it refers to the Church triumphant, as Galatians 4:26 says: *She who is above is Jerusalem the freed-woman: and she is our mother*. We have given as an example a single word; in the same way a single passage could be given and as in the one case so in others.

3. That this book can be said to contain many senses in one text is confirmed by Ezekiel 2:10: *Behold a hand stretched out to me in which there was a rolled scroll and he opened it before me; it was written on within and without*. Scripture 'without' is the literal sense and it is the more evident because it signifies immediately by means of words. Scripture 'within', on the other hand, is the mystical or spiritual sense, which is the more hidden because it refers through the things signified by the words, as has been said . . . .

2. THE SECOND PROLOGUE TO THE *POSTILLA LITTERALIS*:

ON THE AUTHOR'S INTENTION AND ON THE MODE OF PROCEEDING

4. *I saw on the right hand of God seated on the throne a scroll written within and without* (Rev 5:1). As was explained in the previous Prologue this book is holy writing[5] which is said to be written 'without' in respect of its literal sense and 'within' in respect of its mystical and spiritual sense, which in general terms may be divided into three, as has been said: although, under any one of these headings a number of mystical explanations can be constructed. Nonetheless all of them presuppose the literal sense as their foundation; and as a building which tilts on its foundations is destined for collapse, so a mystical explanation out of true with the literal sense should be judged inappropriate and useless—or at least as less appropriate and useful. And so those who would profit from the study of sacred Scripture must needs begin from a grasp of the literal sense, especially since argument may be built only upon the literal sense and not upon the mystical sense, if one wants to settle or clarify any doubt—as Augustine says in his letter against Vincent the Donatist.[6]

5. Furthermore, we should take account of the fact that the literal sense, from which, as we have said, we ought to begin, is much obscured in modern times, partly through the fault of scribes, who, because of the similarity of letters have in many places given readings which vary from what the true text has; partly because of the carelessness of some editors[7] who in many places have supplied punctuation where it does not belong, so that verses have been made to begin and end where they ought not to begin and end, and the meaning of the text is thereby altered—as will be seen by following through below, if the Lord permits—partly because of the quality of our translation, which differs in many places from the Hebrew text, as Jerome has attested

in his work on *Hebrew Questions*[8] and in many other places, and other interpreters, whether in teaching or in writing, say the same. For this reason, according to Jerome in his second *Prologue to Genesis* and in many other places, it is necessary to have recourse to the Hebrew codices in order to establish the literal truth of the Old Testament.

6. Much care needs to be taken in this matter, however, with passages of the Old Testament scriptures which speak of the Godhead of Christ and connected matters; for the Jews have twisted some of these in defence of their errors—as I have explained in part in *Certain Questions on the Divinity of Christ*[9] and will set out more fully, if the Lord permits, when such passages occur. But in those passages where they are unlikely to have altered anything, not having cause to do so, there seems no danger. But when [one is] in doubt, according to the dictum of the blessed Jerome,[10] the safer course is to appeal to the hebrew text as to the original source, so as to be more certain of setting out the truth.

7. It is also as well to know that the literal sense is much disguised[11] by the method of expounding generally handed down in the tradition by those who, though they have had many good things to say, to some degree have hidden the literal sense and the mystical senses by virtue of their multiplication, the result being that the literal sense is almost suffocated, being tangled in so many mystical senses. Furthermore, they have broken up the text into so many fragments and have invoked so many parallels at whim that the mind and the memory are to some degree overwhelmed, turning attention away from the literal sense.

8. These points having been explained, with God's help I propose to rest my case on the literal sense, and I will, from time to time, though infrequently, include the occasional brief, mystical interpretation.[12] Likewise I will call upon the opinions not only of the catholic masters but also of the jewish, especially upon Rabbi Solomon,[13] who among

the hebrew masters is the most judicious expounder of the literal sense, and I will occasionally, though very rarely, include some altogether absurd teachings of the jewish masters, not because they are to be held or followed, but so as to make clear the extent of the blindness which befell Israel, as the apostle Paul tells us in Romans 12[14] (v. 25). For this reason no credence is to be given to the teachings of the jewish masters unless they are consistent with reason and the truth of the literal text.

9. Then again, without any preambles, I proceed immediately to the beginning of Genesis, if only for the reason that I doubt if the rest of my life will be enough in which to expound the whole of holy Scripture. And so I do not wish to dwell on the exposition of the teachings of the blessed Jerome, or of any other master, both because the aforesaid prologues do little enough for the understanding of the books which they introduce, as I see it, and because another brother of our order has given quite adequate prologues to the Bible, and this work is generally available.[15] And so it does not seem to me necessary to set out yet again an account of these prologues, though I have given prologues to some of the books, which I had written before I set out from Genesis. Finally, there is the fact that I am not so well versed in the hebrew or the latin languages that I will be beyond making mistakes in many places.

10. Therefore I declare that I intend to say nothing definitive or assertively except of those matters which have been clearly settled by sacred Scripture or the authority of the Church. As for every other opinion which has been offered, or could be offered, these are to be taken as debatable[16] and as the product of difficult argument, and because of this everything said so far, or to be said, I submit to the correction of Holy Mother Church and of any wise person or pious reader who offers merciful chastisement. Nevertheless, before I proceed to the exposition of the text, I first set out the seven rules for the interpretation of sacred Scripture which Isidore mentions in Book I of his *On the*

Highest Good, Chapter 2.[17] Some call these rules 'keys': because by means of them the understanding of Scripture is unlocked for many.

11. The first of these concerns the Lord Jesus Christ and his mystical body, that is, the Church; for because of the connection between head and body, sacred Scripture in a single text sometimes speaks of both as being the same person, shifting from one to the other—as for example in Isaiah 61:10: *He has dressed me in the clothes of salvation and in the garments of justice he has enveloped me, like a bridegroom adorned with a crown, like a bride bedecked with her jewels.* For what is said in this text of the Bridegroom and so on is understood of Christ, and what is then said about the Bride is to be understood of the Church itself. It is the same with the [first] verse of the Song: *May he kiss me with the kiss of his mouth, for your breasts*[18] *are more delightful than wine.* The words are the Bride's, who longs to delight in the Bridegroom. And it goes on, *your breasts are more delightful . . . ,* these being the words of the Bridegroom praising the Bride. Thus, where readings are connected in this way, the discriminating reader should, in accordance with the first rule, take care to distinguish what is to be attributed to the head and what to the body.

12. The second rule concerns the true body of the Lord, likened to the Church, which is the mystical body of the Lord and is, as we have said, like the fishing net still not drawn into the shore;[19] and so it contains the evil mixed in with the good, until that judgment when they will be separated from one another. And so it is that in sacred Scripture the evil are sometimes commended along with the good with whom they are mixed—as in Hosea 12, where it is said *Israel is a child and I have loved him.*[20] Contrariwise, the good are sometimes reproached along with the evil, as in Isaiah 1:3: *The ox has known its master and the ass its master's crib, but Israel has not known me and my people have understood nothing.*

13. Then again, sometimes in one and the same text are found references both to the good and to the evil, as in Song 1: *I am black but beautiful, daughters of Jerusalem, like the tents of Kedar, like Solomon's hides*; the words are the Bride's, who says *I am black* because of the evil people found in the Church, but because of the good she adds, *but beautiful,* and continues by way of illustration, *like the tents of Kedar,* which refers to the evil ones. For Kedar was the son of Ishmael (this is referred to in Genesis 25) and the Saracens were descended from him. But what follows, *like Solomon's hides,* refers to the good, for by 'Solomon' is to be understood God himself, according to both catholic and jewish commentators. And so his *hides* are those out of which is made his tent in which the good worship God.

14. The third rule concerns the spirit and the letter; and according to this rule a literal and a mystical sense are given in one and the same passage, for the historical truth is to be defended while at the same time it is to be seen as pointing towards a spiritual meaning. This is how the rule is usually explained, though it can also be understood as referring to the literal sense only, as much as to any other sense. In this connection, note that sometimes one and the same text has a twofold literal sense, for example at 1 Chronicles 17,[21] where the Lord says, referring to Solomon: *I will be a father to him and he will be a son to me.* And this is to be read literally of Solomon because he was indeed son of God by adoption in his youth, for which reason Nathan called him *the beloved of God*—see 2 Sam 12:25. Moreover, this authority, *I will be a father to him . . . ,* is invoked by the Apostle in Hebrews 1:5 as said literally of Christ, and this is shown by the fact that the Apostle uses it to prove that Christ was greater than the angels. But proof of this kind cannot be got from the mystical sense, as Augustine says in his letter *Against Vincentius the Donatist*—we have already noted this. So this text was literally fulfilled in Solomon, though less perfectly, since he

was son of God only through grace; and more perfectly in Christ because he was son of God by nature; both readings being, nonetheless, literal, speaking absolutely; though the second reading (concerning Christ) is spiritual and mystical relatively, because Solomon was a type of Christ. . . .

3. PROLOGUE TO THE *POSTILLAE MORALES SEU MYSTICAE*

15. But it should be noted that although sacred Scripture has the fourfold sense previously mentioned, not all are to be found in each place—as is pointed out in *Conference* VIII.[22] For sometimes there is only a literal meaning, as at Exodus 20 [:1], *Hear Israel, the Lord your God is one Lord*; and at Deuteronomy 6:5: *You shall love the Lord your God with your whole heart*. In these passages, and in others like them, no mystical reading is necessary. But some passages have no literal sense, strictly speaking. For example, at Judges 9:8: *The trees went forth to anoint a king to rule over them*, and so on. And at Matthew 5:30: *and if your hand causes you to sin, cut it off and throw it away*. The literal sense is that which is signified by the words, as has been said: and there is no such sense in these passages, nor in others like them. For it would follow that the literal sense of Scripture were false, for trees never did nor could they do, any such thing. Likewise, our Saviour did not suggest that anyone should literally cut off his hand. Rather, in these passages there is a mystical sense which is to be understood of the things signified. For by 'the trees' are to be understood the citizens of Schechem, who made Abimelech their king to rule over them, as is explained in the text itself, and by the hand which is to be 'cut off' is understood any such acquaintance as provides the occasion for a man's downfall—he ought to cut himself off from the company of such. When, however, some teachers say that the metaphorical is the literal sense, this is to be understood in general terms; for where no sense is signified by the words, the metaphorical sense is the primary sense; and so, loosely speaking, it is called the literal sense, since the literal sense, where there is one, is the primary sense; and so, with this in mind, they say that the metaphorical is included in the literal sense. In this spirit, in many places in my writings on the books of sacred Scripture I have called a metaphorical sense 'literal'.[23]

16. Elsewhere in sacred Scripture, however, the text has both a literal and a mystical sense—for example, in Genesis it says that Abraham had two sons, Isaac and Ishmael, and this is true in the literal and mystical senses, for, as the Apostle tells us in Galatians 4:24, the two Testaments were allegorically signified by them. And in the same way, two kinds of son of the same bishop may be signified morally, where one makes good and the other lapses; and signified anagogically are the angels who held firm and those who fell. Again, as was said, the mystical sense is that signified by the things [referred to by the words] and, subjectively speaking, there are many real features of any one thing which may differ greatly from one another. Hence, one thing, speaking subjectively, can sometimes signify many and different things mystically; a lion, by virtue of its steadfastness, signifies Christ—see Revelations 5:5: *Behold, the lion of the tribe of Juda has conquered*; and by virtue of its rapacity it signifies the devil—see 1 Peter 5:8: *Your adversary the devil, like a roaring lion, seeks someone to devour.*[24]

4. THE *POSTILLA LITTERALIS ON THE SONG OF SONGS*

HERE BEGINS THE POSTILLA OF
THE VENERABLE BROTHER NICHOLAS OF LYRA
ON THE SONG OF SONGS

Chapter One

[INTRODUCTION]

May he kiss me and so on.

17. Now that we have dealt with Solomon's first book—in which counsel for the guidance of souls was given—and the second—in which we are encouraged to despise fickle wealth, following from these, here begins the third, which rouses us to the love of a higher happiness, as was more fully explained at the beginning of the first book.[25] There I offered a preface of sorts to all three works.

18. Now the desire for this heavenly bliss arises out of the mutual love by which God and the rational creature love one another, and that is what this book is about, as will be made more fully apparent in what follows. However, a few prefatory remarks should be made here for the better understanding of what follows. The first is that in many places our translation differs from the hebrew text, likewise the chapter headings. The second is that this whole book is written in the form of parable.[26] Nor is it clear to which persons precisely the parable is to be applied in its literal sense[27] and this together with the first difficulty adds to the problems there are with this book. For it would be easy to interpret this work were things as clear cut as they are in Judges 9, where it is said: *Then all the trees said to the bramble: Come and rule over us* (v. 14); there, from the way the text goes on, it is made abundantly clear that this is understood as referring to the citizens of Sechem and to Abimelech, for they anointed him as their king over them.[28] However, none of this is obvious (in the case of

the Song) except that in a general way this work speaks in metaphors of the mutual love of Bridegroom and Bride.[29]

19. Moreover, who this Bridegroom and Bride are is not clear from the text and as a result various readings are given by different interpreters. Some have said that the Bridegroom is literally to be taken as Solomon himself but that the Bride is the daughter of Pharoah, his beloved wife. But this seems not to be true because, granted that this love between Bridegroom and Bride could have been lawful—at any rate if confined within the bounds of marriage, as I have explained more fully in my commentary on 3 [1] Kings 3—it was of a carnal sort and such love often has something not very fitting and unlawful about it; and so the description of a love of this kind seems inappropriate in canonical books of sacred Scripture, especially as they were written at the dictation of the Holy Spirit. In any case, Solomon's knowledge of his love for his wife and of hers for him and of the pleasures such love yields was a matter of personal experience; he did not learn of this love from that revelation of the Holy Spirit which is the reason why hebrew and latin scholars alike list this book among the canonical works.[30] As Jerome makes clear in his *Prologue to Galeatus*: 'it does not seem that it was written to be about a love of this kind'.[31]

20. For this reason the hebrew scholars say that the book speaks in parables of the love of God and the jewish people, whom he espoused when he gave them the Law—as recounted in Exodus 20—thus taking her to himself as his beloved Bride. But catholic interpreters commonly say that the book speaks of the love of Christ and the Church, meaning the Church in its distinction from the Synagogue, for the Church proceeded from the side of Jesus sleeping on the Cross as Eve was fashioned from the rib of the sleeping Adam; in this way both parties strive to turn the letter of the text according to their own purposes.

21. But with all due respect to their judgment, the opinion of either seems in some degree inadequate. In the first

place jewish writers understand the 'Bride' in too narrow a way when they restrict the sense exclusively to the jewish people and the convert Gentiles, while Catholics restrict the sense to the christian people. For there are some things put in this book which are not easily interpreted from the standpoint of its Old Testament status; and there are others which cannot readily be interpreted with reference to its New Testament status. And from this follows another weakness, namely, that the jewish writers awkwardly interpret some things in Old Testament terms which should be understood by reference to the New Testament and similarly Catholics less than felicitously read as having reference to the New Testament some passages which should be understood in an Old Testament sense.[32]

22. But insofar as I will be able to do so, I propose to base my interpretation on the literal sense. And the literal sense is not that which is signified by the words, but that which is immediately meant by the things signified[33]—as is illustrated by the example of Abimelech and the Schechemites referred to above. In this connection, the word *parabola* is derived from *para*, which means 'beyond' and *bole*, which means 'the meaning', for the meaning of words is to signify something other than themselves. Accordingly, in this book the Bridegroom seems to stand for God himself, the Bride for the Church herself, including within its scope the Church of both Testaments. For because men of our own time and those of old share one faith, differing only in greater or lesser degree of explicitness, so there is but one Church, differing only in the greater or lesser degree of its union with God; it is bound in greater union with God in the New Testament era. This is how the Church is understood in the blessed Gregory's seventh homily, where he says: 'Who with greater justice has the likeness of a father of a family than our creator who retains his creatures like servants in his household; who owns the vineyard, that is the universal Church, which is all those from Abel the first just man to the last of the elect who is to be born at the

end of time: then he will give the palm to as many saints as he has favoured.'[34]

23. But the Church understood in this way has existed in different times: in some periods she has offended the Bridegroom; in others she has done his will. Again, the Church is gathered together from different nations, that is, from the jewish and gentile peoples, it contains the just and the unjust, bishops and those subject to them. These, and other like factors, make for the difficulty of this book; for there are frequent shifts from one time-frame to another, from one part of the Church to another, and from the Church to God and back again, all as if in a single literary context. And this is because of the intimate union of Bridegroom and Bride and of the parts of the Church with one another in a single faith, as I have explained in greater detail at the beginning of my commentary on Genesis,[35] on the subject of the rules for the interpretation of sacred Scripture.

24. But the reader should know that even if, as was said, the Church has its origins in the beginning of the world, it first receives the name of Bride specifically at the giving of the Law on Mount Sinai, by virtue of which the people of Israel were betrothed to God by faith and worship, while the other nations fell into idolatry.[36] Hence, when Solomon, writing at the dictation of the Holy Spirit, tells of God's love and the Church's love under the descriptions of Bridegroom and Bride, he begins from the time of the Exodus from slavery in Egypt, for that was when the Law was given. For this reason the book is divided into two parts: the first gives an account of this same love in its Old Testament context; the second in the context of New Testament times. The first part is divided into three sections, of which the first tells of this love as far as concerns the escape from Egypt; the second describes the journey through the desert—beginning from *While the King . . .* (Sg 1:12); the third tells of the crossing of the borders into Judea, beginning at Chapter 4, *I will go* (4:6). Then of these the first is

subdivided into two, for the author first presents the loving plea of the Bride and secondly the gracious response of the Bridegroom, at *If you do not know* (1:8). And then the first of these subdivisions is yet further divided into two, for first of all [Solomon] presents the plea of love and then, beginning at *I am black . . .* (1:5), corrects an error.

[I LITERAL INTERPRETATION[37]]

25. As regards this first passage, the reader should note that the people of Israel—to be understood as referred to by the name 'Bride'—have ardently desired their escape from Egypt[38] so as to be free from a cruel slavery and so as to be able to serve God with greater freedom and to cling to him with greater intensity—as we read in Exodus 3.[39] And this desire is given expression in the words: *May he kiss me with the kiss of his mouth*. In other words: 'O that God would show himself to me by means of signs and loving deeds, as a Bridegroom would to his beloved Bride'.

26. *For your breasts are more delightful than wine*. The hebrew text gives: *For your loves are more delightful . . . .* For the hebrew word given here is ambiguous between *loves* and *breasts*;[40] the jewish authors follow the first meaning, our translation the second. But here the jewish reading seems preferable, for, following the meaning of the hebrew text, the Bride is addressing the Bridegroom and as a form of praise of the Bridegroom the reference to 'breasts' would scarcely be apt. Though you could say that mention of the Bridegroom's 'breasts' refers to the fullness of God's mercy.[41] So, following the hebrew authors, the meaning of *For your loves are more delightful than wine* is that they are more delightful to the palate of the pious soul than is any bodily savour to the bodily palate. And the meaning, following our translation—that is *for your breasts are more delightful than wine*—is that the fullness of your mercies is sweeter to the human mind than wine is to the palate, which of all bodily foods is the best to taste.

27. *The fragrance*—or, in the jewish reading, *the fragrant things*—*of your ointments is above all fragrances,* that is, the fullness of your mercy—alternatively, 'your loves'—gives greater refreshment to the devout mind than any which in a bodily way perfumes the sense of smell.

28. *Your name is oil poured out.* For oil here means the sweet-smelling juice which flows from aromatic trees in Arabia and in the Promised Land and is collected and stored in jars. When it is poured upon a person for his refreshment or health it gives off a sweet smell. For this reason, oil is understood in scriptural contexts to mean, 'good reputation', as the Apostle does when he says in 2 Cor 2:15: *We are the aroma . . . .* So the meaning of *Your name is oil poured out* is that, because of the wonders which God wrought for the sons of Israel in Egypt and in the Red Sea, the reputation of his name and of his goodness is spread to other peoples, with the result that many were converted to the jewish faith.[42] Hence the text continues:

29. *Therefore the maidens have loved you.* Which is to say that other peoples have been converted to your love. For many Egyptians were thus converted and fled from the land of Egypt with the sons of Israel, as can be read in Exodus 12. In this way were Jethro and his household converted when he heard of the wonders which God had done for Israel (Ex 18:10–12).[43]

30. *Draw me after you,* which he did by leading me in great power out of Egypt.[44]

31. *We will run,* by following you in the way of justice, *in the fragrance of your oils*: that is, drawn by the effects of your goodness. In fact, this passage, *in the fragrance of your oils,* does not belong to the text, for it is not found in the Hebrew, but was added by some master or other as an interlinear gloss and was later inserted into the text through scribal error.

32. *the* [*heavenly*] *king has brought me into his chambers* by disclosing to me his secrets through Moses, as is related in

Exodus 3: *and when he had led his flock to the interior of the desert* (Ex 3:1) . . . *and the Lord appeared to him* . . . (Ex 3:2).

33. *We will rejoice and be glad in you*, a prophecy which was fulfilled when, having crossed the Red Sea, they joyfully sang: *We will sing to the Lord, for [he has triumphed] gloriously* . . . (Ex 15:1).

34. *The memory of your breasts*—or alternatively, *your loves*, as the Jewish writers have it—and this is to be read as above.[45]

35. *The righteous*,[46]— that is, the just—*love you* with the love of sons and daughters.

36. *I am black* . . . . Here, following from this last, a mistake of judgement is corrected. In this connection it is worth noting that the Church militant has always contained, does now and will until the end of the world contain, some sinners alongside the just; and alongside the strong, some who are weak. It was in the light of this that the Saviour compared her to nets thrown into the sea, gathering in fish of every kind (Mt 13:47). And so there were some among the jewish people who, enfeebled by their harsh slavery and their patience broken, thought the whole Church to be an offence before God—like an ugly bride before her husband. But although God many times permits his chosen ones to be subjected to trials with a view to their purification and with a view to an increase of merit, he nonetheless refutes the error of the weak by saying, *I am black*, that is, I am shameful before God, in the eyes of the ignorant, *but* in truth *beautiful, daughters of Jerusalem*, that is, you, who are the imperfect ones of the people of Israel on account of which you are called 'daughters', feeble and female in gender.

37. *Like the tents of Kedar*: the tents, that is to say, of the Hagarenes—for Kedar was the son of Ishmael (cf Gen 25:13) who was the son of Hagar (cf Gen 25:12). But the Hagarenes, who are now known as the Saracens, then lived in tents, exposed to the showers and snows of winter and to

the burning sun in summer; as a result they were blackened on the outside, but beautiful within.

38. *Like Solomon's hides.* The reference to Solomon—which means 'peacemaker'—is to be understood of God himself according to jewish writers, for God orders all things with gentleness. But in this context *his hides* refer to the covering laid over the tabernacle in which God is worshipped, for it was made of rams' hides (Ex 26:14); and they were exposed to the rains and floods as the children of Israel were to forced labour in Egypt.

39. *Do not gaze upon me*—that is, do not judge me—*because I am swarthy,* meaning, dark and hateful to God; *it is because the sun has burned me.* For a woman who is otherwise beautiful loses her beauty if she is exposed to the harsh rays of the sun, but loss of beauty of that kind is skin-deep and is due to external causes. And so the meaning of *because the sun has burned me* is that the heat of trials in Egypt has darkened my skin and has given me a shameful appearance. For this reason, Deuteronomy 4:20 speaks of this fire in these words: *But the Lord has taken you and brought you forth out of the iron furnace, out of Egypt*; and so the text continues:

40. *My mother's sons have fought against me,* that is, the Egyptians have afflicted me with harsh burdens, and they are called the sons of the same mother as the Jewish people, because both [peoples] originated from the same land—in the same way as we say that those born in Paris are the children and sons of Paris. Now all the Jews who had entered Egypt with Jacob had died by the time the Egyptians began to persecute them, as Exodus 1 tells us: and so all who remained had been born in Egypt.

41. *They put me in charge of the vineyards,* that is, they imposed servile tasks upon me: and this perhaps in spite of the fact that some of them were themselves slaves assigned to the guardianship of the vineyards by day and by night.

42. *But my own vineyards I have not kept,* meaning that I have not been able to attend to my own tasks with any

ease, being preoccupied with the tasks imposed by the Egyptians.

43. *Show me*: having asked of the Bridegroom the affection of love, here she goes on to ask of him the path that love should take.[47] For some of the Jews, broken by their labours, thought the Egyptians happy and were tempted by their idolatry, and so the Bride asks to be guided away from such mistaken paths saying: *Show me* . . . . And these words are to be interpreted as meaning: 'O you, my Bridegroom, *whom my soul loves, show me at noon*, that is, at the heat of this trial . . .

44. *where you feed* your faithful ones, as a flock', *where you lie down*, that is, where you take your rest in sure faith, thus protecting me from infidelity and idolatry. And so it goes on: *lest I should begin to wander after the flocks*—that is, after the other faithless nations—*of your companions*—namely, of the kings and princes themselves who are in this way called companions of God because they share with him his name. For they are said to be kings and lords as God himself is, as Rabbi Solomon says.[48] But to me it seems better to say that it is the holy angels ruling over the unbelieving peoples who are here said to be the companions of God. So it is that, in Daniel 10:20, the angel who rules over the Greeks is called 'the Prince of the Greeks' and the angel of the Persians 'the Prince of the Persians'. And the blessed Denys[49] says that there were holy angels who are certainly in the company of God, though they rule over the godless nations.

45. *If you do not know* . . . . Having given an account of the Bride's loving request, here, therefore, we are given the Bridegroom's gracious reply to it. And first of all he replies to the second request, maintaining the thread from the immediately preceeding words, and says: *If you do not know yourself, most fair among women*, meaning: 'You, the Hebrew people, beautiful among the other nations on account of your unsullied faith and worship'. *If you do not*

know yourself, that is, if you fear that you will lapse from the true life because of the weak ones among you,

46. *Go out* from the society and companionship of idolaters; for in Proverbs (13:20) it is said *the friend of a fool becomes like one . . . and leave, go follow in the tracks of the flocks,* the tracks, that is, of the men of simple faith, such as were Abel, Schechem, Enoch, and the like,[50] *and feed your kids,* the weak ones of your people *beside the shepherd's tents,* that is, following in the example of the Patriarchs; they, being asked about their occupations, replied: *We are shepherds as our fathers were* (Gen 47:3).

47. *To the horses.* Here, then, he replies to the Bride's first request—which was for the warmth of his love—and says: *I have compared you, my love, to the horses of Pharoah's chariots,* this meaning: I openly declared my true love for you when I sank the pursuing chariots of Pharoah under the Red Sea (Ex 14:29).[51] And then I compared you to my own cavalry—that is, to my angels, whom I love with a great love. Note that in sacred Scripture, the holy angels are often referred to as his soldiery and army, and in the same way here are referred to as 'God's cavalry'. In common usage a troop of horse soldiers is known as 'cavalry'.

[II LITERAL AND ALLEGORICAL INTERPRETATIONS]

Chapter Seven

48. *How beautiful are* .... Having told of the love of Bridegroom and Bride in its reference to the Old Testament, now, appropriately, we hear tell of that same love in its status under the New Testament; and the account comes in three parts, the first of which describes the early development of this status; the second, the expansion of these beginnings, starting at *Come, my beloved* (7:11); thirdly, [in Chapter Eight) once spread abroad, its peaceful establishment.[52]

49. In this first connection, the Bride is described in the parable of a favoured woman. This description differs from that given in Chapter Four where the Bride's beauty is depicted beginning from her head and moving down to her feet; for in this passage the movement is reversed, proceeding from the feet to the head. This is because, as an Old Testament type, the Bride proceeds and comes forth from God, as it were. As a type of the New Testament she is brought from the things of earth to the things of heaven into God. For this reason, the parable of the beautiful woman is first of all stated and then explained. And so in the first place it says *How beautiful*, how exceedingly beautiful, . . .

50. *are your feet in sandals*, for it does much to add grace to a woman's deportment that she should walk with poise and dignity, her feet shod, for it is lacking in modesty to appear in bare feet.

51. *The meeting of your thighs is like a necklace, the work of a master hand*. Here what is referred to is the artistry with which her limbs are crafted, removing every defect of carriage.

52. *Your navel is like a carved bowl*, for it is rounded and well-formed; here *navel* is taken to mean the surface of the belly, for the navel is at its centre. In the Hebrew we

have *Your navel is a burnished vessel,*[53] which refers to the beautiful appearance of the curve of the belly.

53. *Your belly is a heap of wheat,* and, speaking of it in its interior sense, that means that it is fruitful in children; *encircled with lilies,* meaning that it is adorned with marital chastity.

54. *Your two breasts are like two fawns, twins of a gazelle,* for both are full and flow with milk for the feeding of children.

55. *Your neck is like an ivory tower,* straight, like a tower and white, like ivory.

56. *Your eyes are like pools in Heshbon.* According to jewish writers, Heshbon in this context is not the proper name of the city on the far side of the Jordan which is referred to in Numbers 22,[54] where it says . . . *fire went forth from Heshbon,* but is the common noun which means 'a reckoning'. And so the literal meaning is 'Your eyes are like pools in estimation, that is, great is their fame'. *Which are at the gate,* or near the gate, *of the daughters of the multitude*: this refers to Jerusalem, which is called 'the daughter of the multitude' because of being so heavily populated,[55] as is said in Lamentations 1. For there were two pools of water in Jerusalem which much enhanced the city's beauty just as beautiful and clear eyes enhance a woman's. And the eyes are compared to pools of water because they are like water in that if they are hurt, they turn to tears.

57. *Your nose is like the tower of Lebanon,* for it is straight and artfully set on her face, like the tower of Lebanon, erect and strategically situated on the borders of the Promised Land, *overlooking Damascus,* the capital city of the Syrians, who were so often the enemies of Israel.

58. *Your head crowns your body like Carmel,* standing proud as does Carmel in the Promised Land, Carmel which is fertile, or, in other words, fair. As Isaiah says: *The glory of Lebanon has been given to* [*the wilderness*] *and the beauty of Carmel and Sharon* (35:2).

59. *And the hair of your head is like the deep-dyed robes of a king, caught into ringlets*[56] for washing after she has dyed

it; thus is its hue more brilliant in sheen. In this way is represented the fine colouring of the Bride's hair—as the scarlet stuff which is dyed for the robes of kings is of the finest hue. And so the text continues: *How beautiful you are, how fair, my beloved, are your charms. You stand like a palm tree,* erect and tall and *your breasts are like its clusters* swelling with milk.

60. Thus is the Bride's beauty of form described. And in and through this parable[57] which belongs to the literal meaning of the text, the Bride's spiritual beauty is understood as a type of the New Testament. And so the text says:

61. *How beautiful are your feet,* climbing the path of the evangelical counsels, *shod in sandals.* For sandals are made from the hides of dead animals and are a reminder of the death of Christ and of the martyrs; they protect the Bride's feet as she steps steadily on the way of the evangelical counsels; *O daughter of the King*—meaning the Church which, in Revelation (21:2), is called the 'daughter and Bride of Christ' who is ruler of the kings of the earth.

62. *The meeting of your thighs* .... This refers to the coming together of Jews and Gentiles in the one Church of Christ; and this convergence is *the work of a master hand,* that of Christ, who made of the two one thing.[58] *Your belly* ... within which a child is conceived; it is there, in the womb, where a child is nourished before birth; by all this is the Church referred to, fertile in children begotten from Christ himself; and to the fact that they are begotten not in the flesh but in the spirit. As John says (1:13) *who were born not of blood, nor of the will of the flesh* .... And so that belly is said to be *encircled by lilies,* encircled, that is to say, by chastity.

63. *Your two breasts* are the two Testaments, from which the children begotten in Christ draw milk for their growth, as is said in 1 Peter 2:2: *Like new born babies of men, without anxiety long for the milk on which you may grow in salvation. Your neck* ... refers to a faith strengthened by charity. It is charity which joins the Bride's body to the head which is

Christ: *He has made him head over all things for the Church* (Eph 1:22). But this head has a nose, which is the power of discernment by which even today he discriminates between believers and unbelievers, as the nose discriminates between foul and fresh smells. But his eyes are Christ's knowing power; with them he looks favourably upon his people; In John 10:14 it says: *I know my sheep*, as the faithful are called. . . . *are like pools*, for they are filled with tears of mercy.

64. *Your head . . .* , that is, the crown of his head, which refers to the divine nature of Christ; and from this head there flow down the feeling and energy[59] of the spiritual life, first of all into the human nature of Christ and through it to all the members of the Church. And so, the text continues, *like Carmel*, which is fertile, abundant in harvest. *And the hairs of your head* are the Apostles who were the first to join with Christ the Head; and, it says, *like the rich garments of a king*, because for love of Christ the King they were dyed in the red of their own blood by the prize of martyrdom. And on the basis of all this, the passage concludes:

65. *How beautiful you are*: made so by faith within; *how fair*, because of the goodness of your actions, *beloved*, redeemed at so great a price, namely, by the precious blood of Christ. For a thing is dearest which is bought at the highest price; *in your charms*, for the passion of Christ opened the gate to the delights of Paradise for his Bride.

66. *You stand like a palm tree*, erect in justice and drawn up to the height of devout contemplation. *And your breasts are like its clusters*, because they are full with the milk which nourishes the children of Christ and of the Church.

NOTES

1. *Postilla*: a term, Smalley suggests (p. 270), perhaps deriving from *post illa verba*, roughly, 'following the words in question' and denoting a 'continuous gloss interposed between the *loci* of the text'. It thus denotes the kind of commentary excerpted here, as distinct from 'marginal' and 'interlinear' glosses.

2. The preceding passage is a close paraphrase of Thomas Aquinas, see above, *Q.Quodl.* 7, q.6 a.l corp. and a.2 corp.

3. These lines are borrowed from the Dominican, Augustine of Denmark, who composed them c. 1260 in his *Rotulus Pugilaris.*

4. Cf Cassian, *Collationes*, xiv.8, CSEL 13:404–405.

5. *sacra scriptura.*

6. *Ep.* 93.7.24; PL 30:334.

7. *aliquorum correctorum.*

8. *Hebraicae Questiones in Libros Geneseos*, in *S. Hieronymi Presbyteri Opera*, Pars I: *Opera Exegetica*, I, *CCL* 72 (Turnholt, 1959) pp. 1–2. Cf the english translation in *The Principal Works of St Jerome*, trans. W. H. Fremantle, Select Library of Nicene and Post Nicene Fathers of the Christian Church, Vol. 6 (Oxford and New York, 1893) p. 486.

9. A polemical work addressed principally against jewish interpretations of the Old Testament prophecies. There is no modern edition.

10. In his *Preface to the Pentateuch*, PL 28:180A.

11. *multum obumbrata.*

12. Thus, as will be seen, Nicholas reads chapters 1–6 of the Song literally, chapters 7–8 both literally and typologically.

13. Rabbi Shelomoh ben Yishaq, known as Rashi, born Troyes in 1041 and died in 1105 there, where he had established a school of jewish scholars. Best known for his commentaries on the Pentateuch, he was known to the twelfth century scholars as to Nicholas as a 'judicious expounder of the literal sense'.

14. The 1471 edition gives Romans 12; the correct reference is Romans 11:25.

15. Nicholas evidently refers to the Franciscan, William Brito.

16. *scholastice*, i.e., a matter to be settled by disputation.

17. Isidore of Seville. In fact, these are the 'rules' of Tychonius the Donatist, of which Augustine thoroughly approved, see *On Christian Doctrine* III.xxxi–xxxvii (Robertson, pp. 106–117).

18. *ubera*: but see Nicholas' amendment to the Vulgate, n. 28 below.

19. See n. 39 below.

20. The reference is to the Vulgate version of Hosea. In the LXX, 11:1.

21. *Ep.* 93.8, 25; PL 33:334.

22. Cassian, *Collationes*, VIII.iii; CSEL 13:218 219.

23. See my discussion of this passage on pp. 105–107.

24. See Hugh of Saint Victor, n. 7.

25. Nicholas refers to the traditional ordering of Proverbs, Ecclesiastes, and the Song in degrees of spiritual ascent, following Gregory the Great (see above, n. 10) and ultimately Origen.

26. *parabolice.*

27. The fact that Nicholas can speak at all of the *sensus litteralis* of a *parabolum* suggests that *parabolum* means 'metaphor' and that he takes metaphors to be part of the literal sense.

28. Cp. this passage with n. 16 above.

29. *iste liber loquatur parabolice de amore mutuo sponsi et sponse.*

30. There is nothing very surprising about the aprioristic line of argument adopted here. Nicholas' 'literalism' is bound to cause him difficulties with texts whose apparent literal sense is morally distasteful to him. When confronted with such texts, therefore, Nicholas is forced to look elsewhere for the literal significance than in the surface, apparent meaning. And this is one of those passages which shows that, for mediaeval exegetes, 'literal' is not always equivalent to 'obvious'.

31. Unidentified.

32. The whole of nn. 20 and 21 are quoted, verbatim, by Denys the Carthusian in his Commentary, see below, nn. 6–7. In complaining that Nicholas misrepresents the traditions of patristic and mediaeval interpretation, Denys is undeniably justified, though Giles of Rome (see nn. 2–3 above) does represent an exception in offering an exclusively typological, christian interpretation.

33. Once again, Nicholas appears to be following Thomas Aquinas closely. As his illustration from Judges 9:14 above makes clear, Nicholas is here discussing how metaphors function as part of the literal sense. The 'literal' meaning of a metaphor consists in what the metaphor is a metaphor *for*—trees for the Sichimites, a bramble for Abimelech. This is not, of course, to propose a 'literalist' or 'substitution' account of metaphor—that view of metaphor according to which metaphors can always be replaced by their 'literal equivalents', for Nicholas would no more have understood our contrast between 'metaphorical' and 'literal' than would have Thomas Aquinas, for whom also metaphors are strictly part of the literal sense.

34. *XL Homiliarum in Evangelia* I.VII; PL 76:1099–1103. Translation by David Hurst, *Gregory the Great: Forty Gospel Homilies*, CS 123 (Kalamazoo, 1990), Homily 4, pp. 21–27.

35. See above, ¶ 11.

36. Cp. Denys the Carthusian, nn. 18–19 below. Nicholas roots his interpretation of the Song as a parable of jewish history in the central metaphor of the Covenant as betrothal.

37. The heading is mine.

38. The *Expositio Hystorica* likewise sets the Bride's opening request for a kiss against the background of captivity in Egypt. 'Therefore the bride, that is the Synagogue held in captivity, says . . . .' (Prol., p. 53). There is no evidence that Nicholas knew this late thirteenth-century anonymous commentary. The relationship between Nicholas' *Postilla Litteralis* and the *Expositio Hystorica* is through their common debt to Rashi. See my discussion on pp. 115–117.

39. Cf. Denys the Carthusian's critical comment, ¶ 36 below.

40. See *The Vulgate Text and Translation*, pp. 202–204 above. Interestingly, for all his undoubted knowledge of Hebrew, the author of

the *Expositio Hystorica* glosses the unamended Vulgate text's *ubera*, but interprets it as meaning 'mercy'.

41. Cf. Giles of Rome, nn. 8–9 above, and Denys the Carthusian, nn. 29–30 below, who both defend the Vulgate translation, rather aprioristically, as one might expect, given their ignorance of Hebrew.

42. Cp the *Expositio Hystorica*: '*your name is oil poured out*, for in the same way that oil poured out spreads its fragrance afar, so the fame and fragrance of your name (spreads) throughout the whole globe, when the marvels you have wrought in Egypt are heard tell of'. I.3, p. 54.

43. Cp. *Expositio Hystorica*: 'And so, hearing these things, the *young maidens*, that is, the other peoples who are addressed as young maidens . . . . *have greatly loved you*. Thus it was that Jethro, the gentile, blessed God'. I.2, p. 54.

44. *Expositio Hystorica*: ' . . . just as Moses and Aaron drew me and led me out of Egypt'. I.3, p. 55.

45. i.e., as in n. 11.

46. Nicholas' knowledge of Hebrew was evidently not such as to enable him to detect the erroneous Vulgate translation here, see *The Vulgate Text and Translation*, pp. 202–204.

47. Reading the *directionis* of 1496 for the *dilectionis* of 1471. I have not attempted to reflect in English the assonance between *affectum dilectionis* and *effectum directionis*.

48. And following Rashi, the *Expositio Hystorica* glosses this verse: 'for it is not fitting that I should wander after the alien peoples who have their own gods and their own kings and lords, who feed them and rule over them, just as you feed your flocks'. I.6, p. 56.

49. Pseudo-Denys, *CH*, c. 9, 2, 260B, Luibheid, p. 171.

50. *Expositio Hystorica*: 'give thought to your fathers who guarded my law, and follow in their tracks'. I.7, p. 56.

51. *Expositio Hystorica*: '*to my horses*—with which I have fought against Pharoah in the Red Sea . . . .' I.8, p. 56.

52. That is, the constantinian establishment. The author of the *Expositio Hystorica*, anxious to avoid controversy with jewish interpretation, limits the historical reference of the Song safely to the pre-christian era. In this he differs not only from the later Nicholas, but also from his source text in Rashi's commentary, for Rashi reads the Song as having literal reference to jewish history up to his own times in the eleventh century of The Common Era.

53. 1496 edition gives *bacinus clarus*; 1471 gives *bacinus elatus*. Nicholas omits the succeeding phrase of the Vulgate, *numquam indigens poculis*, 'ever filled with wine'.

54. The 1471 edition gives, correctly, 21 (v. 28).

55. Vulgate: *civitas plena populo* (Lam 1:1).

56. *vincta canalibus*.

57. *dictam parabolam*.

58. 1471 refers to Eph 2:13.

59. *sensus et motus*.

Denys the Carthusian

Denys the Carthusian, known as the 'Doctor Ecstaticus' because of the fame of his mystical writings, was born in 1402/3 in Ryckel in modern Belgium. He studied at the University of Cologne, where he became Master in 1424 and appears to have joined the Carthusian Order in Holland in that or the following year.

As befits a monk in the most solitary of all monastic orders, the rest of his life was uneventful, except for a brief period of a year or two around 1451 when he joined Nicholas of Cusa on a missionary tour of the Rhineland, preaching against low standards of morality and piety in the Church—particularly against the unedifying conduct of bishops and priests. Otherwise he occupied a number of offices in his own Order. He was procurator at Roermond from 1432–4, and in 1465 he took charge of a new carthusian foundation at Bois-le-Duc. He resigned from this office in 1469 because of ill-health, returned to Roermond and died there on 12 March 1471. Denys was a writer of extraordinary prolixity and cannot always be excused of a tedious pedantry. He commented on the whole of the Bible and, in addition to the standard commentary on the *Sentences* of Peter the Lombard, wrote commentaries on Aristotle, and on the works of the pseudo-Denys and many works of an ascetical, mystical and homilectic character. Among his best writings, characterised by an unusual economy of style, is his *De contemplatione.* At his best Denys can combine energy of thought with conceptual clarity to a degree which fully justifies his mediaeval appellation.

He was a conservative theologically and eclectic in source, in his biblical commentaries reverting to an older monastic style of commentary in reaction to the new scholarship of Nicholas of Lyra. He drew sympathetically upon the *divus Dionysius,* as he called him, and upon Thomas Aquinas, while in his mystical teaching he was scarcely less enthusiastic for the writings of his compatriot, Jan van Ruusbroec (1293–1381).

I have translated the extracts from his *Enarratio in Canticum canticorum* from volume 4 of the Cologne edition of the *Opera Varia* (1555), but I have made reference from time to time to the Montreuil-Tournai-Parkminster edition of 1896–1935, volume 7 (1898). The paragraph divisions and numbering are my own.

DENYS THE CARTHUSIAN

A DEVOTIONAL CONTINUOUS COMMENTARY ON THE SONG OF SONGS, IN HEBREW CALLED *SIR HASIRIM*

OF CHRIST AND THE CHURCH, OF THE SOUL OF ANY JUST PERSON AND OF THE BLESSED MARY.

Preface

. . . *the bridegroom rejoices over the bride* (Is 62:5)

1. The most blessed John the Baptist, the best man and friend of his Bridegroom, is our witness that the Bridegroom is Christ. For he says: *He who has the bride is the bridegroom.* He adds, speaking of himself, *the friend of the bridegroom, who stands and hears him, rejoices greatly at the bridegroom's voice.* (Jn 3:29) Hence in the Gospel Christ says of himself, *Can the wedding guests fast as long as the bridegroom is with them*? (Mt 9:15). Then, in the Apocalypse we read concerning the chaste and happy wedding, *the marriage of the Lamb has come* (Rev 19:7).[1] But although the most supremely blessed and adorable Trinity as a whole, indeed each divine, eternal and uncreated Person, can be called the bridegroom of each and every rational and intellectual creature, whether in a state of grace or of glory; nonetheless in a special and appropriate way this title belongs and is given to the only-begotten incarnate Son of God as spouse of the militant Church: because bridegroom and bride are usually of the same nature. He, however, not the Father or the Holy Spirit, assumed our nature in the unity of his person.

2. Moreover, although, as we shall see later, it is the Church triumphant and each blessed soul in heaven which is, properly speaking, the bride of the eternal Word and in a higher way than is the Church militant or the soul which is still *in via*[2] (that is, the rational soul in a state of faith and grace), nonetheless, it is commonly agreed that there

is a threefold bride of Christ: namely, the whole universal Church militant, called the 'general' bride of Our Lord Jesus Christ; then, any faithful and loving soul, called the 'individual' bride of Christ; and finally the most blessed Virgin Mary, the mother of Christ, said to be the 'special' bride of Christ. But not only the universal Church, but also any particular[3] church is the bride of Christ and, with respect to any individual can be called the common bride. Consequently, just as the Supreme Pontiff is called the bridegroom of the Church—the bridegroom of the universal Church, as I might say, by proxy,—so bishops can be called the particular bridegrooms of the Churches, each being the bridegroom of the church assigned to him.[4]

3. And so—as from the beginning of the early Church the Holy Fathers and most learned doctors have born witness and written—Solomon, before his downfall and filled with the Holy Spirit, resplendent with the spirit of prophecy, knew in his spirit the mysteries of Christ—his incarnation, his revelation, his preaching, his passion, resurrection and ascension; and he knew why Christ would take all these things upon himself and that he would set the human race free. He knew the number and kinds of the gifts of grace Christ would confer in the present and the gifts of glory [he would confer] in the future; [Solomon knew] how lovingly and intimately he [Christ] would associate and unite himself with them and how ardently and longingly they would await his coming. And he knew with what thankfulness and fervour they would welcome him when he came. And Solomon put together his book about all these things, which, because of its achievements of compression and completeness and [because of] the exalted character of its treatment, and on account of the delightful nature of his heavenly theme, is called the Songs of Songs.[5]

4. From this it may be gathered that they are mistaken who think this work should be read in its literal and historical sense as referring to Solomon and his bride, the daughter of Pharoah, and allegorically to Christ and the

Church.[6] If this were so then the subject matter of this book would be of no worth, sensual and prurient and not spiritual, mystical, most excellent and heavenly; nor would it be a prophetic text, but rather a sort of love song. But it is a book of the highest spirituality and deals with the very purest love which belongs to those who are perfect. In any case, according to Josephus, Solomon took the daughter of Pharoah to be his wife when she was still in her childhood, before she was fourteen years old; and according to other Jewish teachers, even sometime before that. And this book can hardly have been written at that age, but later. Therefore, had he composed those songs literally about himself and the daughter of Pharoah, this book would have been a narrative of past events, not a prophecy of future events, nor could it be a description of a spiritual marriage: and the holy and learned teachers, in whom the Holy Spirit dwells and speaks and through whom the Church chooses to be instructed, witness against this.

5. Finally, since so many and such splendid things have been written about these Songs of Songs by holy and very wise men that there is scarcely time for one man to read them all, I do not intend to delay excessively in the exposition of a very short book, but rather to pluck a little posy from among the flowers of the Fathers and explain clearly any of their more obscure sayings. But to understand what follows, it is necessary to add some preliminary comments.

ARTICLE ONE: *Whether the literal meaning of this book is about God and the Synagogue or about Christ and the Church?*

6. In every field of enquiry it is first necessary to establish what the subject-matter is or what kind of knowledge may be gained from a book in that field: and so we must first decide what this work is about. On this score Nicholas of Lyra gives the following account: *The jewish scholars say that this book speaks in parables of the love of God and of the jewish*

people, whom he espoused when he gave them the Law, thereby taking her to himself as his beloved Bride. But Catholic authors commonly say that the book speaks in parables of the love of Christ and the Church, meaning the Church in its distinction from the Synagogue; for, the Church proceeded from the side of Christ sleeping on the Cross—as Eve was fashioned from the rib of the sleeping Adam; in this way both parties strive to turn the text according to their own purposes.

7. But, saving their better judgment, neither opinion seems entirely adequate. In the first place Jewish writers understand the 'Bride' in too narrow a way, when they restrict the sense exclusively to the Jewish people and the converted Gentiles; while Catholics restrict the sense to the Christian people. For there are some things put in this book which are not easily interpreted from the standpoint of its Old Testament status; and there are other things which cannot readily be interpreted with reference to its New Testament status. And from this follows another weakness, namely that the Jewish writers awkwardly interpret some things in Old Testament terms which should be understood in reference to the New Testament; and similarly Catholics less than felicitously read as having reference to the New Testament some passages which should be understood in an Old Testament sense. Thus Lyra.[7] But his account does not seem to fit the facts particularly as concerns his somewhat unspecific view of Catholic interpreters as saying that this book speaks of the love of Christ and of the Church insofar as the Church is to be distinguished from the Synagogue.

8. For the ancient and most outstandingly holy interpreters insist that this book treats of Christ and of his Church insofar as the Church includes the Synagogue, indeed even insofar as it includes the whole congregation and company of all the elect from the beginning of the world. For of course Origen, who wrote so elegantly about the Songs—as Jerome declared, *in his other writings he surpassed all preceding teachers but in his writings on the Songs he surpassed even himself*[8]—this Origen says: *the Church desires to be married to Christ (the Church, note, being the company of*

all the Saints) so that this Church is like a single person made out of all people, and it speaks out saying: I have all things: I am filled with gifts which, by title of my betrothal I have received before my wedding day. A long time ago, while I was being prepared for my marriage to the Son of the King, the first born of every creature, his holy angels ministered to me bringing the Law in place of the gifts of betrothal. Thus Origen.[9] But it is obvious that he cannot mean the Church except by reference to the person and role of the Synagogue.

9. Moreover Anselm, Archbishop of Canterbury,[10] in the Prologue to his *Commentary on the Songs* writes: *this book must be classified as prophecy (which embraces past, present and future), for it reveals how great was the desire with which the faithful Synagogue sought for and anticipated the coming of Christ, which soon came about. It shows also how great was the joy with which those living in the time of grace welcomed the coming of the Son of God, and in what manner the Church is ennobled by the entry into it of all the nations: which is what we now see.* He also indicates how, at length, the remnant of Israel will be saved, which is to be in the future. Again Anselm says: *this book, this work concerns the bridegroom and bride, that is Christ and the Holy Church both before the coming of Christ and after. For although the patriarchs and prophets and all the faithful before Christ's coming are called 'the faithful of the Synagogue', still, because of the oneness of faith,*[11] *they also can be called the Church.* Then, after this, Anselm adds: *Solomon here begins his treatment of this most blessed subject by showing how greatly the holy Fathers, both before and under the Law, desired Christ's coming and how gratefully he was received by those others in the time of grace.*

10. Moreover, Saint Bernard, at the beginning of his second sermon on the Song says: *So very often, as I think of the burning desire with which the Fathers yearned for the presence of Christ in the flesh, I am touched with sorrow and troubled in myself and now can scarcely contain my tears: I am wearied by the indifference and dullness of our miserable times. For to which of us does the actual revelation of this grace bring as*

much in joy as the promise of it brought in burning desire to the holy ancients? And so Bernard goes on to teach that at the beginning of the Song the words, *May he kiss me with the kiss of his mouth,* are said in the person of those Fathers of the Old Law, that is to say, in the person of the Synagogue, or of the Church which includes the Synagogue. Then Bernard adds: *therefore, their burning desire and their feeling of holy hope speaks to me in those words: May he kiss me with the kiss of his mouth.*[12]

11. Then again, the saintly Gregory, near the beginning of his Commentary on this work, quite explicitly says: *The whole human race, from the beginning of the world to its end, that is to say, the whole Church, we now represent as one single Bride, who has collected its earnest money as a pledge of the spiritual gift through the Law; nonetheless it seeks the* [*actual*] *presence of its Bridegroom and cries: 'May he kiss me with the kiss of his mouth'*.[13]

12. It is thus clear from the witness of so many and such great Catholic Fathers that this book treats of Christ and the Church, not of the Church in its separation from the Synagogue, but as including it; and as including not the Synagogue only, but all the Saints from the beginning of the world, who, before the Law was written, lived under the law of nature.[14] So the Catholic doctors are not to be placed at one extreme of interpretation and set against the Jewish scholars at the other extreme, so that some scholar of modern times can represent himself as occupying the middle ground, as the first to publish a true interpretation of this text. For the later interpreters are the successors of those outstanding teachers I have quoted; and in any case I do not recall reading in any interpreter, well known or worth knowing, that this work speaks of the Church as opposed to the Synagogue and exclusively of the christian people. And even if there were some, with little or none of the authority of those [learned Fathers] mentioned, who do say this, it is not for that reason to be conceded without qualification that 'Catholic interpreters' say it.[15]

ARTICLE TWO: *What sort of people ought to be readers or hearers of this book?*

13. Origen, in his Prologue to the Songs writes: *In the words of the Song of Songs is to be found that food of which the Apostle speaks: Solid food is for the perfect (Heb 5:14). But if anyone who is only a man according to the flesh takes it up, for him there is no little risk and danger from this book of Scripture. Not knowing how to listen to the words of love with pure and chaste ears, he turns everything he hears from the inner man to the outer and bodily powers and feeds in himself the desires of the flesh;* [and] *so, on reading divine Scripture, is aroused to the lust of the flesh. For this reason I warn and advise everyone who as yet is not free from the annoyances of flesh and blood and who has not fled the attractions of material nature, that he altogether refrain from reading this little book and from everything said in it. For they say that even among Jewish people the rule is observed that until a person has reached a developed and mature stage in life they do not allow this book into his hands. But we too accept the same rule from them, namely that all the Scriptures should be given to children by teachers and wise men, including likewise those parts which are called* deuteroseis; *to which category four passages belong, the beginning of Genesis, the first chapter and the end of Ezechiel, concerning the vision of the building of the Temple and this work, the Song of Songs.*[16] This is what Origen says, whose account of the Jewish custom agrees with what Jerome says about Ezechiel, namely that among the Jews no one is allowed access to these four parts of the Old Testament Scriptures until they have reached the age of thirty.[17]

14. Moreover, Gregory says in his Prologue to the *Songs*: *In this book are described kisses, breasts, cheeks, limbs; and Holy Scripture is not be ridiculed because of these words; rather we are to think of the mercy of God, how he wonderfully and mercifully works on us so that by coming down to the words of our shameful love our heart is made to burn in the search of a holy love. But where he humbles himself by his manner of speech there he raises*

us in our minds; we learn from the words of this lower love, with what intensity we must burn with love of the Godhead.

15. *But we must be subtle enough to grasp this, lest when we hear the words of this external love we are moved to things of sense; lest the instrument which is given to lift us up should rather weigh us down. We must seek out whatever is more interior in these bodily, exterior words and, though speaking of the body ourselves be taken, as it were, out of the body. We must come to this wedding of the Bridegroom and Bride enlightened by interior charity and dressed in wedding clothes, lest we be thrown out into the darkness of ignorance (Mt 12:13). He who reads or hears this book, therefore, should have nothing changeable or sensual in his heart so that in his inner person he is a new creation. For this Sacred Scripture is a mountain and any wild beasts which trespass on it will be stoned. (Ex 19:12–13; Heb 12:20). Of course, the* [*wild*] *beasts intruding on the mountain are those who have capitulated to irrational impulses and approach the heavenly heights of Sacred Scripture not as they ought, understanding it in a purely spiritual way but, against reason, are seduced by the cunning of desire.*[18]

16. Moreover the Chancellor of Paris (throughout this work I refer thus to the most learned master John Gerson) in his work on the Song says: *No one should be distracted from belief in the most hidden and pure senses which the smokescreen of the literal* [sense] *disguises in carnality, nor should a person hit the rock of scandal of a foul sensuality. It would be shameful to repeat what I have heard for myself: it would offend pious ears.*[19]

17. You can see what agreement there is among so many very prudent and experienced witnesses about the kinds of people who may be permitted to read or hear this book which, on the surface, seems so very sensual but on a true understanding proves to be very spiritual. They should be people, I repeat, who are reformed, purified of sensual desire, so that they will not, with minds attentive to the descriptions of sensual things, imagine those things of the flesh, but quickly be raised to the things of the mind and spirit. Otherwise they will suffer harm within. In that case,

what is to be done with those many religious and canons and others in Holy Orders who in Church and in the Divine Office[20] are accustomed to hearing or reading these words, though they are not yet thus cleansed, who have hardly attained to a true and spiritual understanding and can scarcely read and hear these words at those times [of the Office] and in Church without indecent thoughts? I think they are to be advised that they should strive as far as possible to understand this book with purity of mind and in its true sense, or at least that they should understand it in general terms and think of all those words as being meant in their spiritual and very pure sense; and they should lift up their hearts to the recollection of God, to thoughts of our Lord Jesus Christ, of his Church and of the glorious Virgin and of their most pure love of each other, thinking of these things at least in general terms; and soon enough they will leave behind them every kind of unbecoming thought.

ARTICLE THREE: *The Explanation of the First Chapter, concerning Christ and the Universal Church.*

18. In many and various ways the almighty and eternal Father God, from the beginning of the world, by means of words and signs, through visions, types, and prophecies, foretold the incarnation of his Son and the liberation of the human race; and from the time of Adam to Moses and the redaction of the written Law, the great patriarchs and holy men—Adam, Seth, Enoch, Noah, Sem, Abraham, Isaac and Jacob—knew of this from the natural law; they, and many other good-living men, whether moved by divine revelation or by the accounts of their ancestors, desired more eagerly than we can guess the coming of the Saviour, his appearance to and redemption of the world.

19. Then, on Mount Sinai, the mysteries of Christ were revealed to Moses; revealed too was how in Christ that promise would be fulfilled which says: *and in your descendants all nations will be blessed* (Gen 22:18), these words being spoken not only to Abraham, but also to Isaac and Jacob—as Moses relates in Genesis. But later, under the Law, the mysteries of the Saviour are foretold and described in the words of David, Solomon, Isaiah and the other prophets much more fully than they were in the natural law, to the extent that the Jews under the Law shared the common and explicit belief that the Saviour of the human race would come into the world; and all of this is in accordance with what Christ said in the Gospel to his disciples: *Blessed are the eyes which see what you see. For I tell you that many kings and prophets and just men desired to see what you see and did not see it, and to hear what you hear and did not hear it* (Lk 10:23–24).[21]

20. And so, in the name of all the faithful people who desired the coming of Christ, whether they were under the natural law or under the written Law, here it is said: *May he kiss me with the kiss of his mouth*: that is, 'Saviour of the world, Son of God, for so long and on so many

occasions promised to me, may he come in person through the mystery of his Incarnation, may he take on my nature in the unity of [his] person, may he show himself to me face to face, speak to me mouth to mouth, may he come to converse among men; and so in the midst of the world work salvation'. From this we may tell how ardently the men of old desired that event: first, from the dignity and excellence of that Bridegroom, whose nobility is so great, who is infinite in beauty, whose wisdom is is completely without limit, whose wealth is boundless, his gentleness unconstrained, his mercy superabundant and his happiness without end or measure. It is therefore not surprising that this Bride should wish to be united and espoused to such a Bridegroom, so great, indeed infinite, in nobility and so delicate to taste.[22]

21. Secondly, we may understand this because of the extent of that Bride's need. For she was condemned to exile, expelled from paradise, burdened by the yoke of sin, in some degree oppressed by slavery and in the power of the devil, denied the joys of eternal bliss, thrown down into the lake of unhappiness and into the mire of the gutter, with no one to lend a helping hand, no one to offer her complete and final redemption. Thirdly, we may think of this in terms of the wonderful, abundant, and saving fruit which is given to the Church by means of the forementioned kiss of this Bridegroom: because by means of it she is freed from all those evils we have referred to, she is brought back into a holy liberty, is made the friend, bride, daughter, heir and consort of her creator, is wonderfully adorned by the gifts of grace. Through this kiss she is made *a holy nation, a people for his possession, a chosen people, a royal priesthood, glorious before all the nations* (1 Pet 2:9).

22. Moreover, just as in that Bridegroom, the Lord Jesus Christ, there are two natures, the divine and the human, so there are two mouths, one divine and uncreated, the other human and created. The divine and uncreated mouth of Christ is his eternal knowledge or wisdom, from which he

has spoken to every well-disposed heart, as the Psalm says: *I will hear what the Lord God speaks to me* (Ps 84:8). Also, in Job 33 we read: *Once God speaks and he does not repeat a second time* (v. 14). For this reason he rebukes certain people through the prophet in these words: *Woe to the rebellious children, that they should carry out a plan, but not one of mine . . . my voice you have not consulted* (Is 30:1–2). Moreover, it is from this uncreated mouth of his that the Only-begotten of God declares plainly, addressing himself to all the blessed in his Father's house, what those good things are in which consists their essential reward. For this utterance is but the revelation in which he shows them himself—his divine essence—clearly for them to see and enjoy. And it is spoken by the whole Trinity in common, glorious above all glories, just as it is attributed also to each of the three adorable and most exalted persons taken singly. For indeed the actions of God *ad extra* are common to the high and individual Trinity of persons. But the eternal Word speaks of his effects directly to the higher angelic minds, through which he illumines the lower angelic minds about such things; and through the holy angels he speaks, in turn, to men, as the great Denys teaches in his books on the *Angelic* and *Ecclesiastical Hierarchies*.[23]

Therefore, when the eternal Word, the only begotten of God, united human nature with himself in a hypostatic union, taking up that human nature into his eternal and uncreated being, then he directly touched, embraced and kissed it, and thus were we too all kissed. Therefore the Apostle wrote to the Hebrews: *For surely it is not with angels that he is concerned, but with the descendants of Abraham* (Heb 2:16). Thence he was seen upon the earth and engaged in converse with men, he kissed us, in his own person he addressed the faithful ones, instructed them and comforted them, reconciling them to his Father God. And so it was his custom to greet his disciples too with a bodily kiss upon their return. This he foretold through Zechariah: *Rejoice and be glad, daughter of Sion, for behold I am coming and I will live among you and on that day many peoples will be drawn near to the Lord* (Zech 2:10–11). For the same reason too, in Baruch 3 it was prophesied: [*He who made the stars*], *this is our God . . . he found the whole way to knowledge and gave her to Jacob his servant and to Israel whom he loved. Afterwards he was seen on earth and lived among men* (Bar 3:36–37).

24. It can also be asked how the Church in her humility was bold enough to demand a kiss from so awesome a Bridegroom, on whom the heavenly hosts wait in fear, whom the Cherubim and Seraphim adore, a Bridegroom of whom we read in Job 37: *he is great in power and judgement and justice, and he is beyond our accounting. Therefore men fear him and all those who are wise in their own conceit dare not contemplate him* (Job 37:23–24). The short answer to this should be that two things particularly arouse the Church to ask for this marital kiss: first, because this most kindly Bridegroom so graciously forstalled her, giving notice of his Incarnation and of his coming in his promise of them, and from this she derives the courage to make her request; the second was the intensely burning charity of the Church for her Bridegroom. But charity frets at separation, is greedy for union, it often takes over our prayers and bursts their bounds and throws itself upon the beloved; and the more vehemently it loves him, the more closely, even intimately, it desires to be united with him. It gives birth to great confidence so that it looks upon the beloved as the beloved rather than as master or superior.[24] To which may be added a third reason, namely her great need, which is not met by the Law. For she is in dire need of a saviour, she can have no salvation except from this Bridegroom. And so this Bride, which is the universal Church, opens the case for her petition and changes from the third to the second person and now speaks to him as if he were present, saying: *for your breasts are more delightful than wine*; but before this, as if speaking to an absent person, she has inserted: *May he kiss me with the kiss of his mouth*: she longingly desires the presence of her Bridegroom and by that longing is placed

so close to him as soon to deserve, in a certain way, his presence. *For the Lord is close to those who call upon him, to all those who call upon him in truth* (Ps 144:18).[25]

25. Furthermore, this Bride knew that her Bridegroom is not confined by time or place, but is present everywhere. And so she confidently speaks to him as to one who is present and in the manner of a prayer addresses the eternal Father of her Bridegroom: *May he kiss me with the kiss of his mouth,* O eternal Father, your only begotten Son. Soon she is even more aroused than before by the love of the Bridegroom and she can no longer restrain herself from talking with him. For a person who loves with the most ardent love alters the manner and style of her speech in accordance with the changing impulses and touches and intensities of her love. Thus Alexander[26] in his Commentary on the Song declares: *love does not restrain the manner of its expression, it does not measure its step.*[27] And so she says: *Your breasts are more delightful than wine.*

26. According to Origen, the breasts of the Bridegroom are to be read as the secrets hidden in the heart or bowels of Christ, that is, they are the treasures of wisdom and knowledge which are hidden within him, by which he nourishes the hearts of his faithful.[28] But it is also possible to interpret the two breasts of the Bridegroom as the two commandments of charity; or again, as the Old Testament interpreted in its spiritual sense and the New; or again as the Saviour's commandments and the evangelical counsels, likewise as his mercy and truth; or, in yet another way, as prevenient and subsequent grace.[29] These breasts are *more delightful than wine,* that is, than the teachings of the Law and the Prophets, more delightful than the harshness contained in the Law in its literal sense, or in the prescribed ceremonies and judgments of the Law. For the gospel Law, which is the law of charity, which contains and confers grace and embodies in actuality what was foretold and promised in the Law and the Prophets, that gospel Law far surpasses the Law which was the law of fear, containing

no grace and bringing nothing to perfection.[30] Hence it is written in John's Gospel: *The Law was given through Moses and truth came through Jesus Christ* (Jn 1:17). For this reason the time of the Gospel Law is called 'the time of grace'.

27. *More fragrant than the finest ointments,* thereby referring to the priceless gifts of grace and virtue, and the sevenfold gifts of the Holy Spirit by which Christ was most nobly anointed in the human nature which he assumed—anointed, filled, and fragrant, as Isaiah witnesses: *The Spirit of the Lord is upon me, because the Lord has anointed me* (Is 61:1). It is to him that we sing in the Psalm: *God, your God, has anointed you with the oil of gladness above your fellows* (Ps 44:7). It is of him that the most holy prince of the apostles speaks in the Acts of the Apostles: *God anointed [him] with the Holy Spirit and with power* (Acts 10:38).

28. Moreover, the breasts of Christ, that is, [his] example, [his] commandments and his evangelical counsels, are the best of all fragrances—meaning the Church's sacraments which are the medicine jars containing heavenly graces. By them violations of the commandments are healed, by their assistance the commandments and the counsels are fulfilled; these, the best of all fragrances, flow from the breast of the Bridegroom, indeed we are told that they flowed from his side, pierced on the Cross (Jn 19:34).

29. One writer[31] has commented on this passage, making particular point of the words, *For your breasts are more delightful than wine.* [He says]: *The hebrew text gives: for your loves are better than wine. The hebrew word given here is ambiguous between 'loves' and 'breasts'. The jewish authors follow the first meaning, our translation the second. But here the jewish reading seems preferable for, following the meaning of the hebrew text, .the Bride is addressing the Bridegroom and as a form of praise of the Bridegroom the reference to 'breasts' would scarcely be apt. So, following the hebrew authors the meaning is that the loves of the Bridegroom are more delightful to the pious soul than any physical taste is to the bodily palate.* 30. My own comment on this is that if the hebrew word is ambiguous between

the two readings, it is preferable to read the Hebrew not as 'loves' but as 'breasts'. Moreover, it seems right to say that Jerome translated the word more aptly as 'breasts', thereby implying a spiritual, not fleshly interpretation.[32] For spiritual breasts do more properly belong to the Bridegroom than to the Bride, since she is fed from the breasts of her Bridegroom, as Cassiodorus mentions.[33] Moreover, Ockham reports Augustine as saying that men properly-speaking have nipples, women breasts, and cows udders.[34] Nonetheless it is usual in Latin to use the one word (*ubera*) to stand for all three. Thus, Hugh[35] says that men have breasts as an embellishment of their bodies; they have no need for them. And so the breasts are quite aptly said to be the Bridegroom's and very gladly does she honour in him what she knows she herself possesses, and by virtue of their likeness in this respect, love sets her on fire all the more intensely.

31. Then she continues to dwell on the praises of the Bridegroom and on the reasons why she desires a kiss of him and again exclaims: *Your name is oil poured out*; for it is not only you yourself, O Bridegroom, who are like *oil poured out*, sweet and resplendent, but even your name, whatever it may be, is sweet to my ears, and by the very mention of your name my soul is given sweetness, it is refreshed, exhilarated, made brilliant with light. What is more, your name, the renown of your great virtue, is spread throughout the whole world, it shines forth and sends out its fragrance; and so throughout the world it is the good odour of God the Father, in fact of the whole superabundantly supreme Trinity. More than that, the preaching of your greatness is poured forth and sweetly smells, like oil streaming forth from a jar; and just as oil floats upon the surface of other liquids, so your name is above all others. And as oil too is a garnish for other foods and alters their taste, so your name is a garnish of the Scriptures and gives a freshness of taste to souls as would a kind of spiritual condiment. Again, oil soothes injuries and wounds; and so

your name, O heavenly Bridegroom, dispels sadness of the heart and heals the wounds of sin.

32. Speaking of the saving properties of this name, the holy angel said to Joseph: *You will call his name Jesus, and he will bring salvation from their sins to his people* (Mt 1:21). Indeed, 'Jesus' means 'Saviour', as Isaiah 45 says: *A righteous God and a saviour, there is none besides me* (Is 45:21). And Hosea 13: *I am the Lord your God . . . and besides me there is no saviour* (Hos 13:4). For indeed it is the work of Jesus Christ in his Godhead to give salvation, through his own proper and uncreated authority, it is in his divine nature to do away with sins, through his own creative activity to infuse the gifts of grace and to grant eternal happiness. For his it is to save, through the humanity he has assumed as the instrumental, meritorious, and higher cause and as mediator and agent of salvation. For in the same way that our body is related to our soul as a living and fitting instrument joined to it; so the humanity of Christ is related to his divinity and to the eternal Word, which assumed that humanity, as an unmediated, living, and fitting instrument of that selfsame Godhead and Word—as Damascene puts it.[36] In addition, how especial, how salutary and effective is the name of this Bridegroom is revealed by the prince of the apostles, who speaks thus: *For no other name under heaven is given to men by which we may be saved* (Phil 2:10). He says, referring to the royal dignity of this name, that it is vessel of election: *God [our Father] has given a name which is above every other name, so that at the name of Jesus every knee is bowed, whether of the heavens, of the earth or of the realms below* (Phil 2:9–10).

33. Again, *your name is oil poured out*, that is, you yourself, O must illustrious Bridegroom, are compared to oil and your goodness exceeds oil in fragrance, your nobility exceeds oil in splendour, your anointing refreshes souls, your mercy heals wounds of body and soul, your consolation soothes the pains of penance and banishes all excessive sadness.

34. *And so the maidens have loved you*: this refers to the particular churches and to souls which are renewed in the Spirit and to the hearts of beginners and to the nations once pagan, proud, fleshly, shameful; they, who through your grace are converted, have become self-disciplined, chaste, and humble. But also, and speaking literally, it refers to the holy virgins, the young maidens among the chosen ones, virtuous young girls, of whom there are many, who not only had contempt for the riches of the whole world, for its pleasures and honours and for bodily adornment, for vanity and for female frivolities; but also underwent the most cruel kinds of death in the most manly fashion and triumphed in great happiness: thus did the sacred Catherine,[37] the most admirable Ursula[38] and others almost uncountable like them, serve you in final perseverance in virginity of mind and of body; and to this day, there are countless such who, in their young maidenhood, leave this worthless world with all its falsehood and enter the conventual life and the holy hermitage and, remaining in perpetual enclosure, are free to enjoy in the Spirit your most chaste embraces.

35. *Draw me after you*. This is to be taken as standing for the Church living under the law of the Gospel—who, knowing that her Bridegroom has come, that the mysteries of human redemption have been fulfilled and that [he] has gone up to heaven, desires to follow him there; but, remembering that her Bridegroom has said *Without me you can do nothing* (Jn 15:5), calls on his gracious help and says: *Draw me after you*, which means: arouse me and take away my indifference, set aflame in me the fire of your love, a love which draws a thing up with it, as fire lifts a thing up on high; give to my tongue the taste of your uncreated and intense sweetness so that I may be joined with you, uniquely and purely, always to be clinging to you, unceasingly sighing for you—thus may I act on that encouragement of the Apostle: *seek the things which are above, where Christ is, seated at the right hand of God. Set your*

minds on things that are above, not on things that are on earth (Col 3:1–2). For I know that you, Lord Jesus, have said, *and I, when I am lifted up from the earth, will draw all things to myself* (Jn 12:32). And again, *No one can come to me unless the Father who sent me draws him* (Jn 6:44).

36. Nor have I any doubt but that God your Father, and you his Only-begotten one, are a single power of attraction, as you are one in your creating. Again, I know that it was truly said by the Apostle: *Not that we are sufficient of ourselves to claim anything as coming from us; our sufficiency is from God* (2 Cor 3:5). See, then, most sweet Jesus, our heavenly Bridegroom, my spirit strives to cleave loyally to you, to take its rest in you, through loving contemplation and contemplative loving:[39] but a thousand obstacles impede me, delay, and hold me back. Our understanding is obscure, reason is weak, the will pulled away by empty and evil things, sensuality drags me down, the daily needs of earthly affairs preoccupy me and hold me captive to things of sense, the objects of external sense seduce me, and armies of vice, the world, and hordes of devils on all sides threaten us;[40] truly I walk among snares, among a regiment of the gravest dangers, but more than that, the weight of miserable flesh presses down on me. What, therefore, must I do, if not have recourse to your most gracious abundance and from the most intimate feelings of my heart pray: *Draw me after you*, do not cease to caress, flood, enlighten, aid, and comfort my heart. For you have said through Hosea the prophet: *With the cords of Adam I led them, with bands of love* (Hos 11:4). Again, through Jeremiah: *I have loved you with an everlasting love, therefore I have had pity on you and I have drawn you* [*to me*] (Jer 31:3). May that drawing take me beyond myself, may the seductive power of every adulterous desire be ever far from me, and every impulse of irrational passion, of deceit and vice.

37. *We will run in the fragrance of your ointments*: that is, when you have thus drawn me, I and my young maidens, and the newly converted to whom I have striven to pass

on the graces given to me, we will quickly draw close to you and run down the way of your commandments, burning with the fire of love. Indeed, nothing is difficult for those who burn with love or to someone who has tasted the teeming variety of your consolations; nothing is more irksome than to be held back from you or to be delayed along the paths of charity. *We will run*, I say, *in the fragrance of your ointments*, that is, in the inward tasting of heavenly gifts, in the grace and effects of the Church's sacraments, in the foretasting of heavenly joys and in the abundance of the gifts of the Holy Spirit. These are the oils, so supremely soothing and limpid; and so as to come to possess them we must follow in the steps above all of holy humility, of patience, meekness and of the cross of Christ, and, with the most blessed Magdalen, be prostrate in real sorrow at the feet of the heavenly Bridegroom and copiously wash them with tears of penitence, and kiss them, and then, through due reparation, through spiritual progress and continual watchfulness of heart, rise up to his hands; thence, in the burning desires of a well-ordered, pure and fiery charity, by means of the unsullied contemplation of unchangeable truth, attain to the most devout and respectful kiss, the kiss of his most pure mouth[41]—which is very different from that contrived kiss of the most holy mouth, which was the traitor's in his great disloyalty.

38. Some attribute these words to the Synagogue, as referring to the exodus from Egypt.[42] This, however, seems inappropriate, because the holy ones of the Old Testament did not desire a liberation chiefly or ultimately from egyptian slavery: rather, they desired redemption from the yoke of sin, from enslavement to the devil, from the guilt of original sin, from the plundering of eternal glory: and the liberation from Egypt was a type of this redemption.[43]

39. Next comes the voice of the Church addressed to the young maidens: *The king has brought me into his chambers*: that is to say, by means of the light and grace of contemplation, he has raised me up to a provisional[44] and obscure

understanding of his wisdom, to a mystical understanding, to sublime ways of knowledge, to the hidden meanings of the Scriptures, to the contemplation of the wisdom of the Trinity above all blessed, concerning the manner in which the human race is saved—through the Incarnation and Passion of the eternal Word. And he has given me a well-founded faith sustained by reasons for believing, and the understanding of a purified mind, so that I may be able to preach the things of faith, to persuade of them, to proclaim them and defend them: it is thus that he has brought me into his sanctuary, into the wide world of his enlightenment, and to the highest step of his wisdom, made me his confidant and his counsellor, my King and my God.

40. More than this, *he has brought me into his chambers,* into the contemplation of the heavenly dwelling places and into the joys of the citizens above, so that I may know not only by faith, but also by a delightful foretaste, through a supernatural disclosure, what is the hope of our calling. Thus may I announce, in the words of my children: *But we, with unveiled face, beholding the glory of the Lord are being changed into his likeness from one degree of glory to another* (2 Cor 2:18). Was not Paul brought into these chambers when he was *caught up into the third heaven,* where he *heard things that cannot be told, which human beings may not utter* (2 Cor 12:2, 4).[45]

41. *We will rejoice and be glad in you*—which means: our heart will be so intensely glad in the contemplation of the wealth of your great glory and in the love of your completely unlimited goodness, not only in the final homeland, but also in our pilgrimage towards it, that that joy reverberates through the body[46] too, as the Psalm says: *My heart and flesh sing for joy to the living God* (Ps 83:2). In the same way we glory now in hope and in the foretaste and pledge of future bliss, as the Apostle says in Romans: *We rejoice in our hope of sharing the glory* [*of the sons*] *of God* (Rom 5:2). And again, *We know that if the earthly tent we live*

in is destroyed, we have a building from God, a house not made with hands, eternal in the heavens (2 Cor 5:1). If, therefore, it seems fitting to take some joy from these lower things of sense, how much more incomparably fitting must it be to rejoice in the source of all good, who is rich beyond all riches and beauty beyond all beauty; in whose complete and infinite possession lies every good that can be desired, everything of beauty; in whom alone lies our salvation. It is of him that the prophet sings in a verse of surpassing sweetness and grace: *In God is my deliverance and my glory; God of my aid and my hope is in God (Ps 61:8). We will rejoice in you,* therefore, O renowned and gracious Bridegroom.

ARTICLE FOUR: *Exposition of the First Chapter: May he kiss me with the kisses of his mouth: On the Individual Spouse.*

42. In the Prologue to this little work I explained how the Bride of Christ is threefold, universal, individual, and special. Thus each soul living in charity is an individual Bride of Christ, espoused to him through faith and charity and vowed to him through the grace of baptism; and so our Lord and Saviour holds her close to him with the arms of love and causes her to bear fruit by the pouring in of virtues. Thus does Augustine say that every soul is a Bride of Christ, or else is an adulteress with the devil: if the soul is in the charity of Christ she is said to be a bride; but if she is in mortal sin, she is known as an adulteress with the devil. And so in this book whatever Solomon writes concerning the Church as a whole (the Bride in the general sense) can be attributed also to the individual Bride tropologically. Since, according to the preceding discussion, the subject of these Songs of Songs is perfect love, these things cannot be said of just any soul which is in charity and grace, but only of the heroic soul, the soul which is divine, perfect, beside itself[47] with love; a line of interpretation followed by the venerable abbot of Vercelli,[48] a man very learned

in the works of the divine and great Denys, but who also translated these works with lucidity of style.

43. And so the contemplative soul once cleansed, set alight with a holy love, not content to rest easy in created things, with all its heart seeking its Bridegroom, the true and unchangeably good, the Bridegroom above all nature and beyond the highest beauty, from the fullness of an absolutely sincere heart, bursts forth into a sweet and love-laden cry: *May he kiss me with the kiss of his mouth*—he, that is, the most tender Bridegroom, who alone satisfies me, who created me for himself; nor can I rest except in him who alone can set all my heart at peace and leave me content.[49] Such is he and so great he is who *kisses me with the kiss of his mouth*; which is to say he gives himself most graciously to me and he is pleased to unite this poor diminished soul intimately to his unrivalled and infinite excellence; touching and casting his light on the highest part of my understanding[50] so that I may contemplate his majesty and wisdom and his utterly boundless truth and beauty; and so too he sets on fire my innermost will and my highest loves so that I may love his unlimited goodness with complete purity, constancy and intensity; so that I may taste his sweetness, an unfathomable, limitless and measureless stream; so that I may rest in his most pure embrace, so that I may be carried away, transformed and absorbed into him and all enraptured, be plunged into the most joyful, vast ocean of his happiness.

44. But how, oh you poor silly little soul, thrust into this heavy weight of matter, tied to the millstone of the body, a soul which on the scale of intellectual beings is as prime matter is among material beings;[51] how can you have the presumption, the boldness even the least self-assurance to ask a kiss of him, of whom the heavens, the earth, the seas are all in awe, before whom the highest of the supreme spirits tremble, beneath whom bow the foundations of the globe? Again, if it would seem presumptuous to ask a kiss, I shall not say of the most glorious Virgin Mary, the mother

of Christ, but even of the glorious virgin Queen Catherine or of Saint Ursula, how much the more so it seems to ask a kiss of the Holy of Holies, the all-powerful King before whom the whole world is like a tiny speck of dust? What do you say to this, oh soul, confined in this exile, in this land of unlikeness,[52] in this vale of tears, where to say that you have no sin is to deceive yourself?

45. THE SOUL'S REPLY: Why do you call me back from the sight of my bridegroom? Why do you hold me back from his embrace? Why do you turn me away from our converse? Why, in this affair which transcends all reason, do you demand an explanation? Do you not know that the eagerness of love is not to be restrained by commonplace decencies? Are you unaware that as the excellence of this bridegroom is so great, so is his honour absolutely infinite? Since when is his love or his kindness any less than his majesty? Did he not himself create me so as to receive that happy kiss of his mouth in the homeland of the Blessed, to see him as he is, to enjoy endlessly his goodness and his sweetness, for the most complete fulfilment, for ever far from all disturbing distractions? He who pours his love into me, he also sets that love aflame and encourages it, and it is he who provokes me and inflames me to beg for the kiss of his mouth. *It depends not upon* [*the*] *will or on effort* (Rom 9:16). Love, fretting at separation, compels me; the thought, indeed the experience of the honour and mercy of the bridegroom, this gives me confidence; and faith too, and the memory of his past goodnesses, these give me life. Was it not he, who, though rich with infinite wealth, rich not in money but in almighty power, and so great that his greatness is without limit, was it not he who for my sake became poor and small? And to be sure, so poor that he had nowhere to lay his head; and so small that he confined himself within the most chaste and most humble womb of a young virgin; and that Unicorn whom no man could withstand was captured by the charity and

purity of just one young girl:[53] and then he gave himself up to death, so that I might become one with him for eternity and that I might be kissed by him. Behold, my heart is like wine that has no vent, like new wineskins it is ready to burst, I must speak that I may find relief (Job 32:19–20). I will speak, therefore, to the Bridegroom and little by little I will recover my breath; and now, provoked by an explosion of desire I will say for the first time, *May he kiss me with the kiss of his mouth*; and a second time, *May he kiss me with the kiss of his mouth*; and a third time I repeat, *May he kiss me with the kiss of his mouth.*

46. ANSWER: Are you not drunk, to speak thus? Have you even no shame? In any case, is not discretion the mother and guide of the virtues, without which even charity falls headlong?

47. THE SOUL: I am indeed drunk, filled with the food and drink of him whose words you will hear later: *Eat, O friends, and drink: drink deeply, O lovers* (Sg 5:1). In short, you seem to me to be ignorant of the rights, of the properties and powers of love. Have you not heard the words of that prophet [Jeremiah] sanctified in the womb of his mother, saying: [*The word of the Lord*] *is in my heart, as it were, a burning fire shut up in my bones and I am weary holding it in and I cannot*? (Jer 20:9) And again: *I am like a drunken man, like a person overcome by wine, because of the Lord and because of his holy words* (Jer 23:9). And if the word of the Lord can so intoxicate and inflame, how much more will his love? Besides, listen to what the holy and gentle Bernard has to say—he knows from experience: *Oh, how great the power of love! Oh, what great strength there is in the spirit of freedom! I am carried away by desire, I am not led by reason. It is not to be thought presumptuous if I am constrained and overpowered by the heart. Shame calls me back; but love overcomes. I am not unaware that the strength of the King loves justice (Ps 98:4); but the command of love does not wait upon justice, nor is it*

moderated by counsel, nor held back by shame, nor is it subject to reason.[54]

48. And so my reply to you is that, in this matter, discretion is to be without discretion: for the source of all discretion is the Holy Spirit, the Counsellor, who fills us to the full, forestalls and inflames us and it is he also who guards us, directs and rules us. But now let disputation be left behind, lest my thoughts be detained any longer from the bridegroom. For indeed, by virtue of my having said, *May he kiss me with the kiss of his mouth*, I feel myself to be touched by him, affected by him, kissed by him: and so, having left you behind, I will speak to him.

ARTICLE FIVE: *An Account of the same Chapter: Of the Special Bride.*

49. The special Bride, she who stands apart from all others, is unique and is the beloved beyond all telling of the heavenly Bridegroom; she is his virginal, most pure and most sacred mother, endowed by her Only-begotten Son himself with an especially luminous faith, pledged by a dowry of the surest hope and caught into the embrace of the most fiercely burning charity, made superabundantly fruitful in overflowing gifts of graces. That is why these songs are read in the Divine Office on the feast days of this Bride. And so a brief account may be given of how it is fitting that they should be found there.[55]

50. Concerning this most glorious and most worthy Virgin beyond compare, chosen from eternity to be the true mother of the true God, it may be said to be a matter of certain belief that she was made holy and was filled with the Holy Spirit in her mother's womb in a manner far excelling the glorious John the Baptist:[56] and of him the angel Gabriel foretold that he would be filled with the Holy Spirit even in his mother's womb (Lk 1:15); and far excelling Jeremiah, to whom the Lord said: *Before I formed you in the womb I knew you, and before you left the womb I*

had made you holy (Jer 1:5); or than any one else whoever, if others there be, who might have been made holy in the womb, always excepting the holy Bridegroom himself, with whom none may be compared.

51. And because in her mother's womb the matchless and most chaste Virgin was filled to the full with gifts from above, as no one else has been, when soon she began to use her reason, she bent herself to progress in them as no one else has done; and because her forechosen soul shone in the presence of the most High with a purity the more excellent, and because she was the more attentive, the more responsive, the more dedicated in her quest for virtue and wisdom of every kind, so hour by hour she was raised higher and was more generously anointed by the Holy Spirit, was bathed in light, set aflame and was able to achieve a stature without equal; and because she was in a unique way of God, she was the more attentive to the word of God; she searched the Law and became learned in it.

52. And, as Ambrose confirms, she doubtless read in Isaiah, *Behold, a virgin shall conceive* (Is 7:14). But more than that, we may gather from the Scriptures that before she conceived the Son of God, she knew of the mystery of the supremely blessed Trinity, she knew that there was a trinity of persons in one God. For when she asked the angel, *How may this be, since I know not man?* (Lk 1:34), the answer she received from the lips of the angel was: *The Holy Spirit will come upon you and the power of the most High will overshadow you. And so the holy One who will be born of you will be called the Son of God* (Lk 1:35). In these words the adorable Trinity is clearly implied, and she understood what the words meant.[57]

53. It seems therefore that we are obliged to believe that she already knew that God, even more, the one and only Son of God, would be made flesh and would suffer to redeem the human race—that she knew these things from the writings of the Law and the Prophets, but especially by means of the Holy Spirit's intimate anointing and

guidance; and there can be no doubt that as she longed for this great redeemer more than any, so she excelled all others in the intensity of her burning love.

54. And although in those furthest depths of her unbounded humility, in which was founded her supreme peace of soul, she could in no way have presumed to think that the Son of God would be made flesh in her, or that she should be chosen for such wonders, nonetheless, when by the angel's message she did come to know that she was chosen for it, that she would conceive the Son of God, moved directly by the Holy Spirit, she believed it completely and also humbly gave her consent and most intensely desired that it should come about. Therefore she said: *Behold the handmaid of the Lord, be it done unto me according to your word* (Lk 1:38).

55. And so it is most appropriately of this best and wisest of virgin girls that, at that moment when she heard from the holy angel, *Behold, you will conceive in your womb*, and then, *the Holy Spirit will come upon you*, that the words may be construed: *May he kiss me with the kiss of his mouth*; that is, the only begotten of God, the heavenly Bridegroom, whom you, O heavenly paranymph, promise to me, you assure me that he will be made incarnate in me and will soon become my son; he deigns to come down to me your poor little handmaiden and unite himself closely and intimately to the substance of my flesh, so that he will take up his body from mine and unite himself hypostatically with it—that is, unite with his uncreated person the rational soul which he will create and, informing this body as it will, achieve a unity of person; thereby his human nature is made to constitute one person with the Eternal Word, assumed by the very Word of God, the only Son of the Father.

56. Again, *May he kiss me with the kiss of his mouth*, that is, may he flood my mind, lovingly and intimately, with the light of his wisdom, may he set it on fire and hold it close to himself in embrace, so that at that moment I may

become and remain worthy to conceive the Lord God, my creator and saviour. What does it gain a person to conceive in the flesh what she has not first conceived in the soul? For I would be more blessed to conceive in solid faith than in the flesh alone. For that motherhood—to be the Mother of God—is a gift of grace freely given, which by itself does not save the person who receives it.[58]

57. Yet again: *May he kiss me with the kiss of his mouth*: that is, he whom the heavens and earth cannot contain, who can be limited within no boundary, fully grasped by no created mind, is made flesh from me, converses with me in gentle tones, is contained in my cradle, is enfolded in my arms, carried in my hands and so he kisses me with the most simple and serene kiss of his mouth. And without doubt you, most loving mother and most modest virgin, with enormous reverence was able to embrace and kiss with the greatest charity the one and only fruit of your virginal womb, the most beautiful and precious baby boy, God born of you, your so very dear child.[59] He too, when a grown man, used to greet his disciples with a holy kiss of the body; and also, when he was a child, he would from time to time gently kiss you, his most holy mother, and cling to your holy neck with his most sacred little arms. And if the eyes and ears of the disciples were blessed because they saw and heard Christ, how much more blessed are you who conceived him and gave birth to him and brought him up with a mother's care, were able to treat him with a mother's authority and to kiss him.

58. *For your breasts are more delightful than wine, more fragrant than the finest oils*. If we follow the line of interpretation followed above [n. 26], these could be the words of the special Bride addressed to her own Bridegroom and Son, who may praise the spiritual breasts of her Son all the more particularly because her mind was nourished, anointed and consoled in so very especially delicate, complete and tender a manner. But they could also be the words of the Bridegroom addressed to his most beloved mother and so

may be read: 'You, O special Bride, mother and virgin, have asked for the kiss of my mouth, and I gladly consent to your request; *for your breasts are more delightful than wine*. This refers to your love, which makes you burn with zeal for the honour of your Creator and to encourage your neighbour with your prayers and example; and it refers to the mercy with which you bring consolation to those who are on the journey and to your desire to give them sustenance. These, I say, *your breasts*, with which you feed me, *are more delightful than wine*, that is, than the strictness of the Law and than any bodily sweetness; *more fragrant than the finest ointments*, that is, than the high contemplation in which you gaze upon the endless nobility of the divine majesty; and than the visible justice with which you carry out all things in order and fittingness'. Again, it may be said of those bodily breasts of the most divine Virgin that they, most blessed as they are, are made almost divine by the continual contact of the adorable, incarnate Bridegroom who sucked from them; they *are more fragrant than the finest ointments*, more fragrant, that is to say, than the most delicious virginal milk, which the Lord of all things took and sucked from them against that hunger and thirst which he freely and in his providence took upon himself and suffered for our sakes.

59. It is told of the holy hermit and famous anchorite Abraam[60] that his grand-daughter was, for a time, led astray and had become a prostitute; and because he wished to bring her back he dressed himself in a soldier's cloak and, disguised as a stranger and a secular, sat down to eat with her in a brothel. And when she put her arms around his neck and began to kiss his face, very quickly she became scented with the delicate fragrance of the holy man's body, a fragrance which his fasting and continence gave to it, so that she too seemed physically to give off the same sweetness. Whereupon she immediately repented. Similar things may be read of other holy men. If that is so, how much more should we piously believe of the most

blessed Virgin, she who is the most blessed, she who excels in self-control, is chaste and most virtuous, that her holy and unsullied body and her breasts made divine, should have given off the sweetest fragrance, especially since such outstanding virtue and purity of soul would naturally flow into and be detectable in the body?[61]

60. *Your name is oil poured out.* It is certain that the name of the Bridegroom tastes all the sweeter to and is poured out the more wonderfully over the heart of the most resplendent Virgin, as she loved the Bridegroom the more ardently, contemplated him with clearer vision and was the more ready to taste it—that is, to the extent to which she was completely free of any disordered affection and fleshly pleasure. For indeed her soul was prepared to taste how sweet was her Lord and was distubed by no unruly passion, was troubled by no delight of the flesh. Alternatively, these words could be addressed by the Bridegroom to the glorious Virgin: *Your name is oil poured out*: that is, 'O dearest mother, within yourself you are completely suffused with interior sweetness, you abound in every mercy, your fame is the most completely unsullied, never do you step through the gates of the holy soul without scattering about you a natural sweetness, the very thought of you revives the soul: and so it is that *young maidens*, innocent and simple souls, those who have but recently be regenerated by conversion and are immature and weak, *have loved you*. For it is you whom every one of the faithful love above any other mere creature, all the faithful love you as their highest and best mistress, the holiest of holy women, their advocate and mother, as their special place of safety and the fellow worker of human redemption, to whom the kingdom of mercy has been entrusted'.

61. *Draw me after you.* Although this most excellent Virgin was most supremely assured of grace, she was nonetheless still a pilgrim on the way and was constantly able to progress and advance in every virtue: and the more humble she became, the more desirous was she to ascribe every

good and every grace and every step forward to her God, in whose mercy and grace she completely and humbly trusted and in her prayers relied. And so when she prayed she said: *Draw me after you*—that is, 'You, God, my Son and Bridegroom, never cease to entice and draw to yourself the desires of my heart with ever greater completeness and with ever more burning love, into ever more lofty contemplation'.

62. Moreover, if the blessed Apostle Paul and many another holy person desired in this life to be dissolved and to be with Christ, with how much more fullness of heart would the blessed Virgin, the most fervent of all, especially after her Son's ascension, have said: *Draw me after you*; that is, 'take me away to the kingdom of your glory and there place me beside you'. Her own assumption being imminent, impatient of a longer separation, she utters those words with the most loving affection. And so, then, her Son disclosed to her through an angel that she would be taken up at once. How often, with what devotion and with what burning love did she speak these words when, after his ascension, she visited the places of her only begotten Son's passion, crucifixion, burial and ascension; how she longed and yearned, sighed for him! How she burned with feelings of holy love!

NOTES

1. Cp. Gregory, n. 8, who uses the same scriptural references.

2. It appears that, for Denys, in principle the anagogical or mystical interpretation is the highest kind, at least of the Song.

3. i.e., diocesan.

4. Denys does not appear to think of the individual soul as 'Bride' in relation to the Church as 'Bridegroom', but of each individual soul as the Bride of Christ in and through the Church as the 'general' Bride of Christ. The pope in relation to the universal Church and the bishop in relation to the diocesan church are as 'Bridegroom' to 'Bride', because pope and bishops are proxy for (*vicarialis*) Christ. So the Church is always female as is the individual soul. We might add that, on this model, the priesthood is always male.

5. Denys gives the plural form as does sometimes Gregory, in n. 6, for example.

6. It is not clear whom Denys could have in mind.

7. See Nicholas of Lyra, nn. 20–21.

8. Jerome, *Prologus, Beati Hieronymi ad Damasum Papam, In expositionem Cantici canticorum secundum Origenem*; PG 13:35–36.

9. *In Canticum canticorum*, I.1; PG 13:84C-D.

10. Anselm of Canterbury is one Anselm from whom this quotation certainly does *not* come. The reference appears to be to *Enarrationes in Cântica canticorum*, until recently thought to be by Anselm of Laon, of which a short version exists in PL 162:1187–1228, where it is thus attributed. The passage quoted by Denys does not appear in the PL text.

11. On this subject, see Nicholas, n. 22.

12. SC 2.1.

13. Gregory, n. 12.

14. See nn. 18–19 below. On the one hand, Denys insists, as here, on the oneness and continuity of the Synagogue—indeed of all human history before Christ—with the christian Church, for the reason that that continuity is the theological basis of the allegorical interpretation of the Old Testament in terms of New. On the other hand, his interpretation of the Song is exclusively allegorical, allowing it no literal sense other than the allegorical, thus evacuating it of any significance in its own terms as Jewish literature; see Article One above.

15. As a matter of fact Denys seems to be right in his assessment of 'Catholic interpreters', at any rate in principle. Ironically, the case of Giles of Rome apart, Denys himself is more open to Nicholas' criticism—which is, after all, directed chiefly at those who devalue the literal sense—than any of the predecessors whom Denys is so willing to defend.

16. Origen, Prologue to *Commentary on the Song of Songs*, in Greer, pp. 218–219.

17. Jerome, *In Ezechielem prophetam*, PL 25:17A.

18. Gregory, nn. 3–4.

19. P. Glorieux, *Jean Gerson, Oeuvres Completes*, Vol. VIII (Paris: Desclée, 1971) p. 579.

20. The litrugical context of monastic interpretation of the Song ought not to be neglected, though Denys' interest here is rather more negative than at n. 49 below. See pp. 162–163 above.

21. Denys' articulation of the 'epochs' of salvation history is as clear as in any of our writers. Nicholas of Lyra's criticism (see nn. 20–21 above) is, however, to the point, since what Nicholas accuses 'Catholic interpreters' of is not that they ignore the pre-Christian epochs but that they devalue the intrinsic significance of the history of Israel in favour of its significance in terms of Christ. And this Denys certainly does.

22. *infinitae dulcedinis*. The Latin *dulcedo* is virtually untranslatable; 'of infinite sweetness' is quite meaningless. In any case 'sweetness' will not do at all; the word is hopelessly undetachable in the modern mind from thoughts of junk, or otherwise politically incorrect, food. Since in practice what the Latin *dulcedo* refers to is what mediaevals thought of as pleasant to a refined palate, it seems best to stick to that core meaning and leave readers to decide for themselves whether that amounts to a sweet or to an astringent gustatory experience.

23. For example: 'That is why they [the heavenly beings] have a preeminent right to the title of angel or messenger . . . . since it is they who pass on to us the[se] revelations which are so far beyond us' *CH*, 4, 180B.

24. Cp Gregory, n. 8.

25. Cp Gregory, n. 13.

26. Possibly Alexander of Neckham, *Expositio super Cantica canticorum ad laudem gloriose et beate Virginis Matris et mysterio incarnationis, Libri IV*, unpublished MS; see Stegmuller, n. 1168.

27. A gloss also found in Giles, n. 9, but derived from the *Glossa Ordinaria*.

28. Origen, *In Canticum canticorum* I; PG 13:87B.

29 See my comment on this passage, p. 129.

30. A harsh judgment of the intrinsic value of the Law, to be compared with the more favourable view found in Thomas Aquinas, see pp. 134–135 above.

31. Nicholas of Lyra, n. 26.

32. Cp Giles of Rome, n. 11. Giles, like Denys, follows the *Glossa* in a notably 'Origenist' ploy of preferring the more difficult reading since it more clearly demands a spiritual interpretation.

33. Source unknown.

34. *viris . . . . conveniunt mamillae, foeminis mammae, pecoribus ubera.* I have been unable to trace the source, whether in Ockham or in Augustine.

35. Source unknown.

36. *On the Orthodox Faith*, III.i-xiii, in *A Select Library of the Nicene and Post-Nicene Fathers*, Vol. 9 (Oxford and New York, 1899) pp. 45–57.

37. Catherine of Alexandria, a legendary saint and virgin, supposedly martyred on a spiked wheel in Alexandria under Maxentius. She appears in mediaeval representations with her wheel, frequently in argument with the philosophers.

38. Another legendary saint, said to have been martyred with anything up to 11,000 companions. A cemetery discovered in Cologne in 1155 was identified with the burial place of Ursula and her companions; thereafter the cult of Saint Ursula was especially popular in that city, the place of Denys' early theological studies.

39. In his *De contemplatione*, I.ii, Denys defines contemplation as a 'loving, spontaneous and sincere knowledge' (*affectuosa, prompta ac sincera cognitio*). Ever ready to synthesise opposed opinions, Denys is a resolute 'intellectualist' in the vexed controversies between 'intellectualists' and 'voluntarists' but concedes to the voluntarist position the importance of love as a necessary condition of intellectual contemplation. Hence the antiphonal formula of his commentary. Compare his moderate intellectualism with the severe voluntarism of Giles of Rome, n. 16.

40. The changes from first person singular to plural are Denys' own.

41. The threefold kiss of feet, hands and mouth, originating in Bernard of Clairvaux (see *Brief Commentary*, nn. 8–10), was by Denys' time a commonplace.

42. The reference is probably to Nicholas of Lyra again, see n. 28, where, however, it is to the previous verse, *Your name is oil poured out*, that Nicholas gives this gloss.

43. Nothing could illustrate more clearly than this disagreement with Nicholas the difference of hermeneutical emphasis on the score of the importance of the primary literal, historical sense.

44. Latin *incerta*, by no means to be translated by 'uncertain'.

45. In this and in the preceding paragraph Denys slips naturally into a 'mystical' interpretation, but the ecclesiological dimension of this 'general' interpretation notwithstanding, this is a distinctly 'individual' reading.

46. It is a favourite theme in Denys' writings about prayer and contemplation that union with God brings about manifold bodily expressions, which Denys holds are a natural and spontaneous overflow of the spirit into the flesh. See *De contemplatione*, III.xi.

47. *ecstatice*.

48. Thomas Gallus, see above.

49. Cf. Augustine, *Confessions, I.1.*

50. *apex intellectus*: the highest point of the highest power of the soul; for Denys, at any rate, the locus in which the divine presence is most intimately and fully to be found. But compare this view with that of Gallus, for whom the *apex mentis* is *affectus* not *intellectus*. See Gallus, n. 10 above.

51. A rather contrived metaphysical hyperbole: 'Prime matter', on the aristotelian account, is matter in its lowest and least differentiated

condition, the materiality of a material thing, as distinct from its 'form'. It is the 'lowest' on the scale of material things, because it is the principle of change and decay of a material thing and the scale of beings, for a Platonist like Denys, is a scale ascending from changeableness to unchangeableness.

52. *in regione hac dissimilitudinis*: a favorite expression of Bernard's, but of pagan neo-Platonic origin; in the pseudo-Denys it is connected with the distinction between 'similar' and 'dissimilar' similitudies, the latter being the likenesses of God which are least like, furthest from, God. See p. 62 above.

53. A reference to the legend of the unicorn which no man may capture by force, but only a virgin may seduce, a common mediaeval mariological and christological symbol.

54. SC 9.2.

55. See my discussion of the liturgical context of allegory, pp. 162–163 above.

56. The primary patron of the Carthusian Order is the Virgin Mary, the secondary patron, John the Baptist.

57. Like Alan of Lille (n. 7), Denys gives a strongly trinitarian reading of the annunciation to Mary and attributes extraordinary prophetic powers to her.

58. *gratia gratis data*, a technical expression denoting the sort of grace we would perhaps call by its older, greek, name 'charism', a grace meant for the edification and sanctification of the Church, not in itself of the recipient—such as prophecy, speaking in tongues, the working of miracles. Such grace is distinguished from sanctifying grace which is, essentially, charity. And as Paul says, charity alone makes its recipient holy (1 Cor 13:3). It is Mary's conceiving in faith which privileges her, not by itself her conceiving in the flesh.

59. An instance, parallel with that in Alan (n. 8), of what Nicholas of Lyra called the 'twofold literal sense' (n. 14): the Shulamite's literal desire for a kiss is read in terms of the literal kisses with which Mary and Jesus may be supposed to have kissed one another.

60. See Sophronius, *The Life of Saint Mary the Harlot*, translated by Paul the Deacon. English translation by Benedicta Ward SLG in *The Harlots of the Desert*, CS 109 (Kalamazoo-Oxford, 1987) 35–56.

61. See note 46 above.

Select Bibliography

A. The Texts, Editions Translated

Alan of Lille, *Elucidatio compendiosa in Canticum canticorum.* Migne, Patrologia Latina, 210.

Alcuin of York, *Compendium in Canticum canticorum.* Migne, Patrologia Latina, 100.

Denys the Carthusian, *Enarratio in Canticum canticorum, Opera Varia.* Cologne 1555. Vol. 4.

Giles of Rome, *Expositio in Canticum canticorum,* in *Sancti Thomae Aquinatis Opera.* Venice 1745. Vol. 1.

Gregory the Great, *Expositio in Canticum canticorum,* ed. P. Verbraken OSB, Corpus Christianorum, Series Latina, 144. Turnholt 1963. See also ed. R. Bélanger, in Sources Chrétiennes, 314. Paris 1984.

Hugh of Saint Victor, *Praenotiuncula de scripturis et scriptoribus sacris.* Migne, Patrologia Latina, 175.

John of the Cross, *El Cantico Espiritual,* in *The Collected Works of St John of the Cross,* ed. and trans. K. Kavanaugh OCD and O. Rodriguez OCD. Washington 1979.

Nicholas of Lyra, *Postilla litteralis in Canticum canticorum.* Rome 1471; *Postillae Morales seu Misticae.* Strasbourg c. 1475.

Thomas Aquinas, *Quodlibetum Septimum,* Quaestio 6, in *Quaestiones Quodlibetales,* ed. R. Spiazzi. Turin: Marietti 1949.

Thomas Gallus, *Thomas Gualterius, Abbas Vercellensis, Commentaires du Cantique des Cantiques,* ed. Jeanne Barbet, Textes Philosophiques du Moyen Age, n. 14. Paris 1967.

Thomas of Perseigne, *Commentarium in Cantica canticorum.* Patrologia Latina, 206.

William of Saint Thierry, *In Cantici canticorum priora duo capita Brevis Commentatio ex S. Bernardi sermonibus contexta.* Patrologia Latina, 184.

B. OTHER PATRISTIC AND MEDIAEVAL SOURCES

Aelred of Rievaulx, *De spiritali amicitia,* ed. A. Hoste, Corpus Christianorum, Continuatio Medievalis, 1. Turnholt 1971.

English translation: *Spiritual Friendship,* Cistercian Fathers Series 5 (Kalamazoo 1977).

Alan of Lille, *Summa de Arte Praedicatoria,* PL, 210;
—. *Anticlaudianus,* ed. R. Bossuat. Paris 1955; trans. by James J. Sheridan, *Anticlaudianus.* Toronto 1973.

Alexander of Neckham, *Expositio super Cantica canticorum ad laudem gloriose et beate Virginis Matris et mysterio incarnationis, Libri IV,* unpublished manuscript cited in F. Stegmuller, *Repertorium Biblicum Medii Aevi* 2:1168. Madrid 1950.

Anonymous of Thirteenth Century, *Expositio hystorica Cantici Canticorum secundum Salamonem,* in S. Kamin and A. Saltman, eds., *Secundum Salamonem: A Thirteenth-Century Latin Commentary on the Song of Solomon.* Ramat Gan, Israel: Bar Ilan University Press 1989.

Anonymous of Fourteenth Century, *The Cloud of Unknowing and Related Treatises,* ed. Phyllis Hodgson, *Analecta*

Cartusiana. Salzburg: Institut für Anglistik und Amerikanistik 1982.

Anselm of Laon (attrib.), *Enarratio in Canticum canticorum*, PL 162.

Augustine, *Confessionum Libri XIII*, ed. Lucas Verheijen OSA. Corpus Christianorum, Series Latina 127. Turnholt 1981.
—. *De doctrina christiana*, ed. J. Martin, CCSL, 32. Turnholt 1962;
English translation: *On Christian Doctrine*, trans. by D.W. Robertson Jr. New York 1958.
—. *De Genesi ad litteram*, PL 34.
De Trinitate, PL 42.

Bede, *In Canticum canticorum Libri VI*, in *Bedae Venerabilis Opera*, Pars II, *Opera Exegetica*, 2B, ed. D. Hurst OSB, Corpus Christianorum, Series Latina, 119. Turnholt 1983.

Bernard of Clairvaux, *Sermones super cantica canticorum*, in *Sancti Bernardi Opera*, 1–2, ed. J. Leclercq, C.H. Talbot, and R. M. Rochais. Rome 1957–1958;
English translation: *Sermons on the Song of Songs*, trans. Killian Walsh OCSO and Irene Edmonds, Cistercian Fathers Series, 4, 7, 31, 40. Kalamazoo 1977–1980.

Bonaventure, *Commentaria in IV Libros sententiarum Magistri Petri Lombardi* in *Doctoris Seraphici S. Bonaventurae Opera Omnia*, Vols I–IV. Quaracchi 1882–1902.

Cassian, *Collationes*, ed. M. Petschenig, CSEL 13. Vienna 1886, and Paris 1958.

Catherine of Genoa, *Purgation and Purgatory*, in *Catherine of Genoa*, trans. Serge Hughes, Classics of Western Spirituality. New York: Paulist Press 1979.

Pseudo-Denys, *Pseudo-Dionysius, The Complete Works*, trans. Colm Luibheid, Classics of Western Spirituality. New York 1987.

Denys the Carthusian, *De contemplatione*, in *Doctoris Ecstatici D. Dionysii Cartusiani Opera Omnia*, IX, *Opera Minora*. Tournai 1912.

Meister Eckhart, *Die Deutchen und Lateinischen Werke*. Stuttgart and Berlin: W. Kohlhammer 1936 -.

Some texts in translation in *The Essential Sermons, Commentaries, Treatises, and Defense*, trans. Edmund Colledge OSA and Bernard McGinn, Classics of Western Spirituality. New York: Paulist Press 1981; *Meister Eckhart: Teacher and Preacher*, ed. Bernard McGinn, with the collaboration of Frank Tobin and Elvira Borgstadt, Classics of Western Spirituality. New York 1986.

Geoffrey of Auxerre, *Expositio in Cantica canticorum, Edizione Critica a cura di Ferruccio Gastaldelli*, Vol. I. Rome 1974.

Jean Gerson, *Super Canticum canticorum*, in *Jean Gerson, Oeuvres Completes*, Introduction, Textes et Notes par Mgr Glorieux, Vol III. Paris 1971.

Gregory the Great, *Homilia in Evangelium*, PL 76.
—. *Moralia in Job*, ed. M. Adriaen, CCSL, 143, 143A, 143B, 1979–85.
—. *Homiliae in Hiezechihelem prophetam*, ed. M. Adriaen, Corpus Christianorum, Series Latina, 142. Turnholt 1971.

Haimo of Auxerre, *In Canticum canticorum expositio*, in *D.Thomae Aquinatis Opera* (wherein so attributed). Venice 1745. Pp. 474–514.

Honorius Augustodunensis, *Expositio in Canticum canticorum*, PL 172:347–496.

Hugh of Saint Victor, *Didascalicon*, PL 176.
—. *De sacramentis*, PL 176.
—. *De virginitate Beatae Mariae*, PL 176.

Jerome, *Letter 53* (to Paulinus) in A Select Library of Nicene and Post-Nicene Fathers of the Christian Church, eds.

H. Wace and P. Schaff, Vol. VI; *St Jerome, Letters and Select Works*. Oxford 1893.
—. *Hebraicae Quaestiones in Libros Geneseos*, in *S. Hieronymi Presbyteri Opera*, Pars I, *Opera Exegetica*, I, Corpus Christianorum, Series Latina, 72. Turnholt: Brepols 1959.
—. *Preface to the Pentateuch*, PL 28.
—. *Prologus, Beati Hieronymi ad Damasum Papam, In Expositionem Cantici Canticorum secundum Originem*, PL 28.
—. *In Ezechielem Prophetam*, PL 25.

John Damascene, *De fide orthodoxa*, PG 94.

Maximus the Confessor, *Ambigua ad Johannem*, PL 122.

Origen, *Commentary on the Song of Songs* in W.A. Baehrens, Die Griechischen Christlichen Schrifsteller der Ersten drei Jahrhunderte, 33. Berlin 1925.
English trans. in R.P. Lawson, Ancient Christian Writers, 26. Westminster, Maryland 1957;
English trans. of *Prologue* in *Origen: An Exhortation to Martyrdom, Prayer and Selected Works*, trans. Rowan A. Greer, Classics of Western Spirituality. New York: Paulist Press 1979.
—. *Homilia in Canticum Canticorum*, in Baehrens, *Origenes Werke* 33. heipzig 1925.

Peter of Celle, *The School of the Cloister*, in *Peter of Celle, Selected Works*, trans. Hugh Feiss OSB. Kalamazoo 1987.

Richard of Saint Victor, *In Canticum canticorum expositio*, PL 196:405–524.

Rupert of Deutz, *Commentaria in Canticum canticorum*, ed. H. Haacke, Corpus Christianorum, Continuatio Mediaevalis, 26. Turnholt 1974.

Thomas Aquinas, *Scriptum super Libros Sententiarum*;
—. *Summa Theologiae*, Latin Text and English Translation, Blackfriars. London and New York 1964.
—. *Quaestiones Disputatae de Veritate*;

—. *In Librum de Divinis Nominibus Expositio*, ed. C. Pera OP. Turin and Rome: 1950.

William of Saint Thierry, *Epistola ad Fratres de Monte-Dei*, ed. R. Thomas OCSO, Pain de Citeaux, 33–34;
English Translation: *The Golden Epistle*, trans. T. Berkeley OCSO, Cistercian Fathers Series 12. Kalamazoo 1980.
—. *Expositio super Cantica Canticorum*, in Sources Chrétiennes, 82. 1962;
English translation: *Exposition on the Song of Songs*, trans. Sr. Columba Hart OSB. Cistercian Fathers Series 6. Kalamazoo 1970.

C. SECONDARY SOURCES

Ackroyd, P.R., and C.F. Evans, *The Cambridge History of the Bible*, Vol. 1, *From the Beginnings to Jerome*. Cambridge: Cambridge University Press 1975.

Allen, J.B., *The Friar as Critic: Literary Attitudes in the Later Middle Ages*. Nashville: Vanderbilt University Press 1971.

Astell, A. W., *The Song of Songs in the Middle Ages*. Ithaca: Cornell University Press 1991.

Barnstone, Willis, *The Poems of St John of the Cross, A bilingual edition*. Bloomington and London: Indiana University Press 1968.

Bell, David N., *The Image and Likeness, The Augustinian Spirituality of William of Saint Thierry*, Cistercian Studies Series 78. Kalamazoo 1984.
—. 'The Commentary on the Song of Songs of Thomas the Cistercian and His Conception of the Image of God', *Cîteaux* 28 (1977) 5–25.

Brenan, Gerald, 'Studies in Genius II: St John of the Cross, His Life and Poetry'. *Horizon*, May, 1947.

Campbell, Roy, *The Poems of St John of the Cross*. London: Harvill 1952.

Capelle, B., 'Les Homelies de Saint Gregoire sur le Cantique', *Revue Bénédictine* 41 (1929) 214–216.

Clark, E. A., 'The Uses of the Song of Songs: Origen and the Later Fathers', in *Ascetic Piety and Women's Faith: Essays on Late Antique Christianity*. Lewiston and Queenston: Mellen, Lewiston, 1986: pp. 386–427.

Casey, M., *Athirst for God, Spiritual Desire in Bernard of Clairvaux's Sermons on the Song of Songs*, Cistercian Studies Series 77. Kalamazoo: Cistercian Publications 1988.

Colish, M.L., 'Another Look at the School of Laon', *ADMLA* 53 (1986) pp. 7–22.

Cox, Patricia, 'Pleasure of the Text, Text of Pleasure', *Journal of the American Academy of Religion* 54 (1986) 241–253.

Dagens, C., *Saint Gregoire le Grand: culture et expérience chrétiennes*. Paris: Études Augustiniennes 1977.

d'Alverny, M.T., *Textes Inédits d'Alain de Lille*. Paris 1965.

de Lubac, H., *Exégèse Médiévale: les quatre sens de l'Écriture*, 3 vols. Paris 1959–1961.
—. *Histoire et Esprit: l'Intelligence de l'Écriture d'après Origéne*. Paris: Aubier 1950.

Evans, G.R., *Alan of Lille: The Frontiers of Knowledge in the Later Twelfth Century*. Cambridge: Cambridge University Press 1983;
—. *The Language and Logic of the Bible: The Early Middle Ages*. Cambridge: Cambridge University Press 1984.

Flint, V., 'The Commentaries of Honorius Augustodunensis on the Song of Songs', *Revue Bénédictine* 84 (1974) 196–211.

Gilson, E., *The Mystical Theology of Saint Bernard*, Cistercian Studies Series 120. Kalamazoo: Cistercian Publications 1990 [originally London 1940].

Glorieux, P., 'Alan de Lille, le Moine et l'Abbaye du Bec', *RTAM* 39 (1972) 51–62.

Grabois, A., 'The 'Hebraica Veritas' and Jewish-Christian Intellectual Relations in the Twelfth Century', *Speculum* 50 (1975) 613–634.

Hailperin, H., *Rashi and the Christian Scholars*. Pittsburgh 1963.

Hanson, R.P.C., *Allegory and Event*. London 1958.

Horn, Gabriel, 'Amour et Extase d'apres Denys l'Areopagite', *Revue d'Ascétique et de la Mystique* 6 (1925) 278–289.

Hourlier, J., 'Guillaume de Saint Thierry et la Brevis Commentatio in Cantica', *Analecta sacri ordinis Cisterciensis* 9 (1953) 105–124.

Jackson, B., 'The Ceremonial and the Judicial: Biblical Law as Sign and Symbol', *Journal for the Study of the Old Testament* 30 (1984) pp. 25–50.

Javelet, R., 'Thomas Gallus et Richard de Saint-Victor mystiques', *RTAM* 29 (1962) 206–233; 30 (+1963) 88–121.

Kerr, F., OP, 'Charity as Friendship', in *Language, Meaning and God*, ed. Brian Davies OP. London: Chapman 1987.

Leclercq, J., *The Love of Learning and the Desire for God*, trans. C. Misrahi. London: SPCK 1978.
—. *Monks on Marriage, A Twelfth Century View*. New York: Seabury 1982.
—. *Nouveau Visage de Bernard of Clairvaux*. Paris: Editions du Cerf; 1976). English translation by Marie-Bernard Said OSB. *Translated as A Second Look at Saint Bernard*. Cistercian Studies Series. Kalamazoo 1990.
—. *Monks and Love in Twelfth-century France*. Oxford: Oxford University Press 1979.
—. 'Le Commentaire bref du Cantique attribue a Saint Bernard', in *Études sur Saint Bernard et le texte de ses Écrits*, ASOC 9 (1953) 105–124.

Lys, D., 'Le Plus Beau Chant de la Creation', *Lectio Divina* 51. Paris 1968.

Matter, E. Ann, *The Voice of My Beloved: The Song of Songs in Western Mediaeval Christianity*. Philadelphia: University of Pennsylvania Press, 1990.

McGinn, B., 'Pseudo-Dionysius and the Early Cistercians', in *One Yet Two: Monastic Traditions East and West*, ed. M. Basil Pennington OCSO. Cistercian Studies Series 2. Kalamazoo 1976.

Meyvaert, P., 'A New Edition of Gregory the Great's Commentaries on the Canticle and 1 Kings', *Journal of Theological Studies* 19 (1968).

Minnis, A.J., *The Mediaeval Theory of Authorship: Scholastic Literary Attitudes in the Later Middle Ages*. Philadelphia: University of Pennsylvania Press, 1988.

Murphy, R. E., 'Canticle of Canticles' in *Jerome Biblical Commentary*, ed. R.E. Brown *et al.* Englewood Cliffs: Prentice Hall, 1968: pp. 506–510.

Nygren, A., *Agape and Eros, A Study of the Christian Idea of Love*, trans. A.G. Herbert. London 1932.

Pope, Marvin, *The Song of Songs*. Anchor Bible 7C. New York 1977.

Rist, J., 'A Note on Eros and Agape in Pseudo-Dionysius', *Vigiliae Christianae* 20 (1966) 235–243.

Roques, R., 'Contemplation, extase et tenebre mystique chez le Pseudo-Denys', *Dictionnaire de Spiritualité* 2: 1885–1911;
—. 'Denys l'Areopagite', *Dictionnaire de Spiritualité* 3: 244–429.

Rorem, P., *Biblical and Liturgical Symbols within the Pseudo-Dionysian Synthesis*. Toronto: Pontifical Institute for Mediaeval Studies, 1984.

Salgado, J-M., 'Les Considerations Mariales de Rupert de Deutz (+1129–1135) dans ses *Commentaria in Canticum Canticorum'*, *Divinitas* 32 (1988) 692–709.

Scalise, C. J., 'The "Sensus Literalis": A Hermeneutical Key to Biblical Exegesis', *The Scottish Journal of Theology,* 42 (1989) 45–65.

Smalley, B., *The Study of the Bible in the Middle Ages.* Oxford: Oxford University Press-Notre Dame: Notre Dame University Press 1962.

Torrance, T.F., 'Scientific Hermeneutics according to Thomas Aquinas', *JTS* 13 (1962) 259–289.

Trigg, J.W., *Origen, The Bible and Philosophy in the Third Century Church.* Atlanta 1983.

Verbraken, P., 'La Tradition Manuscrite du Commentaire de St Gregoire sur le Cantique des Cantiques', *Revue Bénédictine* 73 (1963) 277–288.

Weisheipl, J.A., OP, *Friar Thomas d'Aquino, His Life, Thought and Work.* Washington 1983.

ɪɴᴅᴇx

INDEX TO PART I

Subject Index for Part II: The Texts

References are given to the paragraph numbers of the texts

CISTERCIAN PUBLICATIONS, INC.

TITLES LISTING

CISTERCIAN TEXTS

THE WORKS OF BERNARD OF CLAIRVAUX

Apologia to Abbot William
Five Books on Consideration: Advice to a Pope
Grace and Free Choice
Homilies in Praise of the Blessed Virgin Mary
The Life and Death of Saint Malachy the Irishman
Love without Measure. Extracts from the Writings of St Bernard (Paul Dimier)
On Loving God
The Parables of Saint Bernard (Michael Casey)
Sermons for the Summer Season
Sermons on the Song of Songs I - IV
The Steps of Humility and Pride

THE WORKS OF WILLIAM OF SAINT THIERRY

The Enigma of Faith
Exposition on the Epistle to the Romans
Exposition on the Song of Songs
The Golden Epistle
The Nature of Dignity of Love

THE WORKS OF AELRED OF RIEVAULX

Dialogue on the Soul
The Mirror of Charity
Spiritual Friendship
Treatises I: On Jesus at the Age of Twelve, Rule for a Recluse, The Pastoral Prayer
Walter Daniel: The Life of Aelred of Rievaulx

THE WORKS OF JOHN OF FORD

Sermons on the Final Verses of the Songs of Songs I - VII

THE WORKS OF GILBERT OF HOYLAND

Sermons on the Songs of Songs I-III
Treatises, Sermons and Epistles

OTHER EARLY CISTERCIAN WRITERS

The Letters of Adam of Perseigne I
Baldwin of Ford: Spiritual Tractates I - II
Gertrud the Great of Helfta: Spiritual Exercises
Gertrud the Great of Helfta: The Herald of God's Loving-Kindness
Guerric of Igny: Liturgical Sermons I - II
Idung of Prüfening: Cistercians and Cluniacs: The Case of Cîteaux
Isaac of Stella: Sermons on the Christian Year
The Life of Beatrice of Nazareth
Serlo of Wilton & Serlo of Savigny
Stephen of Lexington: Letters from Ireland
Stephen of Sawley: Treatises

MONASTIC TEXTS

EASTERN CHRISTIAN TRADITION

Besa: The Life of Shenoute
Cyril of Scythopolis: Lives of the Monks of Palestine
Dorotheos of Gaza: Discourses
Evagrius Ponticus:Praktikos and Chapters on Prayer
The Harlots of the Desert (Benedicta Ward)
John Moschos: The Spiritual Meadow
Iosif Volotsky: Monastic Rule
The Lives of the Desert Fathers
The Lives of Simeon Stylites (Robert Doran)
The Luminous Eye (Sebastian Brock)
Mena of Nikiou: Isaac of Alexandra & St Macrobius
Pachomian Koinonia I - III
Paphnutius: A Histories of the Monks of Upper Egypt
The Sayings of the Desert Fathers
Spiritual Direction in the Early Christian East (Irénée Hausherr)
Spiritually Edifying Tales of Paul of Monembasia
Symeon the New Theologian: The Theological and Practical Treatises & The Three Theological Discourses
The Syriac Fathers on Prayer and the Spiritual Life (Sebastian Brock)
The Wound of Love: A Carthusian Miscellany

WESTERN CHRISTIAN TRADITION

Anselm of Canterbury: Letters I - III
Bede: Commentary on the Seven Catholic Epistles
Bede: Commentary on the Acts of the Apostles
Bede: Homilies on the Gospels I - II
Gregory the Great: Forty Gospel Homilies
The Meditations of Guigo I, Prior of the Charterhouse (A. Gordon Mursell)
Guigo II the Carthusian: Ladder of Monks and Twelve Meditations
Handmaids of the Lord: The Lives of Holy Women in Late Antiquity and the Early Middle Ages (Joan Petersen)
Peter of Celle: Selected Works
The Letters of Armand-Jean de Rancé I - II
The Rule of the Master

CHRISTIAN SPIRITUALITY

Abba: Guides to Wholeness & Holiness East & West
A Cloud of Witnesses: The Development of Christian Doctrine (D.N. Bell)
Athirst for God: Spiritual Desire in Bernard of Clairvaux's Sermons on the Song of Songs (M. Casey)
Cistercian Way (André Louf)
Drinking From the Hidden Fountain (Spidlék)
Eros and Allegory: Medieval Exegesis of the Song of Songs (Denys Turner)
Fathers Talking (Aelred Squire)
Friendship and Community (B. McGuire)
From Cloister to Classroom
Herald of Unity: The Life of Maria Gabrielle Sagheddu (M. Driscoll)
Life of St Mary Magdalene and of Her Sister St Martha (D. Mycoff)
The Name of Jesus (Irénée Hausherr)
No Moment Too Small (Norvene Vest)
Penthos: The Doctrine of Compunction in the Christian East (Irénée Hausherr)
Rancé and the Trappist Legacy (A.J. Krailsheimer)
The Roots of the Modern Christian Tradition
Russian Mystics (S. Bolshakoff)
The Spirituality of the Christian East (Tomas Spidlík)
Spirituality of the Medieval West (André Vauchez)
Tuning In To Grace (André Louf)
Wholly Animals: A Book of Beastly Tales (D.N. Bell)

TITLES LISTING

MONASTIC STUDIES

Community & Abbot in the Rule of St Benedict I - II (Adalbert De Vogüé)
Beatrice of Nazareth in Her Context (Roger De Ganck)
Consider Your Call: A Theology of the Monastic Life (Daniel Rees et al.)
The Finances of the Cistercian Order in the Fourteenth Century (Peter King)
Fountains Abbey & Its Benefactors (Joan Wardrop)
A Gathering of Friends: Learning & Spirituality in John of Forde
The Hermit Monks of Grandmont (Carole A. Hutchison)
In the Unity of the Holy Spirit (Sighard Kleiner)
Monastic Practices (Charles Cummings)
The Occupation of Celtic Sites in Ireland by the Canons Regular of St Augustine and the Cistercians (Geraldine Carville)
Reading Saint Benedict (Adalbert de Vogüé)
The Rule of St Benedict: A Doctrinal and Spiritual Commentary (Adalbert de Vogüé)
The Rule of St Benedict (Br. Pinocchio)
Towards Unification with God (Beatrice of Nazareth in Her Context, II)
St Hugh of Lincoln (D.H. Farmer)
Serving God First (Sighard Kleiner)
The Way of Silent Love
With Greater Liberty: A Short History of Christian Monasticism and Religious Orders
The Wound of Love: A Carthusian Miscellany

CISTERCIAN STUDIES

A Difficult Saint (B. McGuire)
A Second Look at Saint Bernard (J. Leclercq)
Bernard of Clairvaux and the Cistercian Spirit (Jean Leclercq)
Bernard of Clairvaux: Man, Monk, Mystic (M. Casey) Tapes and readings
Bernard of Clairvaux: Studies Presented to Dom Jean Leclercq
Bernardus Magister
Christ the Way: The Christology of Guerric of Igny (John Morson)
Cistercian Sign Language
The Cistercian Spirit
The Cistercians in Denmark (Brian McGuire)
The Cistercians in Scandinavia (James France)
The Eleventh-century Background of Cîteaux (Bede K. Lackner)
Image and Likeness: The Augustinian Spirituality of William of St Thierry (D.N. Bell)
An Index of Authors & Works in Cistercian Libraries in Great Britain I (D.N. Bell)
An Index of Cistercian Authors and Works in Medieval Library Catalogues in Great Britain (D.N. Bell)
The Mystical Theology of St Bernard (Etiénne Gilson)
Nicolas Cotheret's Annals of Cîteaux (Louis J. Lekai)
The Spiritual Teachings of St Bernard of Clairvaux (J.R. Sommerfeldt)
Studiosorum Speculum
William, Abbot of St Thierry
Women and St Bernard of Clairvaux (Jean Leclercq)

MEDIEVAL RELIGIOUS WOMEN

Lillian Thomas Shank and John A. Nichols, editors

Distant Echoes
Peace Weavers
Hidden Springs: Cistercian Monastic Women, 2 Vol.

What Nuns Read: Books & Libraries in Medieval English Nunneries (D.N. Bell)

STUDIES IN CISTERCIAN ART AND ARCHITECTURE

Meredith Parsons Lillich, editor

Volumes I, II, III, IV now available

THOMAS MERTON

The Climate of Monastic Prayer (T. Merton)
The Legacy of Thomas Merton (P. Hart)
The Message of Thomas Merton (P. Hart)
Thomas Merton: The Monastic Journey
Thomas Merton Monk (P.Hart)
Thomas Merton Monk & Artist (Victor Kramer)
Thomas Merton on St Bernard
Toward an Integrated Humanity (M. Basil Pennington et al.)

CISTERCIAN LITURGICAL DOCUMENTS SERIES

Chrysogonus Waddell, ocso, editor

Hymn Collection of the Abbey of the Paraclete
Institutiones nostrae: The Paraclete Statutes
Molesme Summer-Season Breviary (4 volumes)
Old French Ordinary and Breviary of the Abbey of the Paraclete: Text & Commentary (2 vol.)
The Cadouin Breviary (two volumes)
The Twelfth-century Cistercian Psalter
The Twelfth-century Usages of the Cistercian Lay-brothers
Two Early *Libelli Missarum*

STUDIA PATRISTICA

Papers of the 1983 Oxford patristics conference edited by Elizabeth A. Livingstone

XVIII/1 Historica-Gnostica-Biblica
XVIII/2 Critica-Classica-Ascetica-Liturgica
XVIII/3 Second Century-Clement & Origen-Cappodician Fathers
XVIII/4 *available from Peeters, Leuven*

Cistercian Publications is a non-profit corporation. Its publishing program is restricted to monastic texts in translation and books on the monastic tradition.

North American customers may order these books through booksellers or directly from the warehouse:

Cistercian Publications (Distributor)
St Joseph's Abbey
Spencer, Massachusetts 01562
tel: (508) 885-8730 ❖ fax: (508)-885-4687

Editorial queries and advance book information should be directed to the Editorial Offices:

Cistercian Publications
Institute of Cistercian Studies
Western Michigan University
Kalamazoo, Michigan 49008
tel: (616) 387-8920 ❖ fax: (616)-387-8921

A complete catalogue of texts in translation and studies on early, medieval, and modern monasticism is available at no cost from Cistercian Publications.